STRANGERS IN THEIR HOMELAND

With love to my wife Doris
My children Elisha, Mirit, Michal and Yael
And all my grandchildren: Gal, Or, Arad, Amit, Itay, Nadav,
Shachar, Aviv, Dor, Shira, and Shani.
A token compensation for the time and attention
I was not always able to give you.

STRANGERS IN THEIR HOMELAND

A Critical Study of Israel's Arab Citizens

RA'ANAN COHEN

sussex
ACADEMIC
PRESS

BRIGHTON • PORTLAND

2 4 6 8 10 9 7 5 3 1

First published 2009 in Great Britain by
SUSSEX ACADEMIC PRESS
PO Box 139
Eastbourne BN24 9BP

and in the United States of America by
SUSSEX ACADEMIC PRESS
920 NE 58th Ave   Suite 300
Portland, Oregon 97213–3786

British Library Cataloguing in Publication Data
A CIP catalogue record for this book is available from the British Library.

Library of Congress Cataloging-in-Publication Data

Cohen, Ra'anan.
    Strangers in their homeland : a critical study of Israel's Arab citizens / Ra'anan Cohen.
    p.   cm.
Includes bibliographical references and index.
ISBN 978-1-84519-267-9 (p/b : alk. paper)
    1. Palestinian Arabs—Israel.   2. Israel—Ethnic relations.   3. Israel—Politics and
government—20th century.   4. Palestinian Arabs—Israel—Politics and government—
20th century.   5. Palestinian Arabs–Israel–Political activity. I. Title.
    DS113.7.C632   2009
    305.892'74–dc22

                                                                                2008031388

Mixed Sources
Product group from well-managed
forests and other controlled sources
www.fsc.org Cert no. SGS-COC-2482
FSC   © 1996 Forest Stewardship Council

Typeset and designed by SAP, Brighton & Eastbourne.
Printed by TJ International, Padstow, Cornwall.
This book is printed on acid-free paper.

Contents

List of Illustrations   viii

List of Tables and Figures   x

Acknowledgments   xi

Foreword by Shimon Peres, President of Israel   xii

*Appreciations by: Professor Shlomo Ben-Ami, Vice President of the
Toledo International Center for Peace; and Professor Joseph Ginat,
Head of Strategic Dialogue, Netanya College*   xiii

Map of Israel   xv

Prologue: Complex Loyalties   1

**1   The Politics of Rift: Models for Analyzing the Case of
    Israel's Arab Citizens**   9
Majority–Minority Relations in Israel: Inclusion or
    Confrontation?   9
        The Consensus Model   10
        The Compromise and Co-operation Model   10
        The Control Model   11
        The Division Model   11
The Case of Israeli Arab Citizens   14
Theoretical and Conceptual Aspects in Electoral Behavior   20

2   Political Supervision and Co-optation   28
The 1948 *Naqba*: Adapting to a New Reality   29
Under Military Administration   30
Early Political Organizations   34
        Allied Arab Lists   36
        Zionist Political Parties   43
        The Israeli Communist party (Maki, Rakah, Hadash)   54
        The *al-Ard* Movement and the Democratic Popular Front   59

3   New Political Movements and Trends   64
First Arab Nationalist Movements   65
Extra Parliamentary Political Organizations   68
    Abnaa al-Balad (Sons of the Village)   72
    The Young Moslems   73
    The Islamic Movement   75
Moving towards a Civil Society   78
    The Land Defense Committee   80
    The National Committee for the Arab Local Authorities
      in Israel   81
    The Supreme Follow-up Committee for the Arabs in Israel   83
    Extra Parliamentary Institutionalization and the
      Emergence of the "Third Sector"   84
New Political Leadership   87
The 1990s: Non-Reactionary Politicization   91
Troubled Politics – Parties Under Threat of Disqualification   105

4   Social Rifts in Arab Politics   113
The *Hamula* – A Social and Political Rift   114
Clan Rifts and Municipal Elections   118
Local Elections between Clan and Party   124
Ethnic and Religious Rifts, and Considerations in Choosing a Party   130
    The Moslems   131
    The Druze   131
    The Christians   132
    The Bedouin   132
    The Circassians   133
Ethnic Voting Patterns   133
    Shefar'am   134
    Sakhnin – The Municipal Arena as an Expression
      of Clan Voting   137
    Umm-al-Fahm – Clan and the Nationalist Vote   138

5   Arab Electoral Power   142
Participating In, and Boycotting, Elections   149
Distribution of Votes in the Israeli Arab Population   153
Ideological and Pragmatic Considerations in Choosing a Party   154
    Nationalist/Ideological Considerations   155
    Pragmatic Considerations   157
Political Trends within the Rifts in Israeli Arab Society   161
    Arab Voters in the Galilee   162
    Arab Votes in the Triangle Area   164
    The Druze vote   167
    Voting Among Galilee Bedouin   170

Negev Bedouin Vote 172
Voting Trends among Christian Arabs 176
Voting Trends in Circassian Villages 178
Voting Trends in Mixed Ethnic Towns 179
Voting in Outlying Settlements 182
Complex Loyalties as Reflected in Voting Behavior 184

Epilogue: Arabs, Jews and the State of Israel –
The Administration, the Establishment and Arab Citizens 189
October 2000 – On the Threshold of a New Reality 189
After the Or Judicial Commission of Inquiry and its Conclusions 194
Decisions on Arab Affairs – Governance in Israel 199
Looking to the Future 209

Postscript 218
The Second Lebanon War and Israel's Arabs 218
The Impact of the Broader Israeli–Palestinian Conflict 221
Israel's Arab Population – Vision for the Future 223

Appendix 227
Results of Elections in Seventeen Election Campaigns
    (Excluding Ethnic Mixed Towns) – Division of Votes between
    the Three Blocs 227

Notes 228

Bibliography 241

Hebrew Bibliography 246

Index 256

List of Illustrations

Illustrations are between pages 91 and 102

1   Independence Day 1950. Reception for Arab dignitaries from the village of Tireh. Among those present were the Regional Military Governor, Goel Levinsky, Regional Commissioner of Police and Zvi Alpeleg, Governor of the southern triangle.

2   Celebrating Israel's sixth Independence Day in Nazareth, with the national flag. May 6, 1954.

3   Prime Minister David Ben-Gurion on a tour of Arab villages in the Galilee accompanied by Sheikh Amin Tarif and MKs Jaber Mu'adi and Saleh Khneifes. July 9, 1959.

4   President Zalman Shazar, accompanied by Catholic Bishop Haldani, entering the Church of the Annunciation in Nazareth. August 22, 1967.

5   Visit of Minister of Religious Affairs, Zerah Warhaftig, together with Yigal Allon and Arab leaders in Kfar Hittin. April 30, 1968.

6   Shimon Peres and Ra'anan Cohen on a visit to Sheikh Hamad Abu Rabia in the Negev, to celebrate his election to Knesset – 1972.

7   Abba Eban and Ra'anan Cohen with Attorney Muhammad Massarweh, who served as Israel's Consul General in Atlanta, USA and a group of young Arab university graduates. April 1974.

8   Protest demonstrations, Land Day, March 30, 1983, commemorating six Arabs killed after land was expropriated in the Galilee.

9   Prime Minister Shimon Peres at an Arab Conference in the Galilee, June 25, 1985.

10 Jerusalem Mayor, Teddy Kollek, with Christian and Moslem Arab leaders at a reception in honor of Argentinean President, Carlos Mennem. Rose Garden, Jerusalem, October 2, 1991.

11 Prime Minister Yitzhak Rabin and Chief of Staff Ehud Barak speaking with Arab residents in a local market, August 1992.

12 Jerusalem Mayor-Elect Ehud Olmert posing during a visit to the old city of Jerusalem shortly after his victory, April 1993. In 2007 Mr Olmert served as the Prime Minister of Israel.

13 Prime Minister Shimon Peres (second from right) and Foreign Minister (left) during a celebration to mark the end of the Moslem holiday of Id al Fiter, February1996. In 2007 Mr. Shimon Peres served as the president of Israel.

14 Prime Minister Benjamin Netanyahuu and Druze dignitaries at the funeral of Dr Darash Maher who fell during an IDF rescue operation in Lebanon, September 1997.

15 Voting in General Elections in the village of Jaljulyeh, May 17, 1999.

16 Protests in Nazareth. Moslems praying on behalf of the mosque next to the Church of the Annunciation, October 15, 1999.

17 Demonstrations in October 2000. Courtesy of *Assenara*.

18 Demonstrations in October 2000. Funeral of one of the casualties. Courtesy of *Assenara*.

19 Israeli Arabs demonstrating outside the Supreme Court in Jerusalem in the course of the Or Commission debates, October 3, 2001.

20 Prime Minister Ariel Sharon, at a meeting with Arab local municipality leaders, December 23, 2003.

21 Sons of Sakhnin football club win the national cup in 2004.

22 A mass rally in Um-al-Fahm, to celebrate the release from jail of Sheikh Ra'ed Salah on July 18, 2005. The Mufti of Jerusalem, Akhrama Sabri and Archimandrit Attala Hanna, spokesman for the Greek Orthodox Church in Jerusalem and Israeli Arab leaders, attended the rally. Courtesy of Itzik Ben Malchi.

23 Inhabitants of Shefar'am storming a bus in which a Jewish soldier launched a murderous attack on Arab passengers, killing four. August 4, 2005. Courtesy of Jenny Mancho Ghosh.

24 Clashes between youngsters and the police in the Druze village of Peqi'in in October 2007, which left several policemen and inhabitants of the village injured.

Illustrations are between pages 91 and 102

List of Tables and Figures

Tables

4.1	Municipal Elections in the Arab Sector in Three Election Campaigns	122
4.2	Results of Mayoral Elections in Umm-al-Fahm	129
4.3	Influence of Regional Rifts on the Arab Vote (not including mixed towns/villages)	141
5.1	Age Profile of the Jewish and the Arab Population	143
5.2	Distribution according to Employment in the Arab Sector	143
5.3	Vote Distribution for Israeli Arab Parties in Two Christian Neighborhoods in Nazareth for the Eleventh Knesset Compared to the Sixteenth Knesset	177
5.4	Voting in Outlying Settlements	183

Figures

5.1	Arab Electoral Power and its Actualization in the Framework of Arab Lists, 1949–2006	147
5.2	Division of Voting among the Three Blocs, 1949–2006, in Percentages (excluding mixed settlements)	160
5.3	Voting Distribution among Galilee Arabs, 1949–2006, in Percentages (excluding mixed settlements)	163
5.4	Voting Distribution in the Triangle, 1951–2006, in Percentages (excluding mixed settlements)	166
5.5	Voting Distribution of the Druze, 1951–2006, in Percentages (excluding mixed settlements)	169
5.6	Voting Distribution among Galilee Bedouin 1951–2006, in Percentages (excluding mixed settlements)	172
5.7	Voting Distribution of Negev Bedouin, 1951–2006, in Percentages (excluding mixed settlements)	174

Acknowledgments

I would like to offer my heartfelt thanks to all those who accompanied me through the various stages of research for this book, for their encouragement, support and solidarity and for their invaluable aid in writing and producing the final manuscript. Thanks to Mr Ashish Mehta, who lives in and loves Israel, Mr Reuven Agassi, Mr Victor Tchenquiz, of London, Mr Haron Dahan, of Baltimore, USA, General (Ret.) Yehuda Halevy and Mr Fouad Mussaffi, of Israel, for their encouragement in publishing this important book for the State of Israel.

Special thanks to the late Dr Reuven Aharoni, who provided me with essential and reliable advice that has so enriched this book. Thanks also to Dr Guy Bechor, who offered many useful comments and provided the final review of the manuscript and to Dr Yitzhak Reiter, who aided me with valuable comments prior to the final manuscript.

Foreword

by Shimon Peres, President of Israel

We shall never be able to come to terms with ourselves so long as Israel's minority populations – in every way our fellow citizens – feel themselves discriminated against. A Jewish state in which there is discrimination is inconceivable. Under such circumstances there will never be peace, or complete equality.

This has been our moral stance from the dawn of time. In the meantime, the world has changed. A person's livelihood is no longer dependent, as in the past, on land, but on science. And it is for this reason that political divisions in the world have lost much of their former importance. Science does not stop at boundaries; armies cannot conquer knowledge. Distances have become obsolete in light of electronic advance, and even racialism is gradually disappearing.

The new economy depends more on relations than on international borders. It is global and, as such, it aspires to reach every corner of the earth where there are people, regardless of skin color, ethnic origin or religion. Because whoever wants to reach many places must have partners in every place.

In any case, modern democracy is not built only on the right of every man to equality, but also on the equal right of every man to be different.

Relations between Jews and Arabs in the State of Israel depend on the ability of all its sectors to enter the new era; only thus can real equality and real peace be achieved.

In his book, Ra'anan Cohen analyzes the existing social rifts and also points out the right solutions to them. His book is built upon a wealth of experience and knowledge, together with a convincing analytical aptitude.

JERUSALEM, April 24, 2008

Appreciations

by Professor Ben-Ami and Joseph Ginat

Professor Shlomo Ben-Ami, Vice President of the Toledo International Center for Peace

This is a groundbreaking study of the dilemma of Israel's Arab citizens. Torn between their loyalty to their Palestinian brethren across the border and their Israeli citizenship, the Israeli Arabs emerge from this important study as a highly politicized community in a desperate search for a proper role in, and access to, the institutions of the State of Israel. Dr. Cohen's thorough study of the electoral behavior of Israeli Arabs is a major contribution to our understanding of the predicament of the Palestinian citizens of the State of Israel in their quest for a way out from their conundrum of torn loyalties. This is a book that both the layman and the expert will benefit from, for it also offers a unique perspective for the understanding of the wider issues of the Arab–Israeli conflict.

Professor Shlomo Ben-Ami is a former Foreign Minister in the Israeli government, and currently serves as Vice President of the Toledo International Center for Peace. He is the author of *Scars of War, Wounds of Peace: The Israeli–Arab Tragedy* (Oxford University Press, 2006).

Professor Joseph Ginat, Head of Strategic Dialogue, Netanya College

Since the beginning of the Zionist enterprise in the Land of Israel, the conflict between Jews and Arabs has affected the lives of both peoples. On a narrow stretch of land there settled two nations who claim full sovereignty. Under these circumstances the Israeli Arab citizens were entwined into a unique situation in which they are a minority group in a homeland of another group but a majority in the Middle East, and at the same time they do not wish to assimilate in the majority group. No wonder, therefore, they find themselves in a complex of loyalties. The State of Israel is by definition the State of the Jewish nation, born during the War of Independence, which the Arabs lost.

This war left the Arabs bitter and wishing for revenge; it also left them with refugee camps and dispersion. The result is a bitter existential struggle which has continued for many years on the background of mighty historical myths, which essentially deny the right of the Jewish State to exist.

Strangers in Their Homeland is the result of unique and extensive research on the Palestinian Arab population in Israel. Its uniqueness lies in the fact that it tells the story of Israel's Arabs from an electoral point of view, through an analysis of voting results in the Arab sector over seventeen election campaigns to the Israeli parliament and two campaigns for direct election of the prime minister.

Unlike social scientists, historians rarely introduce theories into their research. In this respect, Dr. Cohen deviates from the norm and weaves into his book a number of important theories – both from a broad circle of the macro and on the level of the micro – that relate to Arab society itself. This theoretical background adds an important aspect to the analyses included therein and turns them into significant scientific contributions. Indeed, in all the research literature that deals with Israeli Arab society, I cannot bring to mind so large a concentration of numerical data that is of such a high quality and so useful to comprehending the political and social position that Israeli Arabs find themselves in.

I believe that this is the first book on the Israeli Arabs to cover so long a period, and combine such a variety of disciplines: statistics, history, anthropology, political science and psychology. Dr. Cohen's treatment of each subject turns the book into a valuable tool for researchers wishing to study various issues in all the aforementioned spheres.

Alongside the research aspect, the book also presents the special point of view of the author, who has spent many years at the epicenter of political activity, as head of the Labor Party's Minorities Department and, later, as the Party Secretary, Member of Knesset and Cabinet Minister. Dr. Cohen's analysis is sharp and daring, but presents a grim and complex view of reality in the State of Israel. It is hard to contradict his analysis as well as the prophesies that emerge from it. The solutions that Dr. Cohen offers are worthy of deep public and academic debate. While this is an academic and scholarly book, part of its uniqueness lies in the fact that its presentation and writing style will appeal also to the lay reader and not only to academe. The wider the public reading of *Strangers in Their Homeland*, the greater the chance for better understanding and resolution of the complex loyalties of Israel's Arab community and the wider Israeli–Palestinian conflict.

Professor Joseph Ginat is Vice President for International Relations and Research and Head of Strategic Dialogue at the Netanya College. He was previously Head of the Center for Peace Research at the University of Oklahoma, and at an earlier stage of his career he acted as Advisor on Arab Affairs to the Prime Minister of Israel.

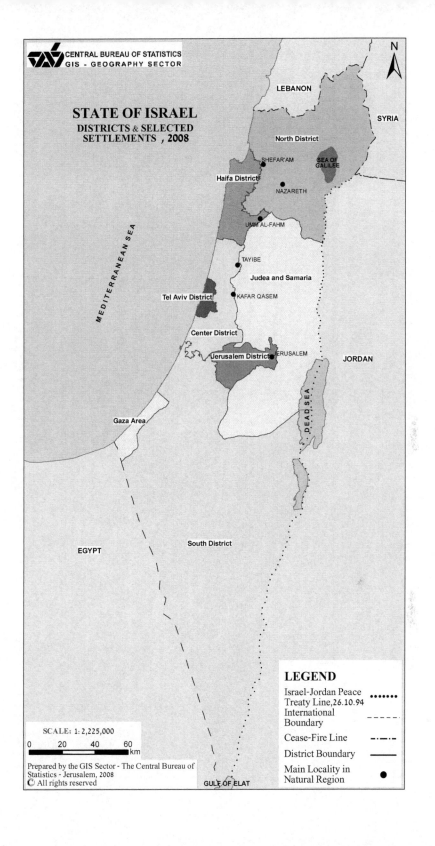

N

STATE OF ISRAEL
DISTRICTS & SELECTED
SETTLEMENTS , 2008

LEBANON

SYRIA

North District

SHEFAR'AM

SEA OF
GALILEE

Haifa District

NAZARETH

UMM AL-FAHM

MEDITERRANEAN SEA

TAYIBE

Judea and Samaria

Tel Aviv District   KAFAR QASEM

Center District

Jerusalem District   JERUSALEM

JORDAN

DEAD SEA

Gaza Area

EGYPT   South District

SCALE: 1: 2,225,000

0   20   40   60
                        km

Prepared by the GIS Sector - The Central Bureau of
Statistics - Jerusalem, 2008
© All rights reserved

GULF OF ELAT

LEGEND

Israel-Jordan Peace
Treaty Line,26.10.94   •••••••
International
Boundary   - - - - -

Cease-Fire Line   —·—·—

District Boundary   ————

Main Locality in
Natural Region   ●

Prologue

Complex Loyalties

My first book, *Complex Loyalties*,[1] singled out the urgent actions that needed to be taken in order to curtail the social, political and economic disparity between Israel's Jewish majority and Arab minority populations. First, the Israeli government must decide on a firm policy regarding Arab-owned lands and put into operation site plans for Arab towns and villages.[2] Second, we must reduce the discrepancy in government grants to Jewish towns and to those inhabited by Arabs.

Eighteen years after the publication of *Complex Loyalties*, practically nothing has been done by the Jewish establishment to alleviate the frustration of Israel's Arab population. Hence the need to reiterate my earlier recommendations in this book.

On the one hand, the Arabs' frustration is deeply internalized – as in the matter of the Arab villages of Ikrit and Bir'am, whose inhabitants were banished in the 1948 War of Independence and have been refused permission to return to their homes ever since. Their case has been bandied back and forth between the courts and the Knesset for 57 years. On the other hand, the Arabs are quite open and outspoken about their frustration. Former prime minister Ehud Barak was very free in his election campaign with grandiose promises to the Arab population. They, in turn, gave him 98 percent of their vote; but Barak promptly turned his back on his Arab voters and reneged on all his promises. He did not even appoint an Arab advisor on Arab affairs.

The rift between the Jews and Arabs was further exacerbated in October 2000, when 13 Israeli Arabs were shot and killed by a police riot squad, in the course of violent demonstrations in support of the second Palestinian *Intifada*.[3] Today, in 2008, this issue is at the forefront of the Jewish–Arab discourse, with the recent decision of the Attorney General to refrain from pressing charges against policemen involved in the shooting. In January 2008 Israeli Arab leaders threatened to bring the case before the International Court in The Hague; if the demonstrators had been Jews, they claimed, the investigation results would have been conducted differently.[4] But with Israeli society still trying to come to terms with the Palestinian issue in general and the Gaza disengagement in particular, there is little time left for dealing with internal problems such as those outlined above, before the Israeli Arab population will become disengaged from Israel's polity, with disastrous consequences.

In 1975 I was asked to head the Labor Party's newly established Minorities Commission. Although politically the position did not offer any great potential, it was a challenge which I accepted with enthusiasm. I was not disappointed, for my tenure with the commission was not only fascinating, but had a major impact on my career. I was given the chance to observe and familiarize myself with Israel's Arab population and to study in close-up the relationships that had developed over the years between it and the country's Jewish population. Later on I devoted my doctoral thesis to the political development and voting trends of the Arab sector.[5] As a result I became thoroughly familiar with the ways in which the establishment dealt with the State's Arab citizens, the Knesset's attitude toward them and concepts developed *vis-à-vis* the Arabs by Israel's party political system. Many were the handshakes and the *Al Marhaba* ("come in peace") greetings, coupled with the hours of discussions with Arab political and community leaders; many were the visits I paid to Arab towns and villages, where I learned much about the worldview and the hopes and aspirations of Israel's Arab citizens.

However, it was not only the Arab side of the equation that interested me. Debates in the Knesset, government sessions and meetings with fellow members of the Labor Party revealed the fears and concerns of Israel's Jewish citizens with regard to events in the Arab sector and allowed me to gain a first-hand view of the motives that guided the Israeli government in defining its attitudes and behavior toward its Arab citizens. This, in some respects, was the most painful aspect of all: I witnessed many old and new government decisions – full of good intentions – that never reached fruition. It became clear that bureaucracy torpedoed most of these decisions, all too often intentionally. I found myself torn between two worlds: the Jewish world to which I belong and the world of the Israeli Arabs, with which I was so involved. I began to understand the depth of the rift between the two.

The future, unfortunately, is not rosy. Israelis, both Jews and Arabs, believe that the State is constantly moving toward clashes between the Arab population and the Jewish establishment. But at the same time, the decision-makers are stuck in a mindset that renders impossible any change, whether in thought or in action, that might help close the gap and lead to equality. A continuation of the present situation sharpens and deepens the Arabs' alienation toward the State, to such an extent that it will not be long before they resort to extensive and open civil disobedience and even violence. The tendency of the Arabs in recent years to turn to the international community for assistance in advancing their cause indicates that such civil disobedience would present a serious challenge to the government of Israel, which would be forced to be constantly on the defensive *vis-à-vis* the pressure to enforce minority rights within the State and civil rights in general.

A number of issues are of particular concern. The first involves the number of Israeli Arabs joining the ranks of anti-Israel terrorist organizations, whether merely to assist terrorists to reach their targets in Israel, or actually to play an active role in attacks on Israelis. Between the 1967 Six Day War and January 2008, "family reunification" has resulted in an estimated 130,000–150,000 Palestinians entering and residing in Israel;[6] some of these individuals were and are involved in terrorist activity. This number may well be much greater and constitutes de facto implementation of the Palestinian "right of return", albeit by the back door. It also harms the numerical and political balance between Jews and Israeli Arabs, two elements whose stability is jeopardized by demographic growth among the Israeli Arab population coupled with reduced Jewish immigration to Israel.

Another cause for concern is the increased radicalization of the Islamic Movement in Israel, especially its northern branch,[7] which acts on behalf of the Hamas and families of suicide bombers in Israel. This activity led to the arrest and imprisonment of the movement's leaders in May 2003. Thus, for example, the Islamic Movement's annual mass rally under the slogan "al-Aqsa is in danger" is used as a platform for across-the-board denial of the Jews' right to the Temple Mount and for harnessing the Moslem world against Israel.

This overt or covert vicious circle of active hostility, which includes reactions on the part of the Israeli Jewish public and government to various phenomena within the Israeli Arab community, will inevitably bring about an uncontrolled clash between two populations living in dangerously close proximity to each other. Recently, several legislative measures against Arab parties and members of the Knesset have succeeded in isolating the Arabs from the country's mainstream political system and reducing their participation in it. This situation, if it continues, will push the Arabs out of the national discourse and, when they feel stripped of the equality enjoyed by other groups in Israeli society, will oust them from it altogether. The situation is exacerbated by Jewish political activists, government ministers and members of the Knesset who periodically come up with extreme and preposterous proposals for the physical transfer of Israel's Arabs.

Under these circumstances, the participation of Israeli Arabs in terrorist acts against Israel encourages and paves the way for proposals to exchange territories, such as those raised at the Camp David negotiations. The idea was that Israel would obtain a legal hold over parts of the West Bank and hand over to the Palestinians the lands around the Halutza Dunes in the North West Negev, east of Gaza. My own proposal at that time was for part of the region known as the "Triangle"[8] to be appended to the West Bank, in return for which Israel would receive blocs of Jewish settlement, in accordance with the agreements that took shape at Camp David. Since the "Triangle" is populated mainly by Arabs and comprises Arab towns and villages that were included in the 1948 Armistice Agreements, such a step could change the demographic balance in the State of Israel and allow those Arab citizens who find themselves living under Palestinian rule to enjoy life in a country with which they share a national, cultural and ideological identity. Such a reorganization of territory, which actually conforms with the geopolitical situation that existed in 1949 in the wake of the War of Independence, might help reduce the points of friction between Jews and Arabs within Israel and create a fair basis for a reciprocal relationship between the two populations. My proposal was based on the same logic that guided President Clinton's plan for an ethnic division of east Jerusalem, according to which "all regions with a predominantly Jewish population would remain under Israeli sovereignty, whereas predominantly Arab regions would come under Palestinian rule". To me, it made sense. Apparently, the idea of territorial exchange is taking root and might even be gaining popularity. According to a poll published on June 25, 2005 on Israel's Channel Two TV, some 54.6 percent of Israel's Jews were in favor of a territorial exchange.

Not only were the ideas presented by myself and others not put into action, they were not even honored by a serious debate. At the moment, I believe that the Arabs are prone to rejecting their vision of integration and are amassing under the flag of political and parliamentary isolation, although doing so will prevent their participation in government and involvement in Israel's society and economy. There seems no imminent or practical solution for mending the Jewish–Arab rift in Israel. Indeed, the feeling is that the situation could blow up at any moment; the consequences are beyond imagination.

This book does not pretend to provide magical solutions for the problems facing the two very diverse populations that share the narrow, overcrowded and troubled strip of land in which we live. Still, if grave mistakes are to be avoided, Jewish and Arab leaders must agree and commit themselves to finding a viable solution that will satisfy their populations, with the appropriate actions taken promptly. Israel appears to be in the midst of a dilemma between complete disassociation from the Arabs (which would entail their transfer out of Israel) and complete assimilation between Jews and Arabs. None of its governments has ever considered a possible middle ground. Moreover, any serious discourse on the matter has always been avoided, as has a clear declaration of intent regarding the Arabs' future in Israel. The transfer issue is raised from time to time, and several parties and political streams have adopted it as their main election platform. Indeed, there is no dearth of politicians and academics in the very center of Israeli politics who support the idea. I believe that great caution should be exercised in raising such an idea. Israel cannot afford to be seen by the rest of the world as a country that banishes its citizens; obviously Arab citizens would never agree to migrate of their own accord. Their leaders have made it very clear that they see themselves as an "inherent minority" – in other words, the land belongs to those who were born here, and the Jewish immigrants are the ones who came from without.

Such a complex reality requires urgent public and governmental action to reduce the points of friction between the two groups. Israel's strategy must focus on minimizing the conflicts to a level acceptable among ethnic groups elsewhere in the world. And, of course, sincere – not patronizing or condescending – steps must be taken to integrate Arab citizens in all walks of Israeli life, to include and involve Arab political parties as equal partners in government coalitions and to appoint Israeli Arab political leaders to operative ministerial positions; only thus can the Israeli Arab population have any kind of influence on the political establishment, alongside Zionist and other sectarian parties.

Since Israeli Arab school-leavers are exempt from military service, I would not rule out some form of national service – possibly consisting of community service within the Arab towns and villages.

Jews and Arabs are destined to live side by side in the Middle East. It seems that a superficially friendly, back-slapping "hummus-labane"[9] relationship is no longer effective in promoting understanding between the two peoples and some significant investment in education is now necessary in order for each side to come to terms with the "other". The initiative for this is mainly in the hands of the Jewish side: for example, Arab language and literature studies must be an integral part of the Jewish schools curriculum. Israel is located in the center of a region where the dominant language is Arabic, yet most of its Jewish citizens are almost entirely unfamiliar with that language. Israelis' ignorance of the Arab language and culture is construed by the Arabs as indifference and arrogance. In Arab culture it is direct personal contact that serves to bond people to each other. The gesture, *mogiamalah*, is the basis of all communication and anyone who is unable to speak the language of the region and to communicate with its inhabitants "at eye level" is seen as alien, unfriendly and arrogant. The chances of such a person being accepted as a legitimate neighbor are negligible.

Jewish school children must be taught the history of the Palestinians and be encouraged to study the Palestinian narrative concerning their conflict with the Jews over the Land of Israel. They must also learn to understand the background of the *naqba*, the Palestinian "tragedy" of 1948, when the State of Israel was established. Israel's Jewish majority must internalize the Arab minority's right to exist by its side, to neutralize the points of friction and to co-operate in building a single civilian society. On the other hand, Israeli Arab citizens must come to terms with the fact that Israel is a Jewish state, which will continue to exist as such and in which they will always be the minority. All this requires a revolution, not only in the leadership's approach, but also in the attitudes of the press, which must devote much more time to exposing the Jews to all aspects of Arab society – and vice versa.

According to a popular myth among the Jewish majority, if and when a solution is found to the Jewish-Palestinian conflict, the conflict between Jews and Arabs in the Land of Israel will also be solved. As I see it, this is a fallacy.

With another step on the long way to a political solution – the Gaza disengagement of August 2005 – completed, there was another outburst of hatred between Jews and Arabs when a fanatic, right-wing Jewish soldier attacked a bus in the Arab village of Shefar'am, killing four innocent civilians. The Arabs had already expressed their fear of becoming the scapegoats of the Israeli right-wingers opposing the disengagement, and this attack was hardly a unique occurrence.[10] Any future political steps of a similar nature, including further withdrawals from the occupied territories, are most probably going to be used by Jewish extremists as an excuse for attacks on Arabs.

The findings described in this book reinforce my theory that the social and economic rift between Israel's Jewish and Arab populations will only deepen if and when Palestinians and Israelis achieve a peaceful solution to their territorial conflict. The removal of the "big" conflict from the equation will highlight the Israeli Arab population's struggle with regard to their personal and public civil status and their position as a nationalist minority. They will strive to realize their own vision of their rights as Israeli citizens. They will focus their efforts on achieving all their civil rights and the State will be unable to continue avoiding these issues against the ever-growing demands of international civil rights organizations.

In Israel, the Arabs' demands for equality will not be welcomed by the Jewish majority and its political representatives. Moreover, such demands will arouse and exacerbate fears of Israel losing its status as a Jewish state. Some Arab citizens are already challenging Israel's Jewish nature and proposing an alternative format for the Jewish homeland – what they refer to as a "state for all its citizens", which ultimately would lead to a two-nation state. I believe that special notice should be taken in this respect of recent sentiments expressed by Arab Knesset members, according to whom the State of Israel is not, in fact, a Jewish state. Such sentiments would suggest that, as far as the country's Arabs are concerned, the State has lost its legitimacy as a Jewish state. Although the demographic balance has remained stable since 1948, such sentiments will increase in the near future, due largely to the waves of Jewish immigrants arriving in Israel over the last decades from the former Soviet Union and Ethiopia. Now, with numbers of Jewish communities dwindling throughout the world, resulting in reduced Jewish immigration to Israel, on the one hand, and the high birthrate among Arabs (helped by state-of-the-art medical facilities not available in Arab countries), on the other hand, the demographic balance is likely to change in the very near future. The possibility should not be ruled out of Israel's Arabs using other methods to realize their nationalist aspirations, with demands ranging from cultural autonomy to a kind of autonomy that is more territorial. Israel will never be able to comply with these demands and must waste no time weighing its relationship with its Arab population.

According to current concepts, the existence of Israel as a state is based on its Jewish majority. It is almost impossible to see Israel, in its present economic position, allocating billions out of its budget to the Arab sector, at the expense of other national objectives. Even today, when decisions have already been taken to devote relatively modest sums toward improving conditions in the Arab sector, things are moving at a snail's pace, or not at all. If a solution is to be found, extensive thought must be invested in the issue at all levels – political, economic, cultural, and demographic. Unfortunately, Israel does not appear to see the urgency of the issue and prefers to leave necessary decisions to the distant future.

A national commission headed by Supreme Court judge Theodore Or published its findings on the October 2000 killings. To me, the most obvious finding is that successive Israeli governments have ignored and discriminated against the Arab sector and, by doing so, have created serious unemployment and poverty which, in turn, have resulted in ongoing discontent and frustration. The conclusions of the Or Commission should not be disregarded; they must become the basis of carefully deliberated planning for future Jewish–Arab relations in Israel. The two societies must not be allowed to evade the task of implementing each and every one of the Commission's recommendations. Only thus can a new reality develop in Israel.

I hope in this book to provide a few creative ideas for reducing the conflict and for understanding the difficult issues involved. I would like to see the development of a common Israeli nationality, one in which all the citizens of this country – regardless of their ethnic background or religion – feel themselves equal members in the Israeli experience. It is my wish that the Arab minority in Israel will come to feel the same as any ethnic minority in any other democratic state in the world which is not at loggerheads with its government; for example, just as German speakers in the southern Tyrol see Italy as their home state, without the need to adopt the national identity of the Italian majority. This is no easy solution to achieve under conditions of ongoing national strife, but it is a value for which all parties must struggle, and for which it is worthwhile overcoming both Jewish and Arab nationalism. The solution will not be achieved by denying the definition of Israel as the Jewish homeland, for such denial will only hinder. In a land where there are, by all accounts, two separate nations, both must be given the respect of self-determination and independence. The right of the Palestinian people to their independence must be realized in a state in which the nationality is Palestinian-Arab, alongside Israel, while those members of this nation who choose to live in Israel must always remain a national minority in the Jewish state.

In order to help resolve the conflict between Israel's Jewish and Arab citizens, I propose the establishment of a public, interdisciplinary, government-linked council with authority to make binding decisions, to manage its own independent budget, and to implement its decisions independently. The proposed council would draw up a plan defining the rights and obligations of all the citizens of Israel on the level of majority-minority relations, with the aim of defining the term "civil equality in the State of Israel". Equality in this respect would consist of national service on behalf of the community, and the setting up of a special authority responsible for establishing joint Jewish–Arab industrial areas. Newly established areas would share equal status with existing industrial areas and parks in Jewish towns, with the objective of establishing a joint, rather than a dependent, economy, as is the case today.

To sum it up, it is my fervent wish to attract maximum attention to the extremely complex relationship between Jews and Arabs in the State of Israel, at the heart of which lies the issue of an Arab minority in a country which is in the midst of an ongoing conflict with the rest of the Arab world. In the words of former deputy health minister Abd al-'Aziz al-Zu'bi, who summed up the problems facing the Arabs: "My nation is at war with my country."

1
The Politics of Rift

Models for Analyzing the Case of Israel's Arab Citizens

Majority–Minority Relations in Israel: Inclusion or Confrontation?

Israel is the only country in the world in which the three great monotheistic religions come together – and with an almost unprecedented passion. Judaism, Christianity and Islam have each defined their own stipulations with regard to this narrow stretch of fertile land that lies along the eastern part of the Mediterranean coast. In doing so, they related to its history, its spiritual importance, its sentimental value, the kind of society that should inhabit it and, of course, its religious and mystic status. Jewish definitions relate to the Godly aspect of Israel and to its national identity ("Promised Land", "Land of Our Fathers"). Christian definitions ("Land of the Bible", "Holy Land") relate to God's renewed pact with the inhabitants of the land via Jesus Christ the Messiah. Islamic definition is based on the understanding of both beliefs as one, combined with the argument that Muhammad's appearance is the event that completed the sophistication of the faith in a single God, through which Islam appropriated for itself ownership of the "holy" land of Israel and its capital Al Quds (Jerusalem).

Whatever the claim may be that each faith purports to have on this land, it will almost inevitably be based on some value that is also at the basis of that faith. It is for this reason that the proliferation of claims leads to confrontations between interests and ideologies of various populations, some of whom have already moved away from the area, such as the Crusaders; yet others established themselves here, and yet others were uprooted and exiled by foreign conquerors, before returning to the land. The results of these processes are tangible to this day in the demographic structure of modern Israel's population, which consists of two main ethnic groups: Jews and Arabs. Although they differ in religious belief, language, culture, social structure and national aspirations, they share one thing: their affinity to this land.

In Israel, Jews are the majority; in the Middle East, however, they are a small minority. On the other hand, although they are a minority in Israel, Arabs constitute the vast majority in the entire region. While Israel is seen by some of the other inhabitants of the Middle East as a foreign political entity, to most Jews the Arabs are a potential enemy.

The side-by-side existence of several ethnic groups is not unique to the State of Israel. The phenomenon is common to the political existence of most countries in the world and especially in the Middle East – and according to many political scientists it considerably limits the chances for a stable democracy.[1] On what, therefore, does the quality of relations between majority and minority groups depend? Researchers of multi-ethnic democracies make use of four main models of public policy created for the purpose of maintaining internal political stability.

The Consensus Model

The approach underlying this model claims that the expansion of education, the industrialization process and the rise in the standard of living will bring about the creation of a new social-economic structure, thereby replacing old ethnic loyalties. Accordingly, the state will strive to form a new comprehensive national identity. The national consensus will be manifested in the creation of national institutions and in encouraging assimilation and the merging of the different ethnic groups into one homogeneous, secular, rational and efficient culture.[2] The geographer Oren Yiftachel maintains that this model is not suitable for countries in which the different ethnic groups are "homeland groups", i.e. they live in their historical homeland areas. Homeland groups tend to isolate themselves more than immigrant ones. For this reason, the consensus model is suitable for immigrant societies such as the USA or Australia, but not for Middle Eastern countries in which the different ethnic groups have lived for generations on the same piece of land.[3]

The Compromise and Co-operation Model

According to this model, the country aspires to preserve the various ethnic identities of its citizens, lend them legitimacy and thus attain a long-term stable democracy. Democracies based on compromise and co-operation use four political principles: relativity, the right of mutual veto, broad coalitions, and autonomy for ethnic minorities, all in order to create widespread loyalty to the state. In cases where ethnic groups are concentrated in specific areas, it can be assumed that giving autonomy to minorities will eventually turn the state into a federation of states – such as is the case in Switzerland, Belgium and Canada.[4]

The Control Model

In this model the majority group, via demographic preferences, tailors public policies to its cultural, economic and political needs, and usually also operates control mechanisms to regulate ethnic minorities. These mechanisms include political supervision, economic dependence and territorial limitations.[5] According to this model, the state tries to preserve its stability by weakening its minorities and making them economically and culturally dependent on the majority. Good examples of this are pre-1968 Northern Ireland and pre-1983 Sri Lanka. Although they were open democracies, the state system in these countries became the almost all-exclusive tool for advancing the interests of the dominant ethnic group. This approach may be effective in the short run, but in the long run it may lead the state into violent confrontation and, ultimately, to disintegration.

It is possible to create a stable, multi-national state using the control model if only all sides adopt the principles of an "improved ethnic democracy", in which full democratic rights are granted to all citizens. Minorities are granted certain limited collective rights, while state institutions and public policy design remain in the hands of the ruling ethnic group. This is what took place in Malaysia after 1969, in Fiji after 1987, and has been the situation in the Baltic States since 1991.

The Division Model

Multi-ethnic societies which are unable to come to a minimal political consensus, and insist on maintaining their religious, cultural and national characteristics, bring about the breakdown of the various control mechanisms. In such cases the only option open to all parties, if they want to prevent violence, is to partition the state. This is what happened during the 1990s in Czechoslovakia and the USSR. Other examples are Singapore's secession from Malaysia, Belgium's secession from Holland, and Mali's removal of itself from Senegal.[6] Additional examples are India, Pakistan and Bangladesh.

What, then, are the causes affecting the stability of multi-ethnic democracies? The first concerns the differentiation between "homeland minorities"[7] and immigrant groups. The former tend to overemphasize their ethnic identity, while the possibility of their integration into the majority society is negligible. When different ethnic groups live in close proximity to each other or even intermingle, no possibility exists for solving the problem through federative or other partition paradigms. Thus territorial separation, which in some cases might be considered a threat to the completeness of the state, in other cases becomes a potential asset and tool through which workable arrangements and a relatively calm co-existence can be attained.

Another component affecting the stability of multi-national states concerns the international diaspora of the groups that make up the state. Thus states in which there is a dual ethnic authority (i.e. the center of authority of an ethnic group is in a neighboring country) tend to be fragile because of the existence of overlapping bodies of authority, which sometimes leads to a conflict between ethnic and civilian loyalties. Northern Ireland, in which the authority centers of two ethnic communities – England and the Irish Republic – rival with each other, is an example for such a complex situation.[8]

Relations between ethnic communities are also influenced by the demographic-spatial aspect when the inflexibility exhibited by the majority in ethnic quarrels is connected to the "annihilation fear" felt by majority members who constitute a minority in a specific area.[9] Examples of this are Sri Lanka, where the Singhalese are surrounded by Tamils in their own country; South India; and also Northern Ireland, where Protestants are surrounded by neighboring Catholics, both in Northern Ireland itself and in the neighboring Irish Republic. Indeed, inter-ethnic conflicts in complex geopolitical surroundings are extremely difficult to overcome.

What is the underlying cause of ethnicity that causes dramatic differences between one group and another? Some believe that ethnicity stems from collective identity and solidarity based on character features such as a belief that they share common ancestors, language, customs, religion, and in some cases also race and color.[10] The Arab ethnic group in Israel features most of the components of this definition: their belief is that of sharing common ancestors, considered the forefathers of the Arab nation; they share the same Arab language; behave according to Arab customs; and most of Israel's Arab population belongs to the Moslem faith, with only a small Christian minority. Israel's Arab ethnic group also has a physical connection with the territory that in the more recent past has become its homeland and been given the name Palestine, and which is known to the Jews as the Land of Israel. Milton Esman compared ethnic politics in the Middle East with similar experiences in other parts of the world. His main deduction is that the implementation and expression of ethnic politics in the Middle East is similar to these in other parts of the third world except that in the Middle East the religious definition in the communal solidarity takes precedence. The ethnic and national identity of the Israeli Arabs stems from the Arabic and Moslem history, which binds them to the Arabic ethnic group in the Middle East and to the large Moslem community in the world. To this one can add the bond to the land of Palestine, which has a symbolic role in the Arabic and Moslem history. Thus at the centre of the ethnic conflict in the Middle East stands the ethnic-national identity and in its wake, communal solidarity, such as in Lebanon, Jordan and Israel.[11]

In most cases, ethnic politics in the Middle East are also connected to majority–minority relations. The idea of differentiating between majorities and minorities was imported to the Middle East from the West and is inseparable from the idea of a representative and parliamentary government.[12] In order for majorities and minorities to co-exist, a basic assumption is that both the political majority and the political minority share a common interest to preserve the political structure with which they are identified, such as the principles of the "political right" or those of the "political left". However, this assumption is cancelled out by the nationalist idea. The moment the political legitimacy of any party stems from its civilian vote and the country's majority population is made up of members of a single nationality, the majority becomes a national majority, which means a fixed and unchanging factor in conflict with smaller groups which are, in themselves, national minorities.

The State of Israel provides a typical example of the way in which political tensions evolve when nationalism combines with ethnicity. According to the accepted definition, Israel is a sovereign state of the Jewish nation, and the Arab minority living in it is a political-nationalistic minority and not only an ethnic minority in the narrow sense of the word. Yet the identity of Israel's Arabs is also influenced by ethnic Arabs in states and national groupings that are more or less at war with the State of Israel.[13] The result for Israel's Arab citizens is an internal conflict that prevents them from becoming full partners in the Jewish national state and in the national consensus on the main issues that shape the political existence of the State of Israel. To a great extent, they present an isolated enclave within the state and are subject to the internal and external pressures that come at them from opposite directions: on the one hand, there are demands – and their own internal desire – to integrate fully into the fiber of the state; on the other hand, they identify with that part of the Arab world which calls them to distance themselves from Jewish society and preserve their national and cultural uniqueness. The term "irredentism"[14] does not reflect the geopolitical reality in Israel. Israel's Arab citizens are born in the country and their national aspirations to entertain direct relations with their brothers across the pre-1967 "Green Line" are not necessarily motivated by a desire to join the political group across that border.

It would appear that ethnic groups who see themselves as having a minority status in a given society would usually try to emphasize their willingness to integrate and make efforts to integrate into the majority society. On the other hand, ethnic groups who consider themselves as belonging to another nation tend to reject their minority status completely, emphasize confrontation and ultimately create conflict between themselves and the majority. Such is the situation in Spain, where the Basques' struggle for autonomy sometimes takes on a violent form and has developed into a general demand for complete separation from Spain, where most of the Basques live. Spanish politics are riddled with deeply rooted nationalist rifts, which become deeper with the increase of Basque underground terrorist activity. These ethnic-nationalist rifts played an important role in the elections of March 12, 2000 and led to the strong electoral support of regional nationalist parties.

As for the relationship between majority and minority ethnic groups in Israel, the question becomes one of whether Israel's Arab citizens represent an ethnic group that adopts the integration approach, or whether they represent a national-ethnic group that adopts a confrontational approach – or are we in fact dealing with a group that has an integrational as well as a confrontational approach? This question, in all its different aspects, is the underlying theme presented in the chapters that follow.

The Case of Israeli Arab Citizens

None of the above models of public policy aimed at maintaining internal political stability fits the situation in Israel, as will be described later. Prior to a discussion of the case of Israel's Arab citizens, I shall try to propose a model to describe the relations among ethnic communities in a state riddled by national tension and claims to democracy.

Israel was created in order to ensure the sovereignty of the Jewish people over its land. Even today, the structure of the state enables the Jewish majority to sustain national institutions which have affinity with institutions and Jews outside Israel, whereas Israel's Arab citizens are prevented from cultivating such affinity with the Palestinians living outside Israel. These Jewish national institutions ruled the Jewish sector during the years of struggle for independence and continued to function side by side with the Israeli government after the establishment of the State of Israel. These Jewish national institutions were responsible for the immigration of Jews from all over the world, for settling them in new towns and villages, and for the acquisition of land on behalf of the Jewish people. In contrast, the Arab minority was cut off from its national institutions and prevented from engaging in activities similar to those of the Jews, with the result that its control over its demographic and economic resources was expropriated from it, for ideological reasons.

In such a state it is possible to achieve internal political stability only through a fitting public policy aimed at creating an integrative model which will define the institutional relations between the two communities. The majority must do its utmost to integrate the minority into government institutions proportionally to the minority's size. In addition, the government has to initiate such institutions that will enable the minority to participate in decision-making concerning the state and its citizens.

The Israeli case, which is unique, is suitable for discussion on the above model and the possibility of its implementation. After 60 years of existence, the government of the Jewish state constantly takes over more and more of the functions of Jewish national Zionist organizations such as the Jewish National Fund and the Jewish Agency. The recognition of Israel by its neighboring countries and a future agreement with the Palestinians might reduce the national tension between the two ethnic communities in Israel, but will increase the civil tension, i.e. the demands of Israel's Arab citizens for equality. A definition of the civilian and institutional relations is needed in the framework of the integrative model in order to reduce the anticipated civil tension.

The Arab minority in Israel perceives itself as an indigenous national minority, as opposed to an immigrant minority.[15] It belongs to the broader category of homeland minorities, or populations that are indigenous to a country but constitute a minority in that country, such as the Tamil in Sri Lanka and the Irish Catholics in Northern Ireland.

After Israel's 1948 War of Independence, a series of local and international events, coupled with the legislation of laws and by-laws (the Law of Return, the Law of Appropriated Assets, the Law of Entry into Israel, the Law for Preventing Infiltration), turned Palestine – the Land of Israel – into the sovereign State of Israel. From a legal point of view, this should have been sufficient. In practice, it seems that it was not; it did not end the struggle between the two very diverse communities. Palestinian Arab demands for sovereignty over the entire land on which the State of Israel sits still exist. In addition to laws, therefore, the State of Israel also needed ideological tools with which to determine its unequivocal right to the land, and it achieved this by emphasizing the historical continuity of Jewish presence and rights over the Land of Israel – what has been defined in the Declaration of Independence as "the historic affinity of the Jewish people to the Land of Israel". Places and localities in Israel were given Jewish names, places holy to the Jews were identified as such, ancient and modern Jewish battlefields were commemorated, as were archeological finds, all for the purpose of proving the Jews' historical right to the land. Israel's history gave the region a tangible Jewish sense of being.

Israel's policies toward the Arab citizens, as expressed in the decisions of the various governments since the establishment of the state, have not deviated greatly from the spirit of the traditional attitude adopted by the country's first prime minister, David Ben-Gurion. During the period when Arabs were under military law, policies were determined by a body known as the "Mapai[16] Committee for Arab Matters", in which central activists of the workers' party participated, together with representatives of all government bodies. The committee discussed desirable policies *vis-à-vis* the Israeli Arab population, and three options were raised. The first option was assimilation – which would have consisted of "Israelizing" the Arabs and obscuring or erasing their Arab identity. The second was liberalization – in other words, inviting the Arabs to participate in Israeli/Zionist institutions, while keeping them as a separate entity. The third option, which was ultimately accepted, consisted of control and supervision – in other words, massive implementation of military law, together with maximum prevention of integration between Jewish and Arab sectors. Israeli Arab residents were not to be made welcome in Jewish communities.

The result was that Arabs were removed from positions of decision-making – a fact that is particularly obvious in areas of management, and especially among the limited representation they were allowed in the organizations dealing with lands and planning. To this day, Israel's Arabs have very little influence on the processes that determine their way of life, the upholding of their civil rights, their economic welfare and their future status; their own bureaucratic institutions have remained to all intents and purposes paralyzed.

This situation remained virtually unchanged after 1984, when successive governments appointed Jewish ministers to be responsible for Israeli Arab affairs. In the absence of a serious and focused discussion on the basic dilemma of Israel's identity, there arose the necessity for a pragmatic solution in which two principles, the particularistic and the universal, interacted in different spheres and at different times, when at each given time one or the other had the upper hand. Thus it is possible to explain the easing up of military administration in the late 1950s and its complete repeal in 1966, and the growth of the universal element among the Jewish public in recent years. On the other hand, the establishment of the Sephardi right-wing ultra-Orthodox Shas political party, the growth of the Islamic Movement, and the 1987 outbreak of the Arab civilian uprising in the occupied territories (*Intifada*) promised the particularistic element a long shelf life.

Israel's policies toward its Arab sector have been shaped mainly by its various prime ministers and, to a far lesser degree, the prime ministers' advisors on Arab affairs.[17] The latter must have been seriously frustrated by the fact that not only were many of their suggestions not put into operation, they were not even raised for discussion. At least from the rise of the right-wing Likud Party to power in 1977, these advisors filled the role of prophets of doom, with their constant warnings that it was only a matter of time before the anti-Arab discrimination, sanctioned by and concealed in the country's laws, would lead to outbursts of violence in the Arab sector. But the politicians passed no decisions and, when some legislation was eventually taken, they got stuck against a process of systematic hurdles.

There was an historical background to this. During the early years of the state, there was a need for military administration, so that decision-making was the order of the day. Yehoshua Palmon, a close associate of prime minister David Ben-Gurion, was given responsibility for carrying out government decisions. But by the time military administration was no longer in operation, the only office through which contact was made between the country's Arab citizens and the civilian establishment was that of the advisor on Arab affairs. Governments no longer took the time to deal with the basic problems of the Israeli Arab population, and their social and civilian status. The advisor on Arab affairs was then free to make proposals that were, to the best of his knowledge, in keeping with the government's view, and these became official government policy. In the absence of a committed operative government framework, a team evolved that consisted of the prime minister's advisor on Arab affairs, the head of the Arab department in the Mapai Party, the head of the Labor Federation Arab department, and the chief of the prime minister's Arab Liaison Department.[18] These departments subsequently increased in strength, and in 1975 the Mapai Arab department metamorphosed into the Minorities Department and was provided with a substantial budget.

The team members consulted with each other and took decisions, which they implemented and co-ordinated, each within his own framework. The government accepted the *modus operandi* of these "Arabists" as if it was government policy. Various government ministers were taken to visit towns and villages in the Arab sector and provided support for the team's activity. The team issued frequent warnings to the government that, in the absence of suitable integration policies, extremism in the Arab sector would continue to increase, and that a far-reaching policy, initiated and implemented by the government, was imperative.

In 1976, in my capacity as chairman of the governing party's Minorities Department, I presented prime minister Yitzhak Rabin with a policy proposal for dealing with the Arab population, which was raised for ministerial discussion and subsequently presented to the government. Although agreement with the spirit of the proposal was unanimous, in practical terms the only decisions to be carried out were those agreed upon by the team.

Upon the establishment of the first national unity government in 1984, I presented a further document, which dealt with a comprehensive policy *vis-à-vis* Israel's Arabs. The document had been drafted after extensive consultations with Jewish and Arab experts from various disciplines and was received with silent agreement; but it was not granted the status of official government agreement, which would have been expressed in actual change in the government's attitude to the Israeli Arab population. The younger generation and university graduates among the Arabs were peeved by the fact that Jews were in charge of Arab affairs and insisted that they could do without this kind of patronization. What they wanted was for Jews and Arabs to be dealt with in the same way. The establishment, on the other hand, saw no urgency in interpreting the changes that were taking place in Israeli Arab society, and any developments were left to chance. Even for cases of political and social unrest, solutions were provided only on a local and temporary basis.

The tensions involved in defining Israel as a Jewish state and its outspoken commitment to democracy and equality between Jews and

Arabs accompany and characterize relations and policies toward the country's Arabs. The Basic Law: the Knesset – which also deals with election platforms – disqualifies any list "which negates the existence of Israel as the sovereign state of the Jewish people". According to the Basic Law: Human Dignity and Liberty, its aim is to "protect human dignity and liberty, in order to establish in a Basic Law the values of the State of Israel as a Jewish and democratic state". The legal paradox manifest in the adjoined words "Jewish" and "democratic" (besides other contradictions – for example, the connection between a person and his private premises, settlement and residential areas) renders the existence of normal and equal relations between the state and its Israeli Arab residents problematic.

The law ensuring the Jewish character of the State of Israel has created a rift between Israeli Jews and Arabs. The exacerbation of the national tension between Israel and the Palestinians brought about the approval of new laws, which only widened the rift. One of the main components of the rift concerns the provision of the Jewish-Zionist character of the state as a governing tool. Therefore, some researchers think that there is not, in fact, a full democracy in Israel. They refer to Israel as an "ethnic democracy", or a "national democracy", or even an "ethnocracy".[19] S. Smooha defines Israel as a unique case of a stable ethnic democracy.[20] I would argue that Israel's governmental structure is one of the factors shaping the Arabs' electoral behavior and their considerations for electing a party. It also creates the "changing votes" phenomenon that is the transfer of votes from the parties connected to Mapai to the Zionist parties and later to national Arab parties. This structure also created the phenomenon of "abstention from voting".

The involvement of Israel's Arab citizens in extra-parliamentary politics is far greater than that of Israel's Jews and is manifested in membership in various nationalist movements and civilian organizations, and participation in demonstrations and strikes, all in order to advance their political interests. By opposing Israel's Jewish-Zionist character, the minority Arab population is prevented from full partnership in government coalitions, notwithstanding the fact that the government structure in Israel assumes the existence of a broad coalition as a condition for managing the government. In spite of visible cracks in the ban against the participation of Arab parties in government coalitions, de facto the situation has not changed, as demonstrated in the 1992 Knesset elections which led to the formation of a Labor-led "unofficial coalition bloc". Arab parties which participated in the formation of the "coalition bloc" supported the government from the outside, thus preventing the establishment of a Likud government.

The Arab voter in Israel, therefore, is constantly required to deal with a multitude of affinities and loyalties such as the family/clan, religious congregation, etc., and various identities, including the Palestinian, the Arabic, the Islamic and the Israeli. Postmodern research presents a paradigm of identity proliferation rather than one of dichotomy. The identities that appear to exist today in various communities are actually a politicization of identity, rather than the essence of identity. Commitment to a specific identity is not static, but depends on circumstances and ideology. There are built-in identities that find their expression in political declarations and other, acquired, identities such as values and personal worldview, which represent an individual's personality.

Another approach has it that Palestinization is an expression of local nationalism, rather than extremism. The Arabs see themselves as a unique nationalist group with its own unique problems (similar to other Arabs in the Middle East, who are "Syrian", "Iraqi", etc.), and they strive to equate their status to that of the Jews and view their struggle for equality as that of a nationalist group. In order to actualize their aspirations, they involve themselves in political life and make use of the tools that the Israeli government and society offer to all citizens of the state. According to this approach, Israel's Arab citizens are loyal to the state and its laws and see themselves as Palestinians only in the sense of showing solidarity with the national aspirations of the Palestinians in the Judea, Samaria and Gaza territories, which are very different from their own. In this respect, for example, although the Israeli Arabs support the establishment of an independent Palestinian state, the vast majority of them would not want to live there.

As their familiarity with the various aspects of the Israeli political system grows, Israel's Arabs are also consolidating their group identity and reinforcing the two components of this identity – the nationalist-Palestinian and the civilian-Israeli. Indeed, Smooha claims that "the new Israeli Arabs" are at once Israelis and Palestinians, and consider being Israeli as tantamount to being Palestinian rather than conflicting with being Palestinian. Arabs in Israel are undergoing a process of politicization which consists of three components: *Israelization* – large-scale integration of Arabs into the social, economic and political Israeli establishment; *internal splintering* – a process of internal pluralism that leads to a fourfold splintering into ideological and political camps;[21] and *Palestinization* – adopting an identity that is nationalistic-Palestinian and supporting the creation of a Palestinian state alongside the State of Israel; at the same time, they are promoting their struggle to achieve this objective and to improve their own civil status in Israel.

Whereas the non-Palestinian Israeli identity is stronger among the non-Moslem minority groups,[22] among most of the Arabs, the civilian-Israeli component in their identity does not necessarily conflict with the nationalist-Palestinian component. According to Smooha, the weight of the civilian-Israeli identity is far greater than other researchers think. These researchers emphasize the national component in the identity of the Arabs as a result of the conflict between Israel and the Palestinians, or as a result of overstressed Palestinization.

Israel's Arab citizens divide the country's space into territorial units which also serve to reflect the different aspects and changing forces in defining their group identity. In this respect, the broad spectrum of opposites and contradictions within the fabric of the Israeli Arabs' identity has created a tolerable *modus vivendi* between their Palestinian identity, their Israeli citizenship and their ethnic affinity.

Their identity consists of four parts: *nationalistic* – their attitudes to various Arab-populated areas in the country, the Palestinian nation and the Arab people; *civilian* – their affinity to the region and to the country; *ethnic-religious* – the way in which they divide Arab areas and mixed Arab settlements into Moslem, Bedouin, Christian and Druze areas; and the *family/tribal system* – where the importance of the nuclear family and its political and social interests overrides the importance of the extended family and the clan because of the transition to urban occupations. In municipal politics, the clan and the extended family continue to be a force to be reckoned with.[23]

There is a clear connection between socio-political changes within Israel and the crystallization of the Palestinian identity of Israel's Arab population. Over the years, the Arabs who remained under Israeli sovereignty moved from a general ethnic Arabic identity to a focused Palestinian identity. This self-identity was the natural outcome of the tension between their collective and personal realities, with the result, in this case, of accelerated politicization and increased willingness to struggle against a situation which, as their individual financial status improved, they conceived as discriminatory. The result was heightened tension between Israeli and Palestinian national identity,[24] which prevented Israel's Arabs from completely identifying with political organizations that were "purely" Palestinian, while blocking any possibility of sympathy for the Zionist establishment. For many years, Israel's Arabs expressed their need for political involvement by supporting local Communist parties who adopted an a-nationalist stand, but took a concrete pro-Palestinian stance.[25]

Thus the Israeli Arabs' struggle to turn Israel into a home for all its people can be seen as an expression of their desire to be an integral part of the state and to end the injustice and discrimination that they experience as an ethnic minority. This, it would seem, is an attempt to reinforce one of the identities adopted by the Arabs – subjects of the State of Israel. Similarly, the struggle to turn Israel into a national home for all its people can be construed as an intent on the part of Israel's Arabs to abolish the state's Jewish character and turn it eventually into an Arab state with a Jewish minority.

It is generally accepted that a population's national identity can be reflected in its voting trends. Thus their electoral behavior illustrates the overruling nationalist component in the identity of Israel's Arabs.

Theoretical and Conceptual Aspects in Electoral Behavior

Research literature dealing with electoral behavior is wide and diverse. Electoral changes relate to changes in political behavior and changes stemming from socio-economic transformation.[26] S. Bartolini and P. Mair claim that electoral stability is actually an expression of two main phenomena: the individual's behavior at the polling station, and lack of structural change in the party system. The political relevance of this stability is reduced to changes it causes in the structure of the political system.[27] Other researchers claim that electoral changes are connected to developments in party systems and the evolution of social rifts.[28]

Most theories on electoral behavior are based on comparative research in Western democracies, which followed demographic processes and economic changes, as well as changes in education and employment. Almost invariably, the most dramatic changes are linked to economic conditions. During the last third of the twentieth century, the West began to rebuild its workforce; there was a drastic decrease in agriculture and a sharp transition to service-providing enterprises. Advanced industrialization led to a decrease in rural populations and a growth in urban centers. Among other things, urbanization meant a greater separation between the home and the workplace. Researchers assumed that as socio-economic characteristics change, so do the characteristics of the public. More readily available education led to an increase in political skills and resources, and created sophisticated communities in numbers unprecedented in the history of democracies. Changes in economic conditions redefined public interests, and the greater the extent of urbanization, the weaker were traditional social nets and old organizational loyalties, all of which reduced the power of the traditional political systems and voting patterns.[29]

At this point we should define the term "rift" in its electoral context. The term refers to a line dividing two different groups. The sharper its edges, the less common are electoral exchanges across this line.[30] The term relates also to subjects of interest, to changes in policy or political identities, which refer to long-term conflicts in a certain society.[31] Social rift can be expressed in the political arena by restraining electoral mobility of the minority. In the Israeli case as well as in other cases of majority–minority relations there is a ceiling obstructing the minority from reaching an effective influential position in politics.

Most studies of Arab society in Israel have focused on the nationalist rift between Jews and Arabs, and have tended to emphasize the ideological and positional content of relevant subjects and downplay the relationship existing between them and social groups. Most researchers have assumed that the rift is a static factor and is not stipulated by time and place. My argument is that political rifts basically appear as reflections of social and economic divisions, and the structure of the rift is defined in terms of social groups and the loyalty of members to their social groups, no less than as a reflection of ethnic, national or religious divisions. My view is that there is a connection between rift and party. The rift is the factor behind the fact that today most Israeli Arabs vote for Arab nationalist parties. The rift itself advances the identity and may be the identity itself. The depth of the rift is determined by the national polity of Israel and by the structure of its regime.

Economic instability and increased unemployment often lead to increased participation in elections along the borders of social and nationalist rifts. According to Zirakzadeh, sharp increases in nationalist voting are connected to economic instability and economic fears. For example, in the 1970s in Scotland and in the Basque region of Spain, when the Scottish Nationalist Party and three Basque parties became, almost overnight, an important electoral force, they increased their share in each of the respective countries by over 15 percent.[32]

Electoral changes also reflect social and political rifts, and some researchers have used a model of social rift to explain electoral changes.[33] In areas where there is a dominant nationalist culture beside ethnic or language populations, a rift is formed between center and periphery. I claim that in order to be integrated into the party political system, a new social rift has to have an institutionalized base, which provides vital political resources such as field workers and election financing. As part of its ideological framework, a social movement that enjoys the support of an institutionalized base will adopt certain positions in order to provide a programmatic basis for the new rift. This is how the Arab population in Israel is behaving. It fortifies the rift by building institutions and creating a basis for a civil society of its own.

Israeli Arab society continues to remain a traditional society, and the most common basis for collective definition is affiliation with a place. The individual's self-definition and social status are determined through local affiliation. A person's home serves as the first definition and reflects the rifts of the place. Most typically, rifts in Israel's Arab society have very high visibility and are connected with identity: segmentation – ethnic, tribal, clan or village[34] – stands out in a count of the number of votes for local Knesset candidates. Those candidates who live in villages with pronounced clan or ethnic rifts enjoyed greater electoral support than the national support rate received by the party they represent.

Notwithstanding the large number of ethnic-based rifts – Moslem (Bedouin and others), Christian, Circassian and Druze – Israel's Arab society is not characterized by the ethnic pluralism accepted in the rest of the world. According to the American sociologist Nathan Glazer,[35] pluralism consists of a variety of religious and ethnic groups each living its unique and separate lifestyle while preserving its customs and its organizational system. In contrast, Israeli Arab society tends to minimize differences in lifestyle, customs and life systems through belonging to the political Arab community.

In the last three decades, various places around the globe have experienced a politicization of rifts according to ethnic, racial and language affiliation, previously hidden by national identities. During the 1970s, the ethnic communities of Scotland, Wales and Quebec were close to achieving constitutional changes in support of separatist movements, and in Belgium the importance of language differences was elevated to such an extent that most voters preferred parties based on language affiliation.

Other countries such as Canada, Malaysia, Cyprus and Sri Lanka also have ethnic and lingual minorities. Studies in these countries have focused on the question of including different national and ethnic groups in one political framework and the implications on the government structure and national frameworks determined by the majority. Studies that deal with the types of democracy existing in countries that are split into ethnic groups touch directly upon our issue, since many researchers have discovered that the political development of the Arabs in Israel resembles that of minorities in Western countries. We shall see in later chapters that in Israel Jews as well as Arabs tended to choose politics of rift and prefer Jewish or Arab parties respectively. All attempts to run Jewish–Arab parties have been short-lived.

The progressive changes that have taken place in Europe since the 1970s resulted in structural changes in the workforce and a smaller working class. By all accounts, this should have taken its toll on support for socialist parties. Also, a shrinking in rural populations should have affected the electoral base of agrarian parties. In fact, support for such traditional political parties remained unchanged until 1970. The question, therefore, should be: If electoral change is indeed caused by social change, why is its influence so latent on the electoral level? In contrast, in the case of Israel's Arabs there is a real correlation between changes in social structure and changes in electoral behavior. During the 1970s the new generation of well-educated Arabs brought about changes in political behavior among the extended families and it was at this time that party political and extra-parliamentary groups began to influence voting trends and political behavior in general. The late 1980s and early 1990s saw the rise of an additional new generation that focused on social activism within the framework of non-profit organizations.

In the democratic political system, fundamental changes are forever taking place. New generations bring into the political environment new interests and talents that influence the political process. These developments create new tensions in the democratic party systems and weaken the traditional socio-psychological connections between voters and parties. Moreover, economic factors are what cause political changes among the modern electorate. Such an accelerated process is taking place among the Israeli Arab society and springs mainly from changes in Israeli Arab local administration. From the 1970s, government agencies started becoming aware of the financial hardships of the Israeli Arab towns and villages, and the Ministry of the Interior unleashed new policies for expanding local government and services and establishing education departments in the local authorities. To a certain extent, these relatively swift socio-economic changes eroded the traditional group and community network. These traditional frameworks did not disappear, however, but adjusted themselves to a changing reality, and the direct contact they were able to maintain with extended families, tribes and the rural population in general resulted in veiled political manipulation. The more homogeneous the communal-social context, the greater the effect of traditional norms on political positions. From this springs the way in which local parliamentary candidates receive significantly greater support than is enjoyed nationwide by the parties they represent.

Electoral and political change is also the result of a qualitative rise in the public's political sophistication. Modern society has led to a tremendous increase in high school and university education, as well as to the diffusion of political information via the media, mainly electronic. This has raised political resources and the cognitive skills of many strata in the population.

Political changes are not necessarily the result of changes in social structure. New issues on Europe's agenda – such as women's rights, the environment and globalization – did not easily find their way into the confines of existing rifts and did not necessarily cause the acceleration of their obsolescence. Some of these new issues may even define the borders of new social rifts. In Israeli Arab politics, the weight of traditional rifts is still strong in spite of attempts to downplay them. The choice of a party is still made according to the boundaries of the main existing rifts – the clan, religious group or social sector, settlement, political left, students and academics, etc. Balad, the only party to raise a new issue – that of civil status – did indeed succeed in garnering votes from all rifts and was elected to the sixteenth Knesset.

The evaluation of political changes will be done by analyzing the election results in the last 55 years. The independent variables were social characteristics and political viewpoints and the dependent variable was the vote for Israeli Arab national parties. The question of whether a social structure becomes less relevant when choosing a party might be answered by the vote for the nationalist Israeli Arab parties. If young voters vote in a way that is significantly different from their parents, then these changes point to a phenomenon of status interest. It should be remembered that a dramatic change has occurred in the demographic structure of Israel's Arab population. Most of today's voters are young and more educated than their parents, and therefore different.

The structural and social changes undergone by Israel's Arab population is due to the influence of the country's Jewish majority, together with population trends imported from Western Europe and the US. It all began as a hesitant change of social and cultural values, increased importance of the nuclear family, slow changes in the status of females, improved living conditions, the development of organized local government, the establishment of political and social organizations and, especially, the constant improvement in formal education since 1977, including a steady increase in university graduates (from 350 in 1960 to 17,000 in 1997 and some 1,200 graduates a year ever since). Education has also been instrumental in bringing about substantial and rapid changes in employment patterns. Agricultural labor – once the main source of income among the Israeli Arab population – decreased to 18.4 percent in the year 2000. By the turn of the century, 19.3 percent of the Israeli Arab workforce was employed in "white-collar" jobs, 50 percent in "blue-collar" jobs.

Possible reasons for the parallel process of social and electoral changes among Israel's Arabs since the early 1970s are the new issues they had to deal with, such as land expropriation, and issues that bridged the social rifts of previous years. In contrast, social change in Europe did not immediately lead to political change because of the slow evolvement of new political generations. The demographic behavior of Israel's Arabs is different. In the 1970s their high birthrate led to the quick growth of a new political generation, which changed electoral behavior and voting patterns. In the early 1990s, a new young political generation came into being, which led again to changes in the Arab party system. Modern Israeli Arab society is very different from that of the 1950s, when the political systems were established. Arabs today are better educated and better informed politically. All of which should mean that there is no longer any reason for Israeli Arab voters to cling to political signals issued by various social reference groups.

Those voters who had already reached adulthood in 1948 are less influenced by the changes and remain attached to their traditional voting behavior patterns. The post-1948 generation is more influenced by social changes. Their offspring joined the voting public before the late 1960s, when the major electoral change took place.

In order to assess the reasons for changes in political affiliation, it is necessary to understand the extent of the changes. Assuming the existence in the country of several different political parties, an index must be drafted outlining political trends at the start of the period, against which a comparison can be made of the end of the period. I have chosen to draft an index of those lists created under the auspices of Mapai, which participated in Knesset elections until their disappearance in 1981.

In this index a vote for Jewish[36] or Arab parties[37] resembles a vote for the political right or left. In Europe the rift between right-wing and left-wing parties was formed in order to define a more obvious social division.

In Israel, such division is devoid of social relevance, although it does have political relevance, which creates a kind of social rift.

At least until the events of October 2000, Israel's Arab voters appeared willing to support the Jewish left, although they did not vote for it substantially. In the political relationship between Arabs and Jews, the Jewish left is seen to favor a political solution to the Israeli–Palestinian struggle and equality for the Israeli Arab minority. The constant decrease in electoral power of Jewish parties among Arabs makes it possible to evaluate the process and reasons for electoral change among the Israeli Arab population.

Different researchers have studied the connection between party affiliation, election participation and electoral stability. It is argued that a person who abstains from voting is less stable from a party political point of view than one who does vote and is more susceptible to the massive political pressure that creates long-term shifts in public opinion.[38] Among Israel's Arabs, party membership has always been marginal. The reasons for this are historical. In the past, Mapam[39] was the only Jewish party to accept Israeli Arab members as far back as the early 1950s. Mapai (forerunner of today's Labor Party), on the other hand, opened its doors to Arab members only in 1970, and then only to those Arabs who had served in the military. Other Arabs were allowed to join only in 1973. On the eve of the sixteenth Knesset elections, only 10 percent of the electorate were members of a political party.[40] The only Arab party to establish a membership list was Rakah, Israel's Communist Party, whose list was always considered very stable. Indeed, because of its small membership, Rakah has no influence on the number of people who participate in elections or on electoral stability. Thus party membership among the Israeli Arab public has little influence on if or how people participate in national elections.

Voting trends among Arabs over a 55-year period and sixteen Knesset election campaigns will serve here as an index for the political behavior of Israel's Arab minority, which is torn between attempts at integration and the isolation that results from solidarity with the Palestinian nation outside the State of Israel. An analysis of voting patterns will be conducted below on two cross sections: national groups and subgroups, which differ from each other in size, but express the variety of rifts in minority populations in Israel and represent the Arabs in the Galilee, Arabs in the Triangle, the Druze community, Galilee Bedouin, Negev Bedouin, the Christian and the Circassian communities.[41]

In a multi-party regime such as Israel's and with a relative voting system that usually requires the establishment of a coalition government, the Israeli Arab electoral vote carries great potential and real weight. One of the questions this book tries to answer is why Arab voters abstain from realizing their electoral potential. Throughout the period covered by this study, this potential is weighed against fourteen Knesset seats. Were proper use made of this potential, the Arab sector could secure substantial achievements. In contrast, the ultra-Orthodox Sephardi party Shas, and the national religious Mafdal parties, with a smaller number of Knesset seats, managed to achieve considerably more on behalf of their voters and on more than one occasion they even determined the formation of a government. But the Israeli Arab public, for whatever reasons, has never succeeded in actualizing its potential. An examination of Knesset campaign results shows that the Israeli Arab Knesset seats have always been distributed among all the parties and therefore have never truly realized their electoral potential.

This trend has seen considerable change in recent years, when the Israeli Arab public has become increasingly aware of its potential, of the ineffectuality of spreading its votes among all the parties, and of the effect this has on their political and social aspirations. Indeed, recent Knesset election campaigns have witnessed a tendency among Israeli Arab voters to support independent Arab lists. Still, a central Israeli Arab party which combines in its political activity a nationalist line and the socio-economic concerns of Israel's Arab population has yet to come into being.

2

Political Supervision and Co-optation

Researchers of Zionist history are united in the opinion that most of the movement's founders were so overwhelmed with the need to revive sovereign institutions and statehood in the Jewish homeland that they did not waste much thought on the eventuality of a Jewish state with an Arab minority. They certainly did not devise a program that included a solution for such a situation and therefore, since the early days of the state, Israel's leaders resorted to various kinds of improvisation in order to deal with the country's substantial Arab population. The country's first prime minister, David Ben-Gurion, tended to set his own minorities policy and, at the most, conferred with only a few of his closest colleagues. While his approach strove ostensibly for equality and security for all, the actual outcome was that the government's policy towards minorities swung between attempts at integrating them into the new state and isolating them. The policy changes that took place from time to time – a sign of the Jewish state's internal struggle between advocates of "gentle" and "strong arm" policies – expressed the desire to give Arab minorities equal rights and duties on the one hand, while emphasizing Israel's security needs on the other hand.

In the early years of the state, Mapai, which was the dominant party in Israel's political system and forerunner of the present Labor Party, set the tone *vis-à-vis* the country's internal and external security policy. This, of course, influenced Israel's long-term relations with the Arab population. By choosing to place the security issue at the very zenith of its internal policy and establishing military administration in predominantly Arab areas, Mapai actually succeeded in isolating the Arabs from the rest of Israel's civilian population. Moreover, some of the Mapai leaders (including David Ben-Gurion, Chaim Weizmann and Arthur Rupin) even went so far as to support a "voluntary transfer" of Israel's Arabs to neighboring countries.

To this day, the Israeli government is unable to make up its mind whether to treat the Arab population as loyal citizens, allowing them to enjoy the equal rights and obligations of the rest of the population, or as a hostile "fifth column" whose sympathies lie out of Israel. Theoretically, Israel's Declaration of Independence promised to protect the individual rights of every citizen of Israel, Jew and Arab alike; indeed, this was expressly laid out in the basic outlines of the first government. The need and desire to apply such democratic principles was more than merely declaratory; it was an approach rooted in Jewish history, when Jews had themselves been a persecuted minority. Now, with a country of their own, Israelis had the opportunity to be generous toward another minority population. Evidence of this attitude is interior minister Yitzhak Greenbaum's visit to Haifa in 1948, when he met with representatives of the Arab community. Clearly confused and ill at ease, he turned to the city's deputy mayor, Haj Taher Karman, and promised one law for all citizens of the state. "The Jews", he said, "have themselves suffered too much to permit themselves to treat the Arabs unfairly."

Israel strove to achieve complete integration of its Arab population and hoped, by developing Arab towns and villages, to close the gap between them and the rapidly developing Jewish settlements. However, these efforts were hindered by the constant vigilance made necessary by the armed Jewish–Arab conflicts and suspicions that Arab–Israeli citizens presented a security risk to the new state. According to Yigal Allon, Israel was in danger from espionage, terrorism and sabotage, guerilla warfare and political struggle on the part of its Arab population. With such an attitude, the only possible action was continued military administration in densely populated Arab areas, together with a land development policy that demanded the expropriation of Arab lands in order to serve the new Jewish towns and regional administration, industrial zones and infrastructure.

The Finance Ministry, Defense Ministry, Prime Minister's Office, Foreign Ministry and – between May, 1948 and July, 1949 (when it ceased to exist) – the Ministry for Minority Populations were all involved in carrying out settlement and development policies. Their attitude toward the Arab population was a direct continuation of the Jewish nationalist approach galvanized during the pre-state, British Mandate "settlement" period: the struggle for territory, a return to "Jewish labor" and a Jewish demographic majority in the Land of Israel.

The 1948 *Naqba*:[1] Adapting to a New Reality

No sooner had the British left Palestine and the fledgling State of Israel prepared to go about the business of establishing a Jewish homeland, than the joint armies of Egypt, Syria, Lebanon, Jordan and Iraq attacked with the intention of "driving the Jews into the sea". By all accounts, they should have succeeded in doing so. But they did not succeed, and the resounding defeat of the Arab armies had a profound effect on Moslems throughout the world and on the Arab population of Palestine in particular. The Supreme Moslem Council in Palestine ceased to exist and its members left for neighboring Arab countries. The Moslem religious leadership, too – the Muftis, Kadis, Ulama'a and all the senior administrators – deserted their communities within the sovereignty of Israel. The Arab political leadership left as well, along with the intelligentsia and the elite urban society. As a result, community infrastructure collapsed. Even before the war, the Palestinian Arab community had been disjointed and lacked any meaningful social and civic institutions; even the Supreme Arab Committee was weakened. To top it all, in 1948 they had to deal with the consequences of a sovereign Jewish state.

To this day, the results of Israel's 1948 War of Independence affect the Israel–Palestine dialogue. As far as the Palestinians are concerned, Israel's Arabs are that part of the Palestinian people who stayed on their land after the State of Israel was established on the "stolen" Palestinian territories. The suffering of Israel's Arab minority, therefore, is part of what is commonly termed the "Palestinian tragedy" and entitles them to be referred to as "the Arabs of 1948" by their brethren across the border.

The dominant issues in the dialogue between Israel's Arab minority and the state's mainstream focuses on the three major outcomes of the 1948 war: the refugee problem, land expropriation policies, and those communities coined by the Arabs as "displaced persons".[2] Israel's Arabs are busy with these issues, which to this day have not been fully resolved and continue to affect relations with the state and the Jewish–Arab discourse.[3] The *Naqba* is deeply etched into the collective memory of Israel's Arabs and has enormous influence on their political behavior.

The Arabs who remained within Israel's borders at the end of the War of Independence were devoid of any kind of political, religious or social leadership. The political organizations of the Mandate period dispersed; the parties, the networks, the headquarters and national committees disappeared. And, as if this were not enough, the establishment of the Jewish state brought Israel's Arabs face to face with a democratic parliamentary system to which they were completely unaccustomed, and which forced them to learn new rules of the game, in an unfamiliar field.

Under Military Administration

The history of Israel's Arabs after 1948 is marked by several junctions, all of which play a crucial role in their collective consciousness and are reflected in their political behavior. Most of the junctions concern one-off events and only one – the period they spent under military administration – was played out over several years.

During the 1948 war, Israel conquered or gained through the Armistice Agreement Arab-populated areas outside the boundaries of the UN partition plan for a Jewish state. The security circumstances were such that there was an obvious need to place these new areas under military administration. Different government authorities had appointed military governors. In 1948, Ben-Gurion decided to bring all military functions together under a central military administration, and the Defense Ministry's Military Administration department was established in mid-August 1948. Renewed battles in the Negev and Galilee regions during October 1948 resulted in an increased Arab population, so that the boundaries of the military administration were extended accordingly.

As part of the temporary government established right after the war, a minister for police and minorities issues was appointed. High on the new ministry's agenda was the rehabilitation of relations between Jews and minority communities, but funding for the ministry was limited, as was its influence on government decisions. The ministry was dismantled in July 1949, after much bickering with other government agencies, which refused to transfer projects and initiatives to its authority. The prime minister's advisor for Arab affairs was appointed in the ministry's place, while so-called "Arab" departments were established in various government ministries in order to address the needs of the Israeli Arab community.

With the cancellation of the Minorities' Ministry, authority to deal with Arab issues was transferred to the military administration, a civil as well as military institution, which took responsibility for the everyday life of Israel's Arabs. Thus the political echelon was freed from the requirement to consider the needs of this particular minority population, how it should be treated and what policy should be adopted towards it. The military administration structures evolved according to the pressures and problems that characterized the course of the War of Independence. They were not set up on a judicial base, nor were they given long-term directives or the tools to develop a general vision of what was expected of them. Only once a truce was agreed upon with neighboring countries (the 1948–9 Armistice Agreement) did the government find time to examine the role required of the military administration and to address the need for a legal framework for this role. Israel sought solutions in the experience of other nations that had to deal with large minority groups and was guided by international law.

The government conducted its relationship with the country's Arab population on three separate levels: the army, represented and authorized by the military administration; civil authorities, which dealt with civil and community matters and represented various government offices; and the populace itself, which was subject to the government's administration and authority.[4] Following the Armistice Agreements, Israel was left with the task of organizing its civil organs of government, and attention was slowly diverted from the management of external conflicts to that of internal co-existence. Once the military administration was organized with the appropriate conduits for the delivery of services, the government began to take care of the population and their everyday problems. As a first step, it took a census of the Arab population and dealt with security matters, mainly stemming from the infiltration of subversive elements from across the border. Next, the government tried to provide solutions for employment, education, health and related problems, and to help people return to normal life, which included finding a way to incorporate the remaining Arabs into Israel's political system.

For the Israeli government, the necessity for military administration was rooted in fundamental distrust and suspicion of Israel's Arab population. It is easy enough to understand, therefore, why five of the six early advisors for Arab affairs were former security and intelligence officers. Attorney S. Jiryyes, one of the founders of *al-Ard*,[5] pointed this out, and agreed that "actually there is a certain measure of truth in the assumption that the military administration was set up for purely security related purposes. It is probable that this institution, which was established during a war between Israel and the Arab states, when the new government was facing serious problems from outside, as well as from its Arab population, whose loyalty to the new regime was questionable, was meant to take care of security issues only."[6]

The main purpose of the military administration was to keep an eye on the Arabs, to limit their movement for security reasons and to prevent them from taking over jobs that Jews could fill. At that time, Israel was absorbing waves of mass immigration – Holocaust survivors from Europe and Jewish refugees from the poor countries of the Middle East and North Africa – and employment was a crucial issue.

The military administration was responsible for perpetuating the gaps in economic development between the Jewish and the Arab sectors, channeling money to Jewish rather than Arab institutions, and implementing a policy of discrimination and restricted credit. It perpetuated the already existent disunity within the Arab population by encouraging communities to split up into rival religious, tribal or regional groups; these disunited groups subsequently became increasingly dependent on the Jewish government. The method of supervision of the military administration caused its politicization, and Jewish political parties – mainly Mapai, Mapam (United Workers' Party) and the Unity of Labor★ – moved in and began operating within the Arab community, mostly in the northern region known as the "Triangle", by involving themselves in matters of municipality and employment. After the 1948 war, with no kind of Arab government remaining in the "Triangle", a leadership of Mapai supporters evolved, from which heads of extended families (*hamulas*), such as Fares Hamdan,

---

★ The Unity of Labor party broke off from Mapam in 1954 and towards the elections of 1965 allied with Mapai to form the Labor Alignment and ceased to exist as an individual entity.

Mahmud Nashif and Diab Ubeid, who had good connections in high government circles, were elected to the Knesset.

In order to obtain the co-operation of the Arab population, the military administration reconstructed pre-war socio-political institutions and local committees headed by *Mukhtar*s, who were made responsible for executing orders issued by the administration. In towns, municipal councils were reinstated and redefined as civil authorities; vacant positions were filled by administration-appointed functionaries. Villages with populations in excess of 800 were placed under the jurisdiction of a committee – operating under the local *Mukhtar* – which consisted of people who were loyal and acceptable to the government. The *Mukhtar* was required to carry out a multitude of tasks, including the traditional job of community leader, which, too, had been adapted to meet the government's needs. Thus, among other things, the *Mukhtar* became responsible for passing on information on the property of absentee landlords, on infiltrators, on people with weapons in their possession, on suspicious persons and criminals, as well as on actual criminal activity. It was the *Mukhtar*'s job to help the governor carry out his own duties, including occasional tax collection; to relay to the local population information issued by the military administration; to register births, deaths and marriages, and to manage a document archive. The committee, which was appointed to help the *Mukhtar*, was responsible for providing the village with municipal services.

Shortly after the onset of military administration, the establishment began questioning the justification of its existence. As early as July 1949, the government submitted a petition to cancel those emergency defense regulations that served as the basis for military administration.[7] Political parties formed a lobby against the military administration. By the early 1960s, Mapam and the Unity of Labor were heading the lobby and arguing that there was no real security value to maintaining military administration and, in any case, it served mainly the political needs of Mapai. Moreover, by being forced to live under military administration, Israel's Arabs had no chance to develop an affinity for the state.[8] While in 1962 the Unity of Labor Party came out strongly in favor of canceling military administration, Mapai and Rafi[9] accepted Ben-Gurion's strong-arm position regarding the Arabs, for reasons of security.[10] When, in 1962, Mapam made its willingness to join the government contingent on canceling military administration, prime minister Levi Eshkol appointed Isser Harel to head a committee to examine the repercussions of the proposed cancellation. Although the committee recommended canceling the military administration in February 1966, only in November 1966 did the Knesset actually confirm it.

The government's willingness to relinquish its supervision and military control of the Arab population meant that the Jewish public and its leaders were sufficiently confident to accept the evaluations of security experts that the situation had improved considerably. Still, notwithstanding the obviously improved standard of living enjoyed by Israel's Arab population under military administration (as compared with that of their counterparts in Jordan, Egypt, Lebanon and Syria), the Jewish establishment followed the military administration's policy of neglect, and virtually ignored the social changes that were taking place within the Arab minority, whose veteran leadership remained across the borders while new tribal heads in Israel took their place. This disregard was typical of the establishment's behavior for years to come, so it was no wonder that the various developments that occurred during the 1970s took Israel's policy-makers completely by surprise.

By taking full advantage of the opportunities provided by the military-political-civilian supervisory system established by the state for its Arab citizens, the Mapai, Mapam and Israeli Communist[11] parties made a considerable contribution to voting trends among Israel's Arab population. The co-operation between the military administration and the various political parties was fruitful. Among other things, the administration followed the movements of workers registered in the labor bureaus, which had been opened by such political bodies as the Arab Workers' Congress (under the auspices of Mapam) and the Land of Israel Workers' Union (under the auspices of the General Labor Federation and the influence of Mapai), all part of government policies that demanded supervision of the Arab public. The labor bureaus remained faithful to and served their parent parties. As the governing party, Mapai created the frameworks, the mechanism and the policy *vis-à-vis* the Arabs, all of which required a political behavior based on integrative voting trends. Mapam and the Israeli Communist Party, two opposition parties when it came to dealing with the Arab public, created the alternative frameworks and a political culture based on nationalist voting trends.

Early Political Organizations

People's most basic political tendencies are expressed in the considerations they make before settling on their choice of a political party; at the general level the result of all these considerations becomes a "voting pattern".

In the past, Israel's Arabs galvanized and adapted their considerations in reaction to the prevailing political establishment, which had a clear position about the Arab minority, and the necessary bureaucratic system to apply this position. The bureaucratic system also undertook the social role of preserving traditional local frameworks in order for them to back the policies of the military administration. Thus Arab society remained a traditional society and the local schisms are to this day the basis for Arab politics in Israel, as will be discussed in the following chapters.

It soon became apparent, however, that the bureaucratic systems had lives of their own and that these did not always conform with the policies determined by government offices. In the early days of the advisor on Arab affairs, these systems developed a unique kind of political behavior in the Arab sector, which was expressed in political organization and the choice of a party both on a local and on a national level. The government did not always intend for this to happen. But it was always the "Arabists"[12] who were employed in Arab matters and, as far as the government ministers and their lackeys were concerned, their word was law with regard to the Arab way of thinking and ways of dealing with this sector. It is possible that the government wished to create a state of conflict, which would provide it with various options for dealing with the Arab sector, and this view is elaborated below.

From the beginning, it was clear to Israel's Jews and Arabs alike that the latter could not opt for full membership in the Zionist political parties – because of the state's Jewish-Zionist character and the fact that most of the parties did not cater to the nationalist aspirations of the Arab public. The Zionist parties, for their part, did not welcome Arab members, and the military administration made it difficult for Israeli Arabs to establish a party of their own and engage in political activities to foster their own national interests. Indeed, no independent Israeli Arab parties were founded during the military administration period. The Israeli Communist Party, the only Israeli Arab party (which was actually joint Jewish–Arab), did not present the Arab voter with a real option. Communist ideology had few followers within Israeli Arab communities and had never been popular among Israeli Arabs and Moslems. Also, the party was under close government scrutiny and many Israeli Arabs were reluctant to involve themselves in activities that could be construed as detrimental to state security.

In Israel, therefore, the Arabs were removed from the center of political influence. Lacking an authentic pattern of democratic parliamentary activity of its own, Arab society largely internalized the political behavior common among the Jewish public. Thus any study of political behavior within Arab society in Israel first requires an examination of the main political orientations of its Jewish counterpart. It is the Israeli party political spectrum, rather than the Israeli Arab lifestyle, that had the greatest impact on the political structure and behavior of Arab society in Israel, which was under constant internal pressure: trying to co-exist with the majority society, coupled with constant conflict over traditional values and the demands of modern political struggle. Indeed, when the Labor and Likud parties formed a political core within Israel's political system, the Israeli Arabs began to gain a measure of influence within that system.

Israel has no clear policy regarding the possible political organization among its Arab minority. In its Declaration of Independence, the state committed itself to ensuring the welfare and political rights of all its citizens regardless of religion or ethnic origin. This commitment, coupled with national, political and social circumstances, justified independent political organization on the part of the Arab population. When such organization did not take place, the electoral potential provided by the Arab population attracted the attention of Zionist parties; but because Arabs could not be expected to identify with the aims and ideology of these parties, they did not accept Arabs as members (there was no problem having them as voters). As Golda Meir said, "[We have] a platform and [we have] principles and I cannot ask an Arab to show interest in Jewish immigration."[13] Still, the Zionist parties were keen to attract the Arab vote.

Most of Israel's Arab population lives in a rural or semi-rural environment, where clan loyalties are stronger than in urban concentrations. This is the direct result of the Arab defeat in 1948, when the majority of the urban elite population escaped, or were banished, across the borders. As a result it was difficult for public systems to develop, out of which a leadership cadre could be elected. The heads of the larger clans therefore became the more prominent among Israel's Arabs. In their attempts to incorporate the Israeli Arabs into the new political system – which was so different from that to which they had belonged during the British Mandate – successive Israeli governments found it convenient to operate via the clan system. Authorities understood that by working with the clan heads, most of whom expressed loyalty and a willingness to co-operate with the new government, it would be possible to control the Israeli Arab population. Leaders of large clans, as well as village *Mukhtars*, exploited their new-found political power to strengthen their own position among clan members and villagers. Their connections with the government and party activists strengthened their social standing: their responsibilities included arranging exit permits for people wishing to move in and out of areas under military administration, providing employment, arranging the unification of families split by national borders, etc. The Arab public, who needed strong representatives to liaise successfully on their behalf, were interested in reinforcing the status of these representatives *vis-à-vis* the authorities, on whom they depended entirely.

Allied Arab Lists

Of the Zionist parties operating in the Arab sector, Mapai and Mapam – and to a lesser degree, the General Zionists[14] – were the most conspicuous. In its quest to attract the Arab vote, and assuming that the Arab public would be reluctant to vote directly for a Zionist party, Mapai devised a system whereby it could profit from the electoral weight of this sector without the Arab voters appearing to be voting for Jews. They achieved this by establishing "allied" political lists under the leadership of the clan heads. The deeply divided Israeli Arab public was interested mainly in day-to-day social and economic issues, so that support for the allied lists formed a channel of communication between it and the government, via their political representatives who headed these lists and who enjoyed access to the government's power centers, the Labor Federation and public institutions. Mapai introduced its allied lists as early as the election campaign for the first Knesset in 1949, thus preventing a practical examination of the theory that Arabs would shy away from voting directly for Zionist parties. Under military administration, totally dependent on the government and with a leadership that consisted almost entirely of *Mukhtars* subject to co-optation, the Arab public accepted their leadership's explanation that giving their vote to the ruling parties – even if these were Jewish-Zionist – was their best bet by far, since these parties were able to provide for many of the people's needs, both on the personal and the communal level.

From the first Knesset elections and until their disappearance from the political scene during elections for the tenth Knesset, 18 allied lists vied for the Arab vote. Most of them were connected to Mapai, the ruling party. The make-up of the lists was usually determined by the mother party according to an ethnic key – Moslem, Christian, Druze and Bedouin, in that order – taking advantage of family and marriage ties and inter-family and inter-clan rivalries for the good of the party. The large al-Zu'bi clan, who inhabit several villages in the Jezreel Valley, provide a good example of the way in which a clan leader, Seif al-Din al-Zu'bi, assured his repeated election to the Knesset, through the vote of his clansmen.

Seif al-Din al-Zu'bi from Nazareth and other clan leaders, most of whom had little or no previous political experience or education, achieved key positions via the allied lists.[15] However, they were not cut out for dealing with the complex challenges they faced and achieved little influence beyond their family, village or region. Nonetheless, they did manage to exploit the allied list system for their own purposes, and, according to Subhi abu Ghosh, "The clan adapted itself to this government tool, so that relations in the village were reflected in the struggle for municipal rule."[16] Leaders were usually put to the test during election years, which the Arab public coined *sanat al marhaba*, or the year of welcome – the time when various candidates would appear in Arab settlements, handing out a myriad of greetings, promises and favors, in the hope of garnering as many votes as possible. Plagued by a fair share of local problems, the Arab community was forced to take a pragmatic stance and, until the seventh Knesset, around 50 percent of the Arab vote did indeed go to the allied lists. It was a situation that, coupled with the rest of the voting system, allowed the clans to preserve their political power in the fact of the social changes and modernization that threatened their standing.

However, as changes within Arab society began to take hold, the allied lists were unable to adapt themselves to the new reality. In some ways the national leadership, fearing a situation whereby the Arab minority would organize itself into a political opposition, contributed to this inability by supporting the clan framework. Thus Arab politics in Israel never became a part of the national mainstream and remained local and divided. In time, as the Arab sector succumbed to modernization, the decreased power of the allied lists became more pronounced. The younger generation made use of the Israeli state education system and gained professional skills that undermined the clan structure. Economic independence made the younger generation increasingly aware of political trends in mainstream Israeli society and gradually removed them from under the political thumb of the clan leaders. As the restrictions of military rule eased (and were cancelled in 1966), the Arabs began moving away from the political power mobilized by the allied party lists. Channels of communication were opened to the various governing authorities and there was no longer a need for middlemen. The time had come for the Arab voters to develop their own political system. Anyone wishing to register a protest or express nationalist aspirations was now able to vote for a party that was considered "nationalist" by the Jewish establishment: the new Communist list (Rakah), for example, which was followed in the late 1970s by Arab parties, including the Progressive List for Peace (PLP), the Arab Democratic Party (ADP) and others. Arabs who were more sympathetic to the Zionist establishment were free to vote directly for Zionist parties.

This change in voting trend prompted the Labor Party – on the eve of the eighth Knesset elections – to adopt a new approach toward its allied Arab lists. One of Labor's strategic decisions involved removing its support for the Co-operation and Brotherhood list headed by Diab Ubeid, in the belief that the list's chances for making it into the Knesset were negligible. Diab Ubeid, who represented the "Triangle" settlements and headed the large Ubeid Abd al-Qader clan from the village of Tayibeh, saw this decision as a personal insult and decided to go it alone. But without the support of the Labor Party, his list failed to make it into the Knesset, proof of the way in which allied lists depended on the mother party.

In place of the Co-operation and Brotherhood list, the Labor Party founded the Arab List for Bedouin and Villagers (ALBV), the first of its kind for Israel's Bedouin community. The new political list was headed by Negev Bedouin leader Sheikh Hamad Abu Rabia. He scored only a moderate victory, however, receiving only 16,400 votes (of which 4,000, a little more than 50 percent of all Bedouin votes, came from the Negev Bedouin tribes).

In order for the list to succeed, the new Arab MKs had to receive certain perks. In the case of Abu Rabia, this consisted of having a telephone line installed, a rare thing in the Negev desert of those days. The phone had to be installed in Abu Rabia's home, the only stone building among a forest of black wool tents, and the cost to the state's treasury was a phenomenal 250,000 IL (the equivalent at the time of $150,000, or over four million

New Israeli Shekels in today's currency). For the country's leaders, the sheikh's house became a place of pilgrimage. The Negev's Bedouin had turned overnight into a hefty political factor, which the establishment could no longer refer to in terms of land and water rights.

As a result of the assistance I gave to the Bedouin political leadership, I received frequent invitations to the Negev, where I went from one *hafla* (feast) to another, from one man's tent to another. On each occasion, Sheikh Abu Rabia would make a point of seating me next to him in the *Sheg* (hospitality tent) and announcing, "This is the man who has reinstated Bedouin honor."

I was not to bask in this success for very long. Elections to the ninth Knesset were looming and the situation, in 1977, could not have been worse as far as I was concerned. My efforts to bring in a younger generation of Israeli Arabs to join the ranks of the Labor Party had succeeded beyond all expectations and the reign of the clan system was on its last legs. The newly established trust between young Arabs and the Labor Party had weakened the allied lists, including Sheikh Abu Rabia's Bedouin list. In the north, things were no better for the list headed by the Moslem representative Seif al-Din al-Zu'bi and his second in command, the Druze Sheikh Jaber Mu'adi. Initially Mu'adi had planned to run independently, but polls showed that the revolution that had begun in the Arab sector had also hit the Druze sector and less influence on the part of clan heads meant less votes for Mu'adi, who would probably be unable to make the minimum vote necessary to admit him to the Knesset.

Mu'adi was forced to join MK al-Zu'bi in a united list, although it soon became apparent that this list, too, had little chance of success. I then had the idea of uniting the Mu'adi – al-Zu'bi list with the Bedouin list in order to ensure the survival of both lists. The united list was headed by the Moslem representative Seif al-Din al-Zu'bi. The second place was allocated, according to tradition, to the Druze Sheikh Jaber Mu'adi. Both made a historical pact in which Mu'adi recognized al-Zu'bi's seniority. However, it was necessary on this occasion to change the arrangement in order to encourage the Bedouin to vote for Abu Rabia and thus get at least two mandates for the united list. The second place on the political list, therefore, was given to Abu Rabia, on the understanding that if the list were indeed to receive only two or less mandates, he would resign his Knesset seat after two years of the Knesset's four-year term and allow Mu'adi to serve a further two years.

The allied lists became less and less relevant and the younger generation of Israeli Arabs no longer appreciated their worth. But they were finally laid to rest in the wake of the murder of Hamad Abu Rabia. The rotation agreement between the members of the united Arab list did not work out well; the list received only enough votes for one Knesset seat and that seat went to Seif al-Din al-Zu'bi, who, after a two-year term in office and heavy persuasion by Jaber Mu'adi, handed over the seat to Sheikh Hamad Abu Rabia, who in turn was supposed to relinquish it a year later to Jaber Mu'adi. Things started to go wrong towards the end of 1980. The Bedouin sheikh explained in various forums that he was the sole representative of the Bedouin community in all of Israel's government institutions. His rationale for overstating his position was the sacred struggle he was leading against the evacuation of Bedouin from their Negev lands. When, at the end of his year in the Knesset, the time came to honor the agreement and relinquish his seat to Jaber Mu'adi, Abu Rabia refused to step down. Mu'adi was mortified. There was more at stake here than the loss of his Knesset seat; he was deeply offended by the affront to his honor. When asked what action he planned to take, he refused to answer. The insult and disappointment were too much for him to discuss.

Abu Rabia, for his part, based his behavior on a loose interpretation of the agreement, according to which, "after one complete year in the Knesset, Abu Rabia's membership in the ninth Knesset will come to an end, and he will be replaced by Sheikh Jaber Mu'adi". He argued that the agreement between them assumed that the list would win two mandates and the circumstance was changed when it received only one. Later, Khalil Abu Rabia, Hamad Abu Rabia's former secretary, tried to reinforce this argument, according to which the agreement was broken by the other side, not by them. Two Arab lists had vied for Knesset seats: the Bedouin, headed by Sheikh Hamad, and the Arab, headed by Seif al-Din al-Zu'bi. The Labor Party decided to unite them because the Israeli Arab list had no chance of making it into the Knesset on their own. It was then agreed, out of respect, that al-Zu'bi would head the list. When al-Zu'bi had a heart attack and was hospitalized, it was only logical that Sheikh Hamad should replace him, but al-Zu'bi begged Hamad from his sickbed to let him continue heading the list and promised to resign the moment he was voted in, thereafter allowing Sheikh Hamad to serve for two years, with Mu'adi following for a further two years. But al-Zu'bi did not keep his promise and postponed his resignation for two years. Subsequently, after heavy pressure from Mu'adi, who also wanted his year in the Knesset, he did step down. The time for Hamad's two years had come and he saw no reason to give them to Mu'adi, because, as he said, he was entitled to his two years. Mu'adi had had his two years when al-Zu'bi sat in the Knesset.

Mu'adi appealed to the legal system for justice, but the court refused to get involved in the political quarrel. Messengers and arbitrators were sent to Abu Rabia, but nothing helped. Abu Rabia made excuses, offered explanations, pretended innocence and used various other tactics. He never actually admitted to having broken the agreement, but he disregarded it. Meanwhile, Sheikh Jaber Mu'adi lost face throughout the entire Arab sector, especially among his Druze followers.

Mu'adi begged me to help him. "We are both in the same party," he said.

I organized meetings between Abu Rabia and senior Labor Party personnel, including Shimon Peres, but no one managed to persuade the sheikh to honor the agreement. I had talks with Abu Rabia and we discussed various forms of compromise and compensation, but nothing helped.

On January 12, 1981, two armed men ambushed Abu Rabia at the entrance to Jerusalem's Holyland Hotel and fired four bullets into his neck. The country was in shock. This was the first assassination in Israel to result from social and political rivalry. The murderers were tracked down almost immediately. Two of Jaber Mu'adi's sons wanted revenge for their father's public loss of face.

The evening before the assassination, I had told a colleague that I believed the quarrel between the two sheikhs could be settled with a generous monetary payment. Now, two of my friends were mortally wounded: on the one hand, there was the murdered Sheikh Abu Rabia, and, on the other, Sheikh Jaber Mu'adi, whose sons faced lengthy prison sentences. I felt the pain of the families and berated myself for believing that a written agreement could override such strong feelings. I could not sleep at night. The next day the media was full of the hunt for the fugitive murderers, who sent messages from their hiding place, hotly denying their involvement in the murder. I was reminded of Cicero's analysis of Julius Caesar's murder: "The Caesar was murdered with manly courage, but according to a childish plan." I used all the means at my disposal in an attempt to persuade the two sons to hand themselves in.

They were arrested three days later, on January 15, and rumors immediately began to circulate about imminent blood revenge. The daily *Ma'ariv* quoted Bedouin leaders as saying alongside Hamad Abu Rabia's grave in the Bedouin township of Kseifeh, "The police will carry out their investigation and we – ours." Jaber Mu'adi replied, in the same newspaper, on the same day, "I am not afraid of blood revenge." The Labor Party, founder of the united political list, feared a clan war, which would leave it severely incriminated; or worse, a religious-ethnic war could break out and the entire Israeli Arab sector would fall prey to it. According to Bedouin tradition, blood revenge can be taken even 40 years after a murder. My job was to stop the feud before it was too late, and I began to organize a lengthy series of meetings with the aim of bringing about a truce between the injured parties. In the end, although I may have succeeded in preventing any further bloodshed, I did not manage to erase the deep hatred between the Bedouin and Druze communities, a hatred that continues to this day.

The murder of Knesset member Hamad Abu Rabia was the crisis that brought about the end of the allied political lists. After serving for a few months in the Knesset, Jaber Mu'adi resigned from politics. He remained the elder secular leader of his community, and for a long time the Jewish elite still visited his home in Yarka on their way to the Druze community, whose political power now had to be reinstated. To this end, I sought ways to connect the older, wiser, experienced leadership with the community's young, educated leaders, who had served in the military and who would be interested in joining the Labor Party and playing an integral role in Israel's mainstream political scene. It was no easy task; the frictions between the Mu'adi family and the family of the community's religious leader, Sheikh Amin Tarif, required me to draw on all my experience in liaising between people. Then, when rumors reached me about a talented young man from the Tarif family, I linked him with the Labor Party's candidate, Riad Hamzi, who agreed to serve as his deputy. Together they took over the local municipality.

In time, the young man, Saleh Tarif, became a Knesset member on the Labor list and subsequently the first non-Jewish government minister. To me, he was a model leader, one with the potential to lead the Arab sector in the future. I helped him become part of the EMET[17] list and did my best to avoid favoritism between the various party contenders. Whenever I visited Saleh or his grandfather, Sheikh Amin Tarif, I made a point of calling on Sheikh Jaber Mu'adi too.

The Labor Party leadership soon adapted itself to the new reality and made some far-reaching policy changes in its campaign for the tenth Knesset. It withdrew its support for sectarian (Arab) parties and encouraged Israel's Arab voters to vote directly for the EMET list. For the first time, three independent Arab lists registered their candidacy for these elections. Not only were these three lists unconnected to Jewish-Zionist parties, they actually provided a serious political challenge to them. Together the three lists won 22,500 votes,[18] but their fate was just like that of Diab Ubeid's independent list and none of them crossed the electoral percentage threshold required to gain a seat in the Knesset. This mutual failure clearly underscored the demise of the personal and allied political list method. Freedom from traditional restraints, better education and a high standard of living joined the increased nationalist awareness that followed the 1967 and 1973 wars to make the independent and allied Arab political lists obsolete. In any case, they could offer no clear political or ideological message, and they no longer had the support of the Jewish establishment.

During the state's early years, Israel's policy-makers focused on developing a puppet Arab leadership that would bow to government decrees and ensure that the Arab vote went to the governing party. In return for their devotion, the Arab leaders were provided with the allied lists, on whose backs they were able to get themselves elected to the Knesset. In retrospect, I believe this policy to have been a mistake. It completely disregarded the changing reality within Israeli Arab society and made no efforts to single out the educated young, politically oriented Arabs, who were loyal to their Palestinian-Arab identity, but also quite prepared to identify themselves as Israelis. These individuals were willing to establish their status among, and co-operate with, the Jewish majority in Israel and to join the national discourse for the good of the two communities. As I see it, Israel missed a golden opportunity by failing to nurture such people as Sabri Jiryyes, Salah Bransah, Muhammad Mi'ari and others, founders of the *al-Ard* movement, who, had they been given the support and encouragement of the establishment, might have developed into a genuine leadership for the Arab population in Israel. Such a leadership would have had the power to create a Jewish–Arab relationship that could have served as a basis for the kind of co-existence that takes into consideration the unique characteristics and needs of both communities.

Zionist Political Parties[19]

During the first few years following Israel's signing of its Declaration of Independence, a situation in which Israeli Arabs could consider voting for Zionist parties would have seemed impossible and illogical. Not too many years later, however, it became quite a plausible option, when those same political parties, for whom the Zionist dream was paramount, began to accept Israeli Arabs as card-holding members. At first, Arab activists had only been useful for getting votes and were not party members per se. Later, however, party officials came to realize that they would have to accept Arabs on an equal and permanent basis and allow them a certain measure of representation. Elsewhere, Israeli Arabs began to realize that by becoming actively involved in the Zionist political system they would have a hand in mainstream Israeli politics and influence in issues that related to their day-to-day lives.

Mapam was the first Jewish party to welcome Arabs into its ranks. Its first experience of Arab politics was during the 1949 first Knesset elections, when it established an allied Arab list – the Popular Arab bloc – similar to those established by Mapai. The list was made up of laborers, farmers and craftsmen from Haifa, Jaffa, Lod, Acre and Shefar'am and was headed by George Nassar, who led a group from Poa'lei Zion Left. He was succeeded by Saleh Ahmad Sa'id, who headed the Arab workers' committee in the Haifa municipality, and Rustum Bastuni. Although the allied Arab list did not make it into the Knesset that year, Mapam included Bastuni in its own list for the second Knesset (1951) and he became the party's first Knesset member. Following the failure of the Popular Arab bloc, Mapam accepted George Nassar's group as members and decided to establish an Arab department with its own elected offices. The department elected a committee headed by Rustum Bastuni, Yusuf Khamis and George Nassar and only in 1954, when the Unity of Labor Party broke away from the Mapam (the issue of Arab membership was one of the catalysts for this break), did Mapam party open itself to the Arab public at large.

Mapam was very active in the Arab sector, both on an ideological and a practical level. At first, it supported a two-nation state in Israel, but it had renounced this position by the early 1950s and espoused the idea of absolute equality for the country's Arab citizens, calling for a drastic reduction in military administration. In 1965, Mapam decided to support the right of return of some of the Arab refugees, but relinquished that position in 1969, when it meshed with Labor (Mapai). For its Arab supporters, a vote for Mapam expressed their nationalist tendencies, without appearing too extreme to the authorities and undermining their wish to be an integral part of Israeli society.

By contrast, there was an ongoing debate within Mapai, and subsequently the Labor Party, between those advocating the integration of Israeli Arabs into the party and those opposing it. Gradually, the party began to accept Arab members, initially into the Labor faction of the General Labor Federation (Histadrut) and, from June, 1970, into the party itself. There was only one restriction, according to which the party was open to members of all minority groups who served in the country's security forces. In 1973 the party passed a decision to open its doors to all Arab citizens residing in Israel who identify with the party's principles and ideology.

In terms of Jewish–Arab relations, 1975 was a difficult year in Israel. The Yom-Kippur War was still fresh in the population's collective memory. On all sides, leaders claimed victory, but the people felt defeated and hopeless. Peace seemed very far away, almost unattainable.

I was completely unprepared for my appointment to head Labor's Minorities Department. My only references were my friendly relations with several figures in the Israeli Arab and Druze sector, and I needed all the support and guidance I could marshal. For half a year, I crisscrossed the country, from north to south, east to west. There was not an Arab settlement in Israel that I did not visit and there was not a single leader with whom I did not have talks. At the end of my study tour I was convinced of one thing: that profound changes were taking place among Israel's Arabs. The traditional clan leadership was losing its hold and its leaders were being replaced by younger, better educated people with a strong nationalist-Arab awareness, who were not prepared to be yes-men to the authorities. I formulated a detailed plan with which to approach the Arab sector and submitted it to the party. It was then presented, via Yigal Allon, to the government. Among other things, my plan pointed out the consequences of the growing frustration among the country's Arab population and the volatile nature of their social and economic situation. I recommended a two-pronged approach: as well as nurturing ties with traditional leaders, the party should explore ways to integrate the younger generation into the Labor Party, before they decided to pursue other forms of political expression that might be harmful to the party as well as to the country.

My plan was not disregarded and earned the support of, among others, Shmuel Toledano, the prime minister's advisor on Israeli Arab affairs, who was opposed to the opinion of my predecessor (Amnon Linn) that the party should provide aid only to "Zionist" Arabs and withhold assistance from Arabs who expressed nationalist aspirations. When I told him that the "Zionists" made up only 3 percent of the country's Arab population, he agreed that there was no reason to discriminate against the others, or to treat them with hostility. The plan also earned the support of Meir Dekel, deputy head of the prime minister's information office, who was responsible mainly for Arab affairs.

The old guard, led by MKs Seif al-Din al-Zu'bi (Moslem) and Sheikh Jaber Mu'adi (Druze), were incensed. Their views were reinforced by a number of Israeli Arab mayors and regional council heads whose power came from the clans and extended families that had placed them in office. On one occasion, realizing that I was determined to move the focus from the so-called "Zionist" Arabs to those who may not have served us all these years but whose nationalist tendencies were not hostile to Israel, Seif al-Din Zu'bi stood up and interjected angrily, "You squeezed us like a lemon and now you throw us away . . ."

Still, there were others in the Arab sector who approved of my plan; people who were very close to major political figures, like Seif al-Din al-Zu'bi's personal secretary, Ihsan Zu'bi, who shared my belief that the time had come to do away with clan heads whose job it was to liaise between the Arab community and the Labor Party. Ihsan complained to me that the traditional Arab public persona had given Labor a mistaken impression of the Arab public in Israel. Likewise, the image of the Labor Party, as well as the state in general, had been distorted in the eyes of the country's Arab public. To me, men like Ihsan were the ideal partners in implementing my plan, and a few days after it was presented I set out on a cross-country tour. My first task was to locate the most suitable people to represent their communities with regard to the Labor Party. I met with dozens of people in the Galilee, the Triangle and the Negev, familiarized them with the party and its goals and what it had to offer them in order to make their political aspirations a reality – as long as these did not contradict the ideals of peace and co-existence.

It was not enough, however, merely to convince Arab intellectuals to join the Labor Party. The party itself also had to open up to the new generation of Israeli Arabs. For a long time I brought local Arab leaders face to face with national and Labor movement leaders in order to draft and pass a decision that would make it possible for Israeli Arabs to register as fully fledged Labor Party members. The initial reaction was always doubt: how can Israeli Arabs be members in a Zionist party? I always had an answer ready: "While we can't ask them to march down Dizengoff Street waving a flag of Israel, we can invite them to join a relationship with us that is not hostile. We can welcome them into the party and, who knows, maybe we'll even make peace with them."

With the approval-in-principle of senior Labor Party members, I set about creating a genuine leadership from among "my" group of hand-picked Arab activists – taking great care not to upset the older generation of clan leaders.

In 1981, I managed to include an Israeli Arab in the Labor Party list of candidates for the Knesset: Muhammad Khalaila from Sakhnin became a member of the tenth Knesset. He was neither a university graduate, nor particularly young, and to the new generation he represented exactly the same generation of yes-men whose influence they were trying to shake off. For the next election campaign, I decided to go for the "real thing", and focused on a man with strong nationalist opinions, a member of the younger generation, who was not connected to any clan.

When Abd al-Wahab Darawsha first came to my office in the Labor Party building, he was a member of a delegation from the Lower Galilee which wanted to reorganize the party's Nazareth branch in order to use it as a base for rehabilitating the city's education and health services. He was nervous and apprehensive. I realized that he anticipated arguments, problems and tension and was expecting to be told that they would only get money if they did what we told them to do. From the beginning, I singled him out as the group's leader. As we parted, I suggested to him and his friends, "Bring all your friends to me. I will not argue with you, as long as you are loyal to the country." My promise to Darawsha was thoroughly tested later, when he began to talk in favor of negotiations with the PLO[20] and a comprehensive peace with a Palestinian state alongside Israel. At that time, concepts such as these were considered a terrible offense in the Labor Party, but I stuck to my promise and, although I disagreed with some of his ideas, I fought for his right to express them.

The Israeli political scene is not in the habit of admitting to mistakes. It was, therefore, not easy for me to get up and admit that Muhammad Khalaila's candidacy and term in office had been a mistake and that I now had a better candidate. It was even more difficult to do so before the Appointments Committee, which consisted of those members of the party leadership responsible for putting together the party's Knesset list as well as for the various appointments within the party hierarchy. The committee's decisions were made according to criteria that were so vague and unintelligible to most party members that it was dubbed the "darkness committee". Having no choice, I was obliged to address the committee and passionately introduced Darawsha as someone capable of connecting the Labor Party with the hopes and desires of the younger generation of the Israeli Arab community.

The Appointment Committee considered my proposal, thrashed it around and even waged a personal attack against me. But in the end, they agreed to adopt it. They were not the only ones who doubted the chances of Darawsha's success or who opposed his appointment. Darawsha had several opponents from among the educated Arab young guard, led by Nawwaf Masalha, who appeared to have some winning credentials of his own. Masalha was an activist in the Labor Federation (Histadrut), a Moslem and a member of the Labor movement's younger generation.

However, information coming in from the Arab street suggested that the advantages accorded to Masalha by the Labor Party leadership were based mostly on his having come of age within the party. As far as the Arab voters were concerned, this was actually a serious disadvantage, because it made him a part of the very establishment they were opposing. The party needed someone from among the voters themselves, who would bring with him the internal revolution that was taking place within Arab society. Darawsha, a school principal, who lived in the Galilee and had no party political past, had a much better chance of being elected than Masalha, who lived in the Triangle and was closely identified with the Histadrut.

Masalha was intelligent enough not bear me a grudge for choosing Darawsha; opening the Labor Party to minority communities was more important to him than any personal competition. As someone who entered the party through the back door, via the young guard, he understood the importance of erasing the clause in the party's rule book according to which only former members of the country's security services, i.e. former soldiers or policemen, were eligible for party membership. Masalha's Jewish supporters – like Haim Ramon and Yossi Beilin – were less tactful and spread hints and threats which made it clear to me that I was jeopardizing my own position in the party if I continued to promote Darawsha. But I refused to give in; to me Darawsha was the best Arab candidate the Labor Party had, and this was all that mattered.

Darawsha was no easy partner, though. Having succeeded in getting his candidacy approved by the Appointments Committee, I then had to deal with the consequences of his opinions. "My people are fighting against my country" – the new Knesset member repeated the catchphrase used by Israel's Arabs and defined the limits of his loyalty to the state: a proud Arab, living in a Zionist state, recognizing its laws and its statutes, but never for a moment relinquishing his people's tradition and struggle for recognition. In retrospect, tolerance did pay off. Over the next two election campaigns, in which I continued to head the Arab department, Labor achieved its best results among the Arab electorate since the establishment of the state: 50 percent of the Arab electorate voted for a Zionist party, most of these for Labor. For me, the real gain was not necessarily electoral, but ideological. Out of a belief that the State of Israel should aim for a multi-cultural society, I felt that we had taken a courageous step toward realizing our dream of co-existence between different communities and peoples, in mutual respect and in a political climate that would allow everyone the opportunity to grow culturally and socially and to express themselves constructively.

Darawsha, however, did not stay for long in the Labor Party. In 1988, he left and founded his own Arab Democratic Party.[21] As he said of the circumstances of his leaving, "I was very disappointed with Labor in respect to social justice for all citizens. Labor joined the Likud in a national unity government under Yitzhak Shamir, who continued his hard line against the Arabs of Israel. Labor Party leaders did nothing to repair the injustice against the country's Arab population since the beginning of the state. Moreover, I was very disappointed with Labor policy. Party heads had made pre-election promises of peace with the Palestinians. Instead, they joined the Likud in suppressing the *Intifada* and continued to ignore the legitimate rights of the Palestinian people. I made several proposals to establish Palestinian-Israeli dialogue and direct negotiations between Israel and the PLO. Labor Party heads, together with the national unity government, went on as before and displayed no signs of responding to my proposals. I had no choice but to resign from the party and establish an independent party through which I attempted to achieve my objectives." Darawsha's departure was very harmful to Labor among the Arab public and the Israeli peace camp. Many of the party's Arab members left to join Darawsha.

For many years, Mapai saw the allied Arab lists as representing the Arab sector and, unlike Mapam (United Workers' Party), did not open its doors to card-carrying Arab members. However, it protected itself by reserving seats for Arab representatives in party committees, without actually accepting them as members. In the end, it can be said that Mapai gained from this on 23 February, 1977, when preparations were being made for the third Labor Party conference. The ongoing struggle between Shimon Peres and Yitzhak Rabin was supposed to be determined. Ostensibly, the powers were equally divided between Peres and Rabin, with party leader Peres very slightly ahead, but it took just a few dozen Arab conference members to tip the balance.

I have always had the deepest respect for Shimon Peres, but Rabin's chances to win the party leadership and head the next government seemed better. Also, one of my closest friends, Yigal Allon, had joined the Rabin camp. Allon was the only senior party member who shared my view of the Israeli Arab problem and believed that it was simply not sufficient to follow a policy of "putting out fires"; rather, an inclusive policy was necessary for co-ordinating relations among the country's different ethnic communities. I was already aware that plans were being drafted by the Ministry of Defense for peace with Egypt,[22] and there was every reason to believe that a Labor government headed by Rabin and Allon would carry them out. But Labor lost the general elections in the summer of 1977 and it was the Likud leader, Menachem Begin, who ultimately made peace with Egypt, according to a plan he received from Moshe Dayan.[23]

Just 24 hours before the Labor Party conference began, I decided to advise the Arabs to support Yitzhak Rabin and, when the votes were counted, it turned out that the Arab vote had made the difference. With 1,445 votes, Rabin won the party's candidacy for prime minister.

Israeli Arabs have been included in the combined Labor Mapam Alignment (Ma'arakh) lists since the elections for the tenth Knesset (1981). The decision for this was made in the wake of an increased awareness of the far-reaching changes taking place in the Arab community, both on the political and the social level, and the fear that a strong Palestinian national identity would result in corresponding political changes within the Israeli Arab community. By allowing them full membership privileges, the leadership hoped to attract politically oriented Arabs who would otherwise opt for independent nationalist Arab parties.

However, there were many in the Arab sector who opposed the *numerus clausus* system used by Labor to limit the membership of less desirable classes of people. Retired police chief superintendent Hanna Haddad, a Christian Arab from the village of Tur'an, was a case in point. In the late 1970s, the Christian community was divided between support for the Israeli Communist (Rakah) Party and the Zionist Labor and Mapam allied lists. In 1977, Labor withdrew its support for Elias Nakhla, the Christian candidate who headed its allied Arab list; in that year Labor also lost its hold on the government, for the first time. Nonetheless, during the following years, the Christians continued to fight, albeit unsuccessfully, for a realistic place on the party list.

In 1981, when Christian and Moslem leaders discovered that Labor had allocated the forty-seventh slot on its list of candidates for the next Knesset to Hamad Khalaila from Sakhnin, they decided to form their own independent list, without leaving the Labor Party. At a national assembly in Acre, they announced the establishment of an independent Christian-Moslem list for Arab Brotherhood, headed by Hanna Haddad. Saleh Diab from Tamra was number two on that list, which won 11,000 votes in the 1981 elections. More than 3,000 votes were disqualified and the list did not make it into the Knesset. Its failure was due in part to fierce competition from the Communist Party, whose platform called for an end to land appropriation and discrimination – both issues tied inextricably with Labor policy. Also, a lack of funds prevented the activists from supervising all the polling stations against election fraud. Hanna Haddad himself had to justify the fact that he was allegedly related to Sa'ad Haddad, head of the South Lebanon Army.[24] In the end, he rejoined Labor and in July, 1995 was elected to the Knesset. He served for 11 months until the Knesset was dispersed.

The rise of the right-wing Likud Party to power in 1977 gave the Arab vote for Zionist parties a meaning that had immediate repercussions on the political map. Arab voters began to attach greater importance to their national struggle and less to clan affiliations, especially because they feared the results of Likud policies toward the Arab sector and the party's attitude

to a possible solution to the Palestinian problem – fears that were somewhat alleviated by the peace agreement Menachem Begin managed to
forge with Egypt. Jews and Arabs alike became aware of the importance of
the Arab vote. While many Arabs wanted to express their nationalist aspirations, they did not necessarily wish to do so by demonstratively voting
for the Communists, and preferred to join the influential political power
centers in Israel. Many Israeli Arabs, therefore, became active in mainstream Zionist parties.[25]

It can be said in retrospect that, since the early days of the state, the
approach taken by the Zionist parties toward the Arab population was
instrumental. Both the Zionist and the religious Zionist parties viewed the
Arabs as no more than a reservoir of votes. They made a point of avoiding
sensitive issues that did not have a broad consensus, such as the character
of the state of Israel and the status of an Arab community in a state that
defines itself as Jewish and democratic. The massive Arab vote for Mapai
during the 1950s and 1960s was based on co-optation of key Arab figures,
including *Mukhtars*, family and clan heads who were able to promise votes
to the governing party. In turn, they enjoyed privileges and first options on
all kinds of development contracts. The parties could do this because it was
they who represented the state's Jewish majority, controlled the state's
resources such as budgets, permits, positions and money that they supplied
to clan heads and other central figures. In this way, government ministries
such as the Interior Ministry and the Ministry of Religious Affairs, which
became the traditional stronghold of the National Religious Party (NRP)
and later Shas (the Sephardi ultra-Orthodox party), were enlisted to get
votes in places where voting for these parties would have seemed unlikely
in terms of the population's political and cultural background. In some
locations, NRP representatives were even voted into the local councils.
These positions of power gave the Zionist parties an advantage over
nationalist Arab parties, which were not part of the government and therefore did not control the national bureaucratic system.

The Zionist parties, especially Labor, never tried to create or define new
political groups with which Israeli Arab voters could identify. Rather, they
accepted the existing splits in Arab society and their campaigning focused
on ethnic and clan rifts. My one and only attempt at including a representative of the younger, university educated generation in the Knesset list
involved Abd al-Wahab Darawsha. It was necessary in that instance to
remove the party's support from the allied lists, which had in any case lost
much of their power. The results were satisfactory and for the first time
since the establishment of the state, Zionist parties received almost half of
the Arab votes for the tenth (1981) and eleventh (1984) Knessets.

The National Religious party (NRP), which had traditionally been
given control of the Ministries of the Interior and Religious Affairs, did
very well in the Arab sector in the elections for the tenth Knesset. Arabs

who voted for the NRP were motivated by practical considerations: these are the two offices with which Arabs are forced to maintain frequent contact on various issues concerning their day-to-day lives. Later, when the balance of power changed and the Sephardi ultra-Orthodox party Shas was given control of these offices, it, too, won a significant percentage of the Arab vote, for the same reasons. But the NRP and Shas parties stopped short of including Israeli Arab candidates on their Knesset lists.

During the 1990s, the Likud and Shas began, like Mapai, to operate among the Arab community, and by the 1988 elections Shas was making good use of its long-time control over the Ministry of the Interior in order to harvest Arab votes. Interior minister Arye Deri, who had tried to solve the financial deficits of the Arab municipalities, presented himself as an Orthodox Sephardi Jew and, as such, he proclaimed that he was in the same boat as the Arabs: both communities suffered discrimination at the hands of a Western regime, governed by secular Israelis. Deri was well aware of the similarity between Shas and the Islamic Movement – both created popular support by building an alternative system of municipal welfare services such as kindergartens, places of worship and health clinics. He translated this similarity into solidarity among religious Moslems and exploited it to its fullest.

In Israel, many Arab university graduates are unable to find employment in their fields, and are obliged to turn to teaching. For many years the Ministry of Education was under the control of the NRP, which was responsible for employing Arab, as well as Jewish, school teachers. This gave it an advantage in the teaching profession – vote for us and we'll give you the best teaching jobs. The Likud used similar tactics, by providing career opportunities within the Druze and Bedouin communities, whose young men serve in the military, police, prison service and other branches of the security forces. The Likud Party went even further in its quest to muster the support of the Arab sector. By assuming that the issue of equality was high on the agenda of the Arab public, the Likud pointed out that its program genuinely attempted to bring about social and economic equality.

The first Arab political party in Israel, the Progressive List for Peace, had a mixed Arab-Jewish membership. Over the years, this, and others like it, gained electoral power until the Likud (a blatantly Zionist party) noticed – for the first time – the special role played by the local Arab parties on the Israeli political map. It was in May 1995 and Benjamin Netanyahu, then leader of the opposition, identified an opportunity to topple Yitzhak Rabin's Labor government, by taking advantage of the planned appropriation of land in East Jerusalem. The Likud harnessed the protest of the Arab MKs for their own needs, made a pact with them and promised them jobs in a future government in return for joining the Likud in toppling the existing Labor government.

As the two-party system of government became rooted in Israeli politics, so the importance of the Arab vote became more obvious. The two largest parties – Labor and Likud – appropriated the lion's share of the country's political center, leaving the fringe to attract groups with more extreme ideologies. In order to form coalitions, both Labor and Likud needed the support of the small fringe parties. But they never turned to the Arab parties, preferring the more or less extreme religious movements, whose ideology appeared closer to that of the political center. The following two examples, however, show that the Arab parties also played an active role in the parliamentary fringe game.

In 1988, Labor wanted to have Shlomo Hillel appointed speaker of the twelfth Knesset. A preliminary count showed that there were not enough votes among the coalition parties to support his candidacy and help was needed from outside. Labor Party leaders were obliged to turn to the Arab parties, although ideologically there was no chance of getting their support. However, I was led to understand that the Arab MKs would vote in favor of Shlomo Hillel if the government would grant municipal status to the large Arab town of Umm-al-Fahm, with all its attendant budgets and concessions, and if progress were to be made in recognizing the various "unrecognized"[26] Arab settlements. The first issue was settled relatively easily with the help of the Ministry of the Interior. For the second issue it became necessary to introduce changes to basic government principles, in order to accommodate a paragraph on the forthcoming convention of a committee of inquiry on the status of these "unrecognized" settlements.

The second example occurred in 1995, when the government decided to expropriate private land in the Arab regions of Shu'fat and Biet Tsafafa near Jerusalem in order to build Jewish neighborhoods on Har Homa. The Arab Democratic Party (ADP) announced immediately that, although the landowners were to receive full recompense, the expropriation was unjust and harmful to the peace process. Moreover, when the Arab Democratic Party submitted a motion of no confidence in the Knesset, the Likud and Netanyahu took advantage of the situation by offering ADP leader Darawsha a ministerial position in the next government, in return for his help in toppling the Rabin regime. Darawsha told me that he would "never join a Likud government because they oppose the Oslo accords and are not ready for talks with the PLO. [The ADP] held lengthy negotiations with Rabin and Peres, until just before the vote was to take place. [The outcome was that] Rabin rescinded the land expropriation and I withdrew my motion of no confidence."

Netanyahu offered lame excuses for his proposed association with Darawsha and claimed that his reasons for supporting the motion of no confidence were different from Darawsha's. "Darawsha asks why they are building on Har Homa," said Netanyahu, "whereas I ask why they are building so little on Har Homa." Ultimately, the Arab MKs did not wish to topple the Rabin government and they certainly had no desire to strengthen Netanyahu; but it remains a political fact that the Arab parties and the right shared a common interest.

The introduction of a split ballot in 1996 – one vote for the Knesset list and another for prime minister – improved the civil status of Israel's Arabs by making it possible for them to vote separately for their prime minister of choice and for their favorite party, be it Arab or any other. The old system never offered the Arabs the opportunity to trade support for a candidate for the office of prime minister for a seat on the coalition bench, since it was not possible to support a candidate for prime minister independently of that individual's party's political list. A typical outcome of this system was the 1992 general election, when the coalition government was supported by Arab MKs who were not part of the government, but joined the political bloc that provided the necessary majority that allowed it to govern. This signaled a growing awareness of the combined political power of Israel's Arab population, but still did not constitute full recognition.

While the term "political bloc" indicated the Arab MKs' outsider status, and the Labor Party and its Arab partners did not feel the time was right for openly joining forces and negotiating political platforms, the fact remains that the direct election split ballot system added power to the Arab MKs, raised the civil status of the Arab community in Israel, and granted them the equality of a voting public that contributed to the election of the prime minister (Ehud Barak received over 92 percent of the Arab vote). The deep disappointment of the Arab public caused by its lack of political influence resulted in a dynamic of frustration. Possibly – and this requires further examination – this dynamic was one of the elements that prepared the ground for the riots of October 2000, following Ariel Sharon's provocative visit to the Temple Mount in Jerusalem, which would not have taken place were it not for Barak's permission.

The double ballot voting system, by which the voter handed in a single envelope with two voting slips, one for the Knesset and the other for the prime minister, was introduced into Israeli politics during the 1996 election campaign. It allowed Arab voters the option of performing their civic "Israeli" duty by voting for their choice of candidate for the premiership; at the same time, issues relating to national and cultural identity were reflected in the choice of Knesset list. The voter was also able to focus on the influence of those issues that were of direct interest to the Arab sector and to demand that the Arab candidates address them. It would appear that in this respect, a definition of the Arab population's identity had turned into an acute need – one which was made more urgent by the fact that, parallel to undergoing a civil process, Israel continued to be specifically Jewish.

Ultimately, by the end of my term as head of the Minorities Department, I was convinced that the allied political lists had to be done away with and that the younger generation of politically aware Arabs should be encouraged to find their place in the Zionist parties. In this way I was sure it would be possible to develop a discourse and dialogue between the two populations, and to overcome the differences between them. The Labor Party did indeed open its doors to the Arab voting population and the results were not disappointing. In the tenth and eleventh Knessets, the Zionist parties (especially Labor) received almost 50 percent of the Arab vote, the highest since the establishment of the state. It was an unprecedented achievement. But the party's offices did not manage to internalize the message passed on by its Arab voters – a message of goodwill and a desire to blend into and become a part of the national consensus. Perhaps the idea of integrating Arabs into the party's mainstream was too hard for its leaders to swallow, and they continued to see the Arabs as unwelcome strangers. Relying on the parliamentary loyalty and co-operation of the nationalist Arab parties in advancing its political, social and economic plans, the Labor Party appears to have unwittingly given up on everything that could be construed as integrating Arabs into its ranks and advancing them politically.

The Israeli Communist Party (Maki, Rakah, Hadash)

In British Mandate Palestine, the Arab Communists maintained a unique tradition of co-operation, albeit difficult, with the Jews. Initially this took place within the Jewish–Arab framework of the Palestinian Communist Party, and later in the Arab-only framework of the League for National Liberation, which for a long time was practically the only active bi-national political platform in pre-State Israel. Once Israel was established in 1948, the Israeli Communist Party (known by the acronym Maki) remained the only political framework representing the interests of those members of the state's Arab population who believed in a bi-national solution to the Palestine issue. Maki soon became the political home of the educated Galilee Christians and received the votes of people who sent their children to study at universities in the Communist bloc, under the auspices of the Communist Party: 50 Israeli Arab students a year were awarded grants to study in Eastern European countries, and by the mid-1980s, more than 1,000 Israeli Arabs had left for the Eastern Bloc countries.

The Communists enjoyed several advantages. The Arab academics and political activists who remained in Israel after the 1948 War of Independence organized themselves into an Israeli Communist Party in 1949. Although – urged by Moscow – the party honored the UN Partition Plan for Palestine, which called for a division of the land between Jews and Arabs, it was able to claim that it had no part in the political decisions that had brought the *Naqba* on the Arab inhabitants of what had formerly been Palestine. All the Communist Party leaders lived in Israel, and Israel's democracy allowed the Communist Party to make claims against the state and, at least until 1950, it continued to demand that Nazareth and the western Galilee be returned to a future Arab state. Moreover, the party possessed the necessary organizational tools and ran a professional trades union in Nazareth, under the name "Laborers' Congress", which was the only surviving pre-war independent Arab organization in Israel.

The weekly *al-Ittihad,* which resumed publication in late 1948, was Maki's Arabic sounding board and one of the tools through which the party tried to expand its influence in as many areas as possible, and in all organizational and social centers in the Arab sector. Although the Communist Party drew most of its electoral support from the Moslem population, its Arab leadership came mainly from among the Christian community, especially the Greek Orthodox community, which was connected to the former USSR. This went back to the days of the British Mandate, when Christians constituted most of the social, economic and political elite of the local Arab population; they were better educated, professional urban dwellers and were more exposed to Westernization than were their Moslem counterparts. However, the party tried to attract Moslems during the 1960s, and indeed such people as Uthman Abu-Ras and later Taufiq Zayad gradually became prominent members of the party leadership. However, it was not until 1973 – the eighth Knesset elections – that the Moslem Taufiq Zayad was elected to the Knesset on the Communist list. During the 1980s, the party made efforts to reach out to the Druze community by laying emphasis on their "Arabness".

For years, the Israeli Communist Party was the only political body in Israel through which Israeli Arabs could express – albeit partly – their desires and dissatisfactions, and wage their political struggle for equal citizenship. All other attempts at setting up an independent political organization (such as *al-Ard,* which broke off from the Communist Party) were strangled at birth. For this reason, an ever-growing number of Israeli Arabs voted for the Communist Party and a large proportion of the Communist Party's leadership came from the Arab communities. As the party became more Arab-oriented, so the Jewish majority in Israel came to identify it increasingly with Arab nationalism.

The Israeli Communist (Maki) Party's basic ideology required of its members that they identify with the Arab nationalist movement. Such a stance made it attractive to Arab voters; Communist ideology was of secondary importance. The fundamental differences between the two ideologies were at the center of the fights between the different blocs in the party – mainly between its Arab and its Jewish members. The party platform was redrafted on more than one occasion and various decisions adopted by its committees had to be toned down in order to accommodate both sides. This, of course, caused a discrepancy between the party's public message and the militant positions taken by some of its members.

Being a political organization and operating within a legitimate parliamentary framework, the Israeli Communist Party was able to reassure and ease the reservations of those Arabs who wished to identify with Palestinian Arab nationalism while continuing to live in the State of Israel. Interaction between Jewish and Arab members also appeared to validate the party's anti-establishment political activity and allowed it to address a larger electorate, including Jews, who could also, at least from an ideological point of view, support the Communist program without worrying about breaking their solidarity with Israel. This situation was bolstered on December 20, 1949 by the decision of the Central Committee of the Israeli Communist Party to support the UN 1947 Partition Plan and the independence of both Peoples within the boundaries of the Land of Israel.

The ideological clashes between Arab nationalist ideology and Jewish nationalist ideology over the Israeli-Arab conflict – which were fueled by interpersonal conflicts among the party's leadership – peaked on the eve of the sixth Knesset elections in 1965, and the Israeli Communist Party split into two separate factions. Two Israeli Communist parties – one Jewish and one Arab – now existed, although the Arab party also had several Jewish members. The "Arab" group, led by Tawfiq Tubi, Amil Habibi and Meir Wilner, separated from the Israeli Communist Party and founded a New Communist List (known by the acronym Rakah). According to the new party, Israel's Arabs were an integral part of the Arab Palestinian nation which has "national rights in Palestine, equal to the national rights of the Jewish people". The vast majority of Israel's Arabs joined the new party because of its political platform. Rakah also succeeded in attracting most of the Israeli Communist Party's voters, and received three Knesset seats. The Israeli Communist Party remained a party of Jewish Communists headed by Shmuel Mikunis, Dr Moshe Sneh and Esther Wilenska, who declared that Israel's Arabs are a national minority and, as such, they would have to struggle for their civil rights in the Jewish state. Following the split, the Israeli Communist Party suffered a resounding defeat in the 1969 seventh Knesset elections and lost four of its previous Knesset seats, remaining with only one. Rakah won three Knesset seats in these elections.

The Democratic Front for Peace and Equality (known by the acronym Hadash) – or, as it was called officially, The New Communist List, Black Panthers and Jewish and Arab Public Circles – merged with Charlie Biton's Black Panther movement, which was active in the poorer Jewish neighborhoods of Haifa and Jerusalem. Biton was even elected to Knesset on an Arab vote, at the expense of an Arab candidate, although the Black Panthers brought no votes from the Jewish public and voices were sounded within Hadash calling for the Panthers to be ousted. As soon as the eleventh Knesset elections were announced in 1984, the party began negotiating with another, left-wing, Jewish movement, called Alternative, headed by Uri Avneri and Professor Matti Peled, and offered it the third place

(Charlie Biton's) on its list. The negotiations failed and Rakah decided to continue its alliance with Biton in order to ensure a balance between Jewish and Arab members on its political list.

The political life of Israel's Arabs underwent a decisive change late 1975, in a process that began on the eve of the elections for the Nazareth municipal council. A body named The Nazareth Committee of Academics and High School Teachers joined with Rakah to form The Democratic Front for Nazareth and brought Rakah a resounding victory in the municipal elections. Nationalist poet and Rakah member Taufiq Zayad was elected mayor with 67 percent of all the votes. The Front's election victory in Nazareth was a turning point for Arab politics in Israel. If, until the middle of the 1970s, it was impossible to organize a wide coalition among Israeli Arabs because of the social rifts in Arab society, the Nazareth model was a sign of things to come and served as an example for the establishment of other political fronts in local councils, and even for a Hadash Knesset list in Nazareth.

Municipal control meant influence and access to budgets. The main thing preventing Rakah from establishing itself in the municipal system was the complexity of social rifts within Israel's Arab community. Whereas on a national level the party was very successful in presenting a public message in defense of Arab nationalism, most of the Arab clan leaders were reluctant to co-operate with Rakah until the late 1960s, for fear of the repercussions such support would bring from the Knesset, upon which local councils were dependent. In order to overcome this hurdle, Rakah began to cultivate ties with traditional circles in the villages, including clan leaders, in the hope of harnessing their help in establishing a united front, which would become a part of Hadash. In return for their support of Hadash in the general elections, Rakah promised its support to these circles in getting their representatives elected to local authorities. Rakah also used this method successfully in gaining control of the National Committee of Arab Municipal Council Chairmen: between 1978 and 1983, the committee chair was a Rakah member.

In the local council elections of November, 1978 the united front lists won 18 out of 54 Arab and Druze municipality chairs and even doubled its council members in many places. This trend became even more established in the 1983 elections, when half of all local Arab council appointments went either to Hadash members or to Hadash-supported candidates.

The secret of Rakah's success among Israeli Arabs was not only its well-oiled and well-financed administration and its intensive campaigning. The real power of the party came from the fact that until 1984 it was the only political party in Israel in which Arabs could openly express their nationalist aspirations. The Israeli Communist Party and, later, Rakah and Hadash (and, again, the Israeli Communist Party within the framework of

Hadash) were not merely political parties; they were also the breeding ground for the intelligentsia, the political leadership and the new, up-and-coming Arab elite in Israel.

The 1970s turned out to be the most impressive decade in the history of the Israeli Communist Party, when it ranked as the only nationalist ideological party on the fringe of Israeli politics. As such, it became the main tool for mutual Israeli–Palestinian protest against government policy after the years of military rule and ethnic-based economic discrimination. The Arab nationalist bloc, in which Rakah figured prominently, began to gain strength in 1977, due to the fact that over the years it had provided one of the few channels in Israel that allowed Arabs to advance politically on a personal level, while the Zionist establishment dug its heels in against any attempt at Arab self-definition, whether individually or in groups. With time, this political force that pushed many a political activist into the welcoming arms of the New Communist List (Rakah) became even stronger within the Arab sector.

A large number of Israeli Arabs acquired education, established themselves financially and helped to formulate a clear position on nationalist issues. At the same time, the Zionist establishment continued to denounce them. In a desire to continue providing these people with a political option, the Israeli Communist Party distanced itself from all political structures that might be construed as Jewish-dominated. In reality, however, the Israeli Communist Party was not able to distance itself from its Jewish voters and its place was taken by the "Front",[27] which provided a fitting answer to organizational needs and to social and political developments for the entire Israeli Arab society.

As long as the USSR existed and was able to give at least modest material assistance to the party itself and to some of its members (such as paying for academic studies in the Soviet bloc countries for the sons of loyal cadres), Hadash was also able to compete with alternative Israeli Arab political organizations that attempted to join the political scene. In return, it received the support of a large group of students, academics and professionals, who, like most Hadash voters, did not necessarily identify with Communist ideology. In the Eastern Bloc, Israeli Arab students received a political education, enjoyed respect and good relations – experiences that stood in complete contrast to the humiliation and estrangement some of them had experienced when interacting with Israeli institutions. For many of them, the revolutionary flavor remained even after the "Front" established itself as yet another political party. A minority of Communist Party members did not view nationalism and Communism as conflicting, and the front organizations that surrounded Rakah on all sides also overcame this contradiction, whenever it arose.

Notwithstanding the never-ending internal bickering over ideology, several diffusive relationships developed within the party, which grew in strength as a result of the constant struggles conducted by Hadash against the other, conflicting streams in Arab society both within and outside Israel. On the one hand, these included the political lists allied with Mapai and, on the other hand, the extreme nationalist Arab movements (*al-Ard* – "The Land", and later *Abnaa al-Balad* – "The Sons of the Village"). In 1984, Rakah faced an even greater electoral challenge, which took the form of the Progressive List for Peace (known by the acronym Ramash), under the leadership of Muhammad Mi'ari. This, too, was an Arab-Jewish party that supported many of the nationalist Palestinian ideologies. Ramash challenged the New Communist Party for pretending to represent the Arab public in Israel, and presented a position that was more extreme than that of Hadash, with the objective of undermining its standing in the Arab sector. In 1992, Ramash disappeared from the political map in Israel.

At the same time as Ramash took up its political activity on the Arab street, a rival that was even more threatening to Rakah arrived on the scene. This was the Islamic Movement. The Islamic Movement constituted a religious problem to the secular Rakah, as well as a new challenge: how could Rakah identify with the PLO and the *Intifada*[28] (in which various groups tried to include also the "1948 Arabs") without being swallowed up by it, and how could Rakah prevent its constituency from being drawn into armed nationalism?

The al-Ard Movement and the Democratic Popular Front

A number of social and political conditions – local as well as regional – which came of age in the late 1950s caused the establishment of radical Arab movements in Israel. Events in the Arab world often aroused reactions on the local Arab political scene and sometimes even caused storms and upheavals on the country's political map: examples were the revolutions in Egypt (July 23, 1952) and Iraq (July 14, 1958), the nationalization of the Suez Canal (1956), and the Egypt–Syria pact (February 1, 1958). Internally, Israel followed a policy that increasingly distanced its Arab citizens from the political establishment and institutions, such as private land appropriation, few employment opportunities and insufficient access to higher education. On top of this, growing numbers of Arabs were killed attempting to cross the border illegally from Israel to its neighboring countries, and the strictly implemented rules of the military administration made for considerable hardship. Great resentment was caused by the pact between Israel, Great Britain and France (at the time of the war in Algiers). Aimed at protecting British and French interests in the Suez Canal, the pact threatened to stall Egypt's attempt to nationalize the Canal. These events on the local political scene were further exacerbated by Egyptian president Jamal Abd al-Naser's pan-Arabic ideology, which was expressed in increased Arab nationalism across the region, all of which made the ground fertile for the growth of radical nationalism among the Arab population of Israel.

Only a few local Arab political groups called for boycotting the Knesset elections. The first was the group led by Elias Kusa, a Christian lawyer, who founded the Arab-Israel Bloc, which he tried to expand in 1955 into a general Israeli Arab movement. The party's main activity consisted of calling on Israeli Arabs to boycott that year's Knesset elections, by handing out flyers and writing protest letters to newspapers. The group did not last long on the Israeli political map.

Two political groups shared a similar fate in the late 1950s and early 1960s, the Arab Front (or Democratic Popular Front) and *al-Ard*, each of which tried to establish an independent Arab party and offered a list of candidates for election to the Knesset. Both failed. All Arab groups established in Israel during this period took the form of opposition to the country's regime. There was a great deal of courage involved in this, in light of the close supervision under which the Arabs were forced to live – i.e. the military administration – and considering that the government was nurturing a traditional, sycophantic leadership and was impatient toward radical independent Arab parties.

The Democratic Popular Front was formed after the 1958 May Day riots, in which local Arab demonstrators clashed violently with police forces, resulting in large numbers of casualties and arrests. The lawyer Elias Kusa, Shefar'am mayor Jabur Jabur and Kafar Yasif local council head Yani Yani established a public defense committee on behalf of the arrested demonstrators. The committee decided to establish a broader Israeli Arab organization to include the Communists and other nationalist groups, under the title "Arab Front". The name was later changed to the Democratic Popular Front (DPF) because of the government's refusal to acknowledge a movement with a nationalist ethnic label. The first meeting of the DPF took place on June 6, 1958 in the Nazareth clubhouse of the Israeli Communist Party, which hosted Communist Party leaders and non-party figures such as Habib Qahwaji, Mansur Kardush, Elias Kusa and Bulus Farah. The latter two later left the Front because they were opposed to co-operation with the Communists. The Front's platform demanded:

1. Cancellation of the military administration.
2. A halt to land appropriations and reinstating appropriated land to its owners.
3. Repatriation of Palestinian refugees.
4. The cancellation of external symbols differentiating between Arabs and Jews in Israel.

From July 1958 to February 1959, the Front established branches in Kafar Yasif, Wadi Nisnas (Haifa), Tayibeh, Ramla, Lod, Be'neh and elsewhere in the Arab sector.

Although the Front raised hopes for change, it ended in ruins due to a combination of external forces that influenced the internal political agenda, including the Soviet Union's support for the July 1958 Qasem revolution in Iraq. The rivalry between Qasem and Jamal Abd al-Naser drove the USSR-influenced Arab Communist parties who supported Qasem away from the nationalist parties who supported Naser. Although many members tended to support Naser, the party adhered to Moscow's line. The DPF, which existed under the auspices of the Israeli Communist Party, did not agree with this policy and a group of young DPF leaders broke away and established an independent Arab nationalist movement in Israel, called simply – even outspokenly – *al-Ard* ("The Land").

The first meeting of *al-Ard* was held in April, 1959. Among its founders were Habib Qahwaji, a Maronite Christian from the village of Fassuta, Mansur Kardush, a Greek Orthodox from the town of Nazareth, Sabri Jiryyes, a Greek Catholic from Fassuta, Mahmud Sarruji, a Moslem from Acre, and Salah Bransah, a Moslem from the village of Tayibeh. Among its members were people with different and even conflicting ideas: leftists, nationalists, socialists, Communists and Naserites. Most were young and many were students, well educated and intellectual; there were also among them businessmen, merchants, farmers and laborers. The movement was not built on a hierarchy and had neither elected institutions nor a clear division of responsibility, yet it succeeded in surviving for many years.

It is difficult to point out an exact reason, but without doubt the movement's attraction lay in the fact that its ideology satisfied many ambitions and combined Arab nationalism with Naserite socialism. The movement's first ideological manifesto was based on Naserism and stated, "The national branch of the Democratic Popular Front is part of the Palestinian people, which is a part of the Arab nation, and will fight for full equality between Arabs and Jews. Israel must recognize that the Arab nationalist movement is the determining factor in the region, dissolve any association with the Zionist idea, recognize the Palestinian people's right to self-determination and permit the return of all those who have left the country."

Already at its inception, the movement had to struggle against three powerful adversaries: the State of Israel, whose authority and borders it did not recognize; the traditional structure of Israeli Arab society, which it perceived as an instrument of the government to control Israeli Arabs; and the Israeli Communist Party, which was part of the Democratic Popular Front and called on the same public for support and therefore endangered the new movement's chances of success. By leaving the Popular Front, the movement expressed its reservations concerning Communist ideology and the acceptance of Naser's ideas on combining socialism and nationalism.

The *al-Ard* movement struggled for six years for legal recognition. In 1965 the movement's leaders tried to submit a list of candidates for the sixth Knesset under the name of The Arab Socialist List. The central election committee rejected the list, claiming that most of its candidates belonged to *al-Ard*, which then appealed unsuccessfully to the Supreme Court. On October 25, 1965, the day on which the Supreme Court handed down its verdict, six years of activity finally came to a close. From then on the members all set out on their own personal political journeys. Jiryyes and Qahwaji left Israel and joined the PLO. Bransah retired from politics and concentrated on establishing a fund for the resurrection of Palestinian heritage in Tayibeh. Kardush left political life temporarily, returning in 1990 to found the Socialist Nationalist Front, with the hope of revitalizing *al-Ard* and *Abnaa al-Balad* ideas. Muhammad Mi'ari, one of the founders of the Progressive List for Peace in 1984, was elected to the Knesset.

Although the *al-Ard* movement disappeared, it left an indelible imprint on Israeli Arab life. Ever since the days of *al-Ard*, there has been a nucleus of Israeli Arabs with a nationalist conscience, who believe that the establishment of an Israeli Arab political party is the only way to express the political and nationalist aspirations of Arabs in Israel. The *al-Ard* movement also aroused in Israeli Arabs a strong tendency to support the kind of independent political bodies that would advance their interests within the Israeli political game. Over the years this tendency has grown, and it will continue to grow as long as Zionist parties refuse to give their Arab voters the feeling that they, too, can truly influence the party's positions and actions.

Government policy neutralized almost all Arab national-political organizations in Israel: it rejected the *al-Ard* Socialist List in 1965; it legislated laws and by-laws to prevent Arab nationalist activity; it closed institutions that fronted for nationalist organizations; it had people arrested and accused of subversive underground activity. All this meant that, officially at least, Rakah remained the sole representative of Israel's Arabs. On the ideological level, however, this was not the case. By denying the existence of *al-Ard*, the government reinforced the movement's claim that it was the authentic political representative of the Israeli Arab sector. In the mid-1970s, other radical groups started appearing, the most prominent of which were the Sons of the Village (*Abnaa al-Balad*) and *al Nahda* ("the resurrection"). Throughout, this period, and in fact since the establishment of the state, Rakah had controlled the radical nationalist left in Arab politics. Since the first Knesset in 1949, its leaders and MKs Amil Habibi, Amil Tuma, Tawfiq Tubi, Saliba Khamis and others constituted de facto the national leadership of the Arab population. Nor was the party's strength harmed by the appearance of new radical political bodies, which belonged to the same left-wing socialist political camp. At first, Rakah tried to harness these new groups to its wagon and involve them in its protest activity. But when the Sons of the Village (*Abnaa al-Balad*) adopted a more extreme and independent stance than Rakah – as a legitimate political party – could permit itself, a fierce ideological struggle took place between the two groups in order to prevent the establishment of a local support infrastructure that would undermine Rakah and erode its traditional power base. Through countless jibes in *al-Ittihad* and other publications, Rakah described the Sons of the Village and other militant groups as irresponsible children, toying with activity that would bring destruction upon them and cause irreparable damage to the whole concept of Arab unity in Israel.

3
New Political Movements and Trends

The meeting after the 1967 Six Day War of the Arab–Israeli community with the Palestinian community in Judea, Samaria (the West Bank) and the Gaza Strip, separated during 19 years of enmity between Israel and the Hashemite Kingdom of Jordan, set two parallel processes in motion. On the one hand, many Israeli Arabs began to re-evaluate their accomplishments compared with those of their counterparts in the West Bank, while, on the other hand, they began to see their identity in a different light. The removal of boundaries exposed Israeli Arabs to a nationalist and politically aware population – the Palestinians – who had gained experience during their struggle against the Jordanian government and had built a Palestinian history and culture based on that struggle. The Palestinians proposed a collective identity, and the Israeli Arabs suddenly found themselves part of it. For this and similar reasons, political processes between the two populations almost always took a one-way course, from the Arabs of Judea, Samaria and Gaza to the Israeli Arabs, not the other way around.

The fragile equilibrium of the Israeli Arabs' identity began to falter. Until 1967, Israeli Arabs had not been called upon to rebel actively against the Israeli government, but rather to wait for the Arab armies to come and liberate them. Not all Israeli Arabs agreed with this attitude of continuing confrontation, and during the Six Day War some volunteered to man vital functions in the Israeli economy left vacant by conscripted Israelis, became blood donors and helped in other ways that expressed solidarity with the state. Israel's victory convinced even the most militant among its Arab citizens that the Arab states were not about to destroy the State of Israel, which would continue its struggle to become an integral part of the reality of the region.

Shortly after the Six Day War, the Arab media, and especially the terrorist organizations, began voicing new political messages, calling upon Israeli Arabs to participate in the Palestinian nation's struggle and to help the Arabs destroy the Jewish state. A real about-turn took place in 1971, when the eighth assembly of the Palestinian National Council (of the PLO), which was held in Cairo, decided to accept the membership of three Israeli Arab citizens who had emigrated from Israel: Sabri Jiryyes and

Habib Qahwaji, both former *al-Ard* activists, and former Rakah member and poet, Mahmud Darwish, who had fled to Egypt in 1971 (and had filled a senior position in the PLO).[1] In April 1972, the Council's political platform was ratified to include the following objectives:

> [to] strengthen national ties with our people in the territories occupied since 1948 as well as those in the West Bank, the Gaza Strip and those outside the occupied fatherland.

> [to] deal with the situation of our people in the 1948 occupied territory and support their struggle to maintain their national identity, adopt their problems and help them unite in their struggle for liberation.[2]

The consolidation of Israel's Arab identity, which had begun in the aftermath of the 1967 war, grew stronger still after the 1973 Yom-Kippur War. The changes brought about by the war sharpened the complexity and division within Arab society in Israel. On the one hand, their solidarity with Arabs in the West Bank and Gaza Strip grew; on the other hand, they became increasingly aware of their status as a large minority population in a Jewish sovereign state.

The first event to signal the growth of a nationalist component among Israel's Arabs consisted of "Land Day" rioting on March 30, 1976. For the first time, Israeli police and defense forces found themselves locked in a violent confrontation with the country's Arab citizens. Six Arabs were killed in the course of demonstrations against the government's plan to expropriate Arab land in order to develop the Galilee; dozens were wounded.[3] Arabs privately owned about 30 percent of the expropriated land and the matter caused great agitation among the entire Arab population of Israel. It raised memories of the large-scale land expropriations of the 1950s and 1960s for the purpose of building the Jewish towns of Upper Nazareth and Carmiel.

First Arab Nationalist Movements

The Israeli Arab population's desire for the kind of political organization that would give vent to their nationalist aspirations and provide an alternative to the Communist Rakah Party was not realized until the eleventh Knesset in 1984. However, the realization of this desire is rooted in the late 1970s. Four members of the Nazareth Committee of Academics joined Rakah to form the Nazareth Democratic Front and were elected in the 1975 municipal elections to the Nazareth city council. Two of them were even appointed deputies to Mayor Taufiq Zayad. The Academic Committee kept its seats in the 1978 municipal elections, but complained that Rakah had taken over the Front and used it to reinforce its own position; it was because of this, too, that the Front had not achieved the political status and power it had hoped for. In 1981, a group of members decided to discontinue the alliance with Rakah and establish a new movement under the name of the Progressive Movement – Nazareth, which campaigned independently in the 1983 municipal elections. The Progressive Movement – Nazareth included former *al-Ard* members, which has been declared illegal. Movement leaders – attorney Kamel al-Dhaher, Dr Rashid Salim and Reverend Riah Abu al-Asal – argued that their movement represented a nationalist stand that was clearer and firmer than that taken by Rakah, which showed its weakness. In the 1983 municipal elections, the Progressive Movement – Nazareth won four out of the 17 municipal council seats, but failed to achieve its goal of breaking the Rakah "Front".

Their relative success on the local front encouraged the movement's leaders to draw up a list for the 1984 national elections. In December 1983, they announced the establishment of a new political party and began negotiations with various nationalist extra-parliamentary bodies, such as the *al-Ansar* group[4] in the town of Umm-al-Fahm. After much deliberation, and prompted by the fear that an independent nationalist Arab party would irk the authorities, it was decided to form a united Jewish–Arab list for parliament. The movement contacted a left-wing Jewish group headed by Matti Peled and Uri Avneri and known as Alternative, together with former members of the left-wing group Sheli, headed by Walid Sadeq. After long-drawn-out negotiations, the Progressive List for Peace (PLP) was born. Muhammad Mi'ari, a former *al-Ard* activist and head of the Land Defense Committee and the Society for the Defense of Security Prisoners, was elected to head the list, and Professor Brigadier General (Ret.) Matti Peled, an expert on Islamic literature, was given second place on the party's list.[5] The new movement's main challenger for a place on the Arab political scene was the Communist Rakah Party, which had, up until then, been uncontested. In order to overcome this obstacle and to attract the Christian Arab vote, which in the past had gone mostly to Rakah, the third slot on the new party's list was allocated to the Reverend Riah Abu al-Asal.

Although the Central Election Committee disqualified the PLP because of its nationalist platform, the Supreme Court allowed the list to participate in the eleventh Knesset elections (1984). The public debate that raged around the disqualification of the PLP engendered considerable support and great sympathy for the party among Israeli Arabs. Since the party had no Communist affinities whatsoever, it was easy for it to establish itself as a radical nationalist party. Young Arabs who loathed Rakah-style Communism; Moslems who were unimpressed by the Christian character adopted by the Rakah leadership; and especially Arab nationalists who had shunned elections in the past – all of these were called upon to help the list gather the number of votes necessary to reach the Israeli Knesset. The newly formed party hinted broadly at its nationalist character and Palestinian roots: its voting slip boasted the letter P for Palestine and it used the colors of the Palestinian flag (black, white, red and green) in its election campaign. The PLP's Knesset campaign ended Rakah's monopoly over the nationalist aspirations of growing numbers of Israeli Arabs.

Unlike other Arab parties, the PLP believed that both Jews and Arabs should enjoy equal political and social rights in Israel. In this the PLP was ahead of its time. When it was first established in the early 1980s, the social and political awareness of Israel's Arab population was at a very low ebb and it was to be ten more years before the country's law courts were required to rule on issues of civil rights, matters that were raised only by political movements established in the early 1990s and wanting to introduce changes to the character of the state. According to PLP leader Muhammad Mi'ari, Arab society had to build its own institutions and entrust them with taking care of various civilian needs. His belief was that the Arabs in Israel are primarily a part of the Palestinian nationalist movement. As a position, this contradicted Rakah's, which emphasized the identity of Israel's Arabs as being a separate national minority within the State of Israel proper.

The great sympathy enjoyed by the PLP prior to the eleventh Knesset elections in 1984, its platform and the way it emphasized its Palestinian nationalism led it to win two Knesset seats and attract 18 percent of all Arab votes, a most impressive accomplishment for a new party. Yet despite this, the movement never really managed to take off. It lacked the financial resources that Rakah received from the Eastern Bloc, was unable to match Rakah's organization and, unlike Rakah, was not in a position to send dozens of high school graduates every year to study in Eastern European universities. Its organization was small, with only a few field workers, and its nationalist message did not translate well into the municipal needs and desires of the local Arab population. At the most, the party's participation in local government elections helped to coalesce the lower ranks of public political activity.[6] In the 1988 Knesset elections, the PLP dropped to 15 percent of the Arab vote and Muhammad Mi'ari was its only MK (this time with no Jewish representation). The PLP continued to emphasize its Palestinian ideology after the elections, but, like Maki in 1965, differences of opinion over national identity caused unrest among its members. Arab members vehemently opposed a reported attempt by Jewish members – mainly Uri Avneri – to gain control of the list. Against this background, Abdallah Badir, PLP leader in the Triangle, left the movement in May 1985.[7]

Uri Avneri was later to say that they had "established a list based on complete parity. In principle, it was clear that we would receive much less votes from Jews and most voters would naturally come from the Arab sector. However, the party's institutions and its Knesset list was not meant to reflect the character of its voting public, but rather to indicate the principle of complete equality between Arabs and Jews. Thus, the movement elected two chairmen; I was one. The list of candidates consisted of an Arab first, then a Jew, then another Arab, and so on." The list suffered attacks by the Communists, who accused Uri Avneri and others of being agents of the CIA and the establishment. According to Avneri, "it was only natural for some people on the list to try to upset the principle of parity and complain that we would never bring in enough votes…"[8]

The PLP ended its political career when it failed to secure any seats during the thirteenth Knesset elections in 1992. This failure was due to several factors, the main one being a feeling among voters that the party's radical nationalism constituted an unattainable ideal. There was also its refusal to unite with the Arab Democratic Party and other political elements, and criticism of the activities of the party and its chairman during the twelfth Knesset, as well as rivalry between Mi'ari and Ahmad Darwish. On top of all this, the idea of a Jewish–Arab political partnership suffered a harsh blow with the forced resignation of the Jewish faction under the leadership of Matti Peled.

The Progressive List for Peace paved the way for the Arab Democratic Party (ADP), headed by former Labor Party member Abd al-Wahab Darawsha. From its beginning the ADP appealed to Moslem voters, so that it was quite natural that, following a period of independent activity, it would join forces with the Islamic Movement as part of the United Arab List (UAL), under the leadership of Abd al-Malik Dahamsha of the Islamic Movement.

Extra-parliamentary Political Organizations

Various events over the ten years since the disqualification of *al-Ard* encouraged Israel's Arabs to seek an organized and legitimate political framework through which to express their nationalist aspirations. The highlight of these events was the 1964 revival of the Palestine Liberation Organization (PLO), which was followed in 1967 with renewed contact between Israeli Arabs and their relations in Judea, Samaria and the Gaza Strip. The 1973 Yom-Kippur War shook Israel's status as an omnipotent military power and brought about an increase in all forms of political activity among the country's Arab population.

Due to the radical ideology of some of the groups in Arab society, which did not conform with the general political consensus, extensive extra-parliamentary activity developed over the years alongside that of officially elected political parties. The struggle of these radical groups focused mainly on issues concerning the nationality, civil status and group rights of the Arab minority in Israel. They all shared a desire to establish a status that did not depend on traditional social rifts.

These extra-parliamentary groups reflected a growing militancy among Arabs and succeeded in uniting different parties – former rivals in other areas – around their common goals, often in the wake of national events such as May Day demonstrations, Land Day strikes, protests over land expropriation, or regional events such as the Naser-inspired anti-Communist attacks in Arab countries. The radical ideologies of these groups often led them into confrontation with the Israeli authorities. Some groups were prosecuted, others declared illegal. Most of them were under constant surveillance by the General Security Services.

Extra-parliamentary political groups affected voting patterns both directly and indirectly by consolidating a camp of loyal radical nationalist voters, while at the same time setting a precedent for the idea of separatism by convincing voters to boycott general elections. To this day, the hard core of the Sons of the Village (*Abnaa al-Balad*) movement not only continues to boycott elections, but conducts a campaign to expand the boycott. The objective of most of these groups was to campaign for Knesset representation; when it became obvious that they would not attain this objective (whether by failing to win enough votes or by being disqualified by the courts), most of them disbanded. Some of the members established or joined other Arab parties, whether individually or with others, but the hard core of these groups tended to remain extra-parliamentary, with little political influence. Such groups include *Abnaa al-Balad*, *al Nahda*, *al-Naser*, etc. For several years, the Islamic Movement was active outside the traditional national political framework of Knesset elections before it began to focus its political activity on gaining control of the Arab local authorities. Some members of the Islamic leadership decided to join traditional Knesset activity, while the more radical northern branch, headed by Sheikh Ra'ed Salah, former mayor of Umm-al-Fahm, continued vehemently to oppose participation in Knesset elections.

Certain political circles in the Arab sector were disappointed with Rakah's position on issues of Palestinian nationalism, finding it to be too moderate. In late 1972, with the approach of the 1973 municipal elections, young, politically oriented people in various parts of the country began organizing themselves into political groups. Some of them had been previously connected to *al-Ard*. In Tayibeh, a group called *al Nahda* ("resurrection", "awakening" or "renaissance") was founded; in 'Ara and Ar'ara a similar group named *al-Fajr* ("dawn") was established; in Tireh were the Sons of Tireh; in Nazareth it was *al-Sawt* ("the voice"); in Sakhnin the group called itself the Sakhnin Progressive Movement; in Mi'elya there were the Sons of Mi'elya for Tomorrow, and so on elsewhere. Ties between these groups were tenuous and, in spite of their common nationalism, they remained unable to agree on various issues, e.g. participating in Knesset elections. For the 1983 local elections, some groups formed the *al-Ansar* ("the supporters") list, while others established local movements. There were further crises before the 1984 Knesset elections, when some activists proposed joining the PLP, while others remained faithful to the principle of non-participation.

In 1990, former *al-Ard* member Mansur Kardush from Nazareth founded the Socialist Nationalist Front, which advocated a Naser-style pan-Arab ideology and called for unity throughout the Arab world and the establishment of socialist regimes. According to the Socialist Nationalist Front, there was no current solution to the problem of Israel's borders and the issue had to remain open to discussion as part of negotiations between Israel and the Palestinians. The Socialist Nationalist Front did not compete in the 1992 Knesset elections and, in fact, remained no more than a group of intellectual theoreticians.

Extra-parliamentary activity was also characteristic of various ethnic political groups. Among the Druze, there was already some organized resistance to Israeli rule in the 1950s, which took the form of opposition to the 1956 national military service law.[9] During the early 1960s, there was fierce dispute within the Israeli Druze population over their national identity and affinity. The result was that the Druze community was split into three groups: one group believed that the Druze are a separate nation, not related to the Arabs; a second believed that the Druze are part of the Arab nation, but enjoy special status in Israel because they serve in the military; a third group considered the Druze to be no different from any other Arab, albeit following a slightly different form of the Islamic religion. The steep increase in protest voting in favor of Rakah in the 1969 elections indicated the relative strength of the different groups and pointed to a shift in power toward the third group.

The early 1970s witnessed the first attempts to establish political groups that were detached from traditional Druze leadership. At the far right of the political spectrum stood the Druze Zionist Circle; the Druze Enterprise Committee stood at the far left. The founders of these organizations were usually educated young men, who grew up either in small families with little wealth and standing, or in the weaker branches of large families. The Druze Zionist Circle was established in 1974 in Daliyat al-Carmel and advocated unreserved support for the Jewish state; because of its Zionist sympathies, it has remained small. Its activities are extra-parliamentary and it is identified with right-wing and centrist parties.

The Druze Enterprise Committee (DEC) was established in March 1972 at the home of Sheikh Farhoud Qasem Farhoud in Rame as a front for the Communist Rakah Party.[10] According to its basic premise, the Druze are an integral part of the Palestinian Arab population in Israel and the same laws should apply to them as to the rest of Arab society regarding military service. The Druze were even called upon to identify with the

Palestinian national struggle. The DEC gained popularity because of its solidarity with the Druze community's feeling of discrimination; being obliged to serve in the military alongside the Jews, they believed (and still do believe) that they deserved to enjoy equality with Israel's Jews. On the other hand, the Committee did not approve of the Israeli government's preferential treatment of the Druze in comparison with the rest of the country's Arab population. Sheikh Farhoud was elected chairman of the Committee and was succeeded after several years by Sheikh Jamal Mu'adi of Yarka. In 1977, the Committee joined the Communist Party's Democratic Front for Peace and Equality and continues, together with a few other Druze activists, to lobby against Druze conscription into the Israeli Defense Forces. Nonetheless, there has been no change in the numbers of Druze conscripts, nor in those refusing to do military service in Judea, Samaria and Gaza. Still, the general consensus among the Druze leadership is that Israel's Druze population must continue to play its part on behalf of Israel's security, and they actively encourage Druze men to pursue careers in the military, police force and prison services.

Druze youngsters balked at the traditional and religious Druze leadership and its control over key positions and, in order to advance their own objectives, they established organizations that were blatantly devoid of any political affiliation – for example, the Veterans' Committee and the Committee for the Management of Druze *Waqf*[11]Affairs.

Among the Christian Arabs, extra-parliamentary activity is fueled mostly by the fear that a decreased birthrate and increasing emigration would result in diminishing political power in areas traditionally considered Christian strongholds (such as Nazareth). The Christians find themselves torn between the desire to be a part of the large Palestinian political community and the need to justify their Israeli citizenship. As a minority among Israel's Arabs they tend to follow, officially at least, a middle-of-the-road ideology that is acceptable to the Moslem majority.

Christians were particularly prominent among the leaders of the radical extra-parliamentary *al-Ard* movement: Mansur Kardush and Shukri Hazen are Greek Orthodox; Habib Qahwaji and Sabri Jiryyes are Greek Catholic. In 1978 Christian Arabs, including the Reverend Riah Abu al-Asal, head of the Anglo-Episcopal community, Khalil Nakhla, Jamal Qa'war, Rashid Salim and Mansur Kardush, helped establish the Palestinian Nationalist Literary Association, *al-Sawt*, to provide competition to Hadash. In 1980, Christian activists were among the founders of the Arab Congress in Israel, which aimed at representing Arab society in Israel but was banned by the authorities.

The following extra-parliamentary movements were especially conspicuous.

Abnaa al-Balad (Sons of the Village)[12]

Founded in 1972 in Umm-al-Fahm by the attorney Muhammad Kiwan, the Sons of the Village movement was the largest and the most militant of the radical local groups mentioned above. The movement did not publicize a political platform of its own and relied for its identity on ties with local nationalist groups, all of whom considered the PLO to be the sole legitimate representative of the Palestinian people.

The Sons of the Village were divided into several sections, all connected to the Rejection Front,[13] which included George Habash's Popular Front for the Liberation of Palestine,[14] and the Democratic Front for the Liberation of Palestine, headed by Nayef Hawatmeh. These shared a common ideology, according to which the entire Land of Israel, from the River Jordan to the Mediterranean Sea, belongs to the Palestinian people and a secular, democratic sovereign Arab state (with the exclusion of Israel) should be established on the entire area of mandatory Palestine. Since Abnaa al-Balad did not see the State of Israel as legitimate, it called for a boycott of Knesset elections.

Ideological disputes between the local groups that supported the Sons of the Village movement prevented it from establishing a formal organizational framework – as did the fear that they would be placed under close surveillance by the government authorities. Instead, the movement preferred to establish non-governmental organizations (NGOs) that would contribute financially on various levels and conduct sporadic activity, especially at the local authority level. The Sons of the Village campaigned in local elections as the National Action Front and in 1978 achieved a record 4,000 votes, with the attendant number of local council representatives. The movement managed to place a single representative in several of the local Arab councils – and in the local councils in Umm-al-Fahm, Tayibeh, Mi'elya and Baqa al-Gharbiyye they succeeded in placing two representatives each. In Kabul, the Sons of the Village representative was elected head of the local council. In 1982, the al-Ansar group broke away from the Sons of the Village over participation in Knesset elections. That year the Sons of the Village took part, unsuccessfully, in the municipal elections.

In the 1983 municipal elections, the movement's representation in some local councils increased to nine seats altogether. When, in the 1989 elections, the Sons of the Village competed in 13 settlements, they lost their two seats on the Umm-al-Fahm council, but gained one in Jatt, Kafar Kanna, Sakhnin, Majd al-Krum and Mi'elya respectively.

The al Hadaf association[15] is active in educational and cultural matters on behalf of the Sons of the Village, publishes literary works and organizes cultural gatherings. Its bi-weekly publication, al-Raya, spouts the views of George Habash's Popular Front for the Liberation of Palestine.

During the mid-1970s, all political activity conducted by Arab students in Israeli universities was overseen by Rakah. Gradually, the Rakah leadership found itself faced with students whose nationalist opinions were more radical than its own. Although, in the 1978 student union elections, the radical students failed to be elected, they convened in December 1978 and decided to establish an alternative to the Rakah-ruled student committees. A manifesto was subsequently published under the name of the Progressive Nationalist Movement, whose members refused to accept Rakah's authority. According to the manifesto, the students demanded the right to define themselves as Palestinians and to extend this right to the entire Israeli Arab population. The PLO – according to the manifesto – was the only legitimate representative of the Palestinian people, and the manifesto called for a "national authority" to be established "in all parts of Palestine, as a transitional solution [in the absence of] peace".

Ideologically, there is no difference between the Progressive Nationalist Movement and the Sons of the Village. Together they share relative success among the Arab student body. Among the Arab university students, the Sons of the Village remain second only to Rakah, and in 1988 they won 4 out of 9 seats on the students' union at Ben-Gurion University. At the University of Haifa, the Nationalist Action Front, a combined list constituting the Progressive Nationalist Movement, the Sons of the Village and the Progressive List for Peace, won 3 out of 11 seats that same year. A similar list won 8 out of 17 seats at the Hebrew University of Jerusalem.

The Young Moslems

One of the results of modernization and Westernization among Arab society is that the younger generation of Israeli Arabs moved away from traditional religion. However, following the 1967 Six Day War, when Israel's borders opened to include Judea, Samaria and Gaza, relationships began to develop between Israeli Moslems and religious movements whose ideologies were based on those of the Moslem Brotherhood. East Jerusalem became the focus of religious proselytizing and Islamic study.

From a social point of view, their return to religion expressed the young people's disappointment with what was taking place in Arab society, their attempt to cope with the dominance of Western culture, or their reaction to the failure of modernization to fulfill their aspirations. The religious preachers and imams from the newly acquired West Bank territories were also instrumental in this process. For years, they had been making the rounds of Israeli Arab villages, mostly in the Triangle; some of them were even employed by the Ministry of Religious Affairs as religious officials, in places where none of the local population could be found to fill these posts. Their activity and presence in the area exacerbated and strengthened waves of religious reawakening against a local background.[16]

The work of Islamic liberation movements in several east Asian countries during the late 1970s and the 1980s, the success of the Shi'ite Islamic
Revolution and Ayatollah Khomeini's rise to power in Iran brought political Islam to the attention of Western leaders and ignited hopes in various
Moslem communities that an Islamic victory was imminent and, with it, a
victory for the Arabs. These events in the Middle East had a profound
effect on the Arabs in Israel and led to a growing movement of "born-
again" Moslems (al-Tha'ibin). Their leaders advocated a return to religion
as a means of defense against Western culture. An example of the ideology
behind these organizations is given below by 30-year-old Humam Natur,
from Qalansawa in the Triangle, leader of a religious group:

> Ideally, the laws of the Koran should – to the letter – become the laws of
> the state of Israel, because the Koran contains everything: politics,
> economics and the rules of society. It is our desire to be allowed to build
> many mosques and religious institutions. Within a few months, maybe a
> year, we shall have a majority in the Arab villages. The wave is getting
> stronger, is increasing and nothing can stop it. They will have no choice,
> they will have to let us establish a Moslem council in the villages and we
> shall live according to the Koran. I am not interested in events within
> Israel, I am keeping track of the Moslem world. In Iran, they have taken
> the right road, but this is still not enough. I believe that we must establish
> something like Egypt's Moslem Brotherhood, here in Israel. The main
> objective of such an organization will be to implement the laws of the
> Koran throughout the Arab sector.[17]

The writer Farouk Mawasi from Baqa al-Gharbiyye described the atmosphere well: "As I see it, this phenomenon is not going to stop, but grows
stronger and widespread, because Islam is the answer to all the ills of this
world."[18]

The al-Tha'ibin movement did not restrict itself to religion and soon
turned its hand to politics. Like the Moslem Brotherhood in Judea, Samaria
and Gaza, the movement established local cells, but, fearing that their
organization might be penetrated by the Israeli authorities, the "born-
agains" concealed any signs that might tie them to the outlawed Moslem
Brotherhood, and chose to be known as "Young Moslems" (al-shabab a-
Muslimin). Their activities during the 1980s bore a religious and social
character. They proselytized and worked to bring young people back to
religion, gave special religious sermons in mosques and tried to gain power
in parents' and students' committees, which they used as a vehicle for
sermons on modesty and single-sex education. They also preached anti-
alcohol messages, demanded traditional, religious weddings, initiated
fundraising for the needy and tried to lay the groundwork for separate,
independent – free of charge or almost free – social and educational

(mostly pre-school) services and health care. It combined pragmatism with ideology, coined the slogan "Islam is the solution", and established itself as an important power in Arab settlements.

An important part of *al-Tha'ibin's* activity was aimed at the secular Communist Rakah Party. The Young Moslems, who claimed that "no ideology exists after the Koran", did not accept the existence of a secular state and wanted to establish an Islamic state run according to Islamic law (the *Shari'a*),[19] in which Christians and Jews would live under the patronage (*Ahl al-dhimma*) of Islamic rule. The ideas of *al-Tha'ibin* fell on fertile ground, especially in the Triangle with its predominantly Moslem population. Leaders identified with the movement soon enjoyed political success: in the 1983 local elections in Kafar Barra, Islamic fundamentalist Kamel Rayyan was elected mayor, and in 1984, Dahud Mahmud al-Jurn was elected to head the local council in Jaljulyeh.

The *al-Tha'ibin* movement was unable to identify with any of the Arab political parties and did not translate its power – successfully tested on the local level – to the nationwide Knesset elections. The new spirit of Israeli Arabs was well described in an article by former Mapam MK Muhammad Watad in the September 1979 issue of *New Outlook*: "The new Islamic religious awakening in the Moslem world has reached a peak [and] is influencing Israel's Arabs, and is part of an international reaction to the moral bankruptcy of contemporary atheist ideologies."[20]

These young Moslems were the first buds that symbolized the awakening of an Islamic stream, from which evolved the Islamic Movement, some of whom participate in Knesset elections and most of whom remain to this day extra-parliamentary.

The Islamic Movement

In early 1981, the Israeli authorities uncovered a fundamentalist Islamic underground group called *Usrat al-Jihad* ("The Family of the Holy War") in the Triangle. The group, which wanted to implement the principles of the Moslem Brotherhood, preached a combination of religious fanaticism and extreme nationalism. Dozens of them were arrested and some were tried and given lengthy prison sentences for terrorist activity. This group became the basis of the Islamic Movement in Israel and developed into a political party with representatives in the Knesset and local and regional councils. The fact that Islam is a framework for a political community, and the Islamic Movement is to all intents and purposes a political movement, substantiates the notion that a connection between Islamic fundamentalist circles and radical political organizations in order to promote common interests is not, under certain circumstances, impossible.

The Islamic Movement that evolved during the early 1980s took over, de facto, the entire organization of the Moslem "ethnic" rift, while the state's control of Moslem religious-ethnic affairs was reduced to management of the *Shari'a* court system. A large number of mosques were built in Arab towns and villages all over the country at the initiative and funding of the Islamic Movement. Members of the Islamic Movement fulfill in them all the religious and managerial functions, while the major mosques ("Friday" mosques) still employ functionaries who receive their salaries from the Ministry for Religious Affairs. The Islamic Movement has gradually become the main supplier of religious services to Israel's Moslem community and the number of mosques under its control is greater than those receiving support from the Israeli government. A large increase in the number of mosques has been noted since the Islamic Movement began taking part in local authority elections; the number tripled from 80 in 1988 to 240 in 1993. By 2003, the two branches of the Islamic Movement operated 43 percent of the 363 active mosques. On the other hand, properties belonging to the *Waqf* have remained mainly under the control of the government, which continues to appoint boards of trustees to maintain and manage them.

The Islamic Movement became one of the main political powers in the Arab sector, especially on the extra-parliamentary level. Its activity combines ideology and pragmatism and blends into the existing conflict in the Moslem arena between the religious and the modern world, between religious concepts and the secular world. In Israel, the Islamic Movement is also the result of a meeting between the Arab minority and Israeli society. The movement is constantly stressing that a return to religion and the laws of Islam are the only way out of the social suffering with which the Moslems in Israel are afflicted. To this end, the movement has established cultural centers, clinics, libraries and aid-for-the-needy funds in those villages where it has taken a strong hold, such as Umm-al-Fahm, Kafar Kanna, Kafar Qasem, etc. All this has helped the movement to establish itself as an important political force among the Arab population. The Islamic Movement first received public recognition when it participated in the February 1983 municipal elections. By this time it was backed by several years of religious and communal activity, which were made possible by the long-standing neglect of the Arab sector by the Jewish establishment, a neglect which brought about a yearning for change, for a new social order, and for answers to ideological issues to which the existing political parties had insufficient response.

On the eve of the twelfth Knesset elections in 1988, there were activists in the movement who proposed joining the political race, whether as an independent Islamic list or as part of a joint Arab political list. In order to avoid internal conflict, it was decided to refrain from running for the twelfth Knesset, and also for the subsequent, thirteenth, Knesset. However, as the elections for the fourteenth Knesset approached, there was an increased demand on the part of the movement's leader, Sheikh

Abdallah Nimer Darwish, to participate, and this caused a split in the movement between the "southern branch", under the leadership of Darwish (until he retired and was replaced by Ibrahim Sarsur), and the extra-parliamentary "northern branch", led by Sheikh Ra'ed Salah.[21] The seeds of the crisis in the movement were sown already during the first *Intifada* (civil uprising),[22] took root after the signing of the Oslo Accords between Israel and the PLO, and matured in the form of the official split in the movement following the decision to campaign for a seat in the fourteenth Knesset in 1996.

By offering its candidacy for the Knesset, the southern branch of the Islamic Movement turned itself into part of the Arab political establishment in Israel.[23] As mentioned above, by that time the Islamic Movement was backed by several years of municipal activity, during which the movement had proved itself to be a pragmatic force with serious influence over the lives of the country's Arab population. It was willing, too, to break down accepted frameworks within the Arab sector's political system. From a structural point of view – containing as it did elected representatives of the major family tribes – it spearheaded the struggle against tribalism that had been initiated by the Communist Party years beforehand.

The entry of the southern branch of the Islamic Movement into the parliamentary arena stepped up the discourse on civil equality between Jews and Arabs in Israel and the problematic issue of a Moslem-Arab minority in a Jewish state. Arab politicians toyed with the idea that they would now be the balancing pivot in Israeli politics. For this reason, perhaps, Darwish presented views that were pragmatic. He came out in favor of two states for two nations and did not work toward a global Islamic state. In an interview he presented these views clearly, even outspokenly: "If such a state did not materialize in the days of the Prophet [Muhammad], should I be the one to make it materialize?"[24]

In the 1989 municipal elections, the Islamic Movement realized its strength by winning five Arab local councils: Umm-al-Fahm, Kafar Qasam, Kafar Barra, Jaljulyeh and the large Bedouin town of Rahat in the Negev. The movement did not get to head either the city or the local council in Nazareth or Kafar Kanna, but became a significant political force in those places nonetheless. Its greatest achievement was winning the mayorship of Umm-al-Fahm, the second largest Arab town in Israel.

In the meantime, the northern branch went on to take a major position in the extra-parliamentary movement and became, de facto, the dominant radical stream in Arab politics. Shortly after the split, the northern branch began concentrating on various forms of activities relating to the Palestinian population, in particular the struggle on behalf of the al-Aqsa mosque on the Temple Mount in Jerusalem, via the organizations established for this purpose, such as the Institute for Humanitarian Aid, the Humanitarian Rescue Committee, and the al-Aqsa Company for the

Rehabilitation and Development of Holy Sites. Their activities included ties with Islamic groups and organizations outside Israel.[25]

Sheikh Ra'ed Salah resigned his post as mayor of Umm-al-Fahm in 2001 in order to become the spiritual and ideological leader of the Islamic Movement and to reduce his ties with the Israeli establishment to the bare minimum. The movement organizes annual mass demonstrations under the slogan "al-Aqsa is in danger", in the course of which harsh accusations are hurled at Israel. The northern branch, therefore, is establishing itself as the Islamic Movement in Israel. Further, as we see it, the southern – parliamentary – branch is an inseparable part of the Islamic Movement in Israel and expresses its basic ideological concepts. It may be assumed that participation in parliamentary affairs is a part of the Islamic Movement's tactics and should not be seen as a result of any fundamental or ideological split. The Islamic Movement's political activity has been accompanied almost from the very beginning by friction with the Israeli authorities.

In 1987, the movement established the foundation called the Islamic Support Committee, in order to support orphans and widows of the *Intifada* residing in the occupied territories. The Israeli authorities closed this committee down because it provided aid to people connected with the Hamas and suicide bombers. So far the committee has reopened and closed several times under different names. Friction with the authorities reached a peak in May 2003, with the arrest of Islamic Movement leaders headed by Ra'ed Salah, on suspicion of exploiting the committee under its various titles for money laundering and passing on funds to Islamic terrorist groups. The arrests aroused equally sharp comments from all the parliamentary and extra-parliamentary Arab groups in Israel. After his release from jail, Sheikh Ra'ed Salah was welcomed warmly by Arab mayors and other public figures, and even today he continues to enjoy the warmth and sympathy of his community.[26] The reason behind this solidarity is the fact that Israel's Arabs see any attack on the northern branch as a direct attack on Islam and on Moslems. The circumstances described above demonstrate the claim that the feeling of frustration and hopelessness in the Arab sector could lead to a violent conflict that will further escalate the tension and lack of trust that are part and parcel of the relationship between the country's two major populations.

Moving towards a Civil Society

The October 1973 Yom-Kippur War, its results and subsequent developments marked an about-turn in the history of Israel's Arabs. After the war, the local Arab population participated, together with the rest of the Arab world, in the process of "rehabilitating their self-respect", as well as committing themselves to the process of strengthening their Palestinian identity. As the image of an invincible Israel was tested, the local Arabs' view of themselves changed from that of a small, powerless minority facing a dominant Jewish majority to that of a large, influential society with its own needs and ideas. Increasing militancy and a desire to influence the centers of power were expressed not only in formal parliamentary organization, but also in local and country-wide bonding with common objectives. More than anything else, this bonding expressed the changes in the way in which Israeli Arab society operated and marked the first steps on the way to a civil society.

This activity emerged, on the whole, from a new factor in Arab society – the educated classes which evolved as a consequence of rising standards of living and improved educational opportunities among Israeli Arabs. It was natural, therefore, that the first organizations to be formed were student unions and academic associations, which focused on solutions for problems particular to these groups. Independent Arab student unions had already begun forming during the late 1960s as a result of their integration problems in Israeli universities and strained relations with the Jewish students. The Arab student unions were separate from the general student body and concentrated on solving problems specific to the Arab student population. The committees even organized social and cultural activities that focused on nationalist issues; they opposed government activity such as land expropriation, which in their opinion was harmful to the Arab public.[27]

The Union of Arab Academics in Israel was founded in the summer of 1971, with the aim of improving the Israeli Arabs' social and cultural living standards (principally by encouraging young people to graduate from high school and continue to university), and to defend their civil rights. To avoid clashing with the authorities, the union leaders firmly denied any affiliation to political bodies. The union did not last for long, however, because internal power struggles and ideological quarrels led to a rift and its eventual dissolution. Other attempts to unite Arab students were similarly unsuccessful.

In 1974, academic and intellectual committees sprang up in several Arab towns and townships such as Nazareth, Shefar'am, Kafar Yasif, etc., and a national high school students' committee was established in April 1974. Arab students' committees were already active in the universities and served as a successful front for the Progressive National Movement and the Sons of the Village. In April 1975, the smaller committees decided to join forces under an umbrella organization to represent all of the country's Arab students, notwithstanding differences of opinion: the Haifa student union was influenced by Rakah, while the union in Jerusalem was influenced by the more radical circles. This situation made common action difficult.

The organizations took pains to emphasize their political non-affiliation and the fact that they did not depend on any political body or parliamentary faction. The fact was, however, that most of them were backed by Rakah. Although ostensibly they had been established in order to deal with specific goals or interests of a certain group, these organizations reacted to almost all political events associated with Israeli Arabs, and provided a strong lobby on their behalf. They also expressed their intention to act, when necessary, as alternative institutions for the Israeli Arab population.

Three groups had a major influence on the extra-parliamentary activity of Israel's Arabs.

The Land Defense Committee

Since the establishment of the State of Israel, expropriation of Arab-owned land was a serious bone of contention and caused strained relations with the authorities. Between 1948 and 1966, when military rule was abolished, the state expropriated lands on which it built new towns and roads, industrial parks and schools. Some of this land was privately owned. At that time, Arab landlords did not have the political thrust to confront the government and accepted their fate weakly. Following the June 1967 war, however, things changed. Land expropriation was an emotionally charged issue and it was, therefore, a simple matter to unite all the Arab political factions around it. Rakah was especially good at exploiting the situation and turned it from a local issue into a national Arab issue, with interwoven nationalist motifs.

The government's 1976 expropriations to furnish the "Judaizing the Galilee"[28] project infuriated the Arab leadership, who saw it purely and simply as disenfranchisement of their lands. In late 1975, Rakah established a new political entity: the Land Defense Committee. Headed by the Anglican priest Shehada Shehada from Shefar'am, the Committee appointed a seven-member secretariat, of which only two were Rakah members. Rakah deliberately lowered its profile in order to create a wider front that could not be identified with any particular political party, and to enable internal unity and co-operation between radical and moderate elements in Arab society.

Agitation among minorities increased steadily and peaked on March 30, 1976, when the country's Arabs held their first "Land Day", when violent confrontations with the police led to several casualties. It had become obvious to me a year earlier that the expropriations would engender mass reaction, in particular since the land was not put to immediate use and the act, at first, appeared pointless. In 1976, I warned that, unlike on other occasions (such as 1966 or even 1956), it would never again be possible to calm things down simply by bribing some *Mukhtar* or other official. In fact, I suggested that on Land Day, it might be a good idea to bring several government ministers to the Galilee region, in order to give the local population a detailed explanation of their plans for developing the region.

On the morning of Land Day, I traveled to Nazareth and stayed at the Labor Party headquarters, where I did my best to soothe tempers and persuade the local population that no dispossession had been intended. My presence, however, was not enough. The Arab leadership took the government's silence to be a confirmation that the intention behind the expropriations was to dispossess them; the people took to the streets. Toward midday, rumors of heavy casualties started to arrive at the Labor Party office. Tempers became more and more frayed and eventually events got completely out of control. I waited for things to calm down, but could do nothing, except watch sadly as my prophecy of the first major rift between the Jews and Arabs in Israel destroyed any goodwill built up by the two communities since 1948.

In protest against government land expropriation, the Land Defense Committee had called for a demonstration on March 30, 1976, together with a general strike in the Israeli Arab sector. Great care and legal advice kept the protest within the confines of the law and allowed the use of legitimate venues for protest rallies and demonstrations. The events of that day – during which six Arab–Israeli citizens were killed – symbolized the Arab population's struggle against the government, and expressed their inherent hostility and nationalist attitude toward the state. Since the Land Day event, the government has almost completely halted the expropriation of Arab land – except for public projects and in return for agreed-upon compensation. The relative success of Land Day raised the pride factor among Israel's Arabs and prodded them into taking further action to protect their civil interests. Land Day continues to be an important occasion on the Israeli Arab calendar and expresses the unity of the Palestinians on both sides of the Green Line. In recent years, it has become a test of organization for Israel's Arabs and a day of memorial rather than a tool for rallying mass action – as it was during the first years following March 1976. The Land Defense Committee has, to a great extent, faded away; its last action was in 1999, over agricultural land near Umm-al-Fahm, expropriated for military maneuvers, regardless of the owners' rights. The Supreme Follow-up Committee for the Arabs in Israel, the main representative of Israel's Arab population, gradually replaced the Land Defense Committee.

The National Committee for the Arab Local Authorities in Israel

In the Arab sector, since the second half of the 1970s, local authorities have gradually become the focus of political activity. Most political bodies, even those that spurned Knesset elections (such as the Sons of the Village), considered local government an effective tool through which to win influence and power.

Establishing the National Committee for the Arab Local Authorities in Israel was a complex process. In June 1970, the first convention of Israeli Arab local authority heads was held in the Galilee with the aim of establishing a lobby to advance their demands in the Local Government Center, the Interior Ministry and other government institutions. Druze municipality leaders participated in the convention, after which a special commission was convened to examine problems unique to Arab local authorities. Headed by Dr Sami Jaraisi, the commission published its conclusions in 1973, pointing to a serious discrepancy between the government aid meted out to Jewish local authorities and that given to their Arab counterparts. The Jaraisi report prodded Arab local authority leaders to demand equal rights.

Fifteen council leaders attended the 1974 convention from the Western Galilee region, and elected a special commission consisting of representatives from Rame, Tamra, Kafar Yasif, Mi'elya, Beit Jann, Sakhnin and Shefar'am. The first meeting of the National Committee for the Arab Local Authorities in Israel was held in Nazareth in February 1974 and was attended by representatives of villages and towns in the Western Galilee, Eastern Galilee and the Triangle. It was the first concentrated effort by local authority leaders from all over the country to prepare a practical plan of action. The central committee, elected in June 1974, requested member status in the Local Government Center.

Initially, the Committee was received favorably by the establishment. Since the 1976 Land Day event, the politicization of Israeli Arab society forced local authority leaders to take a stand not only on municipal, but also on nationalist issues. As the body most representative of Israel's Arab population, the National Committee for the Arab Local Authorities in Israel had a very high profile in the Arab sector and acted as a substitute parliament for Israel's Arabs. When it became apparent that the Committee was dealing with political and national issues and seemed to be exceeding its original mandate, the government broke ties with it and adopted an ambivalent attitude toward it, which ranged from de facto recognition to non-recognition. Until the late 1980s, all contact with the Committee has been made via the Local Government Center, which also includes Arab municipal leaders among its members. Gradually, the government took a more positive stance toward the Committee, mainly because it was a convenient address for police and internal security officials to go to, when they wanted to find a large number of local government officials with whom to negotiate permits for demonstrations and strikes, and organize security arrangements for public events in the Arab sector.

The Supreme Follow-up Committee for the Arabs in Israel

By 1982 the rise in the Committee's power and influence had prompted Ibrahim Nimer Husayn* to establish the Supreme Follow-up Committee for the Arabs in Israel in order to keep track of the government's treatment of the Arab population countrywide. The Committee included members of the National Committee for the Arab Local Authorities in Israel as well as four Arab Knesset members, two from Rakah and two from Labor. The objective was for the Arab community to join forces, to put to full use their dedicated Knesset members through whom they could approach ministers, other Knesset members and Knesset committees.

Committee secretary Abd Anabtawi took advantage of a conversation with me on August 17, 2002 to explain the Committee's ideological platform and its political plans, according to which the destruction by the authorities of illegally constructed houses in the Bedouin neighborhood of Umm al-Sahali next to Shefar'am in April 1998 and the subsequent demonstrations led to changes in the Committee's planned activity. It decided to come out in favor of rebuilding every house destroyed by the government, everywhere in the country. Also, it decided to act on different levels against land expropriation, in addition to accepted forms of protest, and would engage the media to promote its views.

Knowing that the government would reject them, the Supreme Follow-up Committee for the Arabs in Israel set about speeding up plans for expanding areas under municipal jurisdiction. For example, an alternative plan to regional structure plan # 35 was submitted in 1992 and an alternative to plan # 9, clause 2 was submitted in 2001. The Committee was pleased with its achievement, when the relevant authorities accepted several amendments. The Committee also petitioned the Supreme Court after MK Haim Druckman submitted a proposed change in the land law that would make it illegal to sell state lands to Arabs. This was countered by a petition submitted by the Committee to the Supreme Court in 2002, protesting at the destruction of houses across the main street in the southern neighborhood of Majd al-Krum. The aim of the government, according to the Committee, was to cut off the neighborhood from Majd al-Krum and prevent the settlement from spreading southwards.

On the international level, the Committee increased its activity mainly after the events of October 2000, when 13 Arabs lost their lives in the course of violent protests. It has contacts with NGOs, with UN organizations (dealing with civil rights and minority rights) and with foreign embassies.

However, the formation and development of these primary organizations only heralded things to come. Throughout the 1980s and 1990s,

---

* The first Chairman of the National Committee for the Arab Local Authorities in Israel, who was for many years the Mayor of the city of Shefar'am.

institutional processes in Israel's Arab society gained momentum and the number of independent political organizations increased. Many associations began to work in political and semi-political areas such as civil rights, co-existence, internal refugees, etc. It was a process that expressed a change in the political action pattern of Israel's Arabs as well as the formation of additional – some scholars might view them as alternative – power centers to the Knesset and local authorities. Many of these organizations constitute the basis for a certain type of institutional autonomy called for by some Arab intellectuals in Israel. The historian and political scientist Ya'akov Landau[29] argues that all these bodies share a mutual search for a purely Arab framework for political, social and economic activism while expressing disappointment about co-operation with parallel Israeli government institutions. This new-found activism was based on the emerging of new groupings within the Israeli Arab population, mainly young academics seeking empowerment. These new groupings were not identified with traditional social rifts within the Israeli Arab community.

Extra-parliamentary Institutionalization and the Emergence of the "Third Sector"

The formation of new Arab institutions followed a decentralization of activity among the Arab public. Such activity emphasized local intervention and homegrown, autonomous solutions to local problems, on the backs of the NGOs[30] which sprang up throughout the Arab sector and are known as the "Third Sector"; in fact, this type of local activity mirrors similar social forces at play in Israel's Jewish neighborhoods. The organizations are registered with the Ministry of Justice as non-profit associations and are entitled to raise funds in order to finance their activity. Initially, the non-profit organizations were no more than a name and most institutions did not succeed in getting past the formation stage and on to actually contributing to the social area of their choice. The reason for these start-up difficulties stems mostly from the pattern of internal schisms found within the socio-political fabric of Israeli Arab communities and their incessant competition for power and influence. The aim of the founders of these non-profit organizations was to build a new social order, with new power centers and a new and modern agenda within the State of Israel.

The Third Sector organizations have become the main communication channel for Israeli Arabs with the outside world, i.e. the international community. As a result, Israeli Arabs reorientated themselves toward participation in international forums, which were now prepared to consider issues long classified as being internal Israeli affairs. Already in May–July 1992, the advisory bureau for Arab affairs in the prime minister's office published reports under the heading "Israeli Arab Citizens and the

International Community", according to which international bodies received many applications in recent years from Israeli Arabs protesting against discrimination. Diplomatic propaganda efforts on the part of Israeli Arab organizations have so far achieved a statement by US ambassador to Israel William Harrop, on September 3, 1992, in which he declared that discrimination against Arabs in Israel should be part of the agenda in discussions on the US-Israel relationship.[31]

Over the past decade, Israeli Arabs have established organizations that aim to form a nationwide infrastructure. These organizations deal mainly with legal advice, defense and counsel on matters regarding the country's Arab population. By 2005, over 2,000 non-profit organizations were registered, of which at least 300 are active. Most are concerned with equal rights and the attendant political issues: prisoners' rights, displaced persons, land disputes, etc. All are aimed at placing the plight of the Israeli Arab community on the national agenda. These NGOs are involved in political and legal struggles, and local authority leaders seek ways to centralize these struggles within the Israeli Arab community in terms of content and political action. Because of the social status achieved by Arab NGOs, they can now turn to international organizations to gain publicity and funding and to become a part of the public agenda. This new civil consciousness is creating seasoned activists for Arab political parties, thus consolidating local activism with the wider aims of the national political parties. Middle East expert Raphael Israeli calls this phenomenon "sector focusing" and considers it detrimental to Israeli democracy because, according to his view, there are enough political parties to work with.[32] Of course this is an oversimplification, because Jewish parties have not placed Israeli Arab interests high on their political agenda, while existing Arab parties in Israel are marginal and without influence in decision-making bodies. Extra-parliamentary organizations, especially the Supreme Follow-up Committee for the Arabs in Israel, continue to fill a central role for the Arab public in Israel and their importance will only grow. This is so mainly because of the marginal position of Israeli Arabs in parliamentary politics in Israel, and the fact that the Arab parties have remained on the sidelines of civil action and possess no real political power.

Among the oldest of these organizations is the "Galilee Association for Health Research", whose country-wide activity focuses on issues concerning public health, sanitation and the environment. The association was founded by Dr Hatem Kana'na, who worked for the Ministry of Health and is experienced in the field. Much of its activity involves setting down sewage systems and operating mobile health clinics in Bedouin squatter settlements in the Negev and in the north of the country. The association receives support and co-operation from local authorities because of the sewage system projects that it supplies for them, which do not threaten the authority's civic monopoly. In recent years, the association has begun working in other areas and is also active in social and regional research and development.

Among the Arab non-profit organizations registered with the Justice Ministry in 2000, 287 dealt directly with religious matters: the establishment and upkeep of mosques, charity, management of *Waqf* property and religious education. Other popular areas for non-profit organizations are sport and physical education, geriatric care, women's activities, culture and social activities and health and anti-drug programs. In squatter settlements, mainly in the Negev and in the Galilee, associations have emerged that focus on obtaining official recognition for their settlements. Many organizations active among Christian Arabs belong to churches, schools, or deal with religious education.

On national and civic matters the most important organization is *Adala* ("justice") – the Arab legal center for minority rights in Israel, which was founded in November 1996 and is the first of its kind to be managed by Israeli Arab lawyers. *Adala* aims mainly at achieving equality for the Arabs in Israel and defending their civil rights on issues such as land, education, employment, the Arab language, politics, women, culture and religion. In order to achieve its objectives, *Adala* makes liberal use of its right to appeal to the Supreme Court. It also takes advantage of the support of Arab MKs and left-wing Jewish MKs and provides legal advice to NGOs and Arab institutions. *Adala* was deeply involved in the legal aspects of the Or Commission of Inquiry, which was entrusted with investigating the October 2000 riots in which several Arabs lost their lives. It also provided defense representation for Arabs who appeared before the Or Committee.

It is important to clarify the significance of the activity of *Adala* vis-à-vis the position of the Arab community in Israel. According to *Adala*, the individual's autonomy constitutes a goal in itself. However, personal autonomy also necessitates recognition of the collective rights of the group to which the individual belongs. According to *Adala*, Israel's Arab minority is a national homeland minority characterized by its own language, culture, history and collective memory; as such, the view of the collective rights of Palestinian Arabs in Israel is larger than that of cultural, ethnic and religious minorities or immigration groups. Therefore, the struggle of Israeli Arabs is not centered on integration; *Adala* emphasizes group rights and does not consider political and civil rights any less important.

In the sphere of communications, various organizations sprang up, such as *I'lam* ("propaganda") – Arab society's media center, established in 1997 and headed by Salman Natur, Ja'far Farah, Antuan Shalhat and others. *Musawa* ("equality") was established in 1997, following the destruction of illegally built houses in the Bedouin village of Umm al-Sahali near Shefar'am. One of the objectives of *I'lam* was to establish an Arab communication network consisting of professionals with the ability to penetrate the Israeli and international media. *Adala* and the Arab Civil Rights Organization in Nazareth provide European civil rights activists and foreign diplomats in Israel with legal reports on the activity of the Israeli military among the Arab population in Israel.

New Political Leadership

As Israeli Arab society adopted modernization and a new class of young educated people evolved, the more traditional patterns of authority began to fade away. The new leaders do not come from a specific social or economic class, but tend to belong to a similar peer group. They grew up during the period of military administration and are the offspring of the generation that lived through the early years of Israel's independence after 1948. By taking the traditional clan rifts into consideration in establishing their political format, these young people have been able to present a potential focus for independent political activity. Their educational status and skills have provided them with political power within the clan and entitled them to become its representatives. Simultaneously, they have successfully used the clan's power to fill functions in municipal government.

Among the second and third generation of Israeli Arabs, a middle class has developed which enjoys a higher standard of living than their parents. Traditional leaderships have receded into the background and become irrelevant; they have been replaced by individuals who were born into higher living standards and, politically and organizationally, have been influenced by Israeli culture. The second and third generations founded parliamentary and extra-parliamentary Arab parties in Israel, worked within them and took on leadership positions in existing Israeli Arab parties. Although people in this class strove to join the leadership of independent political and community frameworks according to an increasing trend within the Arab population in Israel, on the structural level they were to a certain degree subject to co-opting because of their almost absolute dependence on the Jewish sector in respect to white-collar jobs. Thus, their attitude toward the establishment – the main provider of opportunities for personal advancement and the realization of political power and influence – remains ambivalent.

Pluralism, the obscuring of clan boundaries and global currents in Israel's Arab sector, most of which emerged during the past two decades, eroded the existing clan-based leadership class and organizational weaknesses catalyzed the process. The fact that the traditional Arab leadership in Israel lacked social legitimacy created a situation in which the hundreds of non-profit organizations established in the Arab sector found themselves having to focus on issues that the public and political system are unable to deal with, such as the status of women, equality and community planning, as well as the ongoing debate on the place of the Arab citizen in Israel – all issues which have been discussed for many years within a complex system of political and voluntary bodies which operate internet sites, prepare status papers, operate Knesset lobbies and lobby the Jewish public, maintain contact with international forums and organizations, and keep up a public discussion within Israel's Arab population.

Among the voting public, the status of Arab politics has always been unstable, an instability exacerbated by continued official disdain for Arab representatives coupled with the fringe status of Arab MKs. The Israeli Arab public has never really respected Arab leaders, believing them to be under the influence of social rifts; their ancestry, social and academic status were often held in contempt and they were suspected of nepotism and of pursuing a personal agenda to serve their immediate families and clans, or even of co-operating with the government in return for personal favors. Their marginal status within the Israeli political system seems to prompt Arab MKs and their political lists to adopt extreme positions in order to win the support of potential voters, with the unavoidable result that Israel's Arab citizens are not seen as an organized political entity, sharing a common interest – although most of them share a national identity.

Another factor contributing to the unstable status of Arab politics in Israel is the cultural dissonance within the Arab community. Although the majority agree that there is some institutional discrimination towards them, that complete civil equality has not yet been achieved and that the State of Israel does not fully represent them – and that there is still a need for protests and demonstrations – many Arabs have actually reached an understanding that many of the issues over which their leaders are fighting are never going to be resolved. They have concluded that it is better to maintain a solid and less militant relationship with the Jews, who are quite happy to leave the Arabs to conduct a normal lifestyle, notwithstanding that they can continue to spout slogans protesting against discrimination and in favor of co-existence.

Arab mayors and local council heads made efforts at various times to achieve recognition as the main Arab political leadership in Israel. The absence of an independent Arab ruling structure in Israel created a void that left the local authorities with the status of being the only Arab institutions with official authority and with the financial funding that enabled them to influence their population. Since the group of independent MKs has always been small and disunited, and the Arab MKs in the Zionist parties were never seen as full partners to the Arabs' political struggle, the local authorities were able to demand greater legitimacy as leaders of the Arab population than could the Arab MKs, who were considered suspect – because of the disunited make-up of the Arab political map – and believed to be acting for personal gain and interests.

The leadership that formed and became galvanized during and after the fourteenth Knesset elections included several academics in their forties, new faces to national politics. They also presented a new aspect of the

Israeli Arab community, being bi-lingual as well as bi-cultural. Besides being the sons and daughters of the Israeli Arab culture, they had also adopted the Israeli secular culture and acquired skills that allowed them to move easily in both societies. Men such as Dr Azmi Bishara, Muhammad Zaydan and Atef Khatib placed themselves at the head of the lists they themselves had formed. Four new Knesset members were elected: Abd al-Malik Dahamsha from the Islamic Movement's United Arab List – a lawyer by profession and new to politics; Dr Azmi Bishara from the Democratic National Pact – a philosophy lecturer who had come to politics via extra-parliamentary activism; Dr Ahmad Sa'ad, economist and editor-in-chief of the Arab journal *al-Ittihad*; and Tawfiq Khatib, mayor of Jaljulyeh. Today, the only one not elected at that time, Dr Ahmad Tibi, a physician, well known for his association with the Palestinian Authority, is a leading representative of the new Arab leadership in Israel. Like Azmi Bishara, Tibi is typical of those Arabs who have managed to function well within Israeli Arab society, as well as among the Palestinians, and he serves as a role model.

In spite of impressive personal and professional development, the mobility of Arab political leaders in Israel is quite limited; their paths are blocked by the parliamentary establishment which is controlled by the Jewish majority. In election campaigns involving an obvious ethnic element, the personality of a leader may bring about a distinct rise in votes. In the absence of a leadership capable of fulfilling voters' desires, the number of active voters might well drop. A vicious circle has therefore evolved in which elected members of Israeli Arab parties are few in number and not sufficiently influential on the political scene. Consequently, they have to struggle for a dwindling constituency and their political struggle forces them to take increasingly an radical position, distancing themselves from mainstream Israeli politics. As a result, they find themselves isolated and less effective in the Knesset.

Over the last decade, the Arab leadership in Israel has had significant success in raising political awareness and encouraging political activism among the Arab population. This is especially true if looked at against the background of conflict between the Arab public and the Israeli political establishment, since the beginning of the second Palestinian *Intifada*. From the start, the Arab leadership was interested in social mobility and attempted to re-create a civil society outside the traditional political framework, of the type that the more traditional Israeli Arab leadership had struggled without success to realize within the state's traditional social and legal structure. For this reason, the developing leadership's agenda was from the beginning subject to compromises dictated by Israeli social and political reality. Israeli citizenship served as the highest goal and all their demands were based on the legal and judicial status of this citizenship. Although they made no attempt to internalize Israeli-ness, they did not hesitate to take advantage of it in developing previously camouflaged political orientations and in attempts to break through the framework forced upon them by the government.

Among the early twenty-first-century leadership, Azmi Bishara stood out for being, among other things, a strong proponent of the "state for all its citizens" theory and one of the most eloquent speakers from among the intellectual political stream that supported him. He first entered politics in April 1992 by establishing the "Equality Pact", which later served as the basis for the "National Democratic Pact", on whose platform he was elected to Knesset. Through the "Equality Pact", Bishara tried to present the idea of "a state for all its citizens" as a stepping stone toward autonomy. According to his view, the Israeli state had to nullify the Law of Return and adopt immigration laws similar to those in Western countries. By taking this stance, Bishara made a considerable contribution to the public discourse in Israel. He was also the first Arab leader in Israel to demand recognition for Israel's Arab community as a national minority entitled to autonomy.[33]

Bishara's aim was to promote two far-reaching political and cultural processes: deconstruction of traditional Zionist Jewish nationalism and, simultaneously, construction of a new and modern kind of Arab nationalism. According to Bishara, Zionism did not start out as a national liberation movement, but as one whose objective was to establish a sovereign state with a Jewish majority in a country which had an Arab majority before 1948. To this end, it used colonialist tactics and even saw itself as part of a project to colonize the Middle East. The "two states for two nations" solution, according to Bishara, is temporary. In the long term, the only viable solution for the area between the Mediterranean and the Jordan River is a bi-national state governed by two national parliaments. Thus the country will be the Land of Israel for every Israeli and Palestine for every Palestinian.

Over the past decade, a large group of students and young university graduates has been gaining prominence. Socially, this has all the features of a new peer group, and has been coined by some researchers the "upright" generation, to distinguish them from their parents' "burnt-out" generation and their grandparents' "generation of survivors". The leaders of the "upright" generation demand collective historical justice for Israel's Arabs and are no longer content with the liberalism offered by the Israeli regime.

Today (2008), therefore, the discourse surrounding "a state for all its people" and the idea of autonomy for Israeli Arabs stands at the core of the (Israeli) Arab leadership's political activity and influences their political orientation. This leadership focuses on the Arab MKs, the Supreme Follow-up Committee for the Arabs in Israel, and the struggle for social and civil equality in Israel. The longer it takes for this equality to be implemented, the more urgent the issue for Israel's Arabs and the louder the

1 Independence Day 1950. Reception for Arab dignitaries from the village of Tireh. Among those present were the Regional Military Governor, Goel Levinsky, Regional Commissioner of Police and Zvi Alpeleg, Governor of the southern triangle.

2 Celebrating Israel's sixth Independence Day in Nazareth, with the national flag. May 6, 1954.

3 Prime Minister David Ben-Gurion on a tour of Arab villages in the Galilee accompanied by Sheikh Amin Tarif and MKs Jaber Mu'adi and Saleh Khneifes. July 9, 1959.

4 President Zalman Shazar, accompanied by Catholic Bishop Haldani, entering the Church of the Annunciation in Nazareth. August 22, 1967.

5 Visit of Minister of Religious Affairs, Zerah Warhaftig, together with Yigal Allon and Arab leaders in Kfar Hittin. April 30, 1968.

6 Shimon Peres and Ra'anan Cohen on a visit to Sheikh Hamad Abu Rabia in the Negev, to celebrate his election to the Knesset – 1972.

7 Abba Eban and Ra'anan Cohen with Attorney Muhammad Massarweh, who served as Israel's Consul General in Atlanta, USA, and a group of young Arab university graduates. April 1974.

8 Protest demonstrations, Land Day, March 30, 1983, commemorating six Arabs killed after land was expropriated in the Galilee.

9 Prime Minister Shimon Peres at an Arab Conference in the Galilee, June 25, 1985.

10　Jerusalem Mayor, Teddy Kollek, with Christian and Moslem Arab leaders at a reception in honor of Argentinean President, Carlos Mennem. Rose Garden, Jerusalem, October 2, 1991.

11　Prime Minister Yitzhak Rabin and Chief of Staff Ehud Barak speaking with Arab residents in a local market, August 1992.

12 Jerusalem Mayor-Elect Ehud Olmert posing during a visit to the old city of Jerusalem shortly after his victory, April 1993. In 2007 Mr Olmert served as the Prime Minister of Israel.

13 Prime Minister Shimon Peres (second from right) and Foreign Minister Ehud Barak (left) during a celebration to mark the end of the Moslem holiday of Id al Fiter, February 1996. In 2007 Mr. Shimon Peres served as the president of Israel.

14 Prime Minister Benjamin Netanyahuu and Druze dignitaries at the funeral of
Dr Darash Maher who fell during an IDF rescue operation in Lebanon, September 1997.

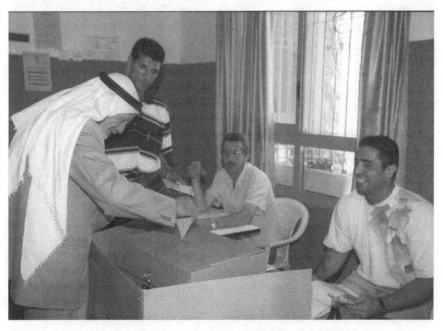

15 Voting in General Elections in the village of Jaljulyeh, May 17, 1999.

16 Protests in Nazareth. Moslems praying on behalf of the mosque next to the Church of the Annunciation, October 15, 1999.

17 Demonstrations in October 2000. Courtesy of *Assenara*.

18 Demonstrations in October 2000. Funeral of one of the casualties. Courtesy of *Assenara*.

19 Israeli Arabs demonstrating outside the Supreme Court in Jerusalem in the course of the Or Commission debates, October 3, 2001.

20 Prime Minister Ariel Sharon, at a meeting with Arab local municipality leaders, December 23, 2003.

21   Sons of Sakhnin football club win the national cup in 2004.

22 A mass rally in Umm-al-Fahm, to celebrate the release from jail of Sheikh Ra'ed Zalah on July 18, 2005. The Mufti of Jerusalem, Akhrama Sabri and Archimandrit Attala Hanna, spokesman for the Greek Orthodox Church in Jerusalem and Israeli Arab leaders, attended the rally. Courtesy of Itzik Ben Malchi.

23 Inhabitants of Shefar'am storming a bus in which a Jewish soldier launched a murderous attack on Arab passengers, killing four. August 4, 2005. Courtesy of Jenny Mancho Ghosh.

24 Clashes between youngsters and the police in the Druze village of Peqi'in in October 2007, which left several policemen and inhabitants of the village injured.

voices calling for a change from a Zionist-Jewish Israel to a "state for all its people". This is not necessarily the discourse conducted by the "upright generation", who seek more radical solutions.

The 1990s: Non-Reactionary Politicization

Over the last two decades the political orientation of the Arabs in Israel has followed two new trends: a political behavior that represents parliamentary segregation and organizational patterns that represent institutional separatism. But this has not led to a radicalization of positions, but rather to a reaction to a number of processes: internalizing and understanding Israeli democracy; perpetuation of the Arabs' status as second-class citizens; deteriorating relations with Palestinians as a result of the first (1987) and second *Intifada* (2000); the failure of Israel's Arabs to become a relevant factor in the peace process between the Palestinians and Israel; and Israel's policy toward its Arab citizens.

A new reality evolved after the Oslo Accords, in which the PLO became a legal entity. This new reality made it possible for Israeli Arabs simultaneously to lobby freely on behalf of the Palestinians and the PLO and to participate in public activity in Israel without the fear of identity crisis. Tibi and Bishara are good representatives of this trend, which has been defined as "politicization without extremism".[34] The political consciousness of Israeli Arabs has become more acute and they are no longer prepared to accept discrimination. Neither have they alienated themselves from the state.

The growing support for Arab parties was especially evident in the 1996 Knesset elections. The new voting system, under the Law of Direct Election, which granted voters the possibility of splitting their vote between the prime minister and Knesset faction, assured the Arab electorate a key role in the elections. The system led to a deeper rift within the Israeli Arab electorate, similar to that in the Jewish sector, and support for the Arab parties rose. The power of existing Arab parties also rose and together they won nine seats, compared with five in the previous Knesset. It seems that the Law of Direct Election produced a rise in voting participation among Arabs (77 percent, versus 69 percent in previous Knesset elections).

For the 1996 Knesset elections, the vote for Jewish parties decreased even further and the vote for Arab parties rose accordingly. This indicates parliamentary segregation, which is a result of the accelerated process of politicization of Israel's Arab society. The parliamentary segregation involved about 67 percent of voters and resulted in a greater number of Arab parties. Those parties that increased their power in the Knesset were precisely those that managed to overcome the rift and unite: Hadash and Bishara's National Democratic Pact (NDP – Hebrew acronym, Balad) parties formed a partnership, as did the Arab Democratic Party (ADP – Hebrew acronym, Mada) and the Islamic Movement, which together formed the United Arab Party (UAP – Hebrew acronym, Ra'am; also known as United Arab List). Five percent of the votes were lost to parties that did not cross the minimum vote threshold.

New parliamentary movements entered the fray and four new Israeli Arab parties announced their candidacy for elections: Ahmad Tibi's Arab Union for Renewal (AUR – Hebrew acronym, Ta'al) was founded in March 1996. Its founders tried to append older political bodies such as the Arab Democratic Party of Abd al-Wahab Darawsha, as well as new movements, such as the Progressive Pact, but the Arab Democratic Party preferred to run for elections with the Islamic Movement. Tibi subsequently left the Union and did not run for a seat in the Knesset. The Arab Democratic Party became a secondary partner in its political union with the Islamic Movement.

Azmi Bishara's Nationalist Democratic Pact consisted of extra-parliamentary movements such as the Sons of the Village, the Equality Pact, Muhammad Mi'ari's branch of the Progressive List for Peace, *al-Ansar* from Umm-al-Fahm, the Socialist Party from the village of Mghar, *al-Nahda* from Tayibeh, and the Tireh Sons. The Nationalist Democratic Pact joined Hadash in the Knesset elections, a partnership which increased the latter's power, and Azmi Bishara was placed fourth on the Knesset list. However, the partnership did not last and was discontinued one year after the elections.

The Progressive Pact also consisted of several extra-parliamentary bodies such as Muhammad Zaydan's Independents' Movement, the Voice of Consent, headed by Negev Bedouin Said Zabarga, and Mi'ari's opponents, headed by attorney Aziz Shehada, who tried, unsuccessfully, to form an alliance with Ahmad Tibi.

The Arab Islamic Bloc was led by Sheikh Atef Khatib from Kafar Kanna, who left the Islamic Movement. Khatib tried to form an alliance with Tibi, but ultimately joined the Arab Democratic Pact/Islamic Movement union.

The hallmark of Israeli Arab parties is their unwavering solidarity with their leaders, which might indicate the leaders' centrality and influence in the street, but also points to organizational and ideological weaknesses in the list the leader heads. These leaders/candidates are not backed by a strong party organization; neither do they consider it necessary to spout a well-founded ideology. The exception, of course, is the Communist Rakah Party, whose leadership still has a collective ideology and an extensive organizational infrastructure; and also the Islamic Movement, which has a unique religious mission and formed an organizational and ideological framework binding to its Knesset representatives.

The small Arab parties failed because they were not sufficiently attractive to the Arab voting public. They tend to center around individuals trying to attract the public's confidence with a platform based almost solely on policy issues, a strategy which has turned out to be insufficient. Lists such as Tibi's Arab Union for Progress and Renewal and Zaydan's Progressive Pact failed for this reason. Politicians who were wise enough to join big political pacts, such as the Nationalist Democratic Pact (with Hadash) and the Islamic Movement with the Arab Democratic Party, did much better in the polls. But these partnerships also had their "stars" – Bishara, Talab al-Sani', Muhammad Baraqa and Abd al-Malik Dahamsha – whose political action is shaped by their personality and exploitation of existing rifts within the Israeli Arab community.

The new political leadership, which had begun to take shape towards the elections to the fourteenth Knesset (1996), was a typical expression of the political changes among Israel's Arab population, mainly since the beginning of peace talks with the Palestinians. There was a feeling among the Arab public that voters were interested in a new leadership to replace their Knesset representatives, who seemed to have lost their vitality. This was made more obvious by the fact that the Arab leadership's center of gravity has gradually shifted from the political parties to the local authorities. Hadash lost its charismatic leader Teufiq Zayad; Darawsha's position in the Arab Democratic Party has become weaker; and Mi'ari, head of the Progressive List for Peace (Hebrew acronyn, Ramash), failed to win a seat in the thirteenth Knesset elections. The Islamic Movement was still hesitant, while Sheikh Abdallah Nimer Darwish made renewed efforts to convince his people to take part in the elections. At the same time Darwish continued to build up his position as spiritual leader of the movement while presiding over 70 non-profit organizations – established and backed by the Islamic Movement – that provided mainly religious, educational and welfare services.

Troubled Politics – Parties under Threat of Disqualification

The political reality brought about by the first Palestinian *Intifada*,[35] the constantly deteriorating security situation, and the worsening of Israeli–Palestinian relations since the outbreak of the second (2000) *Intifada*, have led to a rift in relations between Jews and Arabs within Israel. Since the beginning of the *Intifada* there has been a rise in the number of Arab citizens who have taken part in terrorist activity against Israel. Results of a 2003 poll by the Arab Center for Applied Social Research indicate deep frustration among the Arab population in Israel, who have lost all faith in government policies; indeed, 43 percent of the Arab population even believe that peace between Jews and Palestinians is never going to happen.

It is no wonder, then, that 46 percent of the Jewish population are convinced that most of the country's Arabs support terror; this is, of course, reinforced by the religious and political activity of the northern branch of the Islamic Movement, with its annual rally in Umm-al-Fahm under the slogan "al-Aqsa is in danger".

Under these circumstances, various groups and bodies were called upon to present their positions, supported by "harsh" statistics concerning the trends and movements within the Arab community. According to the Israeli National Security Council (NSC), most Israeli Arabs are not interested in blending into the fiber of the country and show signs of radicalism and even alienation. The growing alienation between Jews and Arabs is jeopardizing social cohesion and internal stability. The NSC has published data according to which, by 2020, the Jewish population west of the Jordan River will be in the minority (45.15 percent) to the Arabs, who will constitute 54.85 percent of the population. Moreover, the alienation, radicalism and separatism among the Arab population form a "crisis scenario" for the State of Israel. According to the Strategic Forum in the Zionist Council of Israel, the demographic issue is of supreme significance to the country's Jewish-Zionist future and its democratic regime; they warn that more importance must be attached to demographic considerations in political agreements or in unilateral decisions, including examining exchange of territory options. The Jewish majority fears that the entry of large numbers of Palestinians from the occupied territories into Israel proper will cause a demographic imbalance and increase the risk of allowing in terrorists. The government and the Knesset have been asked to introduce changes into the citizenship and entry laws, and to restrict the number of Palestinians being granted Israeli citizenship. According to some views, Israel is already a de facto two-nation state, with a minority group that numbers one fifth of the population; within one generation this will rise to over one quarter, just by way of natural growth. Today, these views claim that Israel is populated by two obvious population groups – Jews, who make up the majority, and Israeli Arabs – although the State of Israel is still defined as the sovereign state of the Jewish nation.

In his bi-annual review to the Foreign Affairs and Security Committee (February 12, 2002), General Security Services (GSS) head[36] Avi Dichter included a report that indicated a worrying rise in the involvement of Israeli Arabs in terrorist activity. Since August 2001, 25 different groups of Arab-Israeli citizens have been revealed as having been involved in terrorist activity in the Galilee and the Triangle. Nine of these groups were operated by the PLO; eight were supported by Hamas, three by Hezbollah, three by the Islamic Jihad, and two operated independently. Five terrorist groups were uncovered in Umm-al-Fahm alone, one of which consisted of suicide bombers; three terrorist groups were uncovered in Tamra. During the months of the second *Intifada*, the Palestinian leadership enlisted the support of some of the "1948 Arabs" in its struggle. For example, a 2001 PLO flyer announced, "We are watching, with yearning nationalist eyes, our families and people in the villages and towns for their firm stand since 1948. They are our partners in objective and in fate, partners in a single nationalist dream." To this end, so it would seem, the chairman of the Palestinian Authority convened a liaison committee. These reminder calls to 1948 may have affected the willingness of Israeli Arabs to take part in terrorist activity.

Such a reality was dutifully expressed in parliamentary relations between Jewish and Arab MKs. The election of new Arab nationalist parties and young, assertive Arab MKs added its own aspect to these relations. On a national scale, these new MKs increased their parties' parliamentary activity and aroused the antagonism of Jewish MKs, especially on the right. As the conflict with the Palestinians escalated during the *Intifada* years, so the demands increases to restrict the activity of Arab MKs, who were suspected of over-involvement in the Palestinian struggle in the territories. This situation led to demands for Arab parties to be disqualified from participating in general elections. The Central Election Committee received a request to disqualify Ahmad Tibi and Azmi Bishara, and the Nationalist Democratic Pact, from participating in the upcoming elections to the sixteenth Knesset.[37]

Throughout the tenure of the fifteenth Knesset, such proposals were rife, and were seen by the Arabs as political persecution and attempts at de-legitimization. But the reason behind the stance was that the Jewish majority in the Knesset were deeply concerned by the demographic statistics published by the Central Bureau of Statistics and the implications made by the National Security Council. Among the private members' bills placed before the Knesset was that of Likud MK Israel Katz, according to whose proposal anyone who does not recognize the State of Israel as the sovereign state of the Jewish people would be seen to support armed struggle against the State of Israel, and his or her candidate list would be forbidden to participate in the Knesset elections. Similar proposals came from Eliezer Cohen of the Israel Beitinu party ("National Unity, Israel is our Home"), according to whom every voter in the country must be made to declare his or her loyalty to the State of Israel as being a Jewish state and to respect the country's symbols, its flag and its national anthem. Then there was MK Haim Druckman, who came up with a proposal that state-owned lands could only be allocated to Jews. MK Michael Kleiner (Herut) proposed that Arab citizens of Israel should be encouraged to emigrate to one of the neighboring Arab states. The Knesset busied itself with removing the Parliamentary immunity of Azmi Bishara in the wake of a speech he delivered in Syria, in which he supported the struggle of the Hezbollah; and that of Ahmad Tibi, for entering the refugee camp in Jenin as the April 2002 IDF operation was in full swing.

The northern branch of the Islamic Movement, together with its leadership, were also in danger of being outlawed, due to their activity on behalf of the al-Aqsa mosque and for inflaming the crowds during the annual Umm-al-Fahm meetings under the slogan "the al-Aqsa mosque is in danger", when Israel was accused of planning to tear down the mosque on the Temple Mount in Jerusalem and build a temple in its stead. In February 2002, northern branch leader Sheikh Ra'ed Salah was forbidden from leaving the country because of his declared intention to meet with Sheikh Yusuf al-Qaradawi, the leading preacher of fundamentalist and political Islam. When, in late 2002, a warrant was issued to close down the movement's journal *Sawt al-Haqq wal-huriyya* ("Voice of Truth and Freedom"), Sheikh Kamel Khatib (Sheikh Salah's deputy) stated, in the weekend supplement of Israel's largest daily, *Yediot Ahronot*, that "we are convinced that we have committed no crime and that the establishment has nothing against us that will stand the test of the law courts. All these acts against us are political [...] even if we are outlawed, we shall not go underground, and we shall continue to act in accordance with the laws and traditions of our religion, within the laws of the country. We have a wide network throughout the Arab sector. We run schools, kindergartens, clubs, mosques, and provide educational, social and health services. If someone believes seriously that the movement can be outlawed, he should examine the matter with utmost responsibility. It is important for me to protest against such a step. Such an act may push [our people] to violence. If this happens, we shall place the blame on the government."[38] These words express the plan of action of a social welfare, extra-parliamentary movement that deals in areas in which the government's involvement is extremely restricted. The government's intention to outlaw the Islamic Movement's northern branch was seen by the Moslem public as an affront against the Islamic religion itself. Sheikh Ra'ed Salah and northern branch leaders were indeed arrested in 2003 and accused of maintaining ties with Islamic organizations out of Israel, but they were released in a plea bargain in January 2005. Most of the Arab public in Israel identifies Sheikh Ra'ed Salah's northern branch as being the Islamic Movement, and sympathizes with it, even when voting for other political parties.

At the recommendation of the Attorney General, the Central Election Committee decided to disqualify Azmi Bishara's Nationalist Democratic Pact Party from participating in general elections.[39] The Central Election Committee also decided to disqualify Ahmad Tibi from taking part in the general election, but this was in opposition to the position taken by Attorney General Elyakim Rubinstein and Judge Mishael Heshin. Tibi was accused of denying Israel's Jewish character and supporting terrorism against Israel.

The appeals to the Supreme Court against the disqualification decisions by the Central Election Committee drew the attention of the Arab public, for whom this constituted the "real debate". The issue attracted responses from Arab citizens as well as Jewish and Arab intellectuals. According to historian Adel Manna', "Arab citizens are throwing their lot in with the courts of law, who, for the past couple of years have become the final hurdle before the downfall of Israeli democracy. However, this in itself could well pose an even greater burden on the [Supreme Court], since to many, the courts have become the Arab public's government [. . .]. Many, especially intellectuals and young people, are proud of Bishara and for them this disqualification could be seen as the final straw."[40] As'ad Ghanem wrote in *Ha'aretz* that, although the large majority of Israel's Arabs recognize the existence of Israel, they oppose the regime of discrimination that the Jews built for themselves and established over 50 years. The disqualification of Ahmad Tibi's list and Bishara's Nationalist Democratic Pact join future steps that the state will take against different political and nationalist streams among the Israeli Arab community. According to sociologist Sami Smooha, disqualification of the Arab candidates for the sixteenth Knesset is a political, moral and practical mistake. He views it as a grave move that has harmed the tenuous fabric of co-existence between Jews and Arabs, as well as Israeli democracy and the chances for peace. Since the October 2000 riots, the Knesset has approved statutory amendments that have restricted the political space of the Arab community. Political disqualification only increases the Arabs' sense of alienation from the state, distances them from their Jewish counterparts, and reinforces the hostility of the Jews toward Israel's Arabs.

According to Jamal Zahalqa, who was elected in 2003 to the Knesset on the Nationalist Democratic Pact, "The Arab population's political culture was [previously] undeveloped. But today, the disqualification of an Arab list does not go unmentioned, and *al-Ard* (the Land) remains an open and painful wound in our hearts. Over fifty years, the Arab political system in Israel has built itself around parliamentary circles. If we are pushed outside these circles, we will not simply disappear from the map, rather we shall be forced to operate within ex-parliamentary circles." Here Zahalqa hints that the Arab population has the option of declaring its autonomy and breaking off all relations with Israel.[41] On this subject, Attr. Hasan Jabarin, head of the *Adala Association*, points out that "we are posing the big question: does a state for all its people harm the foundation of the state?" According to Jabarin, "The State of Israel must recognize the equal rights of its Arab citizens both on a civil level as well as the Arabs' rights as a group with the Arab language, Arab culture and the Arabs as a national minority."

The rhetoric that dominated the Supreme Court debates was spiced with political tones and similar explanations to those in which attempts had formerly been made to disqualify the *al-Ard* movement and the Progressive List for Peace. The Arabs believed that the polemic surrounding the disqualification would encourage many of them to go out and vote, but their hopes were dashed when, apart from the Nationalist Democratic Pact, the Arab parties did not increase their representation in the Knesset.

Attempts to disqualify Arab nationalist parties widened the disconnection and disinterest of the Israeli Arab public in Israeli politics. As a result, just a few days before the deadline for submitting party slates to compete in the seventeenth Knesset elections, a new movement formed in the Arab sector in order to organize an election boycott. The Popular Committee for a Boycott of Knesset Elections was established at a meeting of Arab activists and academics in early February 2006 and immediately began calling on the Arab sector to abstain from going to the polls the following month. Instead, the new organization suggested that Arab voters take part in direct elections for a body that would represent the Arab public *vis-à-vis* the state – a kind of "Arab parliament", to replace the Supreme Follow-up Committee for the Arabs in Israel, which traditionally consists of Arab MKs and public leaders.

The testimonies of Arab politicians and academics to the Or Commission provided the most potent expression of their political positions.[42] As well as providing an indication of the political aspirations of the Israeli Arabs, these testimonies are also a reliable forecast of the future relations between Jews and Arabs in Israel. Geographer Rasem Khamaysi told the Commission that the site plans, building, planning, demolition of illegally built Arab homes and non-development of Arab towns and villages all have a long-term effect and could provide a cause for further outbursts in the future. According to him, it is the civil rather than nationalist struggle that is the motive for these potential outbursts.

Political scientist As'ad Ghanem researched the condition of the Arab minority population from a political aspect. In Israel's ethnocratic regime, in which a group's ethnic rather than civilian background provides the key to the distribution of resources and power, the Arabs are prevented from receiving their fair share of government resources and are forced into the kind of hardship that will only worsen if no fundamental changes are made in the country's governmental structure. In his testimony to the Or Commission, Ghanem explained that since Israeli democracy does not enable the Arab minority leadership to achieve their objectives – by making use of the parliamentary tools at their disposal – it might be that the most suitable solution would be wide-scale refraining from participation in Knesset elections and transferring the struggle to extra-parliamentary channels, such as ongoing public protest. He coined his favorite form of protest "public Jihad".[43]

Sociologist Ahmad Sa'di has pointed out the discrepancy between Israel's being a Jewish state and the existence of a Palestinian minority within it. The regime tries to legitimize this situation and claims that a democratic regime can be maintained under such circumstances. According to Sa'di, research on the relationship between the two communities did not disassociate itself from the hostility between the Jews and the Arabs and even contributed to a situation in which the Arabs have been turned into second-class citizens.[44]

Muhammad Zaydan, an independent politician who is considered in some way connected to the Islamic Movement and who has headed the Supreme Follow-up Committee for the Arabs in Israel, was called to testify to the Or Commission hearings as spokesman for the Arab population in Israel. Zaydan said that, although he was a citizen of Israel because he possesses an Israeli identity card, by his own concept he is not a citizen since he is discriminated against and underprivileged, not only economically, but also because he does not share the symbolic capital of the state.

According to the Nationalist Democratic Pact secretary Awwad Abd al-Fattah's testimony, the question of rights is the determining factor. Awwad Abd al-Fattah explained, "At this stage, the Nationalist Democratic Pact is demanding cultural autonomy for the Arab sector. This would mean granting government authority to the Supreme Follow-up Committee for the Arabs in Israel, including responsibility for planning and building, by-laws where necessary and the establishment of universities." Politically, Awwad Abd al-Fattah belongs to the Bishara school of thought, which seeks to demonstrate that the Arab public has internalized the "new discourse". This discourse has succeeded, according to its perpetrators, "to place the Zionist movement into unprecedented distress".

Nationalist Democratic Pact leader Azmi Bishara declared to the Commission that his movement was in favor of establishing national institutions for the Arab minority in Israel, who are entitled to self-determination and collective national rights. The final objective of this process, according to Bishara, is to turn the State of Israel into a state for all its citizens. According to a Nationalist Democratic Pact election flyer, "In the event of a conflict between the two, [Arab] nationalism overrules [Israeli] citizenship." Further, according to the flyer, "A new-generation Arab person knows that, before any other affiliation, he is a Palestinian Arab. It is an ancient cultural tradition and he must deepen his Arab affiliation above all else."

Sheikh Ra'ed Salah, head of the northern branch of the Islamic Movement, expressed the impossibility of a common basis for two sets of values that describe a totally different picture of the same facts and the same statistics. Salah's religious discourse and the legal discourse of Judge Or moved along two paths that would not be reconciled. The view of Jewish history as presented by Ra'ed Salah to the Commission appeared twisted: the Jews have no connection to *al-Haram al-sharif* (the Temple Mount in Jerusalem) and there never was a temple on the mount.

Those people who provided their testimony to the Or Commission, representatives of political movements and intellectual streams among Israel's Arabs, were not prepared to give a clear definition of their national aspirations *vis-à-vis* the State of Israel; indeed, such a definition would have caused them to raise territorial, community or cultural demands, and testifiers feared that such ethnic isolation would be a sure recipe for perpetuating the deprivation and discrimination. They chose, therefore, as Israel's Arabs choose, to evade the issue and rather to talk about equality and to determine a definition according to which equality means doing away with discrimination. This definition usually bypasses the conflict and allows the development of a mutual front. But it also includes a trap, since improved standards of living and an end to discrimination are legitimate national goals that can be achieved – with even greater success – from within the Zionist political parties.

4
Social Rifts in Arab Politics

So far, this debate has focused mainly on the political aspect of the Arab experience in Israel and its various components, including nationalism and religion. However, the voting trends among Israel's Arabs have changed enormously in accordance with the deep changes and adjustments that Arab society has had to undergo in the six decades of Israel's existence.

The political culture that developed within Israel's Arab society has always been based on the great weight attached to real or imagined social rifts. During the British Mandate in Palestine, the old division between the two political camps was based on traditional affinity; one belonged either to the northern tribes (*Qays*) or the southern tribes (*Yemin*), who were in constant conflict with each other. The tension between the two warring sides was based on the conflict between the tribes that settled in the region at the beginning of the Moslem conquest and continued into the rural settlement in the Land of Israel perpetuated by differences in behavior and tradition; many new conflicts were subsequently nurtured, which appeared as "political", "party-associated", or local. Thus, for example, the political struggle between supporters of Hajj-Amin al-Huseini (*al-Majlisiyyn*) and the opposition (*al-Muaridin*), which raged during the time of the British Mandate, was based on social splits between important urban families and the various rural sheikhs. The families and the sheikhs represented different groups belonging – according to association or geographic origin – to *Qays* or *Yemin* tribes; the split lasted throughout the first two decades of the twentieth century and paralleled the ethnic rifts among Moslems, Christian Arabs and the Druze Arabs throughout the country.[1]

As in other societies throughout the Middle East, Arab society in Palestine was based on three main family structures: the nuclear family, the extended family and the clan.[2] The traditional divisions of rural, urban and Bedouin accompanied these distinct structures. The divisions according to religion, clan and social class had an obvious effect on the political orientation of Israel's Arab population, as will be discussed later.

In his study of the extended family in Arab society in Israel, sociologist Majid al-Hajj found that "the lack of political alternatives is what gave the clan its legitimacy as a political factor. Since Arab society was pushed to the edge of Israeli politics, the clan grew into a local institution which was not in conflict with the interests of the Israeli establishment."[3] Further, in traditional societies, political aspirations are based mostly on the tribe, the clan and religious affiliation, rather than on national ideology. Against this background, most political parties active among Israel's Arabs were not considered exceptional.

Successive Israeli governments made a point of maintaining and deepening these ethnic, familial and tribal differences as part of the control system they imposed on Arab society. In fact, pressure on the part of the state turned the various groups into political units, which were manipulated into serving the government's needs. A side effect of this policy was the strengthening of kindred groups during the 1950s and 1960s, as expressed in an increased number of intermarriages (between paternal cousins), in accordance with inheritance laws in Arab society.

Nonetheless, since 1967 there has been a drop in the state's ability at governance, which has resulted in the establishment by the Israeli Arab population of political, civil and local organizations. The clan system, too, has had to adjust to new social and economic conditions and has changed from being a purely kindred organization to a political framework better suited to modern times and to Israel's political system.

The *Hamula*[4] – A Social and Political Rift

The extended family consists of several nuclear families (*dar*), connected by real or imagined blood ties that in early times rallied round a strong leader. In Arab Bedouin society, the basic tribal unit is known as *khams* (a five-generation group of blood relatives);[5] Emanuel Marx has described such a group as a co-liable group, which is expressed mainly in two fundamental ways: blood feuds and mutual aid.[6]

In the village social order common among Israeli Arabs, the responsible group unit is called the "kindred group" and is part of the clan. The clan is a group of people with a common ancestor and a common family name. Over the years, other, smaller family groups, not descended from the founder of the extended family, would sometimes be allowed to join, and several generations later, the newcomers would outnumber the members of the original group.

Over the centuries, extended families settled in villages and endogamous ties were formed between members of the family. Sometimes disputes, financial issues or even demographic growth caused splits in extended families and smaller nuclear groups branched off – but not too far away – from the original extended family base, albeit maintaining ties with the mother village for a certain period. Thus, for example, the original families of Umm-al-Fahm maintain 18 such branches along Wadi 'Ara. Where family ties remain strong, families scattered in other villages would come together in times of danger or need and form a united group with common economic, social and political goals. The extended family structure is most obvious in areas of mutual aid and economic support, blood feuds, filial relations and politics. In any area, most of the land came under the jurisdiction of the larger extended families and provided them with economic and political power. A *Mukhtar*[7] was elected from among the family elders, based on the size of his family, wealth (land and property) and ability. The national Arab leadership evolved from among these *Mukhtars*, who are, by nature, wealthy landowners.

Until the establishment of the State of Israel, the extended family system was central in rural Arab society, and was instrumental in shaping the behavior and values of its members. In the early years of the state, the Israeli government co-operated with the position and influence of the extended family. The military administration supported the elected family heads and treated them as the leaders of Arab society; they, in turn, used their political power to fortify their status in their villages. According to Avner Cohen, who researched rural Arab society in the Triangle during the 1960s, Israel's military administration strengthened the political role of the extended family leadership.[8] However, most sociologists now agree that over the long term, the combination of Israel's economical and technological developments, modernization of the country's Arab community (which has also benefited by these developments) and exposure to Western ideas and interaction with Jewish society has reduced the overall importance of the extended family structure and its political impact. Social and economic processes during Israel's first decades helped weaken rifts between extended families: the reduced status of landowners in the rural hierarchy; the evolvement of an educated professional class and the increased status of the individual in Israeli Arab society; urbanization and local municipal government; a loosening of the extended family framework; and the mutual struggle for civil liberties and representation within Israel's social, economic and political systems.

Yet Arab society's basic, traditional social structure remains to this day. Extended families and tribal differences have become the cornerstone of local authority elections, and the struggle for power on the local level encourages competition between extended families and the various religious groups and political parties.

The 1975 amendment to the Local Authorities' law, which determined a split vote for local council and mayor, resulted in a more complex political game of pacts between extended families and ethnic groups, which in turn contributed to a revived importance of the extended family system. In the early 1990s – and specifically the 1993 municipal elections – a new dimension emerged and gained importance on the political stage, offering an alternative to extended families and religious groups. Young university graduates formed groups that crossed traditional clan, sect and party lines and ran for election. Thus movements such as *Tamra al Ghadd* in Tamra ("Tamra of Tomorrow"), *Mi'elya al Ghadd* in Mi'elya ("Mi'elya of

Tomorrow"), *Abnaa Arrabeh* in Arrabeh, *Abnaa Sha'ab* in Sha'ab and *Abnaa Shafa'amr* in Shefar'am were founded. The success of some of these political newcomers in placing representatives in local councils persuaded the old patriarchs of the clans to choose young and educated candidates to run for election. Young men also took over the leadership of extended families – having been elected by the old patriarchs and in consultation with them. Primary elections ("primaries") became increasingly common within the extended family system and families gained strength on the municipal level.

In Baqa al-Gharbiyye, the Abu-Mokh clan elected its candidate in such primaries in 2003. In Tireh, the Mansur clan elected Iyad Mansur as their candidate against Khalil Qasem. Although the Mansur family makes up 30 percent of the population of the village and the Qasem family only 10 percent, Khalil Qasem managed to get himself elected as local council candidate with the help of seven family lists that voted for him, on the condition that his family voted for their candidates for the local council. And, indeed, each family in the Qasem clan voted for one of the candidates put forward by each of the seven extended families, as agreed upon in advance. That is how a council chairman was elected who was a member of the third largest extended family. In the municipal arena, the extended family's role grew and attempts on the part of educated youngsters at running for office – independent of the extended family – were mostly unsuccessful.[9]

Nimer Awwad, a male nurse from Mazra'a affiliated with the Labor Party, tried to get himself elected to office in the 2004 municipal elections; his clan supported another candidate and he lost. Saleh 'Aqr stood as an independent candidate in Judeid-Makr and lost the election. Sami Sirhan stood on behalf of his clan and was almost elected.

In general elections, too, the extended families played a significant political role, although not necessarily in support of any specific party. Indeed, the vote for different political parties often crossed family lines. It was quite common for the clan to give its support to Mapai and its allied Arab lists, while individuals in the clan opted for Maki or Mapam.

The situation differed in local authority elections, where candidates stood for office under their clan's name. Maki was the only party to run a non-clan list. Individual families often rebelled against clan authority and forged pacts with rival clans. Local authority elections allowed the small clans equal status with the large clan, which needed them to protect its political hegemony. Candidates tried to expand their power and increase their chances of getting elected, especially if they belonged to a smaller family, which is how pacts were formed between the smaller and the larger clans, based mainly on marital ties, common political interests and anticipated returns.[10] For example, Jalal abu Husein ran for mayor in the 2003 local elections in Baqa al-Gharbiyye. He is a member of a smaller clan, which consists of 480 registered voters. In order to increase his power, he forged a pact with three other clans: Atamneh, which gave him 70 percent of their vote; Mawasi, who gave 50 percent of their vote; and 'Aweisat, from whom he received 60 percent of the clan vote.

In villages and towns in which the clan system is strong, it is the clan that determines the way in which its members behave. The way in which they follow the instructions of the clan heads will predetermine the way in which the local authority is run. The voters understand and accept that these are the main codes that govern Arab politics in Israel. Even in those villages and towns in which a large portion of the vote went to national parties, these were supported by clan and ethnic pacts and, indeed, the percentage of voters was especially high. The parties, too, competed on a clan basis and their candidate put forward by a party in fact represented his clan. On occasion, a national party would try to run a candidate via a large clan, but this usually prevented the party from getting the vote of other clans, with the exception of those clans who agreed in advance to run on a joint ticket.

For example, prior to the eleventh Knesset in 1984, in the municipal elections that took place a year previously in Tayibeh, Rakah formed a bond with the Masarwa clan, the adversary of the Hajj Yahya clan. The results of the election were clear: Rakah won 66.5 percent of the Masarwa vote, while the Hajj Yahya gave it only 19.5 percent; the latter had formed a bond with the Progressive List for Peace and given it 64.3 percent of its vote. The Abu-Rayh clan, which consists of about 15 percent of the voting register in Sakhnin, joined Rakah to take 83 percent of the town's votes (voting station #1) in the Knesset elections, whereas the Ghanaim clan's candidate who stood against a Rakah candidate in voting station # 3 gave Rakah only 31 percent of its votes, but gave 47 percent of its vote to the Progressive List for Peace. When a particular political party joined forces with a particular clan, it was very often boycotted by rival clans in the same village.

The Arab parties, therefore, were given the task among the Arab population of recruiting local votes in order to reinforce the support for their lists in the parliamentary elections. The Arab parties contributed to the strengthening of family affiliation as a political option in local elections, because of the political flexibility adopted by them all in respect of the clan's candidate and other associations on the clan's behalf.

The clan's political task and behavior support the theory that defines it as one of the political expressions of the Palestinian Arabs in Israel, alongside the Arab–Israeli, the Communist, the nationalist and the Islamic streams, and defines it as an alternative stream.[11] A number of questions arise from this. Do voting trends indicate the measure of control the clan has on its members with regard to their political affiliation? Is it possible to determine that voting trends in general elections are based on the group interests of the clan, rather than on ideological considerations? The following examination of voting trends along a cross-section of clans is of great importance in analyzing the significance of the political behavior of Arab citizens, especially in determining whether they act like a national minority or according to particular local considerations. The following analyses supply some of the answers to these questions.

Clan Rifts and Municipal Elections

Local government in Arab settlements was influenced mainly by the status of the Arab population in Israel and the social structure in Arab settlements. Between 1950 and 1954, the local municipal authorities active in the Arab sector were those that had been operating during the British Mandate: Shefar'am, which received its municipal status in 1910, Nazareth (1934) and Kafar Yasif (1925). During this period, eight additional municipal authorities were established.

The decision to establish local authorities in Arab villages during this period was influenced by the ethnic and familial composition of village populations. A further 14 local authorities were established in the Arab sector between 1956 and 1960, five of them in the region known as the Triangle and nine in the Galilee region. Twenty-six more local authorities were established between 1960 and 1975.

In September 2000, five local municipal authorities were established in Bedouin settlements in the Negev region of southern Israel. In 2008 there were a total of 76 Arab local authorities in Israel, including two with municipal status (after the amalgamation of several smaller authorities), 62 local councils and 12 towns.

In many ways, the period since 1975 has been characterized by a consolidation of local Israeli Arab municipal rule. Since then, we can talk about local municipal rule that performs most of the main functions that it is meant to fulfill. Local municipal rule has turned out to be the main method for social and political development among Israeli Arabs and the most important avenue for socio-economic mobility, providing employment and promotion opportunities for academics and various professionals in Israeli Arab society. This source of social and economic empowerment for the Israeli Arab professional is especially important when we consider the fact that large segments of the Israeli labor market are still closed to Israeli Arabs.

A number of researchers[12] have pointed out the great importance of local government in Israeli Arab society, and its growing strength, as well as the possibilities it offers to those intellectuals who are interested in working for it, and the contribution it makes to the development of local and national leadership.

There has always been a strong involvement of the clan in local authority matters, even beyond group interests and symbols. Clan/tribal politics is an historic phenomenon in the Arab world and is one of the expressions of tribalism in Arab society. The party political system finds it hard to compete with the clan and is constantly withdrawing, notwithstanding the candidacy of parties in the local arena.

A lengthy study of local political streams in the Arab sector has revealed several phenomena. The 1980s saw a continuous and steady decline in support for lists identified with the extended family. In the 1993 elections, support for such lists picked up again and helped maintain their rule. The reason for this is probably based on the disappearance of the allied Arab lists during the previous decade and the entry into the political arena of nationalist Arab parties in the early 1990s.

Although the strength of the collective is weakened as a result of the increased strength of the individual within the clan, the system did not disintegrate; the clans found themselves having to adapt. The clan's hold on everyday life became looser, but tightened up again during events such as elections, albeit local elections; but the clans were also deeply involved in Knesset elections.

In settlements that had a sound tribal/clan basis, it was the clan that determined the behavior of its individual members. The obedience of elected officials to the instructions of clan leaders shaped the management of local authorities. Voters were aware of these vital codes, which determine Arab politics in Israel. Even in towns and villages in which national parties won a large number of votes, this took place against a background of pacts between religious sects and clans, which led to a 90 percent (and greater) voting turnout. This means that national parties also competed on a clan basis within the Israeli Arab electorate and that the candidate selected by the national parties actually represented his/her clan. Israeli Arab national parties served to mobilize local forces that increased support for their lists in parliamentary elections. Thus the national parties, which adopted a politically flexible position toward the candidate, contributed strengthening family loyalties as a political option in local municipal elections. The Israeli Arab national parties compromised with the existing social structure as a strategic political option in ways that other national (Jewish) political parties could not – with the intention not to change it, but rather to use it for party gains in local and national elections.

The growing significance of the inter-clan rifts in Arab society was not only quantitative, but also qualitative. In 1998, local primaries were held for the first time in several Israeli Arab towns and villages, including Tamra, Sakhnin and Tireh. During the first years after the establishment of the state, the large family clans played an important role in determining candidates for the Knesset and the option of running for Knesset on a clan ticket. For example, the Nashif clan in Tayibeh chose Mahmud Nashif as their candidate for the fourth (1959) Knesset, on the "Agriculture and

Development" list. But the list was beaten by Diab Ubeid, whose clan was larger. Jaber Mu'adi headed a Druze clan in the village of Yarka and represented it for six successive Knesset terms in a joint list with Seif al-Din al-Zu'bi, which was known first as the Democratic List for Nazareth and its District, later to be called the United Arab List in the ninth Knesset. Fares Hamdan of the Abu Mokh clan in Baqa al-Gharbiyye represented his clan in the Knesset between 1951 and 1955. Once the clan lists disappeared (after the tenth Knesset), the space they left was filled by educated members of the younger generation who mixed into the Zionist parties, or established nationalist Arab parties of their own. The clan's status was undermined and the clan came to be seen as an anachronistic tool in the hands of the Jewish authorities that had to be removed from Knesset elections. The clans were no longer able to influence the choice of party candidates for Knesset elections; the parties, on the other hand, grabbed the opportunity provided by the new situation in order to increase their strength, unhampered by obvious affinities to any of the clans. For example, Labor took on Muhammad Watad, a young writer and journalist – although he was from the small Triangle village of Jatt – and he was elected to the tenth Knesset; Labor also nurtured the candidacy of Abd al-Wahab Darawsha, a young school teacher from Iksal, a small village near Nazareth, and he was elected to the eleventh Knesset; Nawwaf Masalha from the Triangle village of Kafar Qara was elected to the twelfth Knesset (1998) on the Labor ticket, on the strength of his reputation as a leader of the younger generation and activist in the General Labor Federation. The clan system became gradually stronger after the 1998 local elections. The younger generation noticed the political advantages of clan-based activity in and out of the villages, and influenced the election of several candidates. In many cases, the youngsters removed the older generation's authority to determine the candidates for political representation, or persuaded them to agree to non-traditional election processes. The law of individual election to a local authority lent greater weight to a candidate's affinity to a large clan or extended family. Once again, the large national parties began courting the clans, and the mayors and elected local council members who had reached office through representing the clans.

Since 1984, the large Zionist parties have held membership drives, and candidates for Knesset are subsequently nominated and elected by the party's registered, card-holding members. This system allowed Arabs to register their membership in the party of their choice, independent of the clan to which they belong and without the need of its approval. Primary elections were also held within the clans, under the auspices of the various family heads, and winners of these elections increased their chances in the general elections opposite candidates who were nominated in party primaries, without having checked their popularity beforehand among the clan. This system left a lot to be desired, since the candidate elected in this way had a greater commitment to his clan than to the other inhabitants of the town or village he was supposed to represent.

The establishment of local authorities reinforced democratic processes on the local level and also formed a base for national politics. The establishment of local authorities also altered the status of relatively weak clans, whose electoral support turned them into desirable partners. The clans all aspired to ensure their position on the municipal council and thus also their control over everyday life in the village. This is illustrated by the multitude of lists competing in the October 1983 elections in 46 Arab and Druze local and municipal councils: 357 lists vied for 470 seats. Only 56 lists appeared under the name of any Knesset party. These statistics are not only indicative of the pressures under which the clan structure finds itself from within, but also underline the schism that characterizes the Israeli Arab community and the difficulties it encounters in its search for a common denominator that crosses clan lines. These difficulties, while providing a handy explanation as to why political parties without authentic clan support encounter almost insurmountable problems in local municipal authority elections, also point at additional forces deepening community rifts around the political identity and function of the clan as an omnipotent and exclusive political unit.

Participation in municipal elections is very high and the number of lists competing is usually larger than the number of seats up for grabs. In the Arab sector, an average of 90 percent of the eligible voters participate in municipal elections, compared to 50 percent in Israel's Jewish sector. In 1993, 628 lists competed for 646 seats; in 1998, 717 lists competed for 667 seats. This phenomenon is unmatched in the Jewish sector. In the Jewish communities, representing 91 percent of Israel's voting register, one list competed for each 3,718 voters, as compared to one list for each 483 voters in the Israeli Arab community. The ratio of voters to competing list is 7.7 times higher in the Israeli Jewish sector where there is no clan influence, than in the Israeli Arab sector where the clan is all-powerful. This phenomenon reflects the political influence of the clan in Israeli Arab society and the socio-political schisms it causes.

The 2003 local and municipal council elections took place in 54 Arab towns and villages (including Ghajar, the Alawi[13] village on the Lebanese border, which had an agreed-upon council head and an agreed-upon list of candidates). Six hundred and seven lists competed for 555 seats and voting participation was especially high: over 87 percent (compared to the Jewish sector, where less than 50 percent of the population voted). All this is proof of the growing strength of clan politics in Israeli Arab society and a return to a ruling position in the towns and villages, after having lost some of its power in previous years to external political movements. The reasons for this change are the disappointment and the apathy amongst Israeli Arabs that followed the failure of party and parliamentary politics to come up with actual gains and influence in the government. Also, it would appear that – in the end – a system of family politics is more suited to the needs of Israeli Arab society, which has adapted itself to modern behavioral concepts, coupled with more traditional norms.[14]

Table 4.1   Municipal Elections in the Arab Sector in Three Election Campaigns

Year	No. of Municipalities	No. of Electorate	No. of Voters	Percentage of Vote	No. of Lists	No. of Mandates	Percentage in the Jewish Sector
1993	58	297,145	263,587	89	628	646	53
1998	59	353,339	320,940	91	717	667	54
2003	54	412,753	356,106	86	594	540	40

Clan voting produced several side effects, according to which the municipal council head or candidate for mayor presents the voters with two lists. The first, or "real", list supports his candidacy and is sometimes actually headed by him, although his name does not appear on it; and the second, "shadow", list is the one on which he is the leading candidate for the position of mayor or council head. The candidate's clan supporters are instructed to vote for him as mayor or council head and also to vote for the "real" list. According to law, the winning candidate will also become a council member, thus increasing the number of members on the council and strengthening his own control over it. The 1998 municipal elections saw 108 "shadow" lists in Israeli Arab villages.

In the 1993 municipal elections, 34 council heads who had not competed for council membership were elected, compared with the Israeli Jewish sector, in which only one such list was successful. By the 1998 municipal elections in the Arab sector, the number grew to 38 candidates elected to head local councils, who were not also council members, as opposed to only one in the Jewish sector. One of the "shadow" lists competing in the 1998 elections was United Eilabun, headed by local council chairman Dr Hanna Swed, a Communist Party member. Since he was elected but his list failed to be elected, he took up his seat as the tenth member of what was intended as a nine-member local council.

A second side effect of clan politics consisted of candidates for mayor or council chairman signing agreements with each other, to divide the five-year term of office between themselves. Since Israeli law forbids political rotation in local authorities, the candidates would agree between them that the winner would resign in mid-term, special elections would be called and the election of the second candidate – usually the only one – would be guaranteed. This is what happened in 1999 in the Druze village of Kisra-Sumei', following the resignation of the local council; likewise in the Druze village of Jatt-Yanuh and the Negev Bedouin settlement of Hura.

The third effect of clan politics consisted of a large number of candidates for the position of mayor, chairman of the local council and a seat on the local council. Clans broke into rival factions and in several towns and villages, such as Kafar Qasem and Tireh, candidates presented themselves in primary elections as the genuine representatives, or the "heart" of their clan. In the 2003 elections in Tireh, 19 lists and 180 candidates competed for 15 seats; in Baqa al-Gharbiyye and Jatt, 19 lists with 212 candidates competed for 15 seats on the joint town council; and 39 candidates competed for 13 seats on the Mghar local council. In many cases, voters were presented with lists of candidates equal to the total number of seats on the municipal council.

The rifts in Israel's Arab society are an expression of inherent weakness and an inability to muster the forces necessary for influencing government policy; these rifts weaken the community and prevent it from becoming a political force active in shaping Israel's socio-political structure. The Arab situation is very different from Jewish parties such as Shas or Agudat Israel, both religious fundamentalist and sectarian, but both with a power base that far outstrips their electoral size.

Local election results, as we have already seen, can be used for diagnosing the status of the clan's political power. In each town or village the lists of candidates are unique; almost none of them share a platform, a slogan or a name in more than one settlement. The lists invariably deal with the problems of one village, never with issues that affect Israel's Arabs in general. Again, this is because the lists were identified with the prominent clans in each village and the competition was over positions of influence.

Inter-clan disagreements or arguments over leadership do not usually spill over into other social or political frameworks outside the clan, even when they cause internal rifts. The size of the clan always influences its political power: the wider its political base, the greater the prestige of its candidate, even when other factors such as personality, financial standing and outside connections come into play. The change to a direct vote for mayor or local council head necessitated combinations or associations between different clans and helped create a leadership whose influence extended beyond clan lines.[15] This new, younger leadership used election tools that had not so far been typical of the Arab sector in Israel, such as creating party platforms and long-term development plans for the town or village. Thus a base was formed for a modern leadership to evolve that went on to take control of the sector. Some clans held primaries in which they chose their political candidate. Others preferred to place educated young men at the head of their lists, in order to attract support from outside the clan. The small-townishness of elections in the Arab sector is sometimes expressed in violent conflict between the supporters of two rival clans (as happened in the village of Jatt in the Triangle), or in cases where a clan is so much in support of a particular candidate as to put an indelible stamp on the party list.

Local Elections between Clan and Party

National political parties, too, have always played a key role in local government in Israel's Arab towns and villages. The voting system in Israel makes the numerical size of the clan very important: the larger the clan, the more votes it can supply the ballot box.

During the 1950s, representatives of Jewish political parties would visit Israeli Arab towns and villages and strike deals with clan leaders over how best to utilize the clans' votes. But structural changes in the economy and the labor market made the clan's economic role almost obsolete and opened the doors for ideological political parties to penetrate the Arab sector and increase their power by addressing the individual directly. Thus was formed a model of ideological and political solidarity that provided a viable alternative to the clan.

The uniting force in local elections in the Israeli Arab sector is the fierce competition over government funds and the resources of the local authority, which is also usually the town's (or village's) largest employer and provider of tenders and contracts. The locals, therefore, are careful not to let outside parties become too involved in local elections. The political parties, for their part, were worried that their participation in local elections would upset the traditional internal structure of the clan and thus hurt their own ability to mobilize the electorate during the national elections. Israel's Communist Party (Maki) was an exception, as was the Islamic Movement in its early days. The Islamic Movement was motivated by a genuine concern for local affairs and tried to win supporters by providing solutions for local problems, mainly in the areas of welfare, education and health.

In the early years of the state, the Israel Workers' Party (Mapai) formed successful alliances with the local Arab leadership through traditional methods such as pacts with the *Mukhtars* and other dignitaries. During the 1950s and 1960s, Mapai galvanized its position among the Arabs through an extensive network of activists. But it would appear that a process of swift politicization and the rise of other forces caused the party to change its tactics and, while maintaining its traditional ties in the Arab sector, Mapai (later the Labor Party) grew concerned by the potential fall of local rule to the Communists or other radicals. Yet the party's connections in the field had not always been stable, especially since its local representatives always kept the option of transferring their support elsewhere and maintained ties with more than one mainstream party. This completely contradicted the situation of the 1950s and 1960s, when a single party was connected to several groups in the same town or village – sometimes even with rival factions – in order to obtain wall-to-wall support in nationwide elections.

Labor was not the only Zionist party to enter the Israeli Arab municipal scene. There was also the right-wing Likud Party, which rose to power in 1977. The centrist party Shinui and the left-wing Meretz Party entered the Israeli Arab municipal scene too. Meretz even established a central municipal team to supervise the election campaign and was active in towns and villages which were considered Communist and Moslem fundamentalist strongholds.

The National Religious Party (Mafdal), which for many years had headed the Ministry of the Interior, established a network of activists and supporters throughout the Arab sector and even won a seat on the Nazareth city council. Although the clan elected the candidate, he took up his seat as the official representative of the Mafdal. The ultra-Orthodox Sephardi Shas Party first appeared in the 1984 Knesset elections and began to involve itself in local elections in the Arab sector after being given control of the Ministry of the Interior.

The Likud Party took advantage of clan rivalry in order to entrench itself politically and gave its support to candidates in return for their own commitment during the general elections. And indeed, the thirteenth Knesset election campaign saw several Arab mayors and local council chairmen come out in support of the Likud – almost certainly in return for promises that if/when the Likud returned to power, it would give priority to solving local problems of their specific town or village.

The Arab parties also involved themselves in local politics and some of them even moved from the municipality to the national arena. The Communists (Rakah was subsequently called Hadash), who had always tried to win seats in local councils and municipalities, established an organizational network in the various towns and villages with which to gain support in general elections; but it never did very well in the local elections.

In contrast to Jewish-supported local lists, Hadash formed its candidate lists by negotiating pacts with such country-wide and local groups as student unions and extended families, which gave their local election platform a national spin. In this way it ensured its position in local municipal councils, which returned the favor in the general elections, although not to a great extent. The fact is that from one general election to another, Rakah lost more and more of its support and was obliged eventually to take in other groups.

The Progressive List for Peace (PLP) grew from a group of former Hadash members and activists in Nazareth who joined together to form a new party after leaving the old one. The list won seats on the Nazareth municipal council and explored additional political opportunities in other towns and villages. Over several election campaigns, it won seats in several other Arab municipalities, and even headed two: Arrabeh and Eilabun.

The Arab Democratic Party (whose Hebrew acronym is Mada), whose founders included several local municipal leaders, set out to work with local activists immediately on its establishment in 1988. Those council heads, who had been re-elected in 1989, downplayed their affiliation with the Arab Democratic Party.

Founded in the early 1970s as an extra-parliamentary movement, the *Abnaa al-Balad* (Sons of the Village) movement concentrated its efforts locally. Although it won seats in various municipalities, its achievements were minimal and the movement never made it into national politics. Political parties, whose focus is on Knesset elections, often support a clan candidate in local elections. In return, the clan finds itself under obligation to the party when general elections come around. However, the clan is not always united in fulfilling this obligation.

The Islamic Movement, which was founded at the beginning of the 1980s, concentrated its efforts initially on local elections and made impressive inroads. This movement rose from 51 seats in 1988, to 59 in the 1993 local elections. Although fiercely denouncing the influence of the clan system, the Islamic Movement relies on the support of individual families within the clan system. The Islamic Movement differs from other parties in that it strives to undermine the clan system. Its candidates rarely represent a single large extended family, but rather individual families or smaller clans. The Islamic Movement also picks individual candidates from large clans, and in the 1988 elections this strategy helped it win the leadership of six local municipal councils. In the 1993 elections, it increased its strength to seven municipalities (Umm-al-Fahm, Kafar Qasem, Kafar Barra, Jaljulyeh, Kabul, Kafar Qara, Kafar Kanna). In elections that were held for the first time in Bedouin settlements in the Negev in September 2000, the Islamic Movement won Kseifeh and Ar'ara, as well as seats in Rahat, where its candidate served in rotation with a Labor Party representative. A series of clashes with the law and a sense of being persecuted led the Islamic Movement to lower its profile in the 2003 elections, and indeed only seven of 594 competing lists included the word "Islamic" in their name. It would appear that the northern branch campaigned only in Umm-al-Fahm, under the name "the Islamic Bloc". Ostensibly, the Islamic Movement presents its public with a more modern view of social structures. In reality, however, it continues in the path of the prophet Muhammad and his "Community of Believers", which undermined the importance of the clan or tribe.

Political parties did not increase their influence significantly in the 2003 elections, as compared to previous elections. The only place in which elections were political and ideological was Umm-al-Fahm, with no one-clan lists contending. The two rival groups consisted of the Islamic Movement's northern branch and the secular National Municipal Alliance, which comprised *Abnaa al-Balad*, Hadash, the National Democratic Party and the United National Alliance of Hashem Mahamid. The Islamic Movement focused its campaign on the arrest of its leaders for security reasons. The northern Islamic Movement kept a low profile for the same reason, and campaigned only in Umm-al-Fahm. And, after 15 years of controlling the municipality, the movement strengthened and won 11 out of the council's 15 seats. The secular group won only four council seats.

The Islamic Movement is not capable of being clan-based, since its Umm-al-Fahm candidate was elected on votes from across the clan board. The winner in the last elections in 2003 is a man who does not hail from any of the town's large clans: Hashem Abd al-Rahman is a member of a small, 30-member clan which originates in Hebron. He is neither wealthy, nor a possessor of social or historical standing. As such, he achieved the greatest victory in the Arab sector. Thus, too, Umm-al-Fahm became the only Arab town in which the mayor's party had the largest number of seats on the council. This is an extremely rare occurrence in Israel's Arab community, being unrelated to clan considerations. Since its rise in the 1989 local elections, the Islamic Movement has managed to build a new elite class and a leadership to replace the traditional leadership class that lost its position and influence. The old order no longer tries to compete with the new leadership, either against the Islamic Movement or against the secular bloc.

The extended family affiliation system of voting, characteristic of the 1989, 1993 and 1998 local election campaigns, differed from that of the 1950s. The old system provided a basis for solidarity and hegemony in Arab towns and villages in Israel; inter-clan rivalries tended to focus on a traditional class system. Nowadays, extended family affiliation is a means for controlling municipal or local councils. Although candidates are still driven by ambition and social standing, they are also aware of the importance of having a good job. In many cases where the mayoral candidate is also a leader of a clan, he is no longer necessarily the oldest member of the clan, nor does he have to be the former *Mukhtar* of the village; usually, too, he is a university graduate. Another new phenomenon is that a large number of extended families – mainly Christian – have established foundations (NGOs), consisting of family members, which serve as an internal support fund and as a framework for inter-clan relationships.

The kind of relationships that developed on a local level between clans and political parties explains why political parties have not become the main framework for local political activity. With the exception of Hadash, all the political parties have neglected the ideological struggle and chosen instead to attach themselves to clans that can deliver votes in municipal and national elections. Typical of this is the Arab Democratic Party, which, by forging political agreements with various clans during the 1993 election, won 45 seats on several municipal councils.

Thus the political parties gained by abandoning ideological platforms and making agreements with clans; they adopted a clan-like mindset and patterns of activity, and their social and national message, whether radical or moderate, was downplayed in order to adapt to the more conservative and traditional attitudes demanded by the clans. Instead of trying to beat the local political game, the Arab parties joined it and chose pragmatism over ideology. Thus, for example, during the 1993 municipal elections, ethnic considerations and traditional structure became important to those parties that wanted electoral power rather than social change. Such political pragmatism led to compromises with the same social institutions (the extended family) that slowed down social modernization in Israel's Arab communities.

The clans, for their part, also found a way to deal with this onslaught of modern politics in order to preserve their political power and prevent the breakdown of the only social framework that provides protection for the individual. They succeeded in thwarting the attempts of young academics to break through ethnic and clan rifts and establish political lists across clan lines. The primaries held in some clans, which were meant to lend a democratic character to clan politics, in fact caused the opposite. They increased candidates' obligations to the clan and created de facto clan parties. Other clans did not even bother to adopt this democratic method and elected their candidates for municipal elections through a "committee" consisting of family heads. As a result, clan affiliation was preserved as a tool for advancing economic interests, and the municipal elections became a factor that empowered conservative instincts and traditional identifications rather than democracy and modernization. Where some clans underwent a process of adjustment to political values, it was expressed by choosing young candidates, who were suitable in terms of their education as well as in terms of their popularity for leading the community and uniting several clans around them.

In Knesset elections, the function of the clan was usually less dominant than in municipal elections. The clans used political parties that sought the Arab vote as a tool in their quarrels with other clans in the village. More than once, a clan made deals with a particular party only because it was the opponent of another party that supported its rival clan. The parties, on the other hand, learned to adapt to "clan politics" and, in many cases, accepted with understanding the refusal of a clan's candidate to identify openly with the party that supported the candidate.

These examples show a clear correlation between clan affiliation and the choice of party, and a parallel correlation between local and general elections. An analysis of voting trends in an extended family shows that, although its social and economic role has weakened, the extended family still fills an important political function. This function is expressed mainly in two areas: the political, which consists of local and national struggles *vis-*

à-vis national parties; and the social, with regard to inter-clan conflicts and feuds. Sometimes there was a connection between blood rivalry and political rivalry.

The local elections in Umm-al-Fahm in 1983 saw a confrontation among the town's four large clans, which constitute some 80 percent of the total voting register. In the second round, Hashem Mahamid, of the Mahamid clan, faced Wajih Mahajna of the Mahajna clan. The Mahamid clan gave its candidate 82 percent of its vote, while the Mahajna candidate received 86 percent of his clan's vote. The following table shows clearly the importance of the clan's position in the traditional political structure and the fact that its members follow its leaders' instructions, so long as the clan continues to be united. A similar analysis was carried out in Sakhnin and Tireh in 2003 and produced a similar picture.

Table 4.2 Results of Mayoral Elections in Umm-al-Fahm[16]

Clan	No. of Votes	Valid Votes	Percent	Wajih Mahajna		Hashem Mahamid	
				votes	percent	votes	percent
Mahamid	2,404	1,939	81	343	18	1,592	82
Mahajna	2,360	2,029	86	1,741	86	288	14
Ighbaria	2,270	1,697	75	888	52	809	48
Jabarin	2,090	1,564	75	533	34	1,031	66
Total	9,124	7,226	79	3,505	49	3,721	51

The division in Nazareth is not according to large and dominant family clans, but according to ethnic-religious background: Christians of various denominations (who make up 40 percent of the population) and a Moslem majority. In the 2003 local elections, Rames Jarrissi, a Christian and a member of a small family who stood on behalf of a national party (Rakah), was elected mayor. The conclusion is that in today's political climate, the only parties able to cross clan lines are Rakah and the Islamic Movement.

Thus what appeared to be a decrease in the power and centrality of the clan system during the 1970s was very short-lived and produced no lasting significant social change within Israel's Arab community. Whereas there was no real change in the clans, change did take place within the political parties, which chose pragmatism and closer co-operation with the clans, even supporting them, if this meant winning local elections. Clan rivalry became integral to the political scene and played an important role in the political game.

During the first years of Israel's existence as a state, the Arab community was governed to a large extent by ethnic and clan rifts. More recently, social and economic changes within the Israeli Arab community have resulted in a reduced influence for these rifts, although they have not disappeared altogether. And during general and local elections, the parties continue to recruit support along the lines of the rifts. Still, the end of the allied Arab lists, which were clearly based on the clans and political interest groups, is proof that the Arab voter is no longer influenced by clan-related issues in choosing his or her Knesset representative. In local elections, on the other hand, the religious, ethnic and clan affiliations continue to exert considerable influence on voting trends.

Political scientists see the evolution of national leadership as a step-by-step process that pauses meaningfully on lower, local rungs of political service to the community before it encourages candidates to try for national office. The local level of political service is seen by political scientists and community leaders as "testing the waters" for the future generation of national political leaders. The voting trends among Israeli Arabs have produced municipal leaders who may not be well suited to lead the community to national accomplishments. Only a few national leaders have come from the local scene. The most typical example is that of Sheikh Ra'ed Salah, head of the Islamic Movement, who became a popular leader as a result of his success as mayor of Umm-al-Fahm, but did not move on to Knesset elections. Moreover, the Supreme Follow-up Committee for the Arabs in Israel, which accumulated political prestige as the most important leadership body in the Israeli Arab community and has expanded its activities as the collective political speaker for the Israeli Arab public, changed as a result of these elections. Fewer representatives were elected because of their party affiliation and more were elected because of paternal lineage. This split into individual factions with tribal rivalry is a sure recipe for municipal deadlock and influences a mayor's ability to make decisions and advance local development programs.

Ethnic and Religious Rifts, and Considerations in Choosing a Party

The non-Jewish population in Israel consists of three major religious communities: Moslems, Christians and Druze. The three share a common ethnic background in that they all belong to the Arab nation. This, however, does not mean that no differences exist among the groups. Among the Christians, various cults and denominations exist as rifts with clear boundaries. The Moslem, Druze and Circassians behave in a similar way, although they tend to seek separate political channels, mainly because they form minority groups within the greater Arab community in Israel, and because of a desire to maintain the social and cultural differences between themselves and the other Moslems. This tendency, of course, served the authorities' desire to keep abreast of events within the country's Arab population. At the center of Israel's "ethnic" policy there stood the principle of "isolation" – i.e. separating the Arab minority from the Jewish majority and keeping it divided within itself, among other things, by preserving the ethno-religious splits. This policy resulted in a somewhat weaker Arab community. Nonetheless, among the different ethnic groups, like the Christians, Druze and Circassians, who were aware of the cultural and social differences between them and the Moslem majority, there has always been a desire to develop their own political frameworks.

The Moslems

At the end of 2006, the Moslem community numbered 1,173,100 and constituted 83.2 percent of Israel's total Arab population; they are the largest and most dominant among the Arab communities and constitute 16.5 percent of the state's total population. The Moslems have a natural annual birthrate of 2.9 percent.[17] The State of Israel has given the Moslem community broad autonomy in all matters of personal status and religion and, for the first time in the history of Moslem presence in the Land of Israel, the Moslems have been defined as a religious ethnic group, one of many.

Before the establishment of the State of Israel, Moslems possessed large quantities of religious property – *Waqf*, including mosques, holy sites, cemeteries, buildings and other sorts of real estate. The state took control of much of the property and appointed a committee of trustees from among the Moslem leaders in the mixed population towns, in which most of the religious property is to be found. In each and every town, religious property has been released into the hands of these committees, who care for them and see to all the needs of the Moslem community. From the very early days of the state's existence, various Moslem groups voiced demands for the removal of the management of holy property and sites from the hands of the National Custodian of Deserted Property and the Committee of Trustees, with responsibility being passed over to an elected "Islamic Council". To this day, the government has not fulfilled such demands, in order to avoid extending the autonomy granted to the country's Arabs.

The Druze

Following its establishment, the state's Druze population numbered 14,800. By late 2006, the number had risen to 117,500, and consisted of 8.3 percent of the entire minority population, and only 1.7 percent of the total population. The community has an annual birthrate of 2 percent. The State of Israel has allowed the Druze community to establish its own institutions and acquiesced to the request of community leaders to recruit its young men into the Israel Defense Forces (IDF). In 1957 the state granted the Druze community the status of independent religion. In 1961 the state recognized the "Spiritual Authority" led by Sheikh Amin Tarif, and in 1962 the Knesset passed the Druze Courts Law, with authority over personal law. In the late 1970s the government relinquished its control over Druze affairs by removing them from the Arab Departments in the various ministries and transferring them to an inter-ministry committee headed by a CEO of the Prime Minister's Bureau, which was established in order to develop the Druze towns and integrate the community into mainstream Israeli life.

The Christians

During and after the 1948 War of Independence, the number of Christians who fled the country was smaller than that of Moslems, so that by 1949 they formed 21 percent of the minority population to remain within Israeli sovereignty. Since then, however, due to a low birthrate and a greater rate of emigration than among the Druze and Moslems, their numbers dropped. By late 2006, the Christians in Israel numbered 120,100 and constituted 8.5 percent of the country's minority population and 1.8 percent of the overall population. Their annual birthrate stood at 1.2 percent. The Christian community is divided into different sects and denominations (Greek Catholic, Greek Orthodox, Latin, Coptic, Mormon, Armenian, and several Protestant sects). Each sect maintains its separate socio-religious organizations around its church and community. The largest Christian sect is the Greek Catholic (about 33 percent of all the Christians), followed by the Greek Orthodox community (30 percent) and the Latin Catholic community (about 16 percent). The only Christian groups to make their mark on Arab politics on a local and a national level have been the Greek Orthodox and Greek Catholic. The small Evangelical-Episcopal community did manage to produce first-class leaders, but these found their place only in the Communist Party.

Most of the Christians (about 80 percent) chose to live in towns or cities, as opposed to about 70 percent of the Moslems, who live in villages. According to the millet[18] system which had been used in the Ottoman Empire, the Christian minorities enjoyed wide latitude in terms of religious and cultural freedom, as well as considerable administrative, fiscal, and legal autonomy under their own ecclesiastical and lay leaders.[19] Unlike the Druze and Circassians, the Christian community was not defined by the State of Israel as a unique minority group, nor did the state differentiate between it and the Moslems who remained within Israeli boundaries; rather, it saw the two ethnic groups (Christian and Arab) as belonging to the Arab minority.

The Bedouin

Although the Bedouin belong to the Moslem community, their behavior is blatantly that of a socio-ethnic rift. They maintain a unique way of life and culture, so that they see themselves as a separate group with needs and interests of their own. In late 2006, the Bedouin community in Israel numbered around 257,000 and was concentrated in two regions: the northern Negev (about 157,000) and the Galilee (about 80,000), with a few moving to the center of the country. About 20,000 Bedouin have settled in Ramla and Lod and a few other Arab villages, especially Tayibeh and Kafar Qasem. The annual birthrate among the Negev Bedouin is amongst the highest in the world and stands at around 4.5 percent.[20]

During the early 1970s, the Negev Bedouin started settling in permanent townships, the first of which was Tel Sheva, which was established in 1960 – although the settlement of the nomadic Bedouin in unsuitably planned permanent stone buildings did not succeed. The town of Rahat was established in 1972 and was quickly populated by groups of Bedouin who worked the land but were not landowners. The peace treaty with Egypt escalated the evacuation of the Bedouin from the Tel-al-Maleh region near Arad,[21] which was destined for the Nevatim air force base. Their relocation in well-planned, modern townships brought about major changes in their traditional nomadic way of life. Today, over 60 percent of the Bedouin population lives in seven permanent towns dotted around the Negev. The remainder continues to live in unrecognized villages and townships, with far-reaching claims to large tracts of land. They are unable to enjoy the pleasures of modern housing, which include sewage, electricity and water, and are at constant loggerheads with the establishment over the future of their lands and improvements in their standard of living.

The Circassians

The Circassians are Sunni Moslems, whose origins are in the Caucasus; the Circassian population in Israel today stands at a little over 3,000 people. Ethnically, the Circassians are different from the other Moslems and strive to emphasize their uniqueness. The group's young men are recruited into the IDF, and a few years ago their leaders asked to be removed from the special education system adapted to the Druze community and to be transferred to the Hebrew education system. They were given the name "Cercess" by their neighbors, although they call themselves "Adiga".[22] In 1864–5, hundreds of thousands of Circassians left the Caucasus in the wake of the war with Tsarist Russia. Sultan Abd al-Hamid II assisted them in settling on lands under his authority, probably because he saw himself as a protector of Islam (for political reasons resulting from his relations with his Russian neighbors), or because he was interested in settling loyal citizens in specific areas of the Ottoman Empire. The Circassians are settled in two villages – Kafar Kamma and Reihaniyye.

The voting behavior of the various groups under discussion in this section is influenced by their ethnic affiliation. The ethno-religious split in Arab society is undoubtedly one of the main reasons why no single all-Arab political party has ever been formed. Traditionally, members of any particular ethnic group were concerned primarily with the interests of the ethnic or extended family group to which they belonged, and did not act out of solidarity with members of other ethnic groups. The ethnic groups themselves constituted not only religious communities, but also independent social entities that did not open their doors to other religious communities that existed in their vicinity. Even when members of other ethnic communities lived in the same villages or towns, as happened in Shefar'am, Nazareth, Rame, Mghar, etc., ethno-religious solidarity rose above feelings of local patriotism and the ethnic group. Ethnic isolation caused changes in political orientation between the various groups and the ethno-religious group became highly influential, both on a local and on a national level.

An analysis of regional voting patterns according to the ethnic affiliation of the population reveals clear voting trends for each ethnic group and region. A possible explanation for this is the dependency of Arab voters on the Jewish establishment, a dependency that caused parts of the Arab public to turn their political activity and their votes toward Jewish parties. At the same time, the growing nationalism among the Israeli Arabs undermined their religious loyalties, although it did not cancel them out altogether.

Among the Druze, politics has always been connected to clan rivalries. With the establishment of the state, there remained four Druze leaders, who headed four large and influential extended families and enjoyed the support of large groups within the community, as well that of the Jewish establishment because of their co-operation during the War of Independence. These leaders were Saleh Khneifes, Jaber Mu'adi, Labib Abu Ruqun and Amin Tarif (who was the Druze community's spiritual leader until his death in 1993). Khneifes, Mu'adi and Abu Ruqun served in the Knesset on Mapai allied lists, and, for over 30 years, were the official leaders of the Druze community in Israel. Since the 1970s, with the growth of a new generation that was influenced by the country's economic development and modernization, the Druze have joined other parties, from both the right and the left. Some Druze, whose feelings of discontent and discrimination were severe, supported the Communist Party. Because it has no separate nationalist aspirations of its own, the Druze community sees itself as different from the other minority groups in the country.[23] Their vote for Zionist parties is influenced mainly by the number of Druze representatives the parties gave them. Thus, for example, the new liberal democrat Dash Party gave Zaydan Atshi the number three slot on its list for the tenth and eleventh Knesset and won a large portion of the Druze vote. The Likud Party, which placed a Druze candidate in a good slot on its Knesset list in the same elections, has won around 20 percent of the Druze vote.

The political activity of the Christian communities has not been connected to family affiliations and has moved in three directions: activity in the Communist Party; activity in the Mapai allied Arab lists; and attempts at establishing independent Christian organizations. Of all the Christian denominations, only the two large communities – the Greek Catholic and the Greek Orthodox – have made their mark on Arab politics on a parliamentary and a local level.

Up to 1973, the Christians and Moslems were represented equally in the Knesset through the allied Arab lists. Since then, no Christians have ever been given a high enough slot on Zionist Knesset lists that would win them a Knesset seat, and those who tried to get elected on independent lists – such as Elias Nakhla and Mas'ad Qasis – failed to do so. Only in the Communist Party were Christian candidates able to reach the top of the list and get themselves elected, but not necessarily as representatives of their community. Following the split in 1965 and the establishment of Rakah, the only Arab members of the party's political bureau and secretariat of the central committee were members of the Christian community.

An analysis of election results according to a regional and ethnic cross section shows that the Moslems spread their votes across the entire party spectrum (with the exception of the Bedouin and Circassians, who tended to vote for Zionist parties). The Druze and Christians, in contrast, tended to vote across a clan-determined line. The Christians have always been influenced by their vicinity. In isolated Christian villages, such as Jish, Fassuta and Mi'elya, most of the vote went to the Zionist parties; unlike those Christians who live in mixed-ethnic villages and are but one community among an overall Arab population.

Out of purely pragmatic considerations, the Bedouin have turned themselves into a reservoir of votes for the Zionist parties. By doing so, they have managed to play a growing and significant role in the political life of the state, to the extent that it was possible to compile an all-Bedouin list to stand for office in the eighth Knesset. Nonetheless, the move to permanent accommodation, and the modernization this brought in its wake, has brought about changes in the traditional voting trends of the Bedouin population; in return, "foreign" political influences have penetrated the community in the form of nationalism and Islamic fundamentalism. As they settled in permanent townships, the Bedouin became exposed to established Orthodox Islam; numerous mosques and religious institutions were built all over the Negev and religious leaders began to teach and deliver public lectures. Within a few years, the Islamic religion had a real stronghold among the Bedouin. Even those who did not live in the recognized permanent townships began leading a more religious lifestyle and praying in improvised tin-hut mosques. These elements were joined by the special problems connected with dissent over lands (common in the Negev) and other issues, which added to this community's already strong sense of discrimination and knowledge that it does not enjoy equality with the majority Jewish population. About 35 percent of the Bedouin continued to live in unrecognized settlements, without drains, running water and electricity; there has been an ongoing conflict with the authorities over the future of their lands and for improved living conditions.

In order to conduct a comparative study of the Arab population's local and national voting trends, a model has been constructed that is based on an analysis of voting trends in three large towns, which illustrates voting trends from ideological, clan-related and ethnic aspects. It should be stressed that the model does not represent the national voting trends among the Arab communities, but various cross sections of the Arab population from the point of ethno-religious affiliation, the social composition of the extended families, geography and kind of town/village. There follows a description of the main characteristics of the towns/villages in the model.

Ethnic Voting Patterns

Shefar'am

The town of Shefar'am, with its wide variety of religious groups, represents an ethno-religious cross section. A close examination of the voting register for the seventeenth Knesset reveals that it consists of 54 percent Moslems, 30 percent Christians, and 16 percent Druze, inhabiting, for the most part, separate neighborhoods.

Relations between the ethno-religious groups have always been good and there is a consensus between the various factions as to the delegation of municipal functions on a religious basis, which makes Shefar'am of particular importance. The town has always been a center for regional activity and it has bred political and academic leaders such as the Druze Knesset member Saleh Khneifes, who served in four Knessets (the second, the third, the fourth and the fifth); the writer Dr Mahmud Abbasi, who served for years as advisor to the minister of education and culture and founded his own list for the ninth Knesset; Prof. Majid al-Hajj, researcher and lecturer at Haifa University; and Ibrahim Nimer Husayn, a traditional leader, for many years mayor and head of the Arab Local Government in Israel. An analysis of voting results according to an ethnic key, in those voting booths whose population is ethnically homogenous, reveals that – for example – in the 1984 general election, 72 percent of the voters in voting station 2,[24] which was placed in a mostly Christian neighborhood, voted for the Arab parties, notably Hadash/Rakah. In the general election for the sixteenth Knesset, most of the voters in voting station 5 were

Christians. The large majority of the vote in this station went to Azmi Bishara's National Democratic Pact list; Bishara is a Christian. Most of the voters in voting station 8 during the eleventh Knesset elections were Moslems; 65 percent of the votes in this station went to Arab parties, as did the Moslem vote in the Triangle. Most of the voters in voting station 18 at the sixteenth Knesset elections were Moslems and the large majority of them (77 percent) voted for Arab parties, again, as did most of the votes in the Triangle. In the eleventh Knesset elections, most of the voters in voting station 11 belonged to the Druze community. Most of the votes here went to Zionist parties. In the sixteenth Knesset elections, most of the voters in voting station 25 were Druze and here, too, most of the vote went to Zionist parties, as did most of the Druze vote countrywide.

An examination of the voting stations following general elections reveals that the voting pattern is constant according to ethnic affiliation. An interesting conclusion arises from this, according to which the Knesset vote among the various ethnic groups matched the overall vote of that group throughout the country.[25] It appears that no single ethnic group influences another when it comes to their vote and that the individual's vote in the ethnic groups conforms with that of the group in general. It appears, too, that there is a certain symmetry between the voting results of members of an ethnic group in a specific town or village and those of all the members of the group on a nationwide level. Moreover, this is especially obvious among the Druze, most of whom give their vote to the Zionist parties.

Sakhnin – The Municipal Arena as an Expression of Clan Voting

The Arab town of Sakhnin, which is situated in the Galilee, is a political and nationalist center. Its population is mostly Moslem, with a Christian minority. Several large extended families live in Sakhnin, the best known of which are Abu Raya, Khalaila, Ghanaim, Zbeidat and Tarabia. These clans compete for control of the town, which was the focus of the first Land Day on March 30, 1976. Among the more prominent figures in the political arena is Hamad Khalaila, who was elected to the tenth Knesset in 1981.

An analysis of the votes according to clans for the eleventh Knesset elections revealed that most voters in voting station 1 were members of the Abu Raya clan; most of the votes in this station went to Hadash. A member of this clan was elected mayor with the support of Hadash. In the sixteenth (2003) Knesset elections, most of the votes at the same station went to Hadash. Most voters in voting station 3 belonged to the Ghanaim clan, the majority of whom voted for the Progressive List for Peace in the 2003 general elections. In the sixteenth Knesset elections most of the voters in station 5, who belonged to the Ghanaim clan, voted for the United Arab party.[26] In the eleventh Knesset elections most voters in voting station 5 were members of the Khalaila clan, and the vote was split between Rakah and the Zionist parties. In the 2003 general elections for the sixteenth Knesset, when most of the voters at voting station 14 were members of the Khalaila clan, the vote was shared by Israeli Arab (especially Hadash) and Zionist parties, much as in the elections to the eleventh Knesset.

Umm-al-Fahm – Clan and the Nationalist Vote

Umm-al-Fahm in the Northern Triangle is at the epicenter of Arab nationalist politics and provides a representative example of an all-Moslem population. Most of the population is economically underprivileged. Four large clans each have an almost equal number of voters: Mahamid, Mahajna, Ighbaria and Jabarin. But it is in Umm-al-Fahm that the extraparliamentary, radical, nationalist political groups, such as *Abnaa al-Balad* and *al-Ansar*, grew and affected political behavior in the region; it is here, too, that the Islamic Movement first emerged and took root. Local politician Hashem Mahamid served in the thirteenth, fourteenth and fifteenth Knessets.

The main area in which the four clans clashed is during elections for the local authority, when everyone wants to win control of the town. In 1983, 82 percent of the Mahamid clan's vote went to its own candidate and 86 percent of the Mahajna clan's went to its candidate. Of these two clans, therefore, most of the voters supported their own candidate; the Ighbaria clan, on the other hand, split their votes between two candidates. Most members of the Jabarin clan supported the Mahamid candidate, in accordance with a pre-agreed pact.[27]

At the latest municipal elections, Sheikh Ra'ed Salah, head of the northern branch of the Islamic Movement and a member of the Mahajna clan, ran for mayor. He had two rivals: Dr Afu Ighbaria and Mahmud Jamal from the Mahamid clan. Since the choice this time was ideological, Ra'ed Salah won over 70 percent of the votes from all clans. In the sixteenth Knesset elections, Hashem Mahamid headed an independent list. In Umm-al-Fahm his list won more than 62 percent of the votes, for two reasons: first, he had the support (albeit not public) of the northern branch of the Islamic Movement; and second, as a local candidate, Mahamid won the support of all the clans. Thus, voting trends in Umm-al-Fahm are clan and party orientated. Since its establishment, the Islamic Movement has managed to garner the support of all the clans and there is no longer any significance attached to the size of the clan in the choice of candidate to head the local municipality.

Local elections are the only ones in which the Arab voter is able to feel on home ground, not only physically, but mainly because of the limited influence of the large national, external parties. Moreover, the local front is almost the only one at which Arab leaders have stood the test of their own constituency.

Notwithstanding the social and economic changes undergone by the Israeli Arab public, social divisions based on clan, geography and region and, of course, ethno-religious affinity, have been maintained. The sectarian and particular considerations have always been woven into political and nationalist considerations to such an extent that it is difficult to discern which of them had the greatest influence. In other words, it is not possible to calculate or describe Arab voting trends simply by examining such obvious criteria as Palestinian national identity, and ignoring the Arab voter's organic affinity for his traditional frameworks hinders the researcher's ability to explain this phenomenon. Moreover, the results of Knesset elections provide the best tool at our disposal for explaining the political swings in Arab society over the years. Election results show us that anyone who voted for a Zionist party (about 30 percent of the electorate) did so purely out of socio-group, pragmatic considerations, which led the voter to the conclusion that it was worth his or her while to support the ruling parties, since they are the ones who have the resources with which to reward those people who gave them their vote. The remaining voters (70 percent) voted for nationalist Arab parties and expressed non-ethnic considerations (such as those who voted for the National Democratic Pact); religious considerations (such as those who voted for the United Arab Party, which they see as representing the Islamic Movement); and mixed political/social considerations (such as those voting for Rakah, the party that stands for office on municipal councils on a larger scale than any other Arab party). The Knesset vote, therefore, is not representative of the Arabs' Palestinian identity, as will be illustrated later.

In the 1999 general election (to the fifteenth Knesset), the ethnic and regional rifts previously mentioned came, once again, to the fore. The ethnic tension between Moslems and Christians reached new heights and expressed itself in the candidates' struggle for high slots on the Arab parties' lists of candidates. The Arab parties themselves had no qualms about exploiting the ethnic rifts. The Communist Hadash Party, for example, followed a clearly ethnic key in composing its Knesset list (number one – Moslem; number two – Christian, etc.). The Islamic Movement is a purely ethnic movement, whose objective is to strengthen the Moslem community. The Arab Democratic Party was established as purely Arab and, unlike Hadash and the Progressive List for Peace, refused to include Jews; even Christian Arabs were not welcome. On the other hand, Azmi Bishara continually tried to downplay his Christian identity and break down the ethnic rift in Arab society. Researchers of Arab society in Israel, Sarah Ozachy-Lazar and As'ad Ghanem, see this as the development of secondary identities and explain it as the absence of Israeli Arabs in the growth processes of the Palestinian nation, on the one hand, and their inability to be accepted as an integral part of Israeli society, on the other.

The renewed ethnic rifts have not drawn Arab society back into the sectarian social structure that the state encouraged for so long, especially during the years of military administration. The more the Arab public continues to develop nationalist political forces within itself, so the boundaries of ethnic rifts are crossed. Thus, for example, the Communists have been quite successful among the Druze; the nationalist Arab parties have integrated many of the Christian leaders and thwarted the establishment of a Christian sector. Ever since the arrival of the Islamic Movement in the political arena, even the Bedouin sector has ceased to be a potential political reservoir for the rest of the parties. In the Bedouin town of Rahat, the Islamic Movement's candidate was even elected mayor in the 2003 local elections.

Several outstanding examples exist of the influence of local, clan and ethnic rifts in elections for the sixteenth Knesset: the Progressive National Pact (PNP) won only 8.2 percent and did not qualify, but Hashem Mahamid, who headed the list, won 63 percent in his hometown of Umm-al-Fahm, beating the mighty northern branch of the Islamic Movement and its stand against Arab participation in general elections. The National Democratic Party won 19.2 percent, but in Kafar Qara, where the candidate was Jamal Zahalqa, the list won 49 percent of the vote; 46 percent voted in Yamma for Fathi Daqqa, number five on the National Democratic Party list; in Tayibeh the united Hadash – The Arab Movement for Renewal (Hebrew acronym Ta'al) list with Ahmad Tibi received 39 percent, against 26.7 percent of the general result. The village of Kafar Kanna can serve as an example of local patriotism. Three local candidates received 90 percent of the vote: Abd al-Malik Dahamsha and Adel Khamaisi, both of the Islamic Movement, received 29 percent, against the United Arab Party's 18 percent, and the National Democratic Pact candidate, Taha Wasel, took 32 percent. This becomes even more significant if we consider the support for Arab candidates in Zionist lists, as compared to the poor support Zionist parties generally enjoy among the Arabs. Ten Arab candidates were present among the first ten places in several Zionist parties: Ghaleb Majadlah (who in 2008 served as the first Moslem minister in the government representing the Labor Party) won 21 percent of the vote in Baqa al-Gharbiyye (Labor won 7.8 percent); Freij Isawi won 20 percent in Kafar Qasem (Meretz won 4.2 percent of the Arab vote); Sami Halabi, the candidate for Am Echad from Daliyat al-Carmel, took 26 percent of the vote, while his list received 5.8 percent. It is clear that among the Druze and Bedouin the ethnic and tribal affiliations remain especially strong: the Bedouin candidate Talab al-Sani' won 51 percent of the vote in Laqyyeh; the Arab Democratic Party candidate Ibrahim al-Umur won 51 percent of the vote in Kseifeh; in Rahat, Musa abu Shaiban, the Islamic Movement candidate, won 40 percent of the vote; Hadash candidate Yusuf Atawna won in 47 percent of the vote in Hura. In the Druze sector, Majali Wahba, the Likud candidate, won 39 percent in Beit Jann; Labor candidate Saleh Tarif won 44 percent in Julis; in Daliyat al-Carmel the Likud candidate Ayub Qara won 15 percent of the vote.

Table 4.3 Influence of Regional Rifts on the Arab Vote (not including mixed towns/villages)

Region	Jewish population	Arab population	Arab voting participation (Percent)	Support for Arab parties (Percent)
Northern District	551,800	603,300	62.0	80.1
Hadera district and Triangle	167,000	134,700	52.4	80.6
Sharon District, Petah Tikva	737,200	95,400	64.0	79.5
Be'er Sheva District, Bedouin	362,300	128,200	46.5	69.7

To conclude, tribe or clan candidates can draw the support of large proportions of their kinsmen, on the condition that the candidate's status in the town or village or within his own milieu is strong and that the clan is socially cohered. This is especially true with regard to the Bedouin and Druze communities.

In recent years we have been witnessing a process whereby Arab candidates on Zionist party lists are unable to win the necessary number of votes to "cover" their own Knesset seat. Nonetheless, these parties continue to place Arab candidates on their Knesset lists – out of national, rather than electoral, considerations.

Further confirmation of the importance of the influence the candidate's area of residence has on the voter's choice of political parties is provided by an analysis of election results for the sixteenth Knesset according to the regions in which Arabs live: the North, including the Galilee and the Valleys, the Northern Triangle, the Southern Triangle and the Negev. With the exception of the Negev Bedouin, inhabitants of these different regions are united in their support for Arab parties, although voting participation differed from region to region. In the Northern Triangle and the Negev, the participation percentage was substantially lower than the national average. In the Northern Triangle, this was due to the Islamic Movement's call to boycott elections; in the Negev, the low participation can probably be explained by local political behavior – a combination of disinterest in Israeli politics, technical problems caused by the distance of voting stations from areas of residence, and protest against the government's policy on lands and settlement.

5

Arab Electoral Power

The term "electoral power" refers to the ability of a specific group to translate the number of its voters into a matching proportional number of seats in the legislature and thus create a situation in which the parties that make up the coalition will have to take the group's interests into consideration.[1] In a voting system such as Israel's, which is based on a national constituency (and not on regional representation), electoral power can have significant influence. The ultra-Orthodox Sephardi Shas Party, for example, won 17 seats in the fifteenth Knesset, which represents almost exactly the Jewish population group that provides its potential voter pool. Shas's ability to influence coalitions and the quality of its legislative achievements for the benefit of its constituency are directly related to its ability to translate its electoral power into real parliamentary power.

Toward the end of 2003, the Arab population of Israel numbered about 1,301,600, of whom 260,000 lived in Jerusalem and 17,000 were Druze living in the Golan Heights. The Arab population constituted about 20 percent of the country's entire population. (Out of this population, 83 percent were Muslims, 8.7 percent were Christians and 8.3 percent were Druze.) Their share of the electorate was 12.6 percent, which results in a potential electoral power of 15 Knesset seats.[2] The natural population growth rate among the Moslems in late 2001 was 3.6, as compared with 1.4 among the Jews. Thus Israel's Arab population is a young population and its age profile differs from that of the Jewish population. Moreover, in the future, it will almost certainly actualize its proportional electoral power to gain as many as 20 or 21 Knesset seats. However, all ethnic groups have seen a clear decrease in birthrate. Thus, for instance, in 2006 the birthrate among the Moslems dropped to 2.9.

The table shows that about half the Arab population is aged below 19, as opposed to only one third among the Jews. Over the years, as the potential of Arab voters increases, this process will necessarily lead to a reduction in Jewish electoral power. According to medium-range demographic forecasts, in 2025 Israel's Arabs will make up 25.5 percent of the country's population and close to 41.6 percent of them will be under the age of 18.

Among Israeli Arabs, 73.8 percent of the population consists of the age group 0–34 years, as compared with 56.1 percent amongst Jews, in 2006. By 2020, the increase in voters aged 18 and above among Israel's Arabs

Table 5.1 Age Profile of the Jewish and the Arab Population[3]

Age range	1995 Jews	1995 Arabs	2001 Jews	2001 Arabs	2006 Jews	2006 Arabs
	No. of citizens					
Population total	**4495.1**	**1,049.8**	**5,025.0**	**1.224.0**	**5,393.4**	**1,413.3**
0–19 years (percent)	32.3	46.4	30.6	46.9	33.2	50.2
20–34 years (percent)	25.5	30.0	26.2	28.9	23.0	23.6
35–44 years (percent)	13.6	10.1	12.1	11.0	11.8	11.6
45 years and older (percent)	28.6	13.2	31.1	13.2	32.0	14.6

would bring them to 20.5 percent of the total electorate, which would give them 25 Knesset seats (out of 120).[4]

The significant changes that have taken place in employment patterns among the Israeli Arab public have brought about changes in the image of the Israeli Arab voter. Over the last decade, the number of agricultural workers has decreased from 20 to 3 percent, while the academic/professional sector has grown from 7 to 20 percent.

The same period has seen a significant change in female labor. Traditionally women were not employed outside their homes. They did, however, work lands belonging to their families. Since the 1980s, a growing number of Arab women have joined the workforce, reaching 22.3 percent in 2006.

The following table shows the significant changes in employment patterns within the Arab sector. The data for 2006 takes into account that at the end of 2006 the civilian labor force in the Arab sector consisted of 295,100 people.

Table 5.2 Distribution according to Employment in the Arab Sector[5]

Branch	1996 No.	1996 Percent	2000 No.	2000 Percent	2006 No.	2006 Percent
Agriculture	8,900	19.4	6,800	18.4	9,100	3.1
Services	30,700	9.3	45,800	11.5	47,700	16.2
Professions	34,400	7.1	51,400	8.5	34,000	11.5
Managers	3,400	4.0	7,200	4.5	6,800	2.3
Industry & Construction	156,300	23.8	164,700	26.6	116,200	39.4
Clerks	10,800	4.3	23,800	6.3	19,300	6.5

Changes such as these affect social, ethnic and clan rifts and play an important role in attempts to establish political movements and parties – both local and national.

Because of Israel's election system, it has always been necessary to form coalition governments, which naturally makes the voting power of each sector extremely important. The potential electoral power in the Arab sector in the seventeenth Knesset was 15 Knesset seats. One would expect the Israeli Arab voters to take advantage of this potential to influence the state's political structure in order to advance their national goals no less than their civil status. In fact, the Israeli Arab vote was split among many political parties and the community did not manage to make use of its electoral power. On the other hand, to this day, the Zionist parties have not dared use this electoral power by introducing an Arab nationalist party into the coalition.

The relative rise of the Israeli Arab electoral power, and the increase in the number of Israeli Arab voters, should have led to two conflicting political developments: the establishment of independent Israeli Arab national political frameworks that do not rely on existing parties, or the integration of representatives of the Israeli Arab community in key positions in existing national parties, in order to take advantage of internal party rivalries. Until the twelfth Knesset, developments tended to favor the latter direction, although the Israeli Arab population seemingly reached the conclusion that in order to play an influential political role on the national scene, they would have to unite and actualize their electoral potential within the framework of a united Arab list. Such a list – given the support of all the country's Arab voters – could have put 15 candidates in the seventeenth Knesset and become a political body with the power to influence the dynamics of national politics. This, however, did not happen; on the contrary, Israeli Arab votes were spread among most of the parties on the Israeli political spectrum. Again, it is hard to avoid the impression that substantial segments of the Israeli Arab voting public are driven not by ideology, but by pragmatism and social rifts, and it is these factors that motivated them to vote for those parties that made it worthwhile for their activists by giving them influence and/or jobs. These "jobs" include, for example, the post of regional school principal, or regional school supervisor, membership on boards of public and private companies and Ministry of the Interior planning committees, the Judiciary, the Treasury, parliamentary advisors on Arab affairs, etc.

In spite of splintering, the Israeli Arab political map has become larger. Today, most Israeli Arabs share a similar agenda *vis-à-vis* their status in the State of Israel and the Israeli–Palestinian conflict. At least on these issues the Israeli Arab political parties can reach a consensus and it is therefore possible to envision them forming a single large party, with the power to influence the political system in Israel.

Major changes took place in Israel's Arab population during three separate periods.

During most of the *first period*, from the first to the ninth Knesset elections, between 1949 and 1977, the Arabs lived under military rule and were forced to experience life as a national and ethnic minority. Throughout this period, the Arab community succeeded in actualizing only 86 percent of its electoral power. However, if we add the Israeli Arab Knesset members elected to the Knesset on non-sectarian national political parties to those elected on the list of the sectarian Israeli Arab political parties, we see that the Israeli Arab community did fully realize its electoral power. This discrepancy can be explained by the fact that during most of this period, the Mapai Party encouraged Israeli Arabs to vote for allied Arab lists, and considered them to be part of its potential voting reservoir. Mapai also made sure that any Arabs who made it to the Knesset on the Mapai list would sing to the Mapai tune. Voter participation among Israeli Arabs was very high during this period and stood at 81.5 percent, higher than the Jewish electorate. The end of this period saw the curtailment of the allied Arab lists and the path was open for new developments on the Israeli Arab political map.

The *second period*, from the tenth to the thirteenth Knesset elections, between 1981 and 1992, saw an increased political awareness, rising levels of education and increased standard of living, together with a growing Palestinian nationalist motif on the political identity of Israeli Arabs. Events such as the land expropriations in the Galilee and the events of March 30, 1976 (Land Day), and the establishment of several Israeli Arab country-wide political parties and extra-parliamentary movements, resulted in voter participation which dropped to around 70 percent, a drop of over 11 percent of the electoral potential of the Arab community in Israel. The allied Arab lists that depended on Mapai/Labor had vanished and the votes of Israeli Arab voters were divided among the Zionist and the Arab parties.[6]

Land Day had a direct effect on the fact that, notwithstanding the increased vote for Arab parties, there was no increase in the number of Arab MKs – because half of the candidates from the leading Arab parties (Hadash and the Progressive List for Peace) were Jews. The lists did not get enough Jewish votes, which meant that in fact the Jewish MKs got in on an Arab vote. Again, the Arabs did not realize their electoral power and placed only five of their representatives in the Knesset.

A new young leadership began to emerge: university graduates with a more radical worldview. At the very time when Israel's Arabs were becoming more politically aware, their realization of their electoral potential dropped to 44 percent. When this is molded to the number of Arab Knesset members elected during this period in the framework of national non-sectarian political parties, we see that electoral power actually stopped at almost 70 percent,[7] illustrating the extent of the Israeli Arabs' tendency to join nationwide, non-sectarian parties. It also combines with the fact that 13 Arab MKs were elected in the framework of these lists – in other words, 37 percent of all Israeli Arab MKs during this period were elected as part of Zionist lists.

The *third period*, which lasted between the fourteenth and the seventeenth Knesset elections (1996–2006), took place in the shadow of extreme and far-reaching events: the peace process with the Palestinians, the al-Aqsa *Intifada* and the riots of October 2000, the Second Lebanon War from 2006. Three election campaigns took place during this period, in which – unlike their forerunners – voters were required to cast two separate votes, one for the prime minister and one for a political party. The system was revoked after the sixteenth Knesset elections and voters were required to cast just one vote. These changes have had grave repercussions on the way Israelis – and Israeli Arabs in particular – vote, and it was during this period that the foundations of Arab civil society were reinforced at the expense of its ties with the Israeli political system. The exacerbations in the Israeli–Palestinian conflict following the breakdown in the Taba Talks,[8] coupled with the outbreak of the second *Intifada*, were instrumental in strengthening the Arab parties.

The Israeli-born Arabs who came of age and joined the voting register during this period appeared to have heightened political awareness. About half of them opted for integration, in the belief that this would increase their achievements in the Israeli political system; they were probably convinced that their political involvement in Israeli government does not necessary contradict their Palestinian national identity, even though the Palestinian issue remains unsettled. In a way, this political behavior challenged the Zionist parties and hinted that the rest of the process depended on the behavior of the Jewish majority.

From the thirteenth to the fifteenth Knessets there was an increased realization of Arab electoral power (from five seats in the thirteenth Knesset to 9 in the fourteenth Knesset, to 10 seats in the fifteenth Knesset). The main reason was the relatively large choice of political Arab nationalist parties. Nonetheless, the Arab voters realized only about 57 percent of their potential electoral power, and only if those Arab MKs elected in Zionist parties are added to the overall number of Arab MKs can it be said that the Israeli Arab community succeeded in actualizing most of their electoral power (86 percent). With the reinstating of the single-ballot voting system prior to the sixteenth Knesset elections, Israel's Arabs realized only 57 percent of their electoral power and the number of Arab MKs dropped, although the number of parties standing for election remained the same. The Arab voters appeared to sympathize most with the more extreme lists, which were threatened with disqualification, but were given permission to stand – almost at the last moment – by the Supreme Court.

Recent years have seen a growing tendency among Arab voters to boycott elections, for example during the sixteenth and seventeenth Knesset polls (2003 and 2006). This is a trend that will probably continue to gain momentum, as Arab voters become more and more aware of the fact that they are not equal partners in Israel's political system and are, in fact, often rejected by it. This fact is clearly illustrated in the actualization of Arab electoral power (figure 5.1).

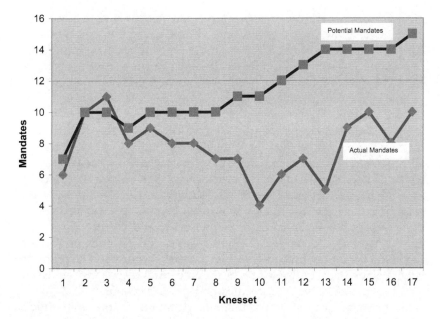

Figure 5.1 Arab Electoral Power and its Actualization in the Framework of Arab Lists, 1949–2006

In summary, it may be said that since the establishment of the state, the Arab sector has actualized nearly 69 percent of its potential electoral power via the Arab lists (allied parties and nationalist Arab parties). With the addition of those MKs elected from within Zionist lists, this number reaches 89 percent.

During the first two periods, Christian voters, with their traditional support of the Communist Party and its offshoots, managed to make full use of the ethnic rift in order to gain access to the Knesset, by co-operating with Mapai's methods for attracting voters. The Druze community began to take advantage of the ethnic rift during the second period, especially because of the part played by Zionist parties such as Likud, Labor and the "flash-in-the-pan" center-democratic party Dash, which arrived in the political arena in 1977, following several years of political corruption, in whose wake the Likud toppled Labor's 19-year tenure in the Knesset.

During the first period, when the allied Arab parties were dominant, the representation of the Christians in the Knesset was four times their actual electoral power. In this period the Druze representation in the Knesset was over twice as large their actual electoral power, and the Moslems were represented only by half of their actual electoral power.

In the second period, Christian representation in the Knesset was somewhat lower, but was still 1.3 times their actual electoral power. When the Zionist Likud Party came to power, the Druze increased their representation in the Knesset to 3.5 times their actual electoral power, while the Moslems still did not manage to actualize all their electoral power.

The ethnic rift was reflected increasingly in real electoral power during the third period. The Christian community was able to achieve twice as much as their real electoral power – a considerable drop as compared to the first period, but slightly more than the second period. Although the Christians and Druze realized more than their real electoral power, Israel's Moslems have never managed to realize theirs fully. Nonetheless, the rise in Moslem Arab representation in the Knesset came in the wake of the growing influence of the Islamic Movement and the new nationalist Arab parties that grew from it. Together, these restored the prominence of Israel's Moslems both in terms of population and in terms of Knesset representation. This process is on an upward trend that will probably continue; such a party, if voted for by the entire Arab electorate, could have won 15 Knesset seats in the seventeenth Knesset elections.

In their continued efforts to unite their community, the Arab leaders established political movements that tried to cross ethnic and clan rifts: *al-Ard*, for example, was formed in order to campaign for Knesset seats. When *al-Ard* was outlawed between the mid-1960s and early 1970s, the Jewish–Arab Communist faction (under its different names: Maki, Rakah or Hadash) did its best to override existing rifts.

Sheikh Abdallah Nimer Darwish, founder of the Islamic Movement, has often said that his ultimate objective is to unite all the political forces in the Israeli Arab community into a single Knesset list. Since neither Rakah nor the Islamic Movement has ever been considered legitimate partners by the Jewish establishment, they have not been able to exert any real influence on Israeli politics. In the eleventh Knesset (1984) the Communist Rakah Party and the Progressive List for Peace only provided a barrier against the possibility of the Likud Party's forming a narrow coalition of its own. On the other hand, these two Jewish–Arab parties were outside Jewish consensus and unable to ensure Labor the ability to establish such a coalition; thus they lost the chance to influence the political map. Still, without the support of Rakah and the Progressive List for Peace, the Labor Party would not have been able to get their candidate, Shlomo Hillel, elected to the position of Knesset chairman of the (1984) eleventh Knesset. In return for their support, the Arab MKs submitted a list of demands to the Labor Party leaders, one of which was fulfilled: Umm-al-Fahm was elevated from the status of local council to municipality.

It was the mass boycott by the Arab electorate which caused incumbent prime minister Ehud Barak to lose to his challenger Ariel Sharon on February 6, 2001. It was also the mass support of the Arab electorate (98 percent) which was instrumental in getting Barak elected in the first place (in the 1999 general election), giving him a comfortable majority and ousting Benjamin Netanyahu. Instead of using this support to settle issues that were of burning importance to the Arab community, perhaps even appointing an Arab minister to his cabinet, Barak chose not to do this and the Arabs were naturally insulted and frustrated.

Participating in, and Boycotting, Elections

According to political scientist Amal Jamal, the Arab population took part in Israel's political process not out of any symbolic or normative motives that would lend legitimacy to the various values represented by this system, but because they saw in the democratic process the only possible way to change the country's attitude toward its Arab public. Participating in the electoral process was a rational act not disconnected from the plethora of circumstantial forces influencing their lives. The nationalist Arab lists have never been included in any coalition, which make them feel that they do not have any influence on the government. This, in turn, also influences the Arab decision to boycott elections. Amal Jamal claims that the rise in voter participation in the 1996 and 1999 elections was due to the fact that voters realized that, under current conditions in Israel, this was their only possibility of achieving anything for their community.[9]

Generally, Israelis participate in elections on a larger scale than their counterparts in other Western democratic countries (78 percent, compared with 50 percent in the USA and Japan, for example). But as their political awareness rose, so did the Arabs' active participation in election campaigns fall. In the state's first general election campaigns, at a time when the Arab population had to adjust to minority status and – for the first time – democratic government, there was an average of 81.5 percent voter participation among the Arab population. It may have been that the Arabs believed that, by voting for the dominant political party, they would garner the favor of the government. Arab participation in elections was especially high during the 1950s and 1960s, when they were living under a military administration that had to carry out the national policies of the dominant Mapai Party, which had ways of drawing the support of the pragmatists among the Israeli Arabs and encouraging them to participate actively in Israel's political process. These circumstances led to a gradual acceptance of the status quo.

The 1977 ninth Knesset elections, which brought the Likud to power, saw a significant decline in voter participation among Israel's Arab community.[10] According to political scientist Asher Arian, it was during this period of rising Arab nationalism that the Israeli Arab voters found themselves confronting a sharp identity crisis, based on the demand of the Jewish majority for Arab support for the Jewish state. For the Israeli Arab community, a boycott of general elections not only provided a way of expressing its dissatisfaction with the political and social processes it had been forced to undergo since the rebirth of the Jewish state, but was also a manifestation of rising nationalist feelings. Arian writes, "Voter abstention in the Jewish as well as Arab sector appears to have different causes. The Israeli Jews' reasons for not voting are usually technical – illness, problems with the voters' list, mislaid I.D. card, indifference, etc. Among non-Jews the decision not to vote is almost always political."[11] Arian based his interpretation of Israeli Arab electoral behavior on a 1973 opinion poll in which half the non-Jewish Israeli participants declared that they would abstain from voting out of ideological reasons. Of the Israeli Jews who declared that they would abstain from voting, only one tenth quoted political reasons.

Increased voter abstention occurred parallel to the appearance of movements such as the Sons of the Village and its successor the Progressive Nationalist Movement, which called on the Israeli Arab public to boycott Knesset elections. According to these movements, voting for the Knesset was tantamount to legitimizing the Zionist state.[12] In an interview with the author in October 1989, Attorney Muhammad Kiwan, leader of the Sons of the Village, said, "Voting for any party, even Rakah, builds and reinforces the Zionist establishment and leaves no room for a nationalist Palestinian organization." Thus, pamphlets in Umm-al-Fahm in June 1981 informed the Arab public "that even the Rakah list [. . .] cannot and will not be able in the near future to change anything about the Zionist reality that affects our existence [. . .] it is clear to us all that the Knesset will not solve our everyday or national problems. [We are therefore obligated] to boycott Knesset elections [. . .] to develop and promote our own nationalism and Palestinian identity and escalate our public struggle."[13] Judging by voter participation during this period, these movements succeeded in influencing the Arab population in Israel, to a certain degree.

In the fourteenth (1996) and fifteenth (1999) Knesset elections, voter participation in the Arab sector rose to almost 75 percent. A possible reason for this is the realization on the part of Israel's Arabs that by establishing an independent political bloc, they could bring about some change in the country. However, the 2003 sixteenth Knesset elections saw a drastic drop in voting participation – due, among other things, to the events of October 2000. Abstention became an ideological issue, with only 59.34 percent of the Arab electorate going to the polls and 40 percent boycotting the elections; it was the lowest voter participation since the first Knesset in 1949. The trend was repeated during the seventeenth Knesset elections. In the Negev, Bedouin voting participation was only 46.5 percent – significantly lower than in the rest of the Arab sector and due to the fact that no solutions had yet been found for land claims, illegal towns and villages and the generally low standard of living among the Bedouin.

The change to a split-ballot voting system in 1996 contributed to a drastic increase in Arab support for the Arab parties. Although the Arab vote was now shared by a larger number of parties, these grew in strength at the expense of votes previously given to Zionist parties. Still, the Labor Party prime ministerial candidates won a landslide victory in the Arab sector: Shimon Peres in 1996, followed by Ehud Barak in 1999, both received some 91 percent of the Arab vote. With the reinstatement of single-ballot voting in the 2003 sixteenth Knesset elections, Labor received 7.8 percent of the Arab vote, and the other Zionist parties together received 20.2 percent, echoing almost exactly the elections for the 1999 fifteenth Knesset.

Ehud Barak based his entire election strategy on his own candidacy for the premiership, in the belief that he would be able to control the Knesset, even if Labor won a few more or a few less seats. The Labor Party was invisible in his election campaign until shortly before election day, when a few party slogans and messages began to appear. Yossi Beilin, who headed the party's election headquarters in the Arab and Druze sector, made sure the Arabs would vote for Ehud Barak, Labor's candidate for the premiership, while using their second ballot slip to express their support for the Arab parties of their choice. Moreover, Labor's Arab HQ made it possible for its Arab activists to campaign on behalf of Arab parties. Most of the Arab votes moved to the Arab parties and never returned. This could be the historic development in the voting trends of the Arab public in Israel.

This strategy, which was supported by Ehud Barak, weakened Labor's standing in the Arab sector and strengthened his own. In fact, Barak undermined almost irrevocably the political power a prime minister needs in order to oversee the Knesset, and gave the advantage to the Arab parties.

Since the state's establishment, Israel's Arab citizens have moved between the "Arab" approach, according to which rights would be achieved through surrender, and the "Western" approach, according to which rights must be demanded. The Arab approach contained little political awareness and a high voting participation, whereas the Western approach was rich in political awareness and supported a low voting participation. Supporters of both approaches eventually realized that a strong political awareness would not necessarily provide the Arab population with the rights it demanded and the result was a massive boycott of the elections to the sixteenth Knesset in 2003 and the seventeenth Knesset in 2006. Only time will tell if this is a permanent phenomenon or a one-off voting trend.

Gradually, disappointment led to the realization that Israeli Arabs have nothing to gain from participation in the Knesset elections. As an alternative, Arab community leaders proposed establishing their own representative institutions and even a separate parliament within their sector. As'ad Ghanem wrote in *Ha'aretz* on February 12, 2001 that if enough voters were to abstain from voting, there would be a possibility of "the election of an Arab-Palestinian political body [as] an alternative national leadership for Palestinians in Israel". The reference here is to the autonomy granted to the Jews under the British Mandate.[14] Elsewhere in the world, the kind of autonomy proposed by Ghanem and Azmi Bishara is almost non-existent. In the Iberian Peninsula, for example, the Basques are demanding an independent republic encompassing all the Basque provinces, including those in France, and are prepared to secede from Spain, the country in which most of the Basques live.[15]

The approach of the sixteenth Knesset elections saw a significant rise in community activity on behalf of an election boycott. The Islamic Movement's northern branch argued that it was inconceivable for Moslems to participate in the election of a governing body that takes its legitimacy from Jewish sovereignty. Sheikh Ra'ed Salah led a public campaign on behalf of an election boycott, refraining from doing so only in Umm-al-Fahm, thus providing silent support to the candidacy of Hashem Mahamid.[16] The Sons of the Village movement wanted to take advantage of the awakening nationalism in order to "convene an Arab parliament that will organize our masses [. . .], determine [our] relationship with the Israeli establishment, and serve as a tool in preventing our masses from being drawn into a shallow and superficial struggle within the Knesset framework."[17] Toward the sixteenth Knesset elections, the Sons of the Village established the Committee for Boycotting the Elections and conducted an election-like campaign to promote their idea: to create a situation in which Israeli Arab Knesset members will be elected by less than 50 percent of the Israeli Arab electorate, thus making it possible to challenge their legitimacy to represent the Israeli Arab community.[18]

It appears therefore that abstention and participation in elections have turned into political-ideological strategies in their own right, and that the election boycott movement gained momentum within the Israeli Arab community. This author believes that most of the election boycotters were potential voters for Arab nationalist political parties.

There appears today (2008) to be a political chasm separating the Arab and Jewish publics. The Zionist parties have lost their former support among the Arab community, yet they still receive 28 percent of the Arab votes. This vote is an expression of personal, clan and institutional connections, or the pragmatic vote of those who still believe in the ideal of co-existence. This author estimates that this voting trend will continue in the future. The Likud Party has decided to focus on the Druze community; Labor continues with its traditional ties and is trying to bring back its former supporters, but appears to be making little headway, and only by fully integrating the Israeli Arabs as equal partners in the political system can any real change be achieved in their voting trends and choice of party.

Distribution of Votes in the Israeli Arab Population

Since the first general elections in 1949, the Israeli Arab sector has always given a measure of support to various Zionist parties from all over the Israeli political spectrum. At least until the thirteenth Knesset, Arab political parties, especially the Arab Democratic Party (Mada) and the Communist Party in its various forms (Maki, Rakah, Hadash), have sought a way into the core of the Israeli political map and to be included in government coalitions. The Arab Democratic Party was very explicit on this. But the Arab parties never succeeded in attracting all the Arab votes. Feelings of alienation and frustration among the Israeli Arab public found expression only in the period following the 1996 general elections; the change to a two-ballot system (one vote for the party and another for the prime minister) intensified this trend and led to a drastic drop in votes for Zionist parties and the establishment of new Arab parties.

The increasingly central role played by Arab parties in the Israeli political arena was accompanied by the slow decline of the Zionist parties – especially Labor – in the Arab sector. The Arab vote for Zionist parties remained stable until the elections for the sixth Knesset in 1965 and approached an average of 30 percent. At that time, votes for Mapai's allied Arab lists reached an average of 52 percent, but that number has dropped gradually ever since; the downward trend was already becoming obvious in the elections for the fifth Knesset in 1961 and gathered momentum in the eighth Knesset elections in 1973. The allied lists disappeared from the political map during the 1984 (eleventh Knesset) elections.

Until its rise to power in 1977, the Likud made no real overtures to the Arab community and any efforts it did make were low key. In contrast with other groups in the Arab population, however, the Likud has traditionally enjoyed considerable support among the Druze community. Since the sixteenth Knesset elections in 2003, the Likud has intensified its efforts in the Arab sector and established party branches in Daburiya, Sakhnin, Tireh and other villages. The Likud leaders believe they can obtain a larger portion of the Arab vote following former prime minister Ariel Sharon's Gaza disengagement plan.[19]

In the fifteenth Knesset elections in 1999, the Arab vote was split among three Arab parties and the Zionist parties. The Arab parties consisted of the Communist Hadash Party and Darawsha's Arab Democratic Party, which, together with the southern branch of the Islamic Movement, formed a joint list under the name United Arab List (Hebrew acronym: Ra'am) and the National Democratic Pact (Hebrew acronym: Balad). Together the three garnered 69 percent of the Arab vote. The Zionist parties won about 31 percent of the Arab vote. The sixteenth Knesset saw an even more pronounced split in the Arabs' electoral base. Ahmad Tibi and his Arab Movement for Renewal (Ta'al) list joined Hadash, which for

the first time did not feature a Jewish candidate. For Hadash this constituted a profound violation of its principles and was testimony to the
reduced importance of the Jewish vote and the party's Communist
ideology.

The National Democratic Pact (Balad) competed on its own for the
first time in the sixteenth Knesset elections (2003) and won almost 20
percent of the Arab vote and three Knesset seats, the greatest achievement in the state's history for an Arab party. The United Arab Party
(Ra'am) remained in a joint list with the Islamic Movement and the Arab
Democratic Party (Mada), but dropped to only 18 percent of the Arab
vote and two Knesset seats, three fewer than in the fifteenth Knesset. This
drop in the party's support is due to the resignation of several key members. Tawfiq Khatib left the Islamic Movement and established the
al-Islah Party, before transferring his support to the Zionist Meretz[20]
Party. Muhammad Kan'an established the Arab National Party, but did
not compete in elections. Hashem Mahamid, who established the
Progressive National Pact (Hebrew acronym: Balam), did not win sufficient votes to cross the election threshold. These splits, together with a
high level of voting abstention, brought the number of Arab MKs representing Arab parties in the sixteenth Knesset down to eight, as compared
with ten in the tenth Knesset (1999). Two Druze representatives were
elected on the Likud ticket, but Labor, the party that had always reserved
slots for representatives of minority communities, did not manage to
place even one. Meretz too did not succeed in electing an Arab representative and, in the final reckoning, the Arabs realized only 57 percent of
their electoral power, which has the potential to secure 15 Knesset seats
in 2008.

Thus, the voting behavior of Israel's Arabs has undergone significant
changes since the fourteenth Knesset elections in 1996. This is expressed
mainly in an obvious tendency to vote for Israeli Arab nationalist parties,
even if this means relinquishing active involvement in Israeli politics. Those
opting for Arab nationalist parties are fully aware that their candidates
would not be partners in government coalitions and would, therefore, not
participate in decision-making forums. The desire of the voters, however,
was to demonstrate electoral separatism; this in turn caused ideological
changes within the political leadership of Israel's Arabs.

Ideological and Pragmatic Considerations
in Choosing a Party

In choosing a specific political party for which to opt, the Arab voter is
faced with a varied and complex list of considerations. According to Asher
Arian, most voters are motivated by ideological factors. Others believe the

subtle differences in emphasis and image between the various parties in Israel are of cardinal importance.[21] Even if they are reluctant to admit it, it would appear that a voter's choice is influenced largely by the candidate's personality and whether that candidate represents a party in government or opposition.[22]

It has been assumed in the past that ideological considerations were not a major factor in the voting behavior of Israel's Arab electorate. According to Gabriel Ben Dor, the issue of identity (belonging) arose and became an important element in the voting considerations of Israel's Arabs after the 1967 Six Day War. Some Arabs accepted the reality of Israel, came to terms with it, considered the state to be legitimate and adopted a sober view of reality in their search for solutions to their problems. Others' concerns with their identity were based mainly on renewed ties with the Palestinians.[23] Arabs whose vote for a Zionist party appeared to conflict with their national Palestinian aspirations were almost always swayed by practical considerations and the fact that they were part of a community. This would explain the thousands of Arab votes for the National Religious Party (NRP) and the ultra-Orthodox Sephardic Shas Party, both of which controlled the Ministries of the Interior and Religious Affairs for many years.

Considerations underlying the voting of Israeli Arabs are therefore complicated and it is difficult to differentiate between the various motives merely on the basis of a statistical analysis of election results. It is obvious, however, that permanent electoral dispersal of votes in the Arab community has encouraged the Zionist parties to compete over the support of this public. During the eleventh Knesset election campaign, Zionist parties seeking Arab support stressed that at the top of their agenda stood a fervent desire for equal rights of all minority populations.[24] It is for this reason that it was only in 1988 that Arab nationalist parties succeeded for the first time in winning 58 percent of the Israeli Arab vote.

In order to understand the above process, one should investigate two sets of considerations that the Arabs utilized when selecting a party.

Nationalist/Ideological Considerations

On the one hand, there is a need to emphasize Palestinian identity, and to promote it among the Israeli Arabs; on the other hand, there is the Arabs' demand for a Palestinian state alongside Israel and an identity that is separate from the Palestinian Arabs. In spite of the aforementioned considerations, until the mid-1980s many Arabs voted for Zionist parties. By voting for a Zionist party, the Arabs were accepting the state and expressing their belief in co-existence between Jews and Arabs, but it was mostly a case of no choice, because there were no Arab parties to vote for.[25] Israel's Arab population was also exposed to political currents in mainstream Jewish society, but it is difficult to examine to what degree this influenced Israeli Arab electoral choices. Nonetheless, the discrepancy between the numbers of votes received over the years by Mapai/Alignment/ Labor and those cast for Herut/Gahal/Likud indicates that Israeli Arab voters preferred the social, economic and political platform of Labor to that of Likud and demonstrated a blend of pragmatic and ideological considerations in choosing their candidates.

Israel's Arabs did not establish political parties or organizations with the intention of furthering social and economic issues relevant to their society. The new Arab parties aimed to enable voters to realize their nationalistic considerations. For many years, Rakah had been the only party associated with any kind of "big ideology" – in this case, Communist ideology. Most of its supporters, however, did not give their vote to this party out of any Communist sympathies, but because of its position on the Palestinian-nationalist issue.

In the early 1980s, the Islamic Movement, whose "big ideology" was Islam, joined the ideological club. Here, too, it soon became apparent that Islamic ideology was greater than the national territory and the Islamic Movement revealed itself as just another sectarian party. The Islamic Movement did not see itself competing for parliamentary seats and soon joined the Arab Democratic Party, an Islamic party established by Abd al-Wahab Darawsha; together they established the United Arab Party (Hebrew acronym: Ra'am). At the head of the United Arab Party's agenda stood social and educational issues, and the party favored a solution that would include the establishment of a Palestinian state alongside the State of Israel. The Islamic Movement's ideology shrank until its main focus was the defense of Islamic holy sites and its supporters acted mainly out of nationalist-ethnic motives. In the end, the United Arab Party – Ra'am – adopted the stance of a religious Moslem party.

With the nationalist issue at the center of the public discourse, the Arab Nationalist parties, including the Islamic Movement, devoted much of their time to the Palestinian-nationalist issue and to the civil and national status of the Arab citizens of Israel, rather than to internal social and economic issues in the Arab sector, such as social-political rifts and the sector's economic situation. The marginality of these issues in the nation-alist Arab parties' political platforms was probably the result of a lack of an independent economic infrastructure in the Arab sector and the Arabs' vision of themselves as connected to the Israeli economy. It is for this reason, too, that no social or economic lobbies ever sprang from within the Arab sector, similar to those in the Jewish sector.[26] The economic problems of Israel's Arabs resemble those of the development towns in the Jewish sector,[27] and most of the Arab parties' efforts were directed at civil rights issues in Israel and at raising the Arabs' status to equal that of the Jews.

The electoral considerations of the Israeli Arabs, therefore, touched on their enduring need to define their attitude to the state and their connection with the Palestinian people. However, in order to turn these nationalist-ideological aspirations into reality, it was necessary to connect with the economic and social aspects of the Arab experience in Israel. Thus the mundane demands and claims of the Israeli Arab public, which encompass such issues as land appropriation, infrastructure, basic services and equal employment opportunities, were expressed in nationalist terms as inequality and discrimination. The Israeli Arabs preferred to wage their struggle via extra-parliamentary organizations rather than through the Arab parties and their elected Knesset members. Only in the late 1990s did the influence of the Arab parties grow and the Arab Knesset members become outspoken in the struggle for equal rights. On this background, it is possible to see both voting for Arab nationalist parties and abstaining from voting as an ideological stance.

Pragmatic Considerations

Arabs who voted for Zionist parties did so mainly out of pragmatic considerations. This author has no statistics to determine how many Arab voters for Zionist parties saw in their vote an ideological expression of their belonging to the Israeli collective, but it is his belief that a very few of these voters saw it as such. A vote for a Zionist party by an Israeli Arab is a clear indication of the existence of social rifts and the need to improve clan status and strengthen relations with the establishment. Moreover, Arabs continued to vote for Zionist parties in order to find favor with the military government, even after the military government was abolished, in order to improve the situation of their village, clan or ethnic group. Their reward consisted of employment and/or various licenses and permits.[28]

In a roundabout way, pragmatism was also tempered by ideology: the leaders of the allied lists were convinced that they were the only ones capable of improving the lot of the Arabs in Israel, and the best way to do this was by co-operating with the establishment. Researcher of Arab society Yitzhak Reiter defined this group as the "moderate camp", for adopting the concept of "real politick" and playing according to the rules of the game set out by the majority.[29]

The abolishment of the military rule in 1966, the rise in education, the changes in employment patterns and the standard of living of the Arab population, as well as the weakening of the social frameworks, brought about a reduction in the pragmatic-personal consideration of the voter. Since the 1970s one can see an increase in the weight of the ideological consideration, out of a wish to influence the Israeli establishment to better the conditions of the Arab minority as a whole. But one should not conclude that there is a direct relation between the passage to ideological consideration and the rise in voting for Arab nationalist parties. Indeed, in some of the "ideological" voters, political awareness has increased in parallel to the wish to take part in the political life in Israel and this was expressed in an enlarged support for the Zionist parties.

It would appear that for many years Israel's Arabs continued to be divided between two sets of considerations – ideological and pragmatic, while each of the sets motivated parts of the voting public to vote for certain party blocs. There has been a clear tendency since the mid-1990s to focus on the ideological considerations, and it is these that today dictate the voting patterns of most of the country's Arab electorate. The reasons for this include the Israeli–Palestinian peace process and changes that took place in the voting system. Since the prime ministerial election campaign focused mainly on the peace process, the Arab parties were able to concentrate on issues that were of particular interest to the population they represented. The dissonance between ideological nationalism and pragmatism was expressed in the divisions within the Arab public as reflected in the choice of their representatives in the Knesset. Although voting trends in the sixteenth Knesset (2003) and seventeenth Knesset (2006) showed no change with regard to the divisions among the Arab parties, there remained the traditional split into three almost equal-sized political camps within the Arab sector that expressed the dilemma involved in choosing between the various options: supporters of Zionist parties (28 percent) – pragmatic vote; supporters of the Communist-secular and Jewish–Arab stream (26.7 percent) – mixed traditional-tribal-ideological vote; supporters of the Arab nationalist radical stream (19.8 percent) – ideological vote; supporters of the Islamic stream (18 percent) – ideological vote. The National Democratic Pact (Balad) MK, Dr Jamal Zahalqa, divides the Arab public into three ideological streams: the left – Rakah voters; the nationalist – Balad voters; and the religious-Islamic – the United Arab Party voters. Zahalqa disregards the Zionist parties, although Meretz could certainly be counted among the left.[30]

The two edges that established themselves on the Arab political map consist of the Islamic stream, which grew in strength since the fourteenth Knesset elections, and the nationalist stream. Until he left Israel under a cloud of suspicion in April 2007,[31] Azmi Bishara took center stage in the latter political stream. Bishara became a part of mainstream Arab politics and succeeded in garnering support for his political ideology from among those who voted for other parties. He also managed to create a dynamic of competition among politicians for the attractive slot in Israeli-Arab politics which promises the voter a struggle for equal rights as well as – so far as this is possible – a struggle to change the very definition of Israel as the sovereign state of the Jewish people to one of a "state for all its citizens". This has become a slogan on the lips of anyone interested in entering political life and, eventually, in running for Knesset at the head of a political body or as part of one of the existing blocs. But let there be no mistake, the two edges – the Islamic and the nationalist – are equally radical and united over the status of the Arab citizens in Israel and a solution for the Israeli–Palestinian conflict.

Whether directly or indirectly, all the Israeli Arab parties have challenged the Jewish character of the State of Israel, and the demand to change its definition into a "state of all of its citizens" is no longer merely an intellectual discussion but a major principle of their political platform. The increased strength of right-wing politics among the Jewish majority and the state's obvious Jewishness may even have boosted this tendency. Thus, for example, in the fifteenth Knesset (1999) Azmi Bishara proposed abolishing the Jewish National Fund and other Zionist institutions, while Ahmad Tibi called for changes in the citizenship law to make it easier for any relatives of Israeli Arabs who have lived out of the country since 1948 to enter Israel.[32] Since the vote for Arab parties is constantly on the rise, it is safe to say that ideological considerations override the pragmatic.

The 1996 election campaign provided the Israeli Arabs with new options for nationalist ideological voting, but surprisingly brought about a greater distribution of the vote. Admittedly, support for the joint Hadash-Balad list increased to 37 percent, as compared with the 23 percent Hadash received in 1992. But by the fifteenth Knesset (1999) elections, Azmi Bishara left to establish a new list with Ahmad Tibi's Arab Movement for Renewal (Ta'al), a split that caused support for Hadash to drop to 22 percent in the 1999 elections.

A new Arab list was established for the 1996 elections under the acronym Ra'am (the United Arab Party), an alignment of the Arab Democratic Party (Mada), the Islamic Movement and Hashem Mahamid's one-man faction. This list won five Knesset seats, due, among other reasons, to the changed voting system. In the 1999 elections the United Arab Party (Ra'am) won 25 percent of the overall vote and 31 percent of the Arab vote. But the alignment did not last long and, when prime minister Ehud Barak stepped down in November 2000, Muhammad Kan'an of the Arab Democratic Party (Mada) and Tawfiq Khatib from the Islamic Movement left to form separate lists.

The pragmatic vote has not yet disappeared completely and is expressed mainly in votes for religious Zionist parties, whose members and cabinet ministers traditionally hold positions that allow them to reward Arab voters with jobs and budgets; thus the Arab support for the ultra-Orthodox Sephardic Shas Party in the 1999 elections. Shas MK David Azulai, who headed his party's Arab election headquarters, saw in the Arab sector an important enough challenge to appoint a senior party official to oversee election activity there. Shas, which for years was entrusted with the Ministry of the Interior, established strongholds in each Arab town and village and rewarded the voters with government budgets and political appointments. In several Knesset elections Shas garnered more than 10,000 votes from the Israeli Arab sector; of course this was a pragmatic vote.

In Kafar Manda, for example, Shas won 27 percent of the votes, more than any one of the Arab parties, due to its association with the Taha clan. There is a long-standing feud between the Taha and Zaydan clans over the post of council head. In supporting Shas, the Taha clan hoped that the Ministry of the Interior would help oust Muhammad Zaydan as chairman of the local council and replace him with a member of the Taha clan.[33] The pragmatic vote has become part of an ideology and the considerations that have entered the voting process are connected with the voters' affiliation to one or another – mainly clan related – social rift.

Election results for the sixteenth Knesset reveal that the critical relations between Jews and Arabs did not cause a significant decline in support for Zionist parties in the Arab sector, although a certain change took place in the way a party was chosen. The United Arab Party (Ra'am), for example, dropped from five Knesset seats to two. But this does not indicate a lack of confidence in the Islamic Movement, the main component in the Ra'am alignment, but rather the result of a call on the part of the northern branch

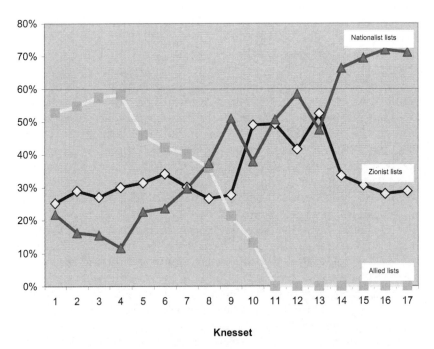

Knesset

Figure 5.2 Division of Voting among the Three Blocs, 1949–2006, in Percentages (excluding mixed settlements)

of the Islamic Movement to boycott the elections. In parallel, the National Democratic Pact (Balad) increased its parliamentary strength from one seat to three, which testifies to the growing alienation of the Israeli Arabs from the Zionist political system and establishment. This author believes that it is incumbent on the state authorities and Jewish public to pay attention to this phenomenon.

The Israeli Arab voter is, therefore, divided by two sets of considerations, the ideological one and the pragmatic/rift one. In the last three election campaigns the tendency was toward the nationalistic-ideological set of considerations. It also seems that the tendency to translate practical problems into terms of inequality and discrimination turned pragmatism into an ideology. The Zionist parties continued to receive part of the Arab votes, while the increased number of Arab nationalist parties has increased the dispersal of votes, as the Arab nationalist parties tried to gather votes from defined rifts in Israeli Arab society.

The phenomena of split votes is a testimony of the political distress of the Arabs in Israel, which stems from a leadership crisis as a result of dissatisfaction at the performance of the Arab MKs in the thirteenth Knesset, as well as a lack of charismatic leaders. In addition, the Arab nationalist parties did next to nothing to improve the interests of the Arab sector.

The Israeli Arab politicians understood that the split phenomenon harms their ability to influence the Israeli political scene and tried to overcome it by creating a common political framework toward the elections to the fourteenth Knesset, but they failed. The failure was a result of fundamental ideological differences between the Communist Party and the Islamic parties, as well as personal disagreements on slots given to one candidate or another and the different traditional rifts in Arab society.

It seems that the Israeli Arab community is politically pluralistic like other groups in Israeli society. If Israeli law-makers will increase voter threshold to two percent or more, the Arab politicians will be forced to compromise and unite, otherwise the Arab sector will not be proportionally represented in the Knesset. On the other hand, if the Arab nationalist parties do unite, the competition between them will decrease and so will the percentage of Arab voters.

Political Trends within the Rifts in Israeli Arab Society

In order to pinpoint specific trends and directions in the political behavior of Israel's Arab citizens between 1949 and 2006, this section provides a statistical and quantitative analysis of voting patterns within the sector. The question was whether a transfer of votes existed from the allied Arab lists to the Zionist parties, or vice versa, and its extent. The analysis was done according to a statistical technique called linear regression equation.[34]

Israel's Arab population is divided into nine main groups, characterized as social rifts. Each rift is analyzed according to three different periods, in order to examine whether there was a variation in voting patterns in each group and if a collective political behavior can be discerned within the group.

These groups are:

1) Galilee Arabs (Muslims)
2) Triangle Arabs (Muslims)
3) Druze
4) Galilee Bedouin
5) Negev Bedouin
6) Christians
7) Circassians
8) Arabs in mixed settlements
9) Arab voters in outlying settlements

Arab Voters in the Galilee

By early 2006, Galilee Arabs made up more than 60 percent of the Israeli Arab voting register (with the exception of Arabs living in mixed Jewish/Arab towns and villages). The Galilee Arab population comprised approximately 40 towns and villages, including Nazareth, Shefar'am, Tamra and Sakhnin. Many of these places are home to Moslems (usually the majority), Christians and Druze. Voting participation is usually higher among the Galilee Arabs than among those elsewhere in Israel – possibly because the Galilee is home to most of the country's political leaders. The Galilee Arab population is motivated to greater political involvement and is aware of its demographic importance in the region; this is apparently the reason why most of the Arab political organizations began in the Galilee region (with the exception of the Islamic Movement and the Sons of the Village movement, which started up in the Triangle).

During the first period (until the ninth Knesset), the average voting percentage of the Galilee Arabs was way above the national average, at 83 percent. This period also showed increased support for the Communist Rakah Party, reaching an average of 32 percent. And this result took place notwithstanding the pan-Arab Naserite movement, which at the time was drawing the masses in other Arab countries to the charismatic personality of Egyptian president Jamal Abd al-Naser.[35]

During the period between the tenth and thirteenth Knessets, voting participation of Galilee's Arabs dropped to 74 percent. Throughout this period the population was often called upon to abstain from voting and to boycott general elections. These calls were exacerbated by outside influences such as the increased influence of the PLO on the international

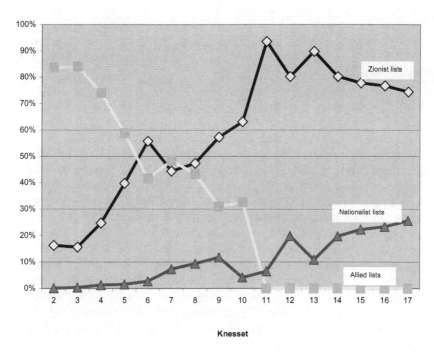

Figure 5.3   Voting Distribution among Galilee Arabs, 1949–2006, in Percentages (excluding mixed settlements)

scene, the 1973 Yom-Kippur War, the dramatic political change that brought the Likud to power in 1977, the Land Day events in reaction to land expropriation, the 1982 Lebanon War, the massacre of Moslems by the Christian militia in the Sabra and Shatila refugee camps in Beirut[36] (Israel's Arabs blamed the State of Israel), and the first Palestinian civil uprising (the *Intifada* of 1987–93). Support for Arab nationalist parties became stronger during this period and reached an average of 59 percent. The Arab allied lists disappeared completely and most of their votes went to the Arab nationalist parties. Some Galilee Arabs voted for the Zionist parties and support for these rose to an average of 37 percent. Moreover, many Israeli Arabs hoped to participate in the national decision-making process and voted for Zionist political parties, whose objectives were to influence coalition negotiations and topple the Likud from power.

During the fourteenth and fifteenth Knesset elections the voting average rose to 78 percent as a result of the new election split-vote system. Voting with two ballots made it possible for voters to enjoy maneuverability and gave them a greater opportunity to advance sectarian interests. The support rate for Zionist parties during this period reached 23 percent, meaning that Arab support for Zionist parties in the Galilee now resembled their support for those parties in the first period. In fact, the Arab

political parties now succeeded in attracting votes previously given to the
Allied lists and even votes given previously to the Zionist parties. The statistical analysis reveals that the shift of most votes was from Allied lists to the
newly formed Arab nationalist parties.

In the sixteenth and seventeenth Knessets (2003 and 2006), voting
participation reached an all-time low of 56 percent. It would seem that the
massive vote boycott during the 2001 special elections for prime minister
had left its mark on the Israeli Arab electorate. The decreased vote was also
fueled by the crisis with the Jewish establishment in the wake of the violent
events of October 2000 and the large number of Arab victims of violent
clashes with the police.

The support rate for the Zionist parties was also amongst the lowest ever
recorded and reached 19 percent. This result was, among others, an
expression of the disillusionment of those Israeli Arab citizens who
supported Zionist parties for practical and even for ideological reasons,
believing that they could influence and reinforce co-existence between
Jews and Arabs. Support for Zionist parties will probably continue to
decline. In the seventeenth Knesset a new Zionist list, Kadima
("Forward"), was formed by former prime minister Ariel Sharon. Under
the current leadership of prime minister Ehud Olmert, Kadima received
only about 4 percent of the Arab vote in the Galilee.

Arab Votes in the Triangle Area

The Triangle population makes up about 25 percent of all eligible voters
in the Arab sector (not including the mixed-population towns and villages).
The entire population of the Triangle is Moslem and concentrated in about
30 large and small villages or towns. The level of voting participation
amongst these Israeli Arabs has always been high, although there have been
many changes over the years.

Until the ninth Knesset (1977), support for Israeli Arab parties stood
at 27 percent on average, probably due to an almost complete lack of representation from the Triangle. Most Arab voters opted for allied Arab lists –
about 42 percent on average, over the entire period and most of the representatives, who were also clan heads, hailed from the larger towns in the
Triangle.

Between the tenth Knesset (1981) and the thirteenth Knesset (1992)
there was a sharp decrease in election participation. This was probably due
to the rise of radical movements such as the Sons of the Village (*Abnaa al-
Balad*) and the Islamic Movement, which called for an election boycott.
The support for Arab nationalist parties in this period increased significantly to about 55 percent, although this was still lower than in the Galilee,
probably because the new Progressive List for Peace did not present a
representative from the Triangle in a prominent slot. The share of the

Zionist parties in the Triangle during this period increased to about 44 percent, compared with only 37 percent in the Galilee. As a result of the split-vote system introduced in the fourteenth and fifteenth Knessets, voting participation rose to an average of 74 percent, notwithstanding the Islamic Movement's call for an election boycott. Support for nationalist Arab parties reached 77 percent, more than in any other part of the Arab sector, probably as a result of the establishment of the United Arab Party before the fifteenth Knesset (1999) elections. In Kafar Qasem, home of Abdallah Nimer Darwish, head of the Islamic Movement's southern faction, which did not join the call for a boycott, the United Arab Party received 51 percent of the votes in the Triangle. There was a sharp drop (to 23 percent) in support for Zionist parties.

Only 54 percent of the Arab electorate participated in the sixteenth and seventeenth Knesset elections, probably because of calls by the northern section of the Islamic Movement and the Sons of the Village for a boycott. Hashem Mahamid was an exception. A resident of Umm-al-Fahm, Mahamid headed an independent Arab nationalist list which won 16 percent of votes in the Triangle, mainly from Umm-al-Fahm. Without this list, voting participation would most probably have been even lower.

Support for the Zionist parties remained nearly stable, about 19 percent compared with 21 percent in elections for the fifteenth Knesset (1999). I believe this percentage was maintained because of support for Amir Peretz's One Nation list, which received 4 percent of its support from the Triangle. By including Nawwaf Masalha (a former Labor MK and resident of the Triangle) in a prominent place on his One Nation list, Amir Peretz secured some of this outcome. Meretz and Labor placed two Triangle residents on their political lists and together received more than 13 percent of the region's votes.

The Communist Hadash Party continued to lead in the sixteenth Knesset elections and garnered 25 percent of the votes. The surprise result of this election campaign was the success of the National Democratic Pact under the leadership of Azmi Bishara, a Galilee Christian. His list won 23 percent of votes; the reason for this might be the fact that Jamal Zahalqa, a Moslem from the Triangle, was placed in the second slot. Under the leadership of Abdallah Nimer Darwish – also a resident of the Triangle – the Islamic Movement won only third place and 16 percent of the votes. It would appear that the boycott called by the Movement's northern section was proving effective. In the seventeenth Knesset the Islamic Movement, under the leadership of Ibrahim Sarsur from the Triangle and under the auspices of the United Arab Party, doubled its support and achieved one third of the votes, and the Communist Rakah Party won only 24 percent of the vote in the Triangle. The New Zionist party Kadima ("Forward"), which won the general elections, received less than 3 percent of the vote in this region.

The shift of votes in the Triangle shows a reverse tendency from that of the Galilee. In the second period, 60 percent of the votes formerly cast for the allied Arab lists moved to the Zionist parties and only about 40 percent to the nationalist Arab parties. The differences in the shift of votes between the Triangle and Galilee communities are based on the culturally diverse populations in the Triangle, which is mostly a village society and therefore more conservative.

Voting patterns in the Triangle appear to be more traditional than those in the Galilee. Until the twelfth Knesset, representatives came only from Labor's allied Arab lists. The clan structure and solidarity in the Triangle is stronger than that of the Galilee and therefore local candidates succeeded in attracting voters to their parties. In the sixteenth Knesset, for example, Triangle residents Jamal Zahalqa received 49 percent of the vote, Hashem Mahamid 63 percent of the votes and Ahmad Tibi 39 percent of the vote. Moreover, Ra'ed Salah, leader of the northern section of the Islamic Movement, did not call for a boycott of Hashem Mahamid in his hometown of Umm-al-Farm. Support for Zionist parties in the Triangle is gradually declining and it can be assumed that it will fall below 20 percent in the next elections.

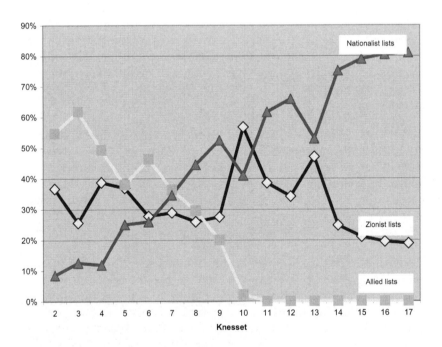

Figure 5.4 Voting Distribution in the Triangle, 1951–2006, in Percentages (excluding mixed settlements)

It seems, therefore, that voting patterns in the Triangle are becoming similar to those in the Galilee, in that the Moslems of the Triangle will vote in a similar way to that of Israel's entire Moslem sector. Previously the Triangle was not as dominant as the Galilee in its representation within the framework of the existing parties and political organizations.

The Druze Vote

Some 117,500 Arabic-speakers living in 20 villages in northern Israel constitute a separate cultural, social and religious community. While the Druze religion is not accessible to outsiders, one known aspect of its philosophy is the concept which calls for complete loyalty by its adherents to the government of the country in which they reside.

Some of the villages in which the Druze live, such as Shefar'am, Isifya and Rame, have mixed populations. Others, such as Beit Jann, Julis, Daliyat al-Carmel, Hurfesh, and Yarka are populated almost exclusively by Druze. Any reference to voting trends in the Druze population concerns only those villages populated almost exclusively by Druze.

The Druze voters tend to be more politically aware than other ethnic groups in the country's Arab community. At the ninth Knesset elections, which showed a significant decrease in voting participation among the other groups, the turnout among the Druze was high and resembled that of the Jewish population. It is noteworthy that at the first Knesset elections, Druze voting participation was even higher than that among the Jewish population and reached an average of 84 percent. Druze support for Arab nationalist parties has always been relatively low, at only 4 percent. However, with the establishment of the Druze Initiative Committee, as a front for Rakah, demanding that Druze youngsters be exempt from compulsory military service in the Israel Defense Forces, there was a slight reduction in subsequent voting participation and a slight rise in support for Arab nationalist parties.

Amongst the Druze the drop in support for allied Arab lists is more noticeable than in the other ethnic groups that constitute Israel's Arab community. Until the eighth Knesset, Druze MKs were elected on allied Arab lists. Sheikh Jaber Mu'adi served in a total of six Knesset assemblies, from the second to the eighth. In the ninth Knesset, he served only part of the term. His allied Arab list was led for most of the time by Seif al-Din al-Zu'bi, a Moslem from Nazareth.

Other Druze lists were also considered allied Arab lists, such as that headed by Saleh Khneifes from Shefar'am, who served in the second and third Knessets, and Labib Abu Ruqun from Isifya, who served in the fourth Knesset. The fact that no change has taken place in the Druze leadership for many years might be the reason for the decline in support for allied Arab lists. Moreover, starting with the eighth Knesset, Druze representatives were given realistic slots on the Dash, Likud and Labor Party lists. Thus, for example, Amal Nasr al-Din was elected on the Likud list to the eighth Knesset, while Shafiq As'ad of Beit Jann and Zaidan Atshi of Isifya were elected to the ninth Knesset on the liberal Dash list. These developments greatly weakened Druze support for the allied Arab lists. The vote shift in the Druze community was towards Zionist parties, which were supported for the entire first period at an average of 38 percent, while at the second Knesset, support for Zionist political parties among the Druze reached only 16 percent.

Rakah Communists tried to infiltrate the Druze sector by handing out grants to students studying in universities in the Eastern Bloc countries. Until 1988, 14 students from the village of Rame were able to study overseas because of these grants. Altogether, 60 Druze students obtained a higher education in Eastern Europe with Rakah financing.[37] Rakah's success amongst the Druze was manifested in parliamentary representation. In elections for the twelfth Knesset, Muhammad Naffa' of Beit Jann was elected to the Knesset on the Rakah ticket. At the end of the second period, support for Arab nationalist parties grew among voters in the Druze community, among other reasons, because of violent confrontations with the police in July 1987 due to land expropriation for the nature reserve surrounding Beit Jann, and because of Muhammad Naffa's slot on the Hadash list prior to elections for the twelfth Knesset.[38]

The third period saw a further decline in voting participation among the Druze electorate, which reached 75 percent. At the same time, there was growing support for the Arab nationalist parties, reaching an average of 21 percent and a less significant support for Zionist parties – 79 percent over the entire period.

In the 2003 and 2006 elections for the sixteenth and seventeenth Knessets, there was a considerable decline in Druze vote participation – 59 percent as compared to 75 percent for the fifteenth Knesset, the lowest since the establishment of the state. The Zionist parties made a much greater effort to garner votes from the Druze community and placed Druze candidates on their political lists. For the first time, two Druze candidates were elected on the Likud list, but neither Labor nor the new central party, Shinui, succeeded in bringing their Druze candidates, Saleh Tarif and Munir Hamdan, into the Knesset. Similar processes took place in the Jewish sector, with disinterest in elections and dissatisfaction with the political establishment. Further, the Druze felt that the state had neglected to take care of their problems, even though they served in the army. With 25 percent of the Druze vote, Labor continued to lead, but in the seventeenth Knesset elections it garnered only 8 percent of the Druze vote. The Likud received only 16 percent in the sixteenth Knesset, but garnered 29 percent of the Druze vote in the seventeenth Knesset, although a Druze candidate was not elected to the Knesset. The newly formed Kadima list campaigned for the first time in the seventeenth election campaign and garnered 20 percent of the vote, introducing the Druze Majali Wahba, who was appointed as deputy foreign affairs minister, in its list. As for Arab nationalist parties, they garnered in the sixteenth Knesset about 23 percent and in the seventeenth 26 percent. It seems that even within the Druze community the Arab nationalist parties are slowly strengthening.

From the data presented we can see that the vote of the Druze was not influenced by their place of residence, whether they lived in the Galilee or in settlements with other ethnic groups, neither were they influenced by national political developments in the Arab sector in the Galilee. The vote of the Druze for Zionist parties was everywhere close to 80 percent. It seems that the compulsory enlistment to the army of the Druze left its impression on the populace as well as on its spiritual leadership. It is possible that if the State of Israel had required compulsory enlistment from all the other ethnic groups, this would have been the picture all over. Now it is too late. The Druze knew to take advantage of the competition between the Zionist parties for their votes, and their representation in the Knesset was always way above their actual electoral power.

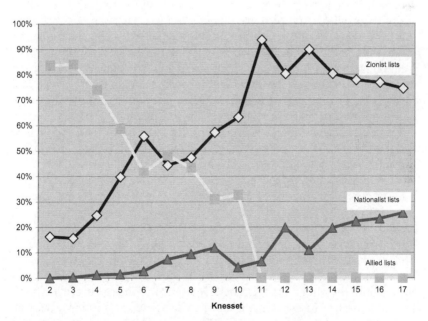

Figure 5.5 Voting Distribution of the Druze, 1951–2006, in Percentages (excluding mixed settlements)

Voting among Galilee Bedouin

At the end of 2006, the Galilee Bedouin community numbered 80,000 people and constitute close to one-third of Israel's Bedouin population and about 6 percent of the country's Arab electorate. Some of them now inhabit new, specially established settlements, such as Arab al-Shibli, Bir al-Maksur, Zarzir, Tuba, Wadi Hammam and Basmat Tab'un. Others still live in unrecognized settlements with no municipal status, a situation that creates not only unrest and bitterness, but also demands for future solutions. The natural outcome is ambivalence towards the state and the political system.

Voting participation amongst the Galilee Bedouin in elections during the first period until the ninth Knesset was surprisingly high and reached an average of 82 percent, and even 93 percent for the fourth Knesset. It is interesting that precisely at the time that Sheikh Hamad Abu Rabia established the Arab List for Bedouin and Villagers, together with Muhammad Husayn Ghadir, a Bedouin from Bir al-Maksur in the Galilee, voting participation dropped – apparently due to tribal and clan rivalries. Bedouin support for Arab nationalist parties during the first period was weak and reached an all-time low average of 7 percent. On the other hand, support for allied Arab lists was high and reached an average of 53 percent during the entire time, and for the fourth Knesset it was even higher, reaching a record 67 percent of all votes from the Bedouin community. Bedouin support for allied Arab lists was slightly higher than that of other Arab groups because of this community's traditional tendency to support the establishment during the early years of the state. Another manifestation of Bedouin support for the establishment was their willingness to be drafted into the security forces, mostly as army scouts earning a salary. A high rate of support for Zionist parties was recorded during the first period, probably as a result of pragmatic or tribal/clan considerations. In the first nine election campaigns there is a correlation between the vote of the Galilee Bedouin to the Zionist parties and the allied Arab list. For example, until the eight Knesset an average of 41 percent of the Galilee Arabs voted for Zionist parties, but in the eighth Knesset a Bedouin allied Arab list appeared which caused a drop to 26 percent in the vote for the Zionist parties.

During the second period, a steep rise in support for Arab nationalist parties began to show among the Galilee Bedouin. This was a direct result of an understanding between the heads of an allied Arab list, according to which Hamad Abu Rabia would be placed at the top of a united north/south Bedouin list for Knesset. He would be followed in second place by Muhammad Husayn Ghadir and had to agree to step down halfway through the term in order to allow Muhammad Husayn Ghadir to serve during the second half of the term. When the time came to carry out the agreement, Hamad Abu Rabia refused to budge and argued that he had not yet finished his mission on behalf of the Bedouin and, in any event, he was functioning as the representative of all Bedouin in Israel. As head of the Minority Department of the Labor Party, I tried to appease Muhammad Husayn Ghadir and offered him different government or party jobs. But he remained adamant that the rotation agreement had to be upheld, if he was not to lose face among his fellow tribe members and supporters. In protest against this broken promise, the Bedouin subsequently voted for Arab nationalist parties. From the beginning of the second period, support for allied Arab lists waned and, as with the other sectors, they disappeared completely. At the same time, support for Zionist parties rose and reached an average of 82 percent (and even 88 percent for the eleventh Knesset).

During the third period voting behavior among the Galilee Bedouin resembles that of the second period. However, there is a steep rise in support for Arab nationalist parties, which reached 46 percent, with a parallel decline in support for the Zionist parties. This reflected increasing nationalist tendencies among the Galilee Bedouin, although they maintained some support for Zionist parties as well.

Examining the shift of votes shows that unlike other Arabs in the Galilee, who transferred their votes to the Arab nationalist parties, the shift was from the allied Arab lists to the Zionist parties. About 90 percent of the votes for allied Arab lists of the Galilee Bedouin were given to the Zionist parties and only about 10 percent to the Arab nationalist parties. This trend started to change in 1998 when the votes shifted from the Zionist parties to the Arab nationalist parties.

The voting participation among Galilee Bedouin for the sixteenth and seventeenth Knessets dropped to an all-time low of about 40 percent. The election boycott was a result of the government's failure to deal with the unrecognized Arab settlements. Bedouin support for nationalist Arab parties increased to a little under 50 percent; especially successful was the United Arab Party, which placed Talab al-Sani', a lawyer from Laqyyeh in the Negev, in its number two slot.

Like the Druze, the Bedouin in the Galilee were not significantly influenced by political developments in their area. Changes in voting patterns were slow and expressed the traditional attitudes in this ethnic group. The tribal structure is still very strong among the Galilee Bedouin, as well as their dependency on the Israeli establishment. A steep drop in voting for Zionist parties is viewed, but still about 50 percent of the votes go to these parties. One can assume that this is a result of their voluntary service in the army. The electoral power of the Galilee Bedouin is relatively low and as a result neither the Zionist parties nor the nationalist Arab parties have a member of this group in their lists to the Knesset.

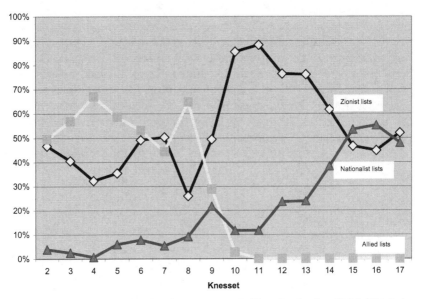

Figure 5.6 Voting Distribution among Galilee Bedouin, 1951–2006, in Percentages (excluding mixed settlements)

Negev Bedouin Vote

The Negev Bedouin, also Moslems (at the end of 2006 numbering some 157,000 people), belong to about 30 tribes, scattered over a wide area in the south of Israel. Formerly nomadic shepherds, the Bedouin are currently in transition from a tribal social framework to a permanently settled society, and they are gradually entering Israel's labor force. This urbanization process started later in the Negev than in the Galilee. About 60 percent of the Negev Bedouin now live in eight new settlements: Tel Sheva, Rahat, Kseifeh, Ar'ara in the Negev, Laqyyeh, Hura, Segev Shalom and Abu Basma, although many still inhabit shanty towns on the outskirts of established Jewish and Bedouin towns. On the whole, the Negev Bedouin community plays a relatively small role in Israeli politics and its members are not usually very active campaigners. There are several reasons for this: for many years the Bedouin population in the Negev was isolated from centers of Arab political activity in Israel, because of geographical distance and social and cultural differences; those Negev Bedouin who still live in unrecognized shanty towns tend not to travel to the polling station where they are registered to vote; because of their lifestyle, these small communities have exhibited a negligible interest in government; traditional Bedouin society disapproves of women participating in activities outside the home, including voting for Knesset elections; and last, if not the most important, the Bedouin are disappointed by the government's policies *vis-à-vis* the ownership of land in the Negev.

At the first two general elections, the voting behavior of the Negev Bedouin was similar to that of other Israeli Arabs. Starting with the fourth Knesset until the ninth Knesset, voting participation decreased; during the first period the average voting participation was about 73 percent.

The Negev Bedouin had to deal with several problems specific just to their community, the most important of being the question of ownership of the land on which they pitched their tents and grazed their herds. According to them and relying on historic arguments, extensive stretches of land in the Negev belong to them. But the state does not recognize their claims, since they are not based on documented proof of ownership. The argument between the Bedouin and the political establishment has existed on different levels throughout the state's existence and, on more than one occasion, caused unrest.

Ostensibly, it is reasonable to assume that this unrest would be expressed in protest voting for nationalist Arab parties, but this is not the case. Between the second and the fifth Knessets, support for these parties never rose above 2 percent. From the sixth to the ninth (1977) Knessets, support for these parties settled at just over 6 percent. Nor did the allied Arab lists receive many votes from the Negev Bedouin, as compared with the support these lists received from the Galilee Bedouin. The remoteness of the Negev Bedouin from Arab centers in the Galilee and the Triangle, as well as their dependence on the state and the Jewish population around them probably influenced their voting patterns. In the second Knesset, only 4 percent of the voters voted for the allied Arab lists, but as of the third Knesset support for these lists gradually rose and in the eighth Knesset, in which a Bedouin allied list competed under the leadership of Sheikh Hamad Abu Rabia, it reached 71 percent, more than in any other previous election.

Their distance from the center of the country, lack of water and shrinking grazing lands due to years of drought, made it necessary for the Negev Bedouin to find alternative sources of income to those provided by their herds of sheep, goats and camels. They became more dependent on the Israeli government than their counterparts in the north. They formed ties with the local Jewish population and their voting patterns were reflected accordingly. Thus, for example, in the second Knesset 95 percent of all eligible Bedouin voted for Zionist parties, mainly Mapai. From the third Knesset on, this dropped to an average of 52 percent throughout the first period. But when a Bedouin list offered its candidacy for the eighth Knesset, support for the Zionist parties dropped to only 23 percent.

During the second period there is a clear drop in voting participation and only 50 percent of the voters turned up to the voting polls in the elections to the tenth Knesset (1981), less than in any previous elections. This continued throughout the second period, probably for ideological rather than technical reasons.[39] Voting trends among the Negev Bedouin indicate that they continue to be disillusioned with Zionist parties, whom, they feel, neglected them and did not take care of their specific problems – mainly the land issue and, later, the illegal settlements and government-sponsored Bedouin towns. These issues never received enough attention under successive governments. During the ninth Knesset, Bedouin support for allied Arab lists was still high, but this dropped sharply until the complete disappearance of these lists. With no allied Arab lists contending, support increased for nationalist Arab parties and peaked at a 29 percent average for the entire second period. At the same time, support for Zionist political parties also rose and reached almost 67 percent. This might be due to the assumption (or hope) that these parties would have enough influence in the Knesset to voice the demands of their voters in ways that were more effective than those used by the allied Arab lists or the nationalist Arab lists.

Figure 5.7 shows two irregular fluctuations in the division of votes in the second period. When the Bedouin allied Arab list disappeared in the tenth Knesset (1981), all its votes moved to the Zionist parties. But the

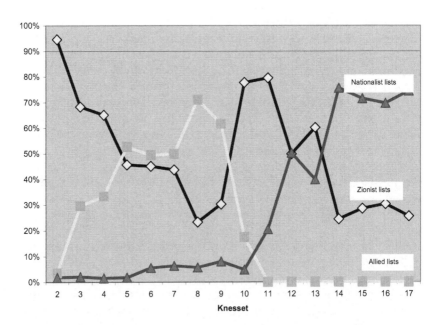

Figure 5.7 Voting Distribution of Negev Bedouin, 1951–2006, in Percentages (excluding mixed settlements)

twelfth Knesset (1988) provided a turning point, after which the Bedouin began opting for nationalist Arab parties. The Islamic Movement, which is very active in communal-religious matters, is successful in attracting the Bedouin to orthodox Islam at a time when the nomad Bedouin are in the process of settling in permanent communities.

By the *third period*, the changed voting system and improved organization within the parties (rather than ideological motives) resulted in a rise in voting participation to about 64 percent. In the 1999 elections the Bedouin of the Negev responded to their alienation and disappointment with the establishment by giving 71 percent of their vote to nationalist Arab parties (as opposed to 5 percent in the tenth Knesset). In the fourteenth and fifteenth Knessets, nationalist Arab lists won about 74 percent of votes, with 62 percent of the ballot going to the United Arab Party and its number two candidate, Talab al-Sani'.[40] On the other hand, support for Zionist parties decreased during this period to an average of 26 percent. Unlike their counterparts in the Galilee, the Negev Bedouin shifted their votes from the allied Arab lists to the nationalist Arab parties.

Participation of voters in the sixteenth (2003) and seventeenth Knessets was the lowest since the establishment of the state (46.5 percent and 44 percent respectively) and the lowest in the whole Arab sector. Voting abstention is not necessarily due to ideological reasons, but because of disappointment that land issues, the matter of the unrecognized villages and the severe economic situation in the Bedouin community have not been resolved. Voting participation would probably have been even lower had there not been two candidates from the Negev Bedouin in the United Arab Party list. In this period the nationalist Arab parties together lost close to 4 percent, but still received about 70 percent of the vote, while the Zionist parties gained about 30 percent.

Following the sixteenth Knesset elections, an attempt was made to examine the differences in voting behavior between the Bedouin "nobility" and the *fellahin*.[41] Unlike the *fellahin*, those families who belong to the tribes that were in the region prior to the establishment of the State of Israel have legitimate – albeit exaggerated – claims to lands throughout the Negev. The *fellahin* wandered up from the Sudan and Arabia and elsewhere in search of employment, and it is they who found it easier to settle in the seven government-sponsored towns; they had only to gain from doing so. The "nobility" was unwilling to accept the conditions dictated by the government and preferred to continue their struggle to regain as much as possible of what they consider to be their legally owned property. Since this property is not registered in the Lands Registry, their claims are easy enough to disregard and they have never elected the right people who could fight for their cause in the Knesset.

Sample ballot boxes in Rahat, Ar'ara in the Negev and Kseifeh indicate that the *fellahin* have a greater tendency to vote for Zionist parties: in

Rahat, 72 percent of the *fellahin* vote went to Zionist parties, as compared with 19 percent of the Bedouin "aristocracy". The Islamic Movement placed a *fellah* from Kseifeh high on its list and 51 percent of that town's voters opted for the United Arab Party, while the National Democratic Pact, which did the same, garnered only 10 percent of the vote. Permanent settlement among the Bedouin community has caused social, economic and cultural changes in the traditional way of life, which influenced their voting patterns. Also, in comparison with the Galilee Bedouin, military service in the IDF among Negev Bedouin is limited. These are the causes for the low rate of election participation and the steep rise in support for the nationalist Arab parties. The situation of the Negev Bedouin could lead to unrest and a severe crisis between them and the state.

Voting Trends among Christian Arabs

At the end of 2008, about 90 percent of Israel's 120,100 Christian Arabs live in urban areas, including Shefar'am, Nazareth and Haifa. Although many denominations are nominally represented, the majority of Israel's Arabs are affiliated with the Greek Catholic, Greek Orthodox and Roman Catholic churches. Since it is difficult to determine their vote distribution with absolute certainty, voting trends based on the results received in two villages populated by the Greek Catholic community are analyzed: Mi'elya and Fassuta. Both these settlements were well connected with the Israeli establishment and have provided candidates for the allied Arab lists.[42] In order to receive a reasonable picture of the voting behavior of the different subgroups in Israel's Christian community, a ballot sampling was analyzed in places with a majority of Christian voters such as Nazareth, Rame and Kafar Yasif. The results show the increasing power of nationalist Arab parties in mixed Christian towns and villages over the periods following the eleventh Knesset.

Voting trends in Mi'elya and Fassuta do not necessarily mirror trends in other mixed settlements, where Christian communities live side by side with Moslems, nor do they mirror voting patterns of the rest of the Christian Arab communities in Israel. Therefore, an analysis of sample ballot boxes in the Orthodox neighborhood in Nazareth was taken after the elections to the eleventh Knesset (1984). The sample showed a high rate of voting (about 77 percent) for nationalist Arab parties. For the sixteenth Knesset (2003), a re-examination of the same sampling showed that 85.7 percent of voters voted for the nationalist Arab parties. Rakah continued to win most of the votes, approaching 64.8 percent, notwithstanding the arrival on the scene of the National Democratic Pact, which took only 19 percent of the Christian vote.

Another sampling of ballot boxes was done in the Catholic neighborhood in Nazareth after both elections. The sample revealed moderate support of the nationalist Arab parties (about 57 percent of the vote on average in the eleventh Knesset and 72.8 percent in the sixteenth Knesset). In villages like Fassuta, Mi'elya or Tarshiha, which are distant from Arab centers, the vote for nationalist Arab parties is even more moderate and the vote for the Zionist parties is higher. In the whole city of Nazareth the nationalist Arab parties garnered a total of 87 percent of the vote, similar to the number in the Orthodox neighborhood.

Table 5.3 Vote Distribution for Israeli Arab Parties in Two Christian Neighborhoods in Nazareth for the Eleventh Knesset Compared to the Sixteenth Knesset

| | Orthodox Neighborhood | | | | Catholic Neighborhood | | |
Knesset	Ballot Box No.	Valid Votes	Arab Parties	Percent	Ballot Box No.	Valid Votes	Arab Parties	Percent
11	7, 8, 9	1,508	1,175	77.9	26, 27, 28	1,714	984	57.0
16	8, 9, 10	1,305	1,119	85.7	16, 17	867	638	72.8

In mixed settlements, which are part of the Israeli Arab population centers, a high percentage of Christians vote for nationalist Arab parties, while in the more outlying Christian villages there is higher voting percentage for Zionist parties.

In Mi'elya and Fassuta the vote for allied Arab lists has undergone many ups and downs. In the second (1951) and third (1955) Knessets, support for these lists exceeded 83 percent, due to the fact that Mas'ad Qasis of Mi'elya was given a high slot on them. Beginning with the fourth Knesset, there was a clear, gradual and moderate downwards trend in support for these lists, until they disappeared altogether. Voting for Zionist parties in Christian settlements, on the other hand, was clearly on an upward trend. In the second Knesset support for Zionist parties reached 13 percent and rose steadily, except for the eighth Knesset, possibly as a result of the 1973 Yom-Kippur War.

In the second period, beginning with the ninth Knesset (1977) to the eleventh Knesset (1984) we witness a steep decline in voting participation similar to the decline in all the Arab sector. The vote for the nationalist Arab parties is increasing all through this period, though it changed from area to area and from one election to the other.

The support of the allied Arab lists continued to decline, even though Hanna Haddad, a Christian from Tur'an, headed a Christian allied list. This author, in his capacity as head of the Labor Party Minorities Department, tried at the time to guarantee Hanna Haddad a slot high on the party's list, but two other Arabs had already been promised such slots. Hanna Haddad, who was sure that he could be elected to the Knesset on an allied Christian ticket, complained that Christians never received suitable representation in

Zionist parties. The author tried unsuccessfully to talk him out of standing. Predictably, the list did not pass the voting threshold.

Support for Zionist parties rose in Mi'elya and Fassuta during the second period – probably as a result of renewed contact with Christians across the border in Lebanon during and after the 1982 war. During this time, a partial vote shift was observed from the allied Arab lists to the Zionist parties. Only about 65 percent of the votes lost to the allied Arab lists went to Zionist parties and there was a clear shift to nationalist Arab parties – probably in protest at the fact that no Christian representatives were given slots in the Zionist parties, coupled with a growing nationalist awareness among Israeli Arabs.

The third period saw a dramatic increase in voting participation in the two Christian villages; 90.5 percent of the eligible voters in Mi'elya and 84.6 percent in Fassuta took advantage of their constitutional rights in the fifteenth Knesset elections. In both locations, during this period, 66.8 percent voted for Israeli nationalist Arab parties, while support for the Zionist parties dropped to 33 percent.

In the sixteenth Knesset (2003) and seventeenth Knesset (2006), voting participation in these villages went down to about 60 percent, as did voting participation nationwide in the Israeli Arab community. Election results were similar to those for the fifteenth Knesset. The nationalist Arab parties won about 60 percent of all votes, while the Zionist parties won about 40 percent.

It may be concluded from the above that the Christian vote remains uniform. The Communist Rakah Party won about 60 percent of the vote, while the party led by Azmi Bishara, who is a Christian, won only about 20 percent. Though Bishara was depicted as a secular, nationalist Arab, he did not succeed in reducing the traditional Christian Arab support for the Communist Party which remains stable since the first Knesset (1949). Since the Christians' influence in Rakah is currently waning, it is possible to assume that the near future will see a shift of votes to other nationalist Arab parties.

Voting Trends in the Circassian Villages

The Circassians, comprising some 3,000 people, are concentrated in two northern villages – Kafar Kamma and Reihaniyye. They are Sunni Moslems, although they share neither the Arab origin nor the cultural background of the larger Islamic community. While maintaining a distinct ethnic identity, they participate in Israel's economic and national affairs, without assimilating either into Jewish society or into the Moslem community.

The support rate for nationalist Arab parties among the Circassians is especially low and, for many years, did not exceed 5 percent. Their support for Zionist parties was traditionally high and for the second and third

Knessets, it stood at over 95 percent. This has to do with the fact that the Circassian community sends its sons to serve in the military and maintains close ties with the Jewish community. The fourth Knesset did, indeed, see a downward trend which reached an all-time low in the seventh Knesset, immediately after the 1967 war, in which Zionist parties won only 45 percent. Beginning with the eighth Knesset, voting for Zionist parties rose again and stabilized at 97 percent. At this time, there was a clear voting shift among the Circassians, from allied Arab lists to Zionist parties – confirming the hypothesis that the Circassian voter chose between two alternatives: Zionist parties or allied Arab lists.

In the sixteenth Knesset (2003) and in the seventeenth Knesset (2006), the Circassians again gave most of their votes to Zionist parties, but for the first time the nationalist Arab parties manage to garner about 18.6 percent of that vote in the sixteenth Knesset.

Altogether, it is obvious that the voting behavior of the Circassians is similar to that of the Druze. Like the Druze, they serve in the army and have integrated in various areas in the country, both factors that appear to have influenced their pragmatic voting considerations.

Voting Trends in Mixed Ethnic Towns

Those Arabs who live in the six mixed towns – towns in which both Jews and Arabs live together and in which the latter are a significant minority – constitute about 12 percent of eligible voters. After the establishment of the state, the "mixed towns" were Jaffa, Ramla, Lod, Haifa and Acre. These were joined by Upper Nazareth, which was established as a Jewish town neighboring Arab Nazareth, but demographic processes and changes in residence patterns turned it, over time, into another mixed town like Tarshiha, which became joined to the neighboring Jewish town of Ma'alot. Lately, Israeli Arab citizens have been taking up residence in towns like Carmiel, Bat-Yam and Be'er Sheba, but the demographic ratio is still small and these cities are not considered mixed ethnic towns.

As well as geographic and social conditions, other factors influence voting patterns and political attitudes, including type of housing in which the individual voters live and distances from political centers of influence, as well as other local factors.

We examined the effect of distance from centers of political activity on the political orientation of the inhabitants of these settlements *vis-à-vis* their choice of parliamentary party. In mixed towns the Arabs are most influenced by their distance from larger Arab centers. For example, while Arabs constitute a minority in the town of Acre, they constitute an absolute majority (65 percent) in the region. Jaffa is part of Tel Aviv, Ramla and Lod are located to the east of Tel Aviv. These three are far removed from the Israeli Arab population centers and the situation there is different. For the Israeli Arab population in Haifa and Upper Nazareth, on the other hand, the situation is more like that of the Arab population in Acre because they are in the Galilee, the place with the largest Arab concentration in Israel. In spite of the differences and social and economic diversity of the Israeli Arab residents in different mixed towns, they can still be related to as one population group, whose most outstanding common feature is its close proximity to the Jewish population.

Besides the characteristics shared by the entire Israeli Arab population in mixed settlements, residents of one town often differ from those in another and, in some cases, one neighborhood can be different from another; thus for example, the slum neighborhoods, such as the Ajami neighborhood in Jaffa, Wadi Nisnas in Haifa, the Old City in Acre and Lod's "railway" neighborhood, as compared with the more affluent neighborhoods in Haifa's Abbas Street or Lod's Neve Yarak.

Arab inhabitants of mixed population towns share several characteristics, such as the formation of large groups of underprivileged people, a high crime rate and a low standard of education; their residents are far from Arab cultural and political centers (except those living in Haifa); they include large groups of rural newcomers; they have closer commercial and economic ties with the Jewish population, mainly at work and in the neighborhood. Sometimes Arabs and Jews live in neighboring streets or even the same housing project.

In addition, differences exist in the demographic mix of Arabs and Jews in mixed towns; for example, in Acre, Arabs made up 15 percent of the town's population in late 2006, while in Tel-Aviv/Jaffa, only 4 percent of the population was Arab, and concentrated mainly in Jaffa. This is very significant in terms of the population's political orientation. There is no doubt that a 15 percent minority population, such as that in Acre, with power to determine who will be elected mayor, will adopt a different political behavior from that of a much smaller minority such as that of Jaffa, whose Arab residents had no real influence on the local political system.

All this affects a community's voting behavior and we might assume that mixed town populations have been influenced by modernization more than have Arab members of close-knit communities. One would assume, moreover, that neighborly relations between the Jewish and the Arab population necessarily lead to more understanding and to a greater "Israelization", or consolidation of an Israeli civic identity.

A study of political choices made by Arab residents of mixed population towns is important because of their electoral weight. It can also distort an assessment of the voting behavior of Arabs in Israel in general. Since most Arabs in mixed population towns cast their ballot in the same voting booths as their Jewish neighbors, there is no accurate method for estimating the Arab vote as opposed to that of the Jewish vote. This is the reason why researchers usually prefer to overlook the mixed population towns. The question is: does daily contact with Jews really influence the voting patterns of their Arab neighbors? Another question is whether Arabs in mixed towns all vote in the same manner and have the same voting patterns, or if different areas have different voting behavior just as residents from one town differ from those of another.

In order to reach a reasonable assessment of the behavior of the Israeli Arab voter in mixed towns, results from several voting stations in neighborhoods with an absolute majority of Arab voters were analyzed. Although this cannot reflect the voting of the entire Arab voting public in the city, it can give an indication of the voting behavior in neighborhoods in which Arabs constitute an absolute majority. Returns in these stations were compared with the overall vote received by nationalist Arab parties in Tel-Aviv/Jaffa; the assumption was that most voters for nationalist Arab parties were Arabs. We differentiated between Tel Aviv/Jaffa and Haifa, in which the Communist Party (Hadash/Rakah) also received Jewish votes, and the other towns where almost no Jews voted for the Communist Party or the nationalist Arab parties. This differentiation helped to fix sample results in Ramla, Lod and Acre, assuming that the difference expresses the voting results of the Arabs in the mixed voting stations which were not included in the sample.

In order to examine the hypothesis on differences between voting in sample ballot boxes and voting in mixed neighborhoods, we examined voting differences between the predominantly Arab old city of Acre and the town's Wolfson neighborhood, which is mixed Jewish and Arab, with Arabs constituting more than half of the population. The socio-economic level of the Israeli Arabs in that neighborhood and in other new neighborhoods in Acre is generally higher than in the town's older neighborhoods. If it turns out that there are no significant differences between voting in these two neighborhoods, the results from the sample voting station will have been considered a reliable reflection of voting patterns.

We also examined whether voting in mixed towns was uniform, with similar voting patterns, or if there are differences between the towns compatible to the differences between the Arab population of one town and that of another town. It was necessary, therefore, to define in detail the special characteristics of each of the mixed towns. Our main assumptions were that the Jewish and Arab voting participation is identical and that most of the votes for nationalist Arab parties come from Arabs. The assessment was that the number of Jews who voted for nationalist Arab parties was negligible and that the votes given to Zionist political parties came from Jews. For example, in the ninth Knesset elections, we examined two voting stations in Ramla. These stations had an 81.9 percent non-Jewish electorate and 829 valid votes. Multiplication of these two data placed the actual number of valid votes at 679. This number was divided between three blocs, thus: all votes received by nationalist Arab parties and allied Arab lists were subtracted from 679. The rest were considered Israeli Arab votes given to Zionist parties. Our sample was chosen from among several voting stations serving non-Jewish voters, where there was an especially high voting turnout.

The examination of voting turnout in Acre showed that support for nationalist Arab parties in that city was even higher than in Nazareth, the stronghold of the nationalist Arab parties. On average, this is the picture in all the mixed ethnic towns, but there are some differences between Haifa and Acre on the one hand and Ramla and Lod on the other. It seems that, while voting for the ninth, tenth and eleventh Knessets in Ramla and Lod was more moderate than in Haifa and Acre, in the sixteenth and seventeenth Knessets support of the nationalist Arab parties exceeded that of Haifa and Acre. The conclusion is that meetings with the Jewish population result in more ideology and radicalism.

Research shows that daily contact with the Jewish population in the mixed ethnic towns leads to increased polarization and electoral support for nationalist Arab parties. The distance from the centers of Arab settlements, residence in homogenous or mixed neighborhoods, or even residence in affluent neighborhoods or slums, had no influence on voting considerations. The support of nationalist Arab parties in mixed ethnic towns over recent years has been higher than in other Arab settlements. It seems that the meeting between Jewish and Arab society allows the Arabs to see the differences in services and infrastructure between Jewish and Arab neighborhoods. The author believes that the government and municipal leaders must act in order to build an equal set of services while taking advantage of the fact that Jews and Arabs alike need the same educational system as well as services and infrastructure in the same town.

Voting in Outlying Settlements

Several Israeli Arab towns and villages exist in locations that are at a distance from the main centers of Arab population. These include towns and villages in the Jerusalem corridor, such as Abu Ghosh, Beit Neqofa, Beit Tsafafa and Ein Rafa. In the upper Galilee, these include Tuba Zanghariyye, Jish, Mi'elya and Reihaniyye. Those on the coastal plain are Jisr al-Zarqa and Furaydis. These settlements are not part of a territorial continuity typical of such areas as the Triangle, Western Galilee and Gush Segev. Settlements outside the geographic population centers of Israeli Arabs usually arouse less interest from the establishment and therefore their inhabitants tend to feel more discriminated against. It could be assumed that these feelings of discrimination would be expressed in protest voting against the Israeli establishment. According to another hypothesis, these settlements, which are far removed from the Israeli Arab centers of political activity, would be less influenced by the nationalist trends characteristic of most settlements in that sector, since their distance increases their dependence on Jewish society and it would therefore be reasonable to assume that their voting would be more moderate.

We examined the accuracy of these two hypotheses by looking at the voting patterns in four remote settlements – Abu Ghosh, Jish, Tuba Zanghariyye and Ein Rafa – over two election campaigns (eleventh and sixteenth Knessets). Far-reaching changes had occurred in the Arab population in Israel in general and in their relationship with the Jewish state in particular during the time between the two election campaigns.

Support for nationalist Arab parties in all four chosen settlements reached an average of 18.5 percent for the eleventh Knesset. This result totally differed from nationwide results, which were 51 percent at the time. Yet a comparison with the sixteenth Knesset revealed that nationalist Arab parties received an average of 47.5 percent in distant settlements, while nationwide they received 72 percent of all Israeli Arab votes. This means that voting for nationalist Arab parties differed in outlying settlements from the national average. The decrease in support for Zionist parties in the sixteenth Knesset comes mainly from the multiplicity of nationalist Arab parties, which included the National Democratic Pact (Balad), the Progressive National Pact (Balam), the Communist Party (Hadash), the United Arab Party (Ra'am) and the list of Asma Ighbariya, all of which won votes from the Zionist parties, but the assumption that voting in outlying towns and villages is radically different from and more moderate than the nationwide voting continues to hold true.

It is easy enough to assume that the presence of nationalist Arab parties in outlying settlements was smaller due to their distance from the main

Table 5.4　Voting in Outlying Settlements[43]

Settlement	Knesset	Eligible voters	Valid Votes	Nationalist Arab (Percent)	Zionist Parties (Percent)
Abu Ghosh	11	1,407	1,007	27.0	73.0
	17	3,130	1,591	74.0	16.0
Jish	11	1,136	761	20.0	80.0
	17	1,954	951	50.0	50.0
Tuba-Zanghariyye	11	1,045	720	0.9	91.0
	17	2,974	980	30.0	70.0
Ein Rafa	11	207	165	17.0	83.0
	17	390	193	49.0	51.0
Total (Average)	11	3,795	2,653	18.5	81.5
	17	8,448	3,715	44.0	66.0

centers of Israeli Arab political activism. Although these settlements experienced no fewer problems than other Israeli Arab settlements (and sometimes even more), Zionist parties enjoyed continuous support in these settlements. This would confirm the hypothesis that geographically removed settlements are more influenced by their Jewish neighbors, who are not a relevant factor in other parts of the Israeli Arab sector. This is probably due to the greater dependence of these settlements on the Israeli establishment and on commerce with their neighbors. This dependence is stronger because of their distance from the hub of Israeli Arab life and also prevents the influence of a more radical majority.

To summarize, an analysis of election results from the viewpoint of rifts in Arab society shows that the Arab vote in Israel can be divided into two main subgroups. The first group (about 72 percent of the Arab voters), which includes Arabs in the Galilee and the Triangle (Christian and Moslem), showed relatively strong support for nationalist Arab parties. The second group includes all the others (Druze, Bedouin and Circassian), who supported mainly the allied Arab lists and Zionist political parties. An examination of Arab voting behavior in Israel must take into account not only the number of eligible voters, but also voting participation according to rifts, especially in light of the fact that, in this community, voter abstention is a form of political statement that should be seen in a different context from voter abstention in the Jewish sector.

Complex Loyalties as Reflected in Voting Behavior

This book deals with the voting behavior of Israel's Arab citizens over 17 election campaigns (from 1948 to 2006), with the aim of providing a comprehensive picture of the identity of this sector of Israel's society.

The finding was that Israel's Arabs are divided between two opposing political directions: integrative and confrontational. The Arabs' voting behavior is based mainly on the dilemma surrounding issues relating to their loyalty to the state and their identity as Israeli Arabs. On the one hand, they are citizens of a sovereign state, which is involved in an ongoing war with a national ethnic group to which they belong – the Palestinian people. On the other hand, they must adapt themselves to the reality of being a minority community in a Jewish state.

It has become clear that political events related to the Israeli-Arab conflict in general and the Israeli–Palestinian conflict in particular influenced the voting behavior of Israeli Arabs. Among these events, the most meaningful was, first, the Six Day War in 1967, which was a turning point in the crystallization of their identity. From a minority group they became once again part of a majority in the area and rediscovered their Palestinian identity. The second event was the 1976 Land Day, which brought them into confrontation with the authorities in Israel by re-examining their civil status in the country. The third event is the outbreak of the second Palestinian *Intifada*, followed by the events of October 2000.

The political history of the Israeli Arabs was divided into three periods in which the influence of these events manifested themselves on the social and political processes that molded and determined their voting behavior.

The first period was 1948 to 1977. At this time the Arab sector was under military government and its main political options consisted of the allied Arab lists under the auspices of the ruling Zionist Mapai (Labor) Party. The only alternative to the allied Arab parties was the Communist Party, and the Arab minority feared to form independent parties. Even the Communist Party could act as an opposition party because it was a Jewish–Arab party. Participation in the election at that time was even higher than in the Jewish sector and the Zionist parties received on average about 80 percent of the votes. In this period the regime molded the Arab settlements in Israel and determined their future. On the other hand, the Israeli government was occupied with the problems of absorbing the new emigrants from all over the world and building the country and did not take the time to consolidate its approach toward the Arab minority and take care of it, almost to the point of ignoring it completely.

Many changes took place in Israeli Arab society in the decade between the Six Day War and the rise to power of the Likud in 1977. The education level rose throughout the sector, employment patterns changed, and there was an impressive rise in the standard of living. These brought about political awareness. Renewed ties with the inhabitants of the occupied Palestinian territories resulted in an awakening of national feeling and solidarity. However, these did not at first influence the Israeli Arabs' voting behavior and the allied Arab parties still played a part in the political arena. It was the 1976 Land Day and the establishment of extra-parliamentary protest movements that signaled a new period in the history of Israel's Arabs.

The second period constitutes the time between 1977 and 1992 and is characterized by the strengthening of the local Arab municipal councils, which produced a younger, better-educated Moslem leadership. In this period the National Committee of Arab Municipality leaders and the Supreme Monitoring Committee for Arab Affairs in Israel were formed. Since the political change in 1977, the Arabs in Israel fluctuated between integrating in Zionist parties in order to promote their civic interests and voting for the new nationalist Arab parties, whose stated aim was to realize national objectives such as the establishment of a Palestinian state alongside Israel. In the 1977 elections, following Land Day, almost half the votes formerly given to the allied Arab parties now went to the Communist Rakah Party. This trend continued until 1981, when the allied lists finally disappeared.

The Arab voter could now follow two parallel courses: the pragmatic integrative course, which was manifested in a vote for a Zionist party, and the ideological national and confrontational course, which manifested itself in a vote for a nationalist Arab party. The Arab voter did not see any contradiction between these two courses, since in an unstable and insecure reality he wished to retain all his options.

A dramatic change in voting patterns of the Israeli Arab sector occurred between 1996 and 2008, which was expressed mainly in political radicalization that came in the wake of deep disappointment. Israeli Arab voters shifted their vote to the nationalist Arab parties, and support for the Zionist parties dropped to a 30 percent low, against the 70 percent support for the nationalist Arab parties. It seems that this will continue in the future because of the survivability of pragmatic considerations in choosing a party. The Zionist parties belong to the establishment, which is able to provide the voters with political functions as well as jobs and status, and some even grant promising slots in their lists for Arab candidates. At the same time, clan rifts are losing much of their influence on voting behavior in the Arab sector, although they remain influential in local and municipal elections. The second *Intifada* that preceded the events of October 2000 resulted in greater voting abstention and fewer than 60 percent of the Arab electorate participated in subsequent elections. This was defined as a symbol of civil and parliamentary isolation on the part of Israel's Arabs, who are aware that the Jewish majority blocks the activity of their Knesset representatives.

The commonly held view that most votes from allied Arab lists went to Zionist parties was disproved by the use of a statistical method that examined vote shifts between party blocs. The hypothesis had been based on the fact that allied Arab lists were established and supported by the Zionist parties, mainly Mapai. Our question was: where did the votes which had been formerly given to the allied Arab lists go once these lists gradually phased out following elections to the eleventh Knesset? An in-depth examination of voting results in the Israeli Arab sector according to blocs reveals that until the fourth Knesset, there was almost no vote shift and fluctuations from one bloc to the other were only marginal. From the fifth Knesset on, there was indeed a vote shift, which differed from group to group: in the Galilee, for example, most votes went from the allied Arab lists to the Communist Rakah Party. This result conflicts with the former hypothesis, according to which there is a vote shift between the allied Arab lists and Zionist parties, and is significant in light of the relative importance of the electoral power of the Galilee Arabs. Voters in the Triangle followed the lead of their counterparts in the Galilee only after the seventh Knesset (1969).

The shift of votes from one major political bloc to another, i.e. from Zionist parties to nationalist Arab parties, expressed a process of reinforcement of the confrontational attitude. The shift also expresses new attitudes, worldviews and generation. The third generation of Arabs to grow up under Israeli sovereignty is well educated and self-confident. Its new leadership is more independent, knowledgeable of the legal system and well versed in the rules of democracy; above all, it is neither complacent nor submissive. Unlike previous generations, the younger generation of Arabs in Israel is familiar with the power of the media and knows how to use it to advance its aims and objectives.

Throughout the period covered by this book, social rifts in Israeli and Arab society have influenced people's choice of political party. The Israeli-Arab rift provided the political means to establish a separate and disunited Arab party system, as well as the infrastructure for social and political movements whose ideologies aim to strengthen the status of the Arabs as a separate national minority. Traditional social rifts in Arab society (clans, tribes and ethnic groups) are responsible for disparity in voting in the Arab sector and the Arabs' inability to form a united front in Israel; in recent years these have been joined by new rifts caused by education and employment.

An attempt was made in this book to provide an answer to the question of why the Arabs have never been able to actualize their electoral power. Our conclusion is that during the first years of the state the Arab minority, which had no real leadership and was not wise in the ways of Western democracy, was forced to adapt itself to the Jewish majority. Most Arab voters knew nothing of the rules of the political game, or of exploiting the advantages of being a minority within Israel's parliamentary system. The Arab minority, therefore, took refuge in traditional social rifts and voted for the allied Arab lists.

An interesting conclusion comes from an analysis of voting patterns among Arab inhabitants of mixed ethnic cities. The general view was that inhabitants of these cities would try to become part of the Jewish majority and that their political orientation would be more moderate than that of their counterparts in the Galilee or the Triangle. The assumption was that living in close proximity with Jews created personal friendships and mutual dependency, which would naturally lead to a more moderate outlook. Also, an urban environment is more influenced by modernization than a rural one, and the hold of the social rifts in the metropolis would be weaker.

In fact, the Arab vote in mixed ethnic cities was characteristically more nationalistic than the rest of the Arab population of Israel. Modernization and exposure to the political behavior of the Jewish majority, together with the democratic tools at their disposal, actually affected their vote in an unexpected way. Possibly, the vote for nationalist Arab parties came in protest at their feelings of alienation and bitterness at the difference in living conditions between Jews and Arabs. Moreover, contact with modern society and exposure to higher education enhanced their national awareness.

The Israeli–Palestinian conflict was also an important factor that Arabs living in mixed population cities took into consideration when choosing a political party to represent them in the Knesset. Exit polls in various neighborhoods showed that the tendency to vote for nationalist Arab parties was typical in slum areas, like those in the old city of Acre; this would suggest that it might be possible to change voting habits by improving economic conditions, even though the national conflict remains unresolved. The importance of voting behavior in mixed ethnic cities lies in the fact that they comprise about 12 percent of the Arab electorate.

It seems that the voting behavior of Israeli Arabs will continue to be influenced by their affinity to an ethnic-religious rift. Abstention will also remain an important tool so long as the Jewish establishment continues to deny Arabs any electoral power. Increasing numbers of extra-parliamentary movements and NGOs will play a central role, and continue to challenge Israel's political system. As the number of voters who abstain from voting increases, so will their representation in Knesset decrease and the ties that bind them to the establishment will gradually be severed, resulting in subversive behavior of extra-parliamentary organizations. Israel will then be forced to form a clear policy toward its Arab citizens – a policy according to which they will be integrated into parliamentary coalitions and appointed to positions in all levels of government.

The main thesis of this book is that by studying the voting behavior of Israel's Arab citizens, we can provide ourselves with a clearer picture of their identity. The fact that the nationalist Arab parties manage to draw more and more voters from one general election to the next is proof of the ever-growing importance of the Palestinian national component in the Israeli Arabs' identity. The nationalist parties give their supporters a political label and sense of belonging, of which they previously felt deprived. By supporting the establishment of a Palestinian state, the Israeli Arab voter becomes part of the greater Arab nation that surrounds Israel. By boycotting Israeli general elections, on the other hand, the Arab voter chooses to take advantage of his/her Israeli citizenship to express dissatisfaction with such issues as discrimination and inequality.

Epilogue

Arabs, Jews and the State of Israel – The Administration, the Establishment and Arab Citizens

The last decade has provided a definitive experience for Israel's Arabs and a learning experience for its Jews. The process began in September 1992 following the thirteenth Knesset elections, peaked during the prolonged strike of Arab municipal leaders toward the end of 1999 and ended in September 2000, with the outburst of the second Arab *Intifada* in the occupied territories.

October 2000 – On the Threshold of a New Reality

In late 2000, 13 Israeli Arabs were killed in riots that were unprecedented in scope in support of the second *Intifada* (which they coined the al-Aqsa *Intifada*). A state commission of inquiry, headed by Supreme Court Judge Theodore Or, was eventually established, but only after a lengthy public struggle, which brought to the fore the depth of frustration within the Arab community since 1998/9.

But October 2000 provided neither a breaking point between Jews and Arabs, nor a change in Arab attitudes to the state. In 1998, Israel's Jews celebrated 50 years of independent statehood and fulfillment of the Zionist dream. To the Arabs, however, this signified 50 years of *Naqba* – the tragedy and humiliating defeat suffered by the Palestinians in 1948.

In September 1998 there was a violent clash between security services and inhabitants in Umm-al-Fahm, protesting against their lands being taken over for military maneuvers.[1] Since the 1950s, various Arab groups, including those displaced from the deserted villages of Iqrit and Bir'am, had been lobbying for permission to return to their former homes. Over time, refugees of other villages, such as Ghabsiyy, Suhmata and others, had joined the protest. The lobbyists' main achievement was to unite all the Arab MKs around the suffering represented by the Association for the Defense of the Rights of the Internally Displaced Persons in Israel, which has been a part of all the Arab parties' political platforms since the 1996 general elections.

Israel's Arabs avoided coining their uprising *Intifada* and began referring to it by its synonym, *Habbeh*, or *Habbeh Sha'abiyya* – "uprising", or "national uprising". Through the use of this term, with its retrospective allusions, Arab intellectuals tried to integrate the riots into the public agenda and to differentiate between it and the Palestinian agenda in the territories occupied by Israel since 1967, with the objective of placing it firmly in the awareness of the Jewish public in Israel. Since the outburst of the violent riots, it has indeed become obvious that this is a civil protest, which hinted at a departure from ongoing apathy, submissive thought processes and behavior and, above all, the awakening of a large and under-privileged minority population from a lengthy sleep and passive acceptance of its situation. The differentiation between the Arab awakening in Israel and the Palestinian *Intifada* in the territories was meant to separate between the objectives of the Palestinian struggle and that of the Arabs of Israel. According to Salem Jubran, editor of *al-Ahali*, "They have an *Intifada* and we have a *Habbeh*. These are two different struggles. The Arabs in the territories are demanding independence, West Bank and Gaza are demanding national rights and the Arabs in Israel are demanding civil rights."[2]

It appeared at first that prime minister Ehud Barak was going to perpetuate the approach of Yitzhak Rabin with regard to the Arab population in Israel. Indeed, Barak's military history was well known to the Arab public, who attributed to him the extermination of leaders and commanders of the PLO and the Fatah in Tunisia and Beirut. But he gave the impression that he was the kind of man who would carry out everything he promised to do. However, during his administration, Barak tended to avoid meetings with the Arab public and, especially, with Arab leaders, which caused considerable bitterness toward him. According to some of the Arab municipal leaders, Barak's attitude to the Israeli Arabs was characterized by a superficial understanding of and an indifference to their needs. Only near to his trip to Camp David in June 2000 did he meet with a group of Arab Labor Party members. The meeting consisted mainly of complaints at his indifference to the Arab public in general and the fact that Arab party members were left out of party activities.

It was decided, before the forthcoming general elections and in the wake of the October 2000 events, to try to repair some of the damage. A conference was arranged for January 2001, to be held in Nazareth, with the objective of coaxing the Arab public to turn out in force and vote for Ehud Barak. Nazareth congresses of this kind took place prior to each general election and habitually drew the mainstream moderates from among the Arab leaders in Israel, and not only those identified with the Labor Party.

This time the congress posed a real challenge to Barak's supporters, who hoped that he would receive a warm welcome and, possibly, a *Sulha* (reconciliation) between him and the Arab sector. However, some members of the election headquarters objected to holding the congress in Nazareth, fearing a renewed outburst of violence and anti-Barak sentiments. It is important to point out that Barak really and truly did understand the necessity for solving the problems and distress of the Arab population, and considered it part of his policies to bring about significant change. In this spirit, he initiated an allocation of four billion NIS for the development of the Arab sector. But the Palestinian *Intifada*, which was at its height during his administration, overshadowed any plans that would have benefited the country's Arab citizens.

Much groundwork was done during the weeks preceding the conference and meetings took place with families of the victims of the October riots, in order to arrange condolence visits for the prime minister. The families refused to meet Barak or a parliamentary delegation sent by him, claiming that his only objective was to win the elections. After the elections, they promised, they would be willing to welcome him. However, once the elections were over, all approaches to Barak went unanswered and he wormed his way out of visiting Arab communities. The results of the conference were minimal. Barak did not succeed in stirring up any real support among the Arabs and a photograph published a few days later of Barak eating in an Arab restaurant in Tireh aroused nothing more than ridicule among Arab voters.[3]

On the political level, the disappointment was soon evident, when the violent uprising in the territories dragged in its wake the downfall of the Barak administration. Indeed, the large majority of Arab voters boycotted the February 2001 special elections for prime minister. Relations between the Jewish majority and the Arab minority in Israel also took a sharp turn for the worse as a result of the events of October 2000. The behavior of the Arab population in Israel changed and the level of violence rose; and the line between the Israeli Arabs and those residing in the occupied territories became obscure. The rise in hostility created by the new reality in Jewish–Arab relations resulted in a growing realization that there would be no return to the previous situation. Demonstrations in support of and in solidarity with the Palestinian struggle turned into an exhibition of frustration and an opportunity for Israeli Arabs to let off steam and fury. Among the Arab population, claims were made that Israel had been discriminating against them and humiliating them for over 50 years. The speakers were all united in the opinion that the days of repression were over and if Israel wished to continue with its previous behavior *vis-à-vis* the Arabs, it would have to exert a measure of strength, whose most obvious results would only be further, more stubborn riots.

It is impossible to understand the events of October 2000 without relating to the obvious economic inequality between Jews and Arabs This inequality is expressed in the way government money is spent; in the discrepancies in infrastructure and health services (and, as a result, life expectancy); in education; and in the way lands are expropriated from Arab landowners. For example, successive governments have made almost no allocation of state land for building and planning in the Arab sector. Local urban plans hardly ever reach the entrepreneurial and approval stage and, from time to time, houses built illegally because their owners had no other choice are destroyed. Dozens of villages have not yet received national recognition and do not enjoy regular water and electricity supplies and other essential services. No plans exist for the establishment of new rural and urban settlements in the Arab sector; Arab representatives are almost never involved in the existing planning committees. Public investments in housing, employment, education and infrastructure lag behind those in the Jewish sector. Between 2000 and 2002, many Arab towns and villages headed the unemployment lists and, of the 25 towns in which unemployment exceeded 10 percent, 17 were in the Arab sector. About 38 percent of Arab families live below the poverty line, as compared to 16.6 percent of the general population in Israel.

Admittedly, recent years have seen a democratization of the Israeli establishment and the Supreme Court of Justice has become the sounding board for many weighty civil issues – except that Arab citizens have come to realize that, although the new Israeli liberalism might be able to promise individual rights, no solution exists to the acute question of collective identity, which appears more insoluble as the Palestinian struggle in the occupied territories escalates. The unavoidable result has been that Israel's Arabs have increased their solidarity with Palestinian nationalism and grown increasingly distant from Israel.

The al-Aqsa *Intifada* in the occupied territories has raised the problematic nature of co-existence between Jews and Arabs. The *Intifada* exposed the fact that of all rifts in Israeli and Arab society, the Jewish–Arab rift is the deepest and most complex. The severity of this rift, according to Dan Suan,[4] lies in the fact that it is the result of the clearest dichotomy: each individual in each of the two societies belongs in the most obvious and objective way to one of the two camps that are divided by this same rift.

The events of October 2000 pushed the Arabs even further onto the country's social sidelines and the new Arab public discourse became more nationalistic and argumentative than ever before, and, as a result, more suspicious and threatening in the eyes of Jewish society. A broad consensus developed among the latter which was shared by most Jews, the political establishment and the military elite, who held that the status of the Arab minority in Israel is a form of security issue: after all, it was Arab citizens who took part in violent demonstrations. This is all reflected in opinion polls: 71 percent of Jewish society is convinced that the "Arab complaints about their conditions in Israel are unjustified"; 62 percent agree with the saying that "Arabs have an exaggerated influence on Israeli politics"; 59 percent agree that "the behavior of the Israeli Arabs is the main cause of tension between Jews and Arabs".[5] The two sides have closed ranks against each other. The Jewish public stopped visiting Arab towns and villages almost entirely and, in response, the Arabs stressed their need to protect their separate national and ethnic identity and even their cultural and geographical boundaries, notwithstanding the fact that, in the end, they did not want to relinquish visits of Jews in their towns and villages.

It would appear that their civil identity did not protect those Arabs who were shot in the course of the pro-*Intifada* demonstration in October 2000. As a result the civil project, devised mainly by Jews who wished to nurture, together with Arabs, a system of co-existence, almost completely collapsed. Arab citizens became embittered by their negative image *vis-à-vis* the Jewish Israelis and Arab intellectuals gave expression to these positions in the Hebrew press. But nothing was sufficient to repair what had been done, in light of the fact that even the good relations between the Israeli left and the Arab citizens had crumbled. What happened was that the Arabs learned that they are citizens of a state in which the majority population is Jewish, and it is incumbent on them to exhibit a willingness and an ability to blend into Israeli society. The only viable solution is for Arabs and Jews to establish a leadership capable of learning lessons from events such as those of October 2000, and to view them as an aim toward co-existence in one country, despite differences between the ethnic groups.

The events of October 2000, which exposed a deep crisis in solidarity with the state and faith in its institutions, have accompanied Israel's Arabs to this day (2008). The deaths of 13 Israeli Arabs aroused a fierce public polemic. An economic crisis, rising unemployment numbers and a fear of the destruction of houses built without planning permission stand constantly in the background and reinforce the feeling of alienation toward the Jewish establishment and public in Israel. In a single blow, the violent outcome of these events changed the agenda of the Arabs in Israel, which now focused on questions of land, the internally displaced persons, the *Naqba* and attempts – in August 2001 – to turn the Supreme Monitoring Committee for Arab Affairs in Israel into an official co-ordinating body, to establish representative and constitutional institutions and to organize themselves as a national minority.

Relations between Jews and Arabs and the Israeli establishment have seen many ups and downs, but since the Temple Mount incident in September 2000, the rift has deepened to the extent of almost complete alienation of the Arabs from the Jewish majority and from the establishment. This rift is going to be extremely hard to bridge; indeed, it is doubtful if it is possible to bridge it at all. Ostensibly, it would appear that the presence of three conditions might make it possible to turn back the wheels of time: a signed peace agreement with the Palestinians, active implementation of the principles of equality between the country's Jewish and Arab communities, and the Arabs relinquishing the "state for all its people" idea. However, until the Arab population is accepted as a full partner in the state – which does not appear imminent – rifts will continue to exist between the Jewish majority and the Arab minority. Under certain circumstances, perhaps, the rifts will not be so deep – but they will not disappear altogether.

October 2000 proved the interdependency of Israel's Jewish and Arab societies. Israel's Arabs should bear in mind that the State of Israel constitutes the realization of the Jewish nation's yearnings for a state of its own, the only state in which Jews are the majority. At the same time, the Jews must remember that their country is not only a Jewish state, but also a democratic state. The majority must understand that for the Arabs, the circumstances that turned them into a minority in the country constitute a national catastrophe, and that their integration into the State of Israel involved many painful sacrifices. It is necessary, therefore, to find ways to reinforce the Arab citizens' feeling of belonging to the state, without detracting from their own culture and community.

There has been a growing feeling among the Arab public in Israel since October 2000 that the time was ripe to demand a drastic change in attitude toward them. Many Arabs – and Jews – believed that relations would now take on new rules, and the Arab public's demands for full partnership in the state's decision-making would become firmer. However, a poll conducted by Sami Smooha and As'ad Ghanem have shown that the October events have actually caused the Arab public to be disinclined to conduct violent struggles, mainly because of the high price such struggles have demanded of them. Thus, in 2001, only 9.5 percent of the Arabs expressed support for illegal violent struggles, as compared with 21 percent in 1999. Either way, the Arab population of Israel is currently in a kind of double marginality: they are not taken into consideration with regard to decisions made by the Palestinian Authority and they have almost no access to the centers of decision-making in Israel, both of which increase their sense of crisis and alienation.

After the Or[6] Judicial Commission of Inquiry and its Conclusions

The decision to establish the Or Commission of Inquiry to examine the events of October 2000 aroused a great deal of unrest among the Jewish public as well as among the Arab public. The Jews saw it as a superfluous move to pacify the Arabs and to diminish the anticipated electoral harm to the Labor Party in the Arab sector, whereas the Arabs looked on the commission with suspicion and found it hard to believe that its conclusions would represent objective justice. The establishment of a commission of inquiry, therefore, did not arouse any great hopes. In my view, the establishment of a state commission of inquiry is not the ideal solution to the situation caused by the events of October 2000. From discussions with various people, it appears to me that Ehud Barak was put under insufferable pressure, both from the Arab public and from the Israeli left wing (headed by MKs and government ministers from Meretz and Labor) to convene a state commission of inquiry. Commissions of inquiry are usually convened in order to find local administrative, mechanic solutions. They adopt bureaucratic and instrumental thought processes and tend to ignore the moral considerations behind the operative decisions taken by the leaders of the systems under inquiry. Such commissions of inquiry aim to examine the way in which the system is functioning, and the compatibility of the activity in question with the law and the general rules of government. They do this by asking such questions as: Did the various levels of decision-makers foresee the outcome of their decisions? Did they carry out the necessary planning and execution? Did they respond efficiently and learn the necessary lessons? But such questions do not deal with the deep processes that determine the character of society. I told the government at the time that I opposed the establishment of a state commission, because it would expose to the public a picture of the Arab community in Israel and its conclusions would be adopted by Arab society in Israel as a "White Paper", with which to condemn the state in the international arena for its treatment of its Arab minority. Instead, I recommended establishing a suitably funded government body, which would make its way toward the Arab public, via meetings and practical initiatives for developing Arab towns and villages, increase employment opportunities in the Arab sector and reduce civil inequality. These, actually, are the issues that concern the Arab citizens and it is they, among others, that brought about the violent outbreaks of October 2000. These issues form the challenge that faces that government and from which it can no longer escape.

Indeed, the Or Commission found itself dealing with a more weighty issue than the matter for which it was convened: that of the inadequate treatment of the Arab population by successive Israeli governments, the same issue that continued to pop up in all its discussions. The issues with which it dealt deviated from the events themselves and the question of who opened fire first. Harsh questions were turned to representatives of the Arab public, decision-makers on the political echelon and police commanders, including: Was it a legitimate democratic demonstration against long-standing deprivation and discrimination? Was it a religious or nationalist outburst? Was it a spontaneous outburst, or was it organized well in advance? Was the outburst for the purposes of civil disobedience, or as an uprising? Did the demonstrators cross the line of legitimate civil dissent?

Did the police see the demonstrators as the enemy and was that the reason why they were so quick to pull the trigger?

For their part, the Arab MKs and other public figures took advantage of the commission, to which they were invited to testify, in order to voice their own truth, which most of the Jewish public refuses to hear and to internalize, a truth that the government, too, has managed to push aside. This truth concerns the condition of the Arabs in Israel, rather than the fatal events which the commission had been convened to examine. The witnesses presented a bill of indictment against the State of Israel blaming the policies of successive governments for their attitude toward the Arab minority population. The senior representatives of the Arab population and its political leaders presented a propaganda line comprised of two main elements: (1) although Israel is a law-abiding state, the Arab population is underprivileged and discriminated against, and therefore it has the right to take legitimate action in order to protest and demand its rights; (2) the Arab public is struggling for its identity and this struggle provides a legitimate basis for its protest.

The Or Commission discussions presented the problematic and complex relationship between Israel's Arab citizens and the establishment. The testimonies of the various offices and institutions exposed the mistakes made by successive governments in dealing with this large minority population – on the matter of land expropriation; building and planning permissions; discrimination in town planning, both locally and regionally; demolition of illegally built housing; discrimination in allocations and infrastructure; allocations for education, etc. Nonetheless, testimonies of Arab representatives show that the problems are deeper than mere discrimination and are connected to their identity and the Arab attitude toward the state. The commission, it would appear, fulfilled a task that no government in Israel had hitherto undertaken, in that it permitted a deep and serious long-term look at the issue of Israel's Arab minority population and investigated the reason behind such violent reaction to the events, whose only objective was protest. The mere fact that Jewish and Arab politicians were invited to testify before the commission, alongside academic experts on Arab affairs, as well as those witnesses who were connected directly with the shooting incidents, is proof that the commission was serious in its desire to examine all aspects of the affair and to reach well-founded conclusions. Moreover, the commission was well aware of the moral aspects of the decisions taken prior to and in the course of the riots, decisions that, by nature, accompany and direct the organization and offices that deal with Israel's Arabs and whose repercussions will inevitably be expressed in the next relationship crisis between the Arab minority and the establishment – a crisis which, I believe, is unavoidable. Thus, since the decision had already been taken to convene it, the commission did well in choosing to deal with the main issues involved in the relations between the Arab minority and the state, rather than to restrict its focus to the riots and the casualties, which were its objective in the first place.

A study of the Or Commission's conclusions reveals that the grave events were the result of profoundly troubling, ongoing factors.

1. An intense confrontation with a large minority Arab population within the Jewish state. The government's treatment of the Arab sector has consisted mainly of neglect and deprivation, with the result that the Arabs suffered from poverty, unemployment, lack of lands, a faulty education system, etc. The ongoing unrest, caused by all these, reached its peak in October 2000.
2. Next was the political-ideological radicalization process that the Arab sector has been undergoing over the last decades. These processes were expressed, among others, in various forms of solidarity and even support for the Palestinians against the State of Israel. The radicalization process was also tied to the growing strength of political Islamism in Israel in the period leading up to October 2000.

The Israeli Arab leadership failed to take advantage of the power these factors and events generated to fulfill their community's legitimate democratic demands. For the first time an accusing finger was pointed directly at Arabs. And, indeed, the commission determined that Sheikh Ra'ed Salah, as mayor of Umm-al-Fahm and subsequently head of the northern branch of the Islamic Movement, has, since 1998, been responsible, time after time, for advocating and encouraging the use of violence as a means for achieving objectives and denying the very legitimacy of the State of Israel. Thus also with regard to Azmi Bishara, head of the National Democratic Pact (Balad) faction in the Knesset, and Abd al-Malik Dahamsha, head of the United Arab Party (Ra'am) faction and member of Knesset. As for Jewish–Arab relations, the commission pointed out that the events placed a greater distance than ever between the possibilities of achieving co-existence and widened the rift between the two groups. It did not, however, reach any conclusions against any of the Arab witnesses who came to testify.

A close examination of the Or Commission's findings confirms the claims raised in earlier chapters, especially with regard to various government policies concerning the country's Arab citizens. The commission gave official authority to core issues in Jewish–Arab relations in Israel. From now on, it will no longer be possible to wriggle out of dealing with the commission's conclusions. The administration will be forced to implement at least some of the commission's decisions and the Arabs will see them as an historic document and a precedent in any legal petition or appeal to international civil rights organizations. For Israel's Arabs, the report is a definite sign of a new reality.

The Or Commission used its conclusions as a mirror to be placed before both the Israeli government and Arab society. The Or Commission was, after all, the most senior governmental forum to be convened since the beginning of the state to focus on issues concerning the Arab public and its status in Israeli society. It determined that the October 2000 events were not undetached from a broader reality, and from historical and political processes. In this respect, the commission's stance *vis-à-vis* the Arab population and its leaders is connected to two aspects: first, it relates to the past, to the study of the events and the history of the State of Israel with regard to the Arab citizens; and second, it touches on the future and lessons learned.

It would appear that *"Adala* – The Legal Center for Arab Minority Rights in Israel"*, which has been active since 1996, is keeping alive the battle over the Or Commission on behalf of the Arabs. Adala has been helped by Irish lawyers, well versed in Ireland's experience in this kind of commission of inquiry.[7] With the start of the Or Commission, *Adala* began taking testimonies. They passed on information to the press, claiming that evidence presented by the police was false, in order to cause the commission to focus not only on those who carried out the shooting, but also on the suffering of the Arab sector. In short, *Adala* attempted to broaden the commission's scope. It is impossible to defend Sheikh Ra'ed Salah without discussing the al-Aqsa mosque. It is not possible to defend the "sayings" of Abd al-Malik Dahamsha without also taking into account the demolition of Arab houses.[8] It is not possible to defend Azmi Bishara without discussing civil issues. Hasan Jabarin, Director General of *Adala*, described the commission and its discussions as "yes, it was a court, historical and political". *Adala*'s attorneys followed the discussions of the commission and even prepared their own conclusions, including "alternative conclusions", under the heading "Law and Politics in Front of a Commission of Inquiry". It is my belief that the Or Commission lent legitimacy to *Adala*, as a body that stands guard and defends the civil rights of the Arab minority in Israel, and, since then, *Adala* has indeed led a legal battle for protecting these rights in Israel and in the world.

In its report, the Or Commission arrived at those reasons believed to be the cause of the protest rally in October 2000: historic discrimination – since 1948 – and socio-economic discrimination were deemed to be the cause of the relationship crisis between the Jews and Israel's Arabs, a crisis that was sparked in the wake of the violent incidents in the territories. *Adala* adds the discriminatory allocation of lands as another central cause. As for the immediate reasons, *Adala* concludes that Ariel Sharon's August 28, 2000 visit to the Temple Mount in Jerusalem is what actually ignited the protests.

It is not easy to determine for certain whether Israel, in convening a government commission (the first of its kind), has missed the boat with regard to repairing past injustices. The October riots, the overreaction of the police (which are excused as being a reaction to the rioters themselves), the obvious influence of the Islamic Movement (which doesn't cease warning of Israel's so-called intention to attack the al-Aqsa mosque), the rhetoric of incitement of the Arab MKs, the perpetual nibbling away of the Israeli Arabs' Israeli identity, the unfulfilled promises of the government to the Arab sector and the terrorist cells in Israeli Arab homes, especially during mid–2001 – all these issues testify to the vast rift that continues to grow between the two societies.

Decisions on Arab Affairs – Governance in Israel

Israel's political system is characterized by an extremely centralized administrative authority and a divided Knesset. Policies are mostly the responsibility of the prime minister, while the Knesset works and influences the political content via coalition politics. The power of the large parties has dropped and the party system has become multi-focused. The split sharpens the coalition government's difficulties in governance. The 1996 and 1999 elections, with the direct vote for prime minister, brought about a deep rift in the Knesset and the lack of a single major party. Fifteen parties were elected to the 1999 Knesset and the smaller ones increased their ability to receive large and disproportionate chunks of the government pie. Most of the government's energies and resources were invested in fulfilling coalition promises. The political establishment grew more sectarian and the political parties focused on specific issues or in fulfilling their jobs as representatives of particular interest groups. Under these circumstances, the Arab sector was pushed to the sidelines. In any case, the Arab parties had never been part of the political game, nor were they taken into consideration in the coalition wheeling and dealing.

Over the years, most government decisions were managerial and instrumental; the Arab population was considered only with respect to security, economics, health, education, law and religion. Most decisions relating to Arabs were negative and usually involved committees and teams recommending methods of law enforcement and increased control over the Arab sector. Most decisions were ad hoc responses to sudden crises or tensions, or from political considerations. Events such as the 1967 Six Day War, the 1973 Yom-Kippur War, the 1987 *Intifada* and the first Gulf War, which had a dramatic psychological effect on the Arab sector, did nothing to induce successive governments to deal with issues relating to Jewish–Arab relations in Israel. It was only the highly charged riots of October 2000 that drew the government's attention and forced it to begin thinking of possible solutions. But these drew criticism from Jews and Arabs alike and the rift between the two communities only deepened.

One potential solution worth mentioning is the 1962 five-year plan to develop the infrastructure in the Arab towns and villages. The objective of the plan was to "raise their consumer level and living standards, so that their low standard of living does not become a source of hate". And, indeed, some of the villages received roads, public buildings and other infrastructure work. It was an important, though limited, act and expressed a little of what was included in the original program. According to the historian Yair Boimel,[9] it seems that the decision-makers had no real intention to implement the plan in its entirety. As part of the debate to cancel the military administration in 1966, discussions were held on the status of the Israeli Arabs. Twenty years later, two significant discussions took place in the government on the same subject: I initiated the first in 1984, during the premiership of Shimon Peres. The discussion was based on plans prepared by an interdisciplinary steering committee comprising Jews and Arabs, and provided an in-depth analysis of the major issues and suitable solutions. In fact, the discussion did not provide any real results, and the program remained on paper only. The second discussion, in 1989 (during the Shamir government), was initiated by the minister in charge of Arab affairs, Ehud Olmert. Neither the *Intifada* in the territories, nor events such as "Land Day" and the riots of October 2000, yielded any constructive solutions, other than jacked-up preventive measures and yet another declaration regarding a government program for the benefit of the Israeli Arabs.

The prime minister's office is the place in which the decision process takes place and through which dealings with ministers and ministerial committees are channeled. It is also the place where senior civil servants and other administrative personnel carry out their work. But interaction with the specific interest group – the Arab citizens themselves – was usually limited. Unlike the advisers and assistants on media, military, economical and political affairs (many of whom used their talents and ambitions to follow distinguished careers), the advisors on Arab affairs in the prime minister's office and in various other government offices were mostly second-level civil servants, and their expertise on Arabs affairs became a disadvantage when they tried to move up the political hierarchy. Activity in the Arab sector never could provide a ticket to inclusion on the Knesset candidate list. Too many Jews see people who work with Arabs as belonging to and being part of the Arab sector and tend to treat them with suspicion. Most of the ministers entrusted with Arab affairs were not included among the senior government members. Nawwaf Masalha, former MK and member of Histadrut (Labor Federation) committees, often said to me, "It's a pity. So long as you are involved in the Arab sector, the Jews won't allow you to reach any senior position. To them, work with Arabs is a stain."

The resentment and suspicion felt by many Jews toward Arabs – the result of decades of Israeli-Arab conflict – are what created this attitude. And thus cultural differences and suspicion remain the reason why only people with a military background, or "Arabists", join the bureaucratic system that deals with Arab affairs.

The *modus operandi* typical of successive governments in Israel consists of the establishment of committees and teams. Throughout its years of activity, the Bureau for Arab Affairs never achieved the respect or even legitimacy of the Arab public, which saw it as patronizing. Thus, since 1984, different government ministers have been appointed to deal with Arab affairs. Ostensibly, this constituted an upgrade in attitude to the Arab sector. In fact, it was the same thing, with different dressing. Advisors on Arab affairs continued to serve the government, except that now they were ensconced in new ministerial offices.

The Barak and Sharon governments tried to activate a number of groups to deal with the Arab population. On March 18, 2001, the government decided to establish a ministerial committee for the Arab sector, under the chairmanship of government minister Saleh Tarif, a Druze who represents a minority group in the Arab sector. At first the idea was for "the ministerial committee to prepare a comprehensive plan for solving the distress of the Arab population and follow its progress, while maintaining consultations with elected heads of the Arab public". Similar ministerial committees had been convened by earlier governments. Other committees and subcommittees for Bedouin affairs in the south also acted under government auspices and were chaired by whoever was the current general manager of the government. In the wake of the October 2000 rioting in Arab towns and villages within Israel, the Barak government decided on November 20 the same year to establish a Department for Affairs of Arabs in Israel, which was to act alongside the Ministerial Committee for the Arab Sector. One week later, on November 29 – probably under the influence of those events – the government decided to draft a proposal regarding the structure and authority of the central body entrusted with dealing with Bedouin affairs. The team was never convened, nor did it even present any plans and, with the fall of the Barak government, all that remained of the decision was a piece of paper. The new government under the premiership of Ariel Sharon did not even acknowledge it.

It was only in the late 1980s that the Israeli government began to understand that it was its job to initiate an extensive, long-term regional development plan for the Arab sector, because the level of services and infrastructure was way below that of the rest of the country. But it was only in the mid-1990s that the government of Israel decided to implement an ongoing plan for developing and advancing the Arab population. A separate plan was prepared for each of the different ethnic groups within the Arab sector. In 1995, a plan was drafted for the Druze and Circassian sector; in 1998, the plan was drafted for the Bedouin of the north; in late 2000, the Barak government decided on the most extensive plan ever prepared for the entire Arab sector, which was to cost the economy some NIS 4 billion over the years 2001–4. The decision stressed that this was a national emergency plan for the development of the Arab sector in Israel and its main objective was to reduce social discrepancies at all levels. The plans were accompanied by government decisions and commitments to carry them out and were supposed to involve significantly increased resources to be channeled into the Arab sector. Also, government ministers promised to push forward various related plans, but almost nothing was actually done.

A typical example is the government's plans for the unrecognized Bedouin villages in the Negev. The government had always believed in transferring the Bedouin population to orderly, urban settlements. But the Bedouin were uncooperative. The eight government-established townships soon turned into hotbeds of unemployment and crime, and many Bedouin refused to uproot and move into them, preferring to remain in the areas they considered their own. Thus many Bedouin families congregated in settlements devoid of municipal status, lacking government recognition and basic services: electricity, water, roads and health and welfare services. The gap in welfare and community services was soon filled by the Islamic Movement, which introduced an efficient infrastructure of essential amenities, in Umm-al-Fahm, for example. The result was the rapid Islamization of the Bedouin population.

In 1985, as chairman of the Labor Party's Minorities Department, I took upon myself the task of explaining this reality to the country's leaders and attempted to bring about a change in government policy *vis-à-vis* the Bedouin people and their lands. I consulted with legal and real estate experts and formulated a position on the lands issue. I tried to advance the concept that, even if there was no official basis to the Bedouin claims to lands in the Negev, it is impossible to ignore their squatters' rights – which resemble those of sitting tenants in key-money apartments and houses. I believed that compensation must be provided to the "Diaspora" Bedouin in the form of money or substitute land. The government should establish suitably planned settlements for them, including all necessary services; these settlements should be provided with enough land to cover the inhabitants' long-term needs (given their 5.5 percent per annum reproduction rate), in order to prevent the population from taking over additional lands. Today, the Bedouin are spread over more than half a million acres of land in dozens of spontaneously established settlements, devoid of all government recognition. My plan would enable the return of most of the lands under dispute (nearly 200,000 acres), which the Bedouin claim as their own.

I also recommended establishing an administrative body which would concentrate the authorities of all the various government offices involved in dealing with the Bedouin sector; the advent of this body would enable immediate solutions to relevant issues and prevent the need for negotiating between different offices. And, indeed, in the early 1980s, the Operational Administration for the Law of Lands Purchase was established, which signaled the beginning of a serious improvement in the relations between the government and the Bedouin population. The administration's first task was to evacuate the Bedouin from Tel-al-Maleh (Tel Malhata), followed immediately by the more painful issue of moving the Negev Bedouin population to permanent settlements. I was involved in the establishment of the Bedouin towns of Hura and Laqyyeh, which were designed to accommodate the needs of the inhabitants, with whom I had close contact. Over time, the Administration for the Advancement of the Bedouin Issue – which I had recommended at the very beginning of my tenure as head of the Labor Party Minorities Department – developed out of the Operational Administration.

The turning point in official attitudes to resettling the Bedouin came in 1995 – on a declaratory level, at least. The Ministry of Housing proposed allocating funds for developing and planning four additional urban settlements for the Bedouin (each of which was to house between 5,000 and 12,000 inhabitants), and seven rural, agricultural villages (in which some 1,500 families would be settled). However, the plan was restricted to those areas under the auspices of the Housing Ministry; the Bedouin themselves were not involved in its drafting, nor were they asked to agree to it. Moreover, the plan did not include water allocations for agriculture, grazing grounds, or industry to fulfill the Bedouin's demand for employment. On the other hand, the plan for the southern region under the authority of the Interior Ministry did not reflect any change in policy toward the Bedouin issue, but continued to push settlement in the existing Bedouin townships. There was obviously no fixed government plan for this population. Still, during 2000, the villages of Darjat and Umm Batin were recognized as permanent settlements and in 2001–2 there was a decision-in-principle to establish seven additional settlements; in August 2002 a plan was approved for the establishment of Be'er Hail (Bir Hadaj) and Beit Pelet, which were meant to provide a prototype for modern rural-agricultural settlements. In April 2003, a long-term plan was approved, once again, for development in the Negev Bedouin sector. In an attempt to attract the inhabitants of villages currently spread over large areas and implement the government's right to the land, the plan consists of developing seven settlements which did not have municipal status. The Ministry of the Interior decided, in July 2003, to appoint a regional council – under the name Abu Basma – for the Bedouin villages, to include under its auspices eight villages, all of whom received lands in 2005, on which to establish a settlement.[10]

Most of the decisions and agreements signed with representatives of the Arab sector during the 1990s stressed the central role played by the Ministry of the Interior in examining the needs of the population, as well as in initiating and planning the development of the local Arab authorities. The ministry was supposed to locate the budgetary problems of these authorities and to find ways for pushing the plans forward and implementing the government's policies for reducing the gap between the Arab sector and the rest of society. Already in August 1991, the government had entrusted the Ministries of the Interior and Finance with preparing a five-year plan for the Arab sector. But in his 2001 report, the state comptroller revealed that the development plan had never even been galvanized.

Things started to change somewhat in 1992, in the wake of processes that led the Rabin government to the Oslo Accords. In August 1994 the government and representatives of the Arab community decided to establish a committee under the auspices of the Ministry of the Interior, in order to examine various problems with which local and regional authorities in the Arab sector had to contend. In effect the committee did not formulate a document summarizing its findings, not to mention conclusions, and, in fact, stopped operating. In January 1997, another agreement on the same matter was signed between the government and the Arab local authorities; but this time, too, the government and Ministry of the Interior failed to fulfill their part in the agreement.

December 1999 saw another agreement between representatives of the Ministry of the Interior and the Ministry of Finance, in consultation with a committee of the heads of Arab local authorities. According to this agreement, the relevant government offices were supposed to present a four-year plan for carrying out projects in the Arab settlements. The plan was supposed to be presented between January and March 2000 and to include projects relating to infrastructure, development, industry and employment. But in October 2000 the government decided on an ongoing, inclusive plan for the development of the Arab settlements and, this time, the job of fulfilling it was given to an interministerial team, headed by the prime minister's office.

Of all the five-year plans, only that aimed at the Druze and Circassian sectors was almost fully funded, although its implementation was quite faulty. The government relinquished its authority and the distribution of funds became, in part at least, a political-economic tool in the hands of the Forum for the Heads of Druze and Circassian Local Authorities, a member of the plan's administrative committee.

Although the government took many positive decisions regarding Israel's Arab sector, many of them remained unfulfilled. Presumably, some of the civil servants who were supposed to carry out the government's decisions reckoned that the government did not wish for its decisions to be fulfilled and that they were merely declaratory. The non-fulfillment of government decisions can also be explained by the fact that "all the political spectrum" did not include the Arab parties, or a single Arab MK from the Zionist parties. The Arabs in Israel have always filled a separate category, both with regard to their parliamentary presence and by the way they were conceived as a potential electorate. There appears to be in the government a desire to break down the wall between Jews and Arabs, and to bring about change by drafting decisions to the benefit of the Arab population. But since the Arabs are not party to the decision-making process, or involved in carrying out the plans, they remain reserved and critical. It is my belief that the best way to move forward on this issue is to draft a Jewish–Arab social pact that will define the civil rights and obligations both of the Jews and of the Arabs in Israel. The government should then approve the manifesto, adopt it, and it would thereby become a basis for the country's policies toward the Arabs.

I have discovered that 610 decisions have been taken on the matter of Israel's Arab population since the establishment of the state. Only 78 of these were taken during the tenure of the military administration (1948–66). During this period, the establishment reigned completely and firmly over the Arab public and did not see the need to discuss and make decisions that might bring about any improvement in the Arabs' conditions, or even to promote political issues. To this may be added the fact that no factor was found that drew the Israeli Arab public into open conflict with the authorities. Against this background, 1952 was an exceptional year, in that during those 12 months, nine decisions were taken with regard to the Israeli Arabs. Most of these dealt with the way in which the various government offices treated them under military administration, and with the lack of co-ordination between the different departments in the military administration and the civil servants in the Arab sector. Things changed significantly between 1967 and 1991. During this period, the government took 263 decisions on Arab-related issues. This makes it obvious that successive governments of Israel were guided by the approach that the Arab issue was to be dealt with only as a result of regional or internal circumstances, and not to promulgate long-term plans unless the matter required a decision. Thus, between 1967 and 1968 alone, 36 decisions were taken, mainly as a result of the Six Day War, which resulted in open boundaries to the Gaza Strip and the West Bank and to a renewed (and worrying) meeting of the Arabs of Israel and their Palestinian relatives in the territories.

The 15 decisions made during 1972 were influenced mainly by the weakened monopoly of the Communist Rakah Party and the establishment of the Sons of the Village movement; and also by the fear of growing Arab nationalism in the country and by the growing awareness among the Arabs of their civil rights. A manifestation of these was the decision to establish a public committee to examine the level of municipal services in the Arab sector. Other decisions included the employment of Arab graduates and land issues in the Negev, as well as the matter of integrating the Arab population into the life of the state. The first two years of the Likud administration (1977–8) were relatively silent, with only nine Arab-related decisions taken. The Likud, it appeared, wanted to study the matter and to set a policy of its own *vis-à-vis* the Arab minority population. After some time, the Likud decided to choose a policy that was defined in words as "involving the Arab population in the life of the country". The result of this choice was discord between the CEO of the Prime Minister's Office, Eliyahu Ben Elissar, and the advisor on Arab affairs, Moshe Sharon, which resulted in the resignation of the latter, whose proposal to integrate Arabs and disband the Advisor's Bureau was completely ignored. Nor was Moshe Sharon's successor, Binyamin Gur-Arye, able to bring his plan to the attention of the government. And, for the first time, a minister, Simha Ehrlich, was appointed to supervise Arab affairs. There was no doubt at all that the prime minister himself had no direct interest in the Arab issue.

The year 1987 saw 22 decisions on Arab matters, the result of activity on the part of Moshe Arens, minister for the Arab sector. Arens announced his intention to achieve full integration of the Arab citizens in the life of the country and during that year the government held a debate on the status of the Druze population. The *Intifada* that broke out in the territories during December 1987 did not raise any debate on possible repercussions for the Arab population of Israel, and throughout 1988, notwithstanding such events as the general strike in the Arab sector that began on November 15, only one decision was taken, on the initiative of the Supreme Monitoring Committee for Arab Affairs in Israel. A significant about-turn took place only in 1992, and from then until April 14, 2002, the government produced 269 decisions on the country's Arab population, resulting from changed attitudes toward the Arab population following the Oslo Accords and NGO activity, especially on civil rights issues.

The government took a large number of decisions during 2000 and 2001, as compared with previous years. On January 27, 2000 the government adopted the plan to update urban plans for Arab towns, with a budget of NIS 28 million. The plan, which aimed at improving relations with the Arab population, did not include the Bedouin settlements in the country's south, nor was it ever carried out. The October riots brought about more government decisions of this kind.

The picture remained grim and is reflected yearly in the state comptroller's report. According to the 2001 report, some 48 percent of the Arab towns and villages have no master plan for development and there is a severe lack of reserve lands for public needs, which makes it impossible for any long-term plans to develop. The state comptroller blames the Ministries of the Interior and Finance, both of whom failed, over the years, to fulfill most of the government's various decisions. Sami Isa, chairman of the local council at Kafar Qasem on behalf of the Islamic Movement (southern branch), who discovered that the plan for local development that he had helped draft with the Ministry of the Interior had not been implemented, went so far as to announce the implementation of an independent development for the village. Although the plan was not approved by the planning authorities, Isa permitted the inhabitants to build according to its outlines, announcing that "life is stronger than planning permission".

The Or Commission report reinforces the claims made in this book with regard to successive governments' treatment of the Arab population of Israel. For example, the conclusions reveal the lack of an effective governing system in all matters pertaining to the Arab sector. According to the Or Commission, there has been a constant increase in the alienation between the Arab minority and the Jewish majority since the establishment of the state, and "this is a strategic danger of the first order".[11] Although the commission's report points out the basic conditions for the strained relations between Arabs and Jews, the plan published by the government shows no change in attitude. Moreover, the prime minister made it conditional on "co-operation on the part of the Arab sector and its leadership in such a way as to make possible the creation of an ideological infrastructure for real co-existence".[12]

In adopting the conclusions of the commission that it itself established, the government could have implemented them immediately, but it chose, instead, to evade practical decisions and to establish another ministerial committee "for conducting a thorough study of the conclusions of the Or Commission report, and presented the government its own opinions regarding the rest of the conclusions detailed in the report".[13] This is one more example of Israel's problematic governance. As has already been stated, the government tries to avoid having to contend with issues that require decisions and implementations, reasoning that a too-swift process of change in the status of the Arab population could upset the state's dominantly Jewish character. Naturally, this infuriates the Arabs and deepens even further their mistrust of the Jews. The Lapid Commission gave its full support to the Or Commission's conclusions and even added practical recommendations of its own, including the establishment of a government authority to deal with problems involved in planning and building, budgets, discrimination, participation in government offices, and the authority to supervise the implementation of government decisions. We must now wait and see if this authority, if it is, indeed, established, has the ability to see to the implementation of the Or Commission recommendations, as they were adopted by the Lapid Commission, whose recommendations the government, on its part, also adopted. In the meantime, unsurprisingly and typical of government behavior in Israel, a supervisory committee established by the Council for National Security has been entrusted with the task of following up the conclusions of the Lapid Commission. In other words, a twisting, winding course has been created on the way to perpetuating the existing situation, at the base of which lies a blatant unwillingness to change the current reality.

Israel is faced with a picture of disorganized governmental activity in everything concerning the Arab population, and faulty governance in face of the fact that the civil service does not always implement government decisions to the full. All this has taken place over a period of time that saw the development of a civil society and the establishment of institutions and organizations that promote civil rights and maintain international connections in order to put forward issues concerning the minority Arab population in Israel and the latent discrimination against it. The state appears to continue to respond to events rather than plan for the future. For example, one week before the Or Commission published its report – and with timing that was not coincidental – the Ministerial Committee for the Non-Jewish Sector released an "extensive plan aimed at improving conditions for Israel's Arab citizens, redefining their status and integrating them in [Israeli] society and in the state". Once again, the program presented declaratory or administrative clauses, of the kind that had already been adopted many times before. For example, "rules will be determined with regard to suitable representation for the Arab population in the civil service and in government offices". It seems that the only novelty here is the introduction of a new body to "deal" with Arab affairs – the Council for National Security on the Matter of the Non-Jewish Sector, which is supposed to be part of the Ministerial Committee for the Non-Jewish Sector.[14]

It is important, therefore, to say clearly that successive governments' management of Arab citizens since the establishment of the state has never been decisive and has constantly evaded decisions regarding the civil and political status of the country's Arab minority. Israel's Jewish identity and image have always consisted of political/constitutional blocks that prevented the country from changing its policies with regard to its Arab population and Jewish–Arab relations. These blocks prevented the government and the establishment from adopting the kind of focused and clear-cut policy which would inevitably have caused conflict between political adversaries and upset the concepts of leading members of the establishment. No government would have been able to take serious, long-term decisions on land allocations, or the return of local Arab displaced people to villages destroyed in 1948, or to introduce changes in the state's symbols and the Law of Return. Moreover, there has never been a leadership willing to change basic values necessary for integrating the Arabs. The practical results of these blocks are alienation and mistrust between Jews and Arabs.

It was not only Jews and Arabs, as individuals, who created moral/ cultural blocks that kept them apart from each other, but also the establishment. Thus it has been possible for the authorities to take advantage of legal loopholes and to favor the Jewish majority when it came to settlement and allocation of government funds. It was easy, too, not to be too hasty in implementing decisions, or to be over-generous when there was no special fondness for or friendship toward Arabs; not to mention, of course, the distance caused by the profound cultural differences between Jews and Arabs.

For their part, the Arabs were influenced by their circumstances and by their need to reinforce the Palestinian component in their identity, as a result of which their Jewish counterparts felt threatened and suspicious. The rapid Islamization of Arab society strengthened further the mistrust and mutual alienation. The Jews learned the advantages of living in a Jewish state that fulfills their national wishes and of raking in its economic fruits, and developed an ethnocentric attitude that was soon given legal backing. Any chance, therefore, of bridging the social, cultural and nationalist gap was thwarted. Influenced by regional and internal events, the Jews continued to stress the demographic danger posed by the Arab population and some even demanded a transfer of all the Arabs, or territorial exchange, in order to maintain the state's Jewish image. Moreover, laws aimed at limiting the civil and political status of the Arabs achieved parliamentary support and the presenters of these laws were not prevented from doing so, even though some of them were blatantly discriminatory. The Israel-Palestine conflict, which has not been resolved to this day, has sharpened the position of both sides – Jewish and Arab. Among the Jews, the right wing has increased its support and, among the Arabs, the Islamists and those who support a radical stance against the state and its authorities have grown stronger. These positions are the result of a lengthy historical, nationalist conflict and decades of educational brainwashing. The political/constitutional blocks have taken root on the administrative level, obstructing most operative decisions. Among the politicians, these blocks have become a political agenda.

In Israel's socio-political reality, these blocks are ineradicable and no policies are capable of covering up for them. It is possible, therefore, only to propose solutions that do not deviate from the paradigm that conceives Israel as a Jewish and democratic state and, even then, there will be no significant change in Jewish–Arab relations; on the contrary, there can only be a honing of the friction between the two populations. The proposals put forward below cannot provide a solution to the basic regional and internal processes in which Israel finds itself, but they are an attempt to find a way to bring normality to the country's civilian life.

Looking to the Future

Since 1993, the year in which the Oslo Accords were signed between Israel and the PLO, Jewish–Arab reality in Israel has been in turmoil. The feeling that peace is within reach has awakened fears and hopes that are expressed in the two communities in accordance with the political orientations of the two; the ideological aspirations and security traumas carved in the experience of them both. Facing peace, Israeli society has become increasingly involved with itself and even more divided. The country's Arab citizens, on the other hand, move between the equality option and the exclusion option. The government, the establishment and the political parties have become more liberal and democratic, but they are also in a vice, pressed between the Arab population on the one hand, and, on the other, an ongoing social crisis which has deepened the rift between right and left. Above all else, the last 15 years reflect the changes undergone by the Arab population, Jewish–Arab relations in Israel and the contribution of the political system to this situation.

Two processes have been chasing each other within Israel's Arab population, in the wake of the peace process – "Israelization" and "Palestinization". These processes are ostensibly contradictory, but are actually complementary. A unique synthesis now exists of Palestinians and Israelis, which expresses itself in localizing the national struggle. In other words, casting an Israeli component into the Palestinian national struggle; adapting the Israeli Arabs' struggle to their civil reality; and harnessing a minority with a blatantly Palestinian identity to the struggle of its group national identity within the Israeli reality. But the "Israeliness" of Israel's Arabs has its limits. This is obvious from the stance they are taking on the government's "Disengagement Plan" – Israel's evacuation of the settlements in the Katif bloc and the Gaza Strip – as well as Ehud Olmert's 2006 "Realignment Plan".[15]

On this subject, it appears that Arab citizens do not see themselves as a part of the public discourse, even though an Israeli withdrawal from the territories is part of the political ideology of the entire Arab public. According to historian Adel Manna' and sociologist Aziz Haidar, the Arabs fear the downfall of democratic rule in Israel, believing it would have an adverse effect on them. They prefer, therefore, not to intervene, or even to make themselves heard on anything concerning the withdrawal. But above all, the Arabs of Israel appear to fear that the withdrawal will cause the state to be more "Jewish", which will mean less civil rights for them, and there may even be talk of territorial exchanges with the Palestinian Authority (in which areas with an Arab majority population will be handed over to the Authority). Aziz Haidar adds that, with the return of the Jewish settlers to Israeli territory, the Arabs will become the Jews' Palestinians; the internal conflict with the Arabs will just grow stronger.

Thus the Arabs might wish to remain Israelis. And this, as I see it, is their dilemma. On the one hand, as the political process moves forward – and the convergence plan is part of that process – so will the fear of the country's Arab population increase and as a consequence they will alienate themselves even further from Israeli society. On the other hand, it is obvious that they wish to remain in Israel as part of Israeli society, but they prefer to stay on the sidelines, watching the internal Jewish struggles, and fearing for their future.

The combined processes of "Israelization" and "Palestinization" have also motivated the Arab leadership in Israel – both political and intellectual – to doubt the foundations of Israeli reality. They have begun to point out the supposed discrepancy between Israel being at once Jewish and democratic. MK Ahmad Tibi put it quite picturesquely: "Israel is a democratic state to the Jews and a Jewish state to the Arabs." As'ad Ghanem[16] has said that the two main tests of a democratic regime – equality before the law and defense of the minority – do not exist in Israel and because of this Israel is not a democratic state. This was followed by more outspoken complaints from Arab leaders and intellectuals, and calls for a change of the regime in Israel. Until such a time as Israel becomes "a state for all its people", these individuals demand some kind of autonomy for the Arab minority and the necessary ideological infrastructure to accommodate their demand. Although this idea is still exclusively adhered to by Arab intellectuals, the Arab leadership is trying to establish civil institutions and organizations (NGOs) as a basis for a Palestinian society in Israel.

The Islamic Movement has taken practical steps in this direction. Sheikh Ra'ed Salah is pushing forward with the "autonomous society plan", whose objective is "an integrative society that manages its own institutions and life, a society free of the pressure that threatens it on the part of the Israeli establishment". In the Kuwaiti weekly *al-Mujtama'a*, he laid out the main points of his program, which he described as the basis for the establishment of a "state within a state".[17] In effect, some of the institutions in the plan – education, welfare, culture, sport and religious services – are already provided by the Islamic Movement. The sheikh appears to be trying to combine Islamic ideology into his aspirations for increased political and social power for the Islamic Movement. Although this is accepted by his own followers, it is not shared by the Arab public at large.

Many of the Arab political bodies, as well as many intellectuals from among Arab society in Israel, are not in a hurry to define their national aspirations in the State of Israel, since such a definition would have led them to put forward demands for territorial, cultural and social autonomy. Many fear that such ethnic separatism would provide a formula for perpetuating their disadvantage and discrimination. Israel's Arabs have chosen, therefore, a definition according to which equality means no more discrimination. This definition has in a sense bypassed the conflict and enabled the creation of a united front; but it also incorporates a trap. After all, improved living conditions and an end to discrimination are both legitimate national objectives, well worth working for; but if this work is carried out within frameworks provided by the Zionist parties, the results might even be successful.

In an attempt to grab a defensive position, it would appear that Jews and Arabs in Israel have each become entrenched in opposite corners. Also, the Arabs are moving fast toward parliamentary and civil isolation. The Arab MKs are finding themselves pushed to the political and parliamentary fringe. Because they are irrelevant and lacking in power and influence, they are forced to become ever louder and more provocative,[18] especially on issues that do not relate directly to their constituents, namely the Arab voters, who hang no great hopes on their political influence, but seek alternatives in the form of self-government, dissociation from the establishment, building independent institutions and maintaining a separate political community.

Here it is worth presenting the position taken by Nadim Rouhana,[19] which, today, reflects the mainstream intellectual and political elite within Arab society in Israel. According to Rouhana, the highly explosive nature of the Israel-Palestine conflict is a result of the fact that the Palestinian Arabs are a homeland nation. The focus of the Palestinian nation's collective identity is its ties to its homeland; in other words, the territory between the river (Jordan) and the (Mediterranean) sea. Thus the Palestinian people's struggle is not necessarily over the establishment of a Palestinian state in the territories. The fact is that they refused to receive 92 percent of the West Bank, as offered to them at the Camp David negotiations. From the point of view of a homeland nation, such a state could never solve the refugee problem, or their return to their homeland; nor can it organize the presence of the refugees in their homeland. For this reason, too, Israel's Arabs will refuse to move to territories defined as a Palestinian state, because – according to them – they are already sitting on their own land in their homeland.

The civil status of Israel's Arabs has become a critical issue among international groups and NGOs. The United Nations, too, is showing interest in the relationship between the Jewish majority and the Arab minority in Israel. In a May 2003 report, the UN Civil Rights Commission calls on Israel to reduce the social, economic and cultural gap between Jews and Arabs and to recognize the Bedouin settlements scattered throughout the Negev region.

Three options face the state of Israel and its Arab citizens:

1. *Status quo*: Israel will continue trying to maintain Jewish seniority and the image of a democracy according to its own concept. This is a model of the "ethnic democracy" which exists today. In time, this model will almost certainly result in reduced exclusivity of the Jewish majority and improved living conditions for the Arab minority. But this option does not define the majority-minority relations in Israel and leaves an opening for perpetual arguments on the rights and status of the Arabs in the country.

2. *Integration:* This option would enable Israel to adopt a process of democratic change, during which the Arabs will gradually be granted full equality, at the cost of some blurring of the country's Jewish image. Although, under certain circumstances, this option can be realized, it is not desirable because this would lead, ultimately, to a two-nation state.

3. *Dissociation:* Israel would continue to maintain ethnic domination at the expense of equality. In such a case, the Arab sector will probably consider isolationist options, in other words, dissociation without emigration. The meaning of this is that the Arab population would opt for dissociating itself from the governing system. This is a dangerous option for the future of Israel and action must be taken to avoid it.

The dialectics behind the definition "Israel as a democratic, Jewish state" requires Israel to move toward a new model. There is reason, therefore, to propose a recipe for future relations between Jews and Arabs in the State of Israel, one that would take into account the options described above and be based on a structure founded on policies involving the Arab citizens in the distribution of power and resources. Such a structure would mean granting cultural autonomy to the Arabs, sharing resources with them, ensuring equal opportunities and distribution of power and allowing them to advance economically, socially and politically. In addition it would mean giving them the authority to manage regional planning policies.

Before describing the structure of the proposed model, it is worth describing some of the issues that appear to undermine the security of the Jewish majority in the future of the Jewish state:

1. *The demographic issue:* the natural birthrate of the Arab population is significantly higher than that of the Jews, so that by 2025 the Arab population will constitute about 25 percent of Israel's population, compared with today's 19 percent. Statistical data show that the Arab population's birthrate in 1980 stood at 3.4 percent, while at the end of 2003, it was 3 percent. The drop parallels the raised living standards and improved education opportunities among Israel's Arabs. Further investment in improving living standards in the Arab sector and a further rise in education levels will – ostensibly – result in further drops in the birthrate, as has taken place in other parts of the world.

2. *Islamism and "born-again" Islamists:* A movement of return to religion has grown since the early 1980s, drawing in its wake streams of Islamism that took advantage of the spaces (welfare, education) left empty by the Israeli establishment. Some Islamists even call for electoral boycotts. So far, the Islamic Movement has

not succeeded in gaining mass support, but with no improvement in the conditions of the Arab public and a solution to the Israel-Palestine conflict, the Islamic Movement could well be returned to the center of the political map, which will greatly increase the fears of the Jews.

3. *Palestinian nationalism and peace with the Palestinians*: Since 1967, Israel's Arab citizens have gradually come to view themselves as Palestinians; this has been reinforced by Israel's recognition of the PLO and the understanding that followed the Oslo Accords that there is no alternative to the establishment of a Palestinian state. The fact of their being Palestinians reinforces the ties between Israel's Arab citizens and their counterparts across the border. On the one hand, the possible establishment of a Palestinian state as a solution to the conflict will cause Palestinian nationalism to be less effective inwardly, even directing it to more external channels. But on the other hand, a situation of peace will increase the Israeli Arabs' struggle for equality and an equal share in the national wealth. The State of Israel will probably be unable to cope with this situation and there will arise new social and political crises, which could undermine Israel's Jewish identity and international status.

4. *"A state for all its people"*: This idea has been gaining ground since the 1990s among the Arab public and even among parts of Jewish society. This is a political balloon that has to be set loose. There is no contradiction between Israel being a Jewish state with a democratic regime, and it being a state for all its people. It is the right of a national state – such as the state of Israel, the state of the Jewish nation – to preserve its special symbols of flag, insignia and national anthem, and the Law of Return and all the other components that ensure its continued existence as the Jewish state. The place the idea has taken in the public and political discourse shows weakness and evasion on the part of Israel's national leadership in confronting it.

5. *Building institutions and civil society*: The Arab population in Israel is undergoing a stepped-up process of building its own institutions, similar to that of the Jews in pre-state days, under the British Mandate. The Arabs are building an infrastructure for an independent civil society within the State of Israel and are being helped by international forums and organizations in funding their activity, and in putting forward their political and civil agenda. They use collective strategies that emphasize their status as a national minority with rights according to international charters. This is taking place because successive Israeli administrations have failed to fulfill the communal and civil needs of the country's

Arabs; as a result they are obliged to create alternatives and to penetrate the international arena. Israel is therefore shown in a very negative light, as a country that does not conform with internationally accepted standards.

6. *Migration to Jewish towns and cities*: Rising standards of living and the influence of Jewish society have led Arab newly-weds and middle-class families to seek housing solutions in Jewish areas, which had hitherto not been considered "mixed population", where, they believe, they will enjoy better quality municipal services and their children will receive a higher level of education; such a flow of emigration may well change the character of Jewish towns. The Supreme Court decision on the civil rights of Israeli Arabs to purchase land in any town or village they choose will probably encourage many people away from overcrowded Arab towns into new developments, and thus undermine Israel's housing policies and the country's control over public spaces.

I believe that the Jewish majority is not about to agree to changes in Israel's political regime. The regional conflicts in general, and especially that between Israel and the Palestinians, are not likely to be solved in the near future and will continue to affect the relations between Jews and Arabs. The issues just raised will continue to accompany us in the future and will influence the two communities. My proposed plan, therefore, can overcome the blocks in Israeli society and push forward policies whose objective is to reduce points of friction, while preserving the Jewish character of the State of Israel. Only thus can a fair and reasonable relationship be built between Jews and Arabs.

The following is a two-part plan. Part I deals with structural and organizational changes on decision and administrative levels; Part II details political-economic issues that require a solution.

Part I – The inter-social level

1. *A social charter*: The government will establish a small committee of Jewish and Arab community heads – public and intellectual leaders – in order to draft a Jewish–Arab social charter. This charter will determine agreed-upon rules on issues of dissent between the administration and Arab and Jewish citizens. Once it is adopted by the government, the charter will become a binding administrable document.

2. *Coalition*: The political system must relate to the Arab parties as legitimate partners in a government coalition. Considerations for inviting them to join a coalition should involve a far-reaching view of the national and social benefits, and the necessity to turn the

Arab population into a positive and important partner, with much to contribute.

3. *Status of a national minority*: Legal recognition of Arab citizens as an Arab-Palestinian minority. Such recognition involves granting a measure of political autonomy (e.g. a supervisory committee on Arabs should be given the authority to represent Arab affairs); and granting cultural and educational autonomy (e.g. granting the Arab education branch of the Ministry of Education the same measure of organizational, budgetary and educational autonomy as is granted to the state religious education system).

4. *National service*: The State of Israel is still in the middle of a conflict with the Palestinians, which makes it impossible to draft the country's Arabs into compulsory military service; moreover, the Arabs themselves are opposed to military service. In order to protect the Arab public's civil rights, as well as their obligations, it is necessary to decide on a framework for compulsory non-military national service, with a focus on their community's needs. So as to keep objection to the minimum, a suitable basis has to be created that will take in as many youngsters as possible, Arabs and Jews, in order to create a melting pot at a time of peace.

5. *Recognizing Arab culture*: The division between Jews and Arabs is due in no small measure to the fact that many Jews know nothing about the culture and language of the Arabs. It is necessary, therefore, to build a school curriculum in Jewish schools, to include study of the Arabic language and Arab culture.

Part II – The political–economic level

1. *Regional policy*: In regions with a significantly large Arab population, the Arab inhabitants should be given the chance to design their space: planning, development and management of their lands and other lands allocated to them by the state for their needs. In return, the matter of illegal housing will be settled and all new building and construction will require formal planning permission. The government will grant preference to the completion of all planned building in Arab towns and villages. In these areas, modern new towns must be built that can serve as centers for receiving government and regional services, and also as centers for employment and culture, in the hope that these towns will attract everyone seeking improved living standards.

2. *Joint Arab–Jewish industrial areas*: It is imperative to draft a policy encouraging the integration of Arab industry into the national economy. Such integration can reinforce a sense of belonging among the Arab population and a feeling of solidarity with the

state. To this end, therefore, the government and Jewish and Arab local authorities should establish several joint industrial areas in the vicinity of Arab towns and villages. The Ministry of Commerce and Industry must establish a funding body for financing small businesses, as part of Arab industry, in order to create Jewish–Arab co-operation, to take advantage of skilled manpower in the Arab population and to provide employment opportunities.

. *Settling the Bedouin land claims:* The Negev has Israel's only large land reserves. A large proportion of these lands is being taken over by the region's Bedouin inhabitants, a fast-growing population due to their above-average birthrate. The state missed the chance to settle the land ownership issue when it was still possible to do so at a much lower cost. Today, the government is facing a financial time bomb and is no longer able to evacuate the Bedouin from their lands without presenting them with acceptable settlement solutions that will accommodate their needs and their lifestyle. The state must now co-operate with Bedouin public leaders in order to plan additional towns and villages for those who are still living in unrecognized villages and to reach a final settlement that will put an end to the various land claims.

4. *Structural changes:* The government must establish a ministerial office whose sole job consists of preparing and implementing an emergency plan for reducing the inequality and social gaps between Jews and Arabs. The office will be granted all the necessary authority to oversee the allocation of funds to the Arab population from various government offices. I believe that, without a government office, headed by a government minister (although there will always be those who claim that this is only a revival of the advisor on Arab affairs post), it will not be possible – in the current Israeli bureaucratic atmosphere – to implement any of the aforementioned suggestions.

The future of Israel's Arabs does not rest in their hands alone, but will be influenced to a significant degree by the actions of the Jewish majority. The status of the Arab population in the state and in its political system is among the most burning issues on the agenda of the Jewish majority. The problems outlined in this book cannot be ignored, and they must be faced with courage. It can only be hoped that the explanations of this very complicated situation, and the proposals made, will provide a positive contribution to raising people's awareness to the problematic majority-minority relations in Israel.

Postscript

From the summer of 2006, three important developments impacted Jewish–Arab relations in Israel: the war in Lebanon; the resumption of the US-led peace negotiations between Israel and the Palestinians; and the Arab minority elite's future vision manifestos.

The Second Lebanon War and Israel's Arabs

The second war in Lebanon erupted in the summer of 2006, when the Lebanese Shi'ite organization, Hezbollah, abducted two Israeli soldiers and rained rockets over northern Israel. Once again, the Arabs of Israel faced an identity crisis. Although the Arab community was equally hard hit by the war, many of its leaders voiced sharp criticism against Israel and demanded an immediate end to the hostilities. On the other hand, there was very little criticism from Israel's Arabs against Hezbollah leader Hassan Nasrallah, and indeed some Israeli Arabs even spoke out in his support. Moreover, in defiance of Israeli law, which forbids Israeli citizens from traveling to enemy states, three Arab MKs from the National Democratic Pact Party, together with two former MKs, traveled to Syria after the war for a meeting with Syrian president Bashar Assad, an active partner in the conflict between Lebanon and Israel. They were arrested on their return and questioned by the police.

The war, which has been termed in Israel the "Second Lebanon War", differed from all of Israel's other wars since the 1948 War of Independence. Most of these took place on enemy territory, beyond Israel's borders. The only one in which the home front was affected, the 1991 Gulf War, was when Iraq's Saddam Hussein fired Scud rockets at Israel, causing damage only to the Jewish population. During the Second Lebanon War, Hezbollah was less discriminate and fired rockets on Arab towns and villages, causing havoc and a mass migration of inhabitants, as well as loss of life. Hezbollah rockets fired from Lebanon killed 39 Israeli citizens, almost half of whom were Arabs.

In response to the daily attacks from Lebanon, the Israeli Arab media virtually ignored these victims. Most of the Arab public felt and expressed pleasure and even pride at Hezbollah's success in hitting deep into Israeli territory; they were happy that Israel was unable for over a month to overcome a weaker adversary. Any anger against Nasrallah related mainly to the fact that Israel's military response to his attacks had caused so much damage to Lebanon's infrastructure. Israel's Jewish population was very surprised that so few Arab voices were heard condemning Nasrallah for firing rockets against Arab towns and villages in Israel; many Israeli Arabs felt that Israel was responsible for the war.

The Arabs' stance exacerbated that of the Jewish majority, who saw their fellow citizens appearing to take the side of the enemy. The war caused an even greater rift between the country's Jewish and Arab citizens, leaving the Mediterranean conflict firmly between the two camps. The conflict was sharpest in the northern town of Haifa, which has always been a model of co-existence between the ruling Jewish majority and the Arab minority. After Hezbollah rockets had killed several inhabitants of Haifa, Nasrallah called on the town's Arabs to leave – and there were those who did. Haifa's Arab deputy mayor, Walid Hamis, who was outspoken in his condemnation of Israel throughout the war, was later dismissed from his post.

Israel's Arabs took an active stance in this war, in contrast to their passive approach during previous wars with its neighbors, or the war in the Persian Gulf. The Second Lebanon War was an example of the Arab community's move toward nationalist extremism and their solidarity as a nationalist minority within Israel. Although the Arabs constitute a minority in Israel, Israel is itself a tiny minority within the Arab world (over 300 million) that surrounds it. Does the Israeli Arab community see itself as a part of the Arab majority in the region, or as a minority in a Jewish state? And in that respect, the Jewish majority may be asked whether it sees itself as having the power of a majority, or does it conceive itself as threatened by the Arab majority in the Middle East? And what are the consequences of this two-way reality?

In an era of global communications, the Israeli Arabs are finding themselves connected to the larger Arab world and their solidarity with Arab nationalism is constantly rising. Moreover, Arab satellite TV has a vast audience in the Persian Gulf: *al-Jazeera* is the most popular television channel in Israel's Arab sector and has greatly affected their sympathy toward Hezbollah. Many Israeli Arabs participate in Arab Internet talk-backs and, by joining the regional majority, have gained a renewed self-confidence and identity, and a sense of belonging to a huge regional Arab and Moslem hinterland. This renewal usually comes at Israel's expense. Thus a conflict of interests has developed, even with regard to their language: should they invest energy in learning Hebrew, the language of the workplace and their only chance of really "making it" in Israel, or would it be more beneficial to extend their boundaries with the Arabic language, the language of the region, the language of their national and cultural yearnings?

Thus Israeli Arabs are caught between a clash of two collective definitions. On the one hand, they feel themselves part of the overall Moslem majority in the Middle East. On the other hand, it is this broader sense of belonging that intensifies their collective local identity as Palestinian Arabs within a Jewish state. Israel's Arabs have chosen to settle these adverse identities by combining them: they are part of the Arab majority in the Middle East, they are part of the State of Israel, and they are a local Palestinian community within Israel. It is probable that in the near future most of Israel's Arabs will support an Arab leader in order to promote their status within the Arab world. It is not surprising, therefore, that the National Democratic Pact Party, under the leadership of self-exiled former MK Azmi Bishara, currently promotes a pan-Arabic ideology and does not see itself as a local Arab party.

In 2006, the Arabs of Israel had their first taste of Katyusha rockets and terrorism. For the first time they faced a predicament that had previously been the exclusive domain of their Jewish counterparts: death, loss, and personal and collective responsibility. For the first time they experienced first-hand what it meant to be a victim of Arab terrorism. Paradoxically, they felt what it meant to be an Israeli. Their awareness as Israelis was carved in blood, as was their Palestinian identity. It is a paradox they are struggling to come to terms with. It is no simple dilemma. For example, whose suffering should they identify with: that of the Lebanese, admittedly fellow members of the Arab nation, but far away across the border, or the family and friends of the slain Jews, alongside whom they live? Is it distance that brings about awareness, or is it awareness that brings about distance?

It's a hard decision to make at the individual level. When no battles raged between Israel and its Arab neighbors, the country's Arabs were able to identify with both sides, who were, anyway, supposed to be making peace with each other. But in times of conflict, extremism and war, they are forced to choose sides, a feat almost impossible to accomplish. Hitherto, most Israeli Arabs were satisfied with stressing the importance of peace in the Middle East. This position allowed them to put Israel or the Arab world to the side, and to talk about the personal benefits of living in peace with the Arabs of the region, with the State of Israel and, first and foremost, with themselves. But events such as the Second Lebanon War once again bring forth a decision of choice. Israel's Arabs have discovered, yet again, the bitter fact that they are not necessarily a bridge to peace between Israel and the Arab world. Even worse, when vociferous Israeli Arabs decry the political and military reactions of the Jewish majority, the general Arab–Israeli rift inevitably widens. The Israeli Arabs thereby once again become part of the problem rather than part of the solution.

The question then is, why are the Arabs of Israel so unwilling to identify with the state, since, for the first time since its establishment, there exists a Jewish–Arab meeting of interests away from the Middle East battleground? The reason appears to be that the Arab street sees Hezbollah and its leader as a hero who has achieved strategic successes against the IDF and damaged its image. Still, the fact is that Hezbollah is no more than an extension of a non-Arab and non-Sunnite Iran, which aspires to take control of the whole Moslem world and to achieve hegemony over the entire Middle East in Radical Islam's first step on the way to conquering the Western world.

The processes described above are the reason why the Israeli Arab leadership has attached itself to those Arab states that support Hasan Nasrallah – the Shi'ite Hezbollah leader – rather than Western leaders, who, knowing that Hezbollah is not a Lebanese national movement but a long arm of Iran, either condemn or ignore him. Based on this confederacy, can it be said that, in the wake of the Second Lebanon War, Israel's Arabs and their leaders are being drawn into the Shi'ite area of influence? It is impossible to tell. In recent years, any violent conflict involving Israel reinforces the solidarity of the country's Arabs for the other side, albeit these Arabs pay a high price for supporting the enemies of the state. On the other hand, successive governments have made no real efforts to encourage Arab citizens to share a sense of belonging to the country.

The Impact of the Broader Israeli–Palestinian Conflict

The relations between the Arab minority and the Jewish majority in the State of Israel are tied irrevocably to the broad Israeli–Palestinian conflict, a conflict charged with emotional and cognitive forces throughout the Arab world and more broadly among 57 states, the majority of whose populations are Moslem. The fact that the US supports Israel hinders American policy in the Middle East and America's war against world terrorism, since this support increases the hostility of the Arab street toward the US and against the West in general. The US, therefore, is very interested in promoting a solution to the Israel-Palestine conflict, or in preserving the peace process and preventing further regression into war in the region, if a solution is not feasible in the foreseeable future.

The visit of US President George W. Bush in January 2008 to Israel and the Palestinian Authority was intended to advance the negotiations between the two parties in the conflict and to bring about a signed agreement by the end of 2008. However, the split in the Palestinian Authority between Hamas, which controls the Gaza Strip, and the PLO (Fatah), which controls the West Bank, raises doubts as to the possibility of making practical progress, although as far as Israel is concerned, the talks are meant to culminate in the signing of a "shelf agreement".[1]

Until the 1990s, it was still possible to perceive among Israel's Arab community an acute need for progress toward an Israeli–Palestinian solution. It was generally assumed that a peaceful end to the conflict would alleviate the Israeli Arabs' identity problems, would remove their obstacle of dual loyalty and would open the door to their complete integration into Israeli society. Today the situation is different. Since the 1991 Madrid Conference, whose objective was to promote the peace process between Israel, the Palestinians and the Arab states, Israel's Arabs have come to the conclusion that the peace process, even if it succeeds in its objectives, will not solve their problems. Issues such as expropriated property, the return of the 1948 refugees to their home villages, the right of return of family members of Israeli Arabs: all these are not addressed within the framework of a peace agreement between Israel and its neighbors. According to the Israeli Arabs, the PLO relinquished these demands in return for the establishment of a Palestinian state and sees this population as a burden with extreme demands that might cause Israeli public opinion to refuse to agree to further significant compromises. Thus the Israeli Arabs and the Palestinians find themselves holding opposing positions, a situation that, too, hinders the possibility of achieving any kind of political arrangement. Indeed, the Palestinian Authority chairman, Mahmud Abbas,[2] has made frequent mention of the Israeli Arab issue, hinting that they must not burden the establishment of an independent Palestinian state by joining the *Intifada* or by presenting extreme demands, including the reinstatement of all the deserted Arab villages within the State of Israel, or rescinding the state's Zionist character. According to the Palestinian Authority, the Arabs in Israel are entrusted with using their vote to promote an Israeli–Palestinian peace agreement, as they did in 1993, when the votes of the Arab MKs assisted in approving the Oslo Accords.

In November 2007, on the eve of the Annapolis Conference, initiated by President Bush in order to advance an Israeli–Palestinian peace agreement, the Supreme Follow-up Committee for the Arabs in Israel decided to call on Mahmud Abbas to refrain from recognizing the State of Israel as a Jewish state. The call was echoed throughout the Arab minority in Israel, who wish to turn Israel into a two-nation state. In response, Israel's foreign minister, Tzippi Livni, said that a future Palestinian state is supposed to provide a solution for the Palestinian people as well as the Arabs of Israel, and the establishment of a Palestinian state should also fulfill their national aspirations. In other words, the establishment of an independent Palestinian state would provide a source of identity for Israel's Arab citizens, in the same way that Israel provides a source of identity for the Jews of the world. Livni's sentiments were misconstrued as a call for the Arabs of Israel to remove themselves to a future Palestinian state and aroused the anger of the Arab leadership, who claimed that the foreign minister was making plans for expelling the Israeli Arab population.

Israel's military activity against terrorist organizations in the Gaza Strip during the early months of 2008, which resulted in the death of 120 Palestinians and a reduction in the supply of merchandise to the Strip, featured strongly in the Arab and international media. To Israel's

Arabs, these events constituted aggression against the Palestinians.

Israel's Arabs see every attack by Israeli security forces against the Palestinians as an attack on themselves and their nation and, on occasion, on their own families. This further alienates them from the state. On the other hand, the country's Jewish public, exposed to the Arab MKs' incitement and denouncements of the state and its activity in the occupied territories, has lost its tolerance for its Arab counterparts. For example, when Qasam and Grad rockets were fired on the southern Israeli town of Sderot in early 2008 and a south Jerusalem Arab inhabitant carried out a terrorist attack on Jewish students at the Rabbi Kook Center, not a word of protest was heard from the Arab leadership. Instead of providing a bridge between Israel and the Palestinians, the Arabs of Israel find themselves in an ever-widening chasm of interests between themselves and the Jewish state and, no less significantly, between themselves and their Palestinian brethren.

It is for this reason that President Bush's 2008 visit to Israel and the Palestinian Authority and the Annapolis initiative have aroused equal doubts among Jews and Arabs in the State of Israel. Most of the population in Israel is skeptical with regard to the success of this initiative, because of the very weighty rifts between the Israelis and the Palestinians. The Israeli–Palestinian conflict will continue to reflect on the internal relations between Israel's Arab minority and Jewish majority and will make it difficult for the government to carry out a corrective policy that would provide full equality for the Arab minority in the State of Israel.

Israel's Arab Population – Vision for the Future

As noted above, the events of October 2000 and their repercussions were a watershed in the Israeli Arab population's attitude toward the state and its institutions. The existing crisis of confidence between the Arab public and the Israeli establishment was intensified and a new direction in the struggle to achieve recognition as a national minority has been adopted. Israel's Arab political and academic leadership now bases its activity on the fact that recent years have seen a growing awareness in the world to the status of Indigenous Minority Groups,[3] and various organizations within the United Nations (including the United Nations Development Program) are currently concerned with the civil rights of minority groups. As a result, prominent members of the Israeli Arab population managed to put the minority rights of Israel's Arabs on the agenda of several of these international organizations.

Among certain circles within the Jewish majority in Israel there is a growing awareness of the need for a constitution that would settle the legal status and human rights of all sectors in Israeli society. Many people are convinced that the state should seek a clearer expression of the fact that the Arabs form a large minority population within it, and the idea for Israel to become "a state of all its citizens" is now being voiced more often in the Jewish sector. Growing awareness in the world to minority rights and debates on the issue in international forums are causing waves in Israel; Israel's international status and closer relations with the UN are exposing it to international decisions on civil rights issues. The growing tendency for ethnic conflicts in various countries to attract international intervention means that these are no longer considered merely the concern of the countries in which they take place. However, it is still too early to evaluate whether the international community will intervene in the internal ethnonational conflict in Israel.

The process of "internalization" of the Arab minority in Israel involved also a serious debate regarding the political vision of Israel's Arabs as a national minority in a country that identifies itself as both Jewish and democratic. Between December 2006 and March 2007, four constitution-like documents were published by Israeli Arab leading NGOs detailing the Arab minority's vision for its future in Israel.[4] There was little new in the documents with regard to content; the novelty lay in the identity of the authors: a group of intellectuals, mostly connected with academia, affiliated with the mainstream of Arab politics in Israel today, under the auspices of the Supreme Follow-up Committee for the Arabs in Israel. The three documents evolved from a feeling that the Arab citizens in Israel had to take action on their own behalf, at a time when the Jewish majority was making moves toward drafting a constitution and not involving them. Today Israel's Arab citizens strive to match their situation to that of national and ethnic minorities in other countries, whereas previously their debate had focused on discrimination and deprivation – with such issues as the shortage of school classrooms in the Arab sector, insufficient infrastructure, and too little representation in public administration. Apart from a handful of radical intellectuals, Israeli Arabs had been generally reluctant to raise demands for autonomy, or for recognition as a national minority, for fear that the Israeli authorities would use this as an excuse to discriminate against Arab institutions.

The 2006 documents all focus on the historical narrative that stresses the fact of Israel's Arabs being an Indigenous Minority in their homeland and their right to conduct their own affairs in matters of education, culture and religion and to establish their own national institutions.

One of the more sensitive issues dealt with by the documents is that of land and the demand for greater involvement of Israeli Arabs in planning and construction committees and preparation of special site plans to settle the problems of *Waqf* properties and unauthorized Arab towns and villages.

However, alongside their criticism of the State of Israel, the documents do not refrain from pointing out problems within the Arab community.

Arab society continues to be patriarchal, a traditional clan system is the accepted form of leadership. Political and social movements in the Arab sector deal only with the "big issue" and avoid an extensive debate on such socio-cultural matters as the status of women. In contrast, the documents offer a development strategy with the aim of creating solidarity and quality of life, raising the status of women, encouraging involvement in social issues and civil values and a collective identity; all with the objective of reducing the social rifts in Arab society.

The documents all deal with the erosion of the unique Arab Palestinian identity caused by close proximity to Jewish culture, and the detachment of local Palestinian culture from the Arab and Islamic "mother culture". It is necessary, therefore, to initiate a debate on the Israeli Arabs' cultural relations with the state, with the West and with the international community. Tools must be created in order to tighten ties with the Palestinian nation and the Arab peoples. The documents also call for the establishment of an elected national institution to deal with these issues.[5]

Current visions for the future raise a demand for "consociational democracy" by granting each group in Israel the right to veto decisions made by the other side; the Arabs would be prepared to recognize the fact that Israel is at most a "joint motherland" to the two nations (Jewish and Arab), thus denying Israel's definition that it is the sovereign state of the Jewish nation. According to the semi-constitutional documents, Israel should be a two-nation state, since its population consists of a Jewish majority and a large Arab minority. As the authors of the papers see it, the current condition of Israel's Arab population is rooted in the fact that Israel is a Jewish national state and the problem can be solved only by the removal of Israel. According to them, it is necessary to bestow collective rights on Israel's Arabs, including equal immigration and their share in the state's resources, until such a time as their vision of Israel's removal is realized. Another demand is for the state's symbols to express the existence of the Arab minority and for changes to be made to the national flag and anthem.

The question of Israel's definition was a bone of contention a few years before the four above-mentioned documents were published. Between 1999 and 2000, a series of discussions were held between Jewish and Arab intellectuals in an attempt to draft a charter that would provide a new approach to Jewish–Arab relations in Israel.[6] The debates, which reached a dead end over the definition of Israel's identity, revealed that the Jewish–Arab rift is too multi-faceted for attempts on the part of Jews and Arabs to overcome the discrepancy between Israel's definition of itself as a Jewish state and its concept of itself as a democracy to succeed.

The publication of the four documents in late 2006 and early 2007 may lead to a genuine process of Jewish–Arab dialogue and perhaps make it possible for Israel's Arabs to view themselves as part of the state. On the other hand, the roots of the conflict continue to spring up in all aspects of life in the country and the intensified conflict between Israel and the Palestinian Authority undermines relations between Jews and Arabs in Israel.

If but a few of this book's recommendations are carried out, and if the Arabs are permitted to feel a part of the Israel experience, there is still a prospect for a positive change in Israeli Arab attitudes toward the Jewish state. Eventually, we may hope for a change in Israel's Arabs' attitude to the Israeli–Palestinian conflict, and a move toward more understanding of the state's policy and its Jewish majority outlook. If this were to be the case, it would likely bring about changes in voting trends among Israeli Arabs, and even public expressions of solidarity with the State of Israel.

Appendix

Results of Elections in Seventeen Election Campaigns (Excluding Ethnic Mixed Towns) – Division of Votes between the Three Blocs

Knesset	Date	Eligible Voters	Valid Votes	Percentage	Arab Nationalist Parties	Percentage	Allied Arab Lists	Percentage	Zionist Parties	Percentage
First	25.1.1949	30,620	24,126	78.79	5,277	21.87	12,756	52.87	6,093	25.25
Second	30.7.1951	69,268	68,145	86.44	9,444	16.24	31,872	54.81	16,829	28.94
Third	20.7.1955	76,682	67,926	88.58	10,533	15.51	39,000	57.42	18,393	27.08
Fourth	3.11.1959	82,721	69,605	84.14	8,107	11.65	40,586	58.31	20,912	30.04
Fifth	15.8.1961	91,225	75,410	82.66	17,090	22.66	34,620	45.91	23,700	31.43
Sixth	2.11.1965	100,715	89,555	80.89	21,208	23.68	37,742	42.14	30,605	34.17
Seventh	28.10.1969	127,469	103,891	81.50	30,832	29.68	41,758	40.19	31,301	30.13
Eighth	31.12.1973	147,933	113,836	76.95	42,611	37.43	40,932	35.96	30,293	26.61
Ninth	17.5.1977	173,974	127,726	73.42	64,632	50.97	27,715	21.33	35,379	27.70
Tenth	30.6.1981	211,293	141,959	67.19	53,719	37.84	18,659	13.14	69,581	49.01
Eleventh	23.7.1984	239,229	176,115	73.62	89,255	50.68	0	0.00	86,860	49.32
Twelfth	1.11.1988	283,647	202,462	71.38	118,389	58.47	0	0.00	84,073	41.53
Thirteenth	23.6.1992	343,283	234,030	68.17	111,242	47.53	0	0.00	122,788	52.47
Fourteenth	29.5.1996	404,230	304,262	75.27	202,061	66.41	0	0.00	102,201	33.59
Fifteenth	17.5.1999	434,009	322,157	74.23	223,609	69.41	0	0.00	98,548	30.59
Sixteenth	28.1.2003	506,004	300,268	59.34	216,036	71.95	0	0.00	84,232	28.05
Seventeenth	28.3.2006	569,299	308,639	54.21	219,730	71.19	0	0.00	88,909	28.81

Election to the Prime Minister Office in the Years 1996–1996

Knesset	Date	Number of Voters			Labor's Candidate			Likud's Candidate		
		Eligible Votes	Valid Votes	Percentage	Candidate	No. of Votes	Percentage	Candidate	No. of Votes	Percentage
Fourteenth	29.5.1996	404,230	304,262	75.2	Peres	275,442	90.5	Netanyahu	28,820	9.5
Fifteenth	17.5.1999	434,009	322,157	74.1	Barak	295,159	91.6	Netanyahu	26,998	8.4
Special	6.2.2001	473,825	72,560	15.3	Barak	53,090	73.2	Sharon	19,470	26.8

Notes

Prologue: Complex Loyalties

1 Tel Aviv, Am Oved Publishers, 1990 (Hebrew).

2 In the 60 years of the State's existence, successive governments have avoided defining the boundaries of, and setting site plans for, Arab towns and villages. The natural population growth within the Arab population has forced many Israeli Arab citizens to build their homes on the outskirts of, or even outside, their towns. Today, there are around 150,000 illegally constructed houses in the Arab sector, on Arab-owned land.

3 *Intifada* is a civil uprising, often involving violence. The second *Intifada* began in October 2000, and Israeli Arabs came out in support of the Palestinian *Intifada* in the occupied territories.

4 Hadash Organizes a Petition for International Commission of Inquiry into the Events of October 2000, *Ha'aretz*, February 2, 2008.

5 Ph.D. Thesis, Tel Aviv University, 1989, "The Political Developments of the Arab Minority in Israel, as Reflected by Parliamentary Voting Patterns – 1948–1984."

6 A. Sofer and G. Shalev, "Claim for Return," Haifa University Press, July 2004 (Hebrew).

7 The Islamic Movement in Israel consists of two "Sections". The Southern Section is congregated mainly in the southern part of the "Triangle" and has representatives in the Knesset. The Northern Section, which predominates in the northern part of the "Triangle" and the Galilee, is more radical and incites the Moslem world against Israel.

8 Once referred to as the "Little Triangle", this is a concentration of Israeli Arab towns and villages adjacent to the Green Line, located in the eastern Sharon plain among the Samarian foothills. The name derives from the "triangle" of settlements visible from an aerial view. Prior to the 1948 Arab–Israeli War and Israel's establishment and sovereignty over that area, it was referred to as the "Little Triangle" to differentiate it from the larger "Triangle" region between Jenin, Tulkarm, and Nablus, so called due to the extensive anti-Jewish attacks there during the 1936–9 Arab revolt. Soon after the area was transferred to Israel from Jordan as part of the 1949 Armistice Agreements, the term was expanded to include the entire area around Umm-al-Fahm rather than just the towns of Kafar Qasem, Jaljulyeh and Kafar Barra, and the "Little" appendage quickly fell out of common usage. From Google.com; ref. Triangle (Israel).

9 Hummus and labane are local fast foods. "Wiping" a plate of these foods

with a piece of pitta bread is considered a sign of camaraderie when done by two or more people sitting down together.

10 In 1990 an Israeli opened fire at a bus stop, killing seven Arabs. In 1994, American-born Dr Baruch Goldstein entered a holy site in Hebron and murdered 29 Moslem worshippers.

1 The Politics of Rift: Models for Analyzing the Case of Israel's Arab Citizens

1 M.R. Haug (1967), 30–294; M. Esman and I. Rabinovich (1988), pp. 3–9.
2 M. Gordon (1975).
3 O. Yiftachel, based on M. Gordon (1975), pp. 84–111.
4 A. Lijphart (1977).
5 S. Smooha (1980), pp. 256–280; O. Yiftachel (1988), pp. 76–104.
6 S. Waterman (1987), pp. 151–170; O. Yiftachel (1988), pp. 87.
7 Homeland minorities are national ethnic groups settled on land that is considered their homeland, as opposed to groups in other countries that are not their national home and to which they emigrated for historic, political or economic reasons.
8 D. Horowitz (1982), pp. 329–350.
9 E.H. Crighton and M.A. MacIver (1991), pp. 127–142.
10 M. Esman and I. Rabinovich (1988), p. 3; G. Ben-Dor (1988), p. 71.
11 M. Esman (1988), p. 287.
12 E. Kedourie (1988), p. 26.
13 A. Yaniv and M. Al-Haj (1983), pp. 145–149.
14 Irredentism – a political principle or policy directed toward the incorporation of a territory historically or ethnically related to one political unit but presently subject to another.
15 Former MK Azmi Bishara in an interview with *Ma'ariv*, May 5, 2000.
16 Hebrew acronym for Israeli Workers' Party, whose first leader was David Ben-Gurion. The current Labor Party evolved from this socialist workers' party.
17 For more on the prime ministers' advisors on Arab affairs, see Benziman and Manzour (1992).
18 Between 1975 and 1985 these were Shmuel Toledano, Ra'anan Cohen, Ya'akov Cohen and Meir Jarah (Dekel) respectively.
19 A. Ghanem, N. Rouhana and O. Yiftachel (1988), pp. 253–267.
20 S. Smooha (1998), pp. 172–202.
21 The camps described by Smooha relate to political affiliation of Israeli Arab citizens, and they are divided into "committal" – Arabs belonging to Zionist political parties; "reserved" – those who hold positions somewhere between Zionist parties and the nationalist opposition (this camp came to the fore with the establishment of the Arab Democratic Party in 1988); "dissidents" – supporters of the Israeli Communist Party (known since 1977 as Hadash) and the Progressive Peace List; and the "deniers" – these are represented by the Sons of the Village, who demand a secular democratic state in all the territories of traditional Palestine.
22 According to a 1995 poll conducted by Smooha, 90.2 percent of the Druze,

60.1 percent of the Christians and 48 percent of the Moslems see themselves more as Israelis than as Palestinians. See, S. Smooha (2001), pp. 288–290. (Hebrew)

23 Schnel (1994).

24 See I. Kaufman (1995).

25 Until the ninth Knesset, most of the Arab vote went to the Israeli Communist parties. After the ninth Knesset, and especially from the fourteenth to the seventeenth (current) Knesset, there was a drastic change in voting patterns in the Arab sector, which reflected the Arab population's disappointment with their treatment by the Jewish state. From 50 percent support for the Zionist parties, the Arab vote dropped to 30 percent; the remaining 20 percent went to nationalist Arab parties. There was also a marked drop in voter participation after the fourteenth Knesset, another reflection of the Arab population's dissatisfaction.

26 R. Dalton (2002).

27 S. Bartolini and P. Mair (1990), p. 4.

28 R. Dalton, S.C. Flanagan and P.A. Beck (1984), pp. 454–460.

29 N. Franklin, T. Mackie, H. Valen et al. (1992); Dalton et al. (1984).

30 S. Bartolini and P. Mair (1990), p. 41.

31 N. Franklin, T. Mackie, H. Valen et al. (1992).

32 C.E. Zirakzadeh (1989), pp. 319–399.

33 Dalton et al. (1984).

34 Bartolini (1990), p. 172.

35 N. Glazer (1957).

36 They are sometimes referred to as "Zionist parties".

37 This category includes also Communist parties and the Jewish–Arab Progressive List for Peace. In research literature these are also called "nationalistic parties".

38 A. Campbell et al. (1960), pp. 89–119; P. Kloppner (1982), pp. 112–141.

39 The United Workers' Party,

40 According to data received from the three major Jewish parties, at the end of 2002, the Labor Party had 21,454 Arab members, Meretz had 10,570 and Likud had 12,078. No data is available for Rakah, but according to estimations, Arab members should not exceed 2,000 in number.

41 Data relating to Knesset election campaigns is based on summaries provided by the Central Election Committee.

2 Political Supervision and Co-optation

1 *Naqba* is the Arabic word for catastrophe. *Naqba* Day is the annual day of commemoration by Palestinians of the anniversary of the establishment of Israel in 1948, thus commemorating the dispossession of their people.

2 The reference is to Arabs who left or were forced to leave their towns or villages, but remained within the State of Israel.

3 There is dispute as to the number of Palestinian Arab refugees from the 1948 war. According to the Arabs, these numbered between 900,000 and one million; Israel argues that the number could not exceed 520,000. UN officials place the number at 726,000. According to UNWRA the number of

refugees living in camps in 2001 was 1,203,828 and the entire refugee population stood at 3,709,514.

4　The military administration officially began on October 21, 1948 and ended on November 8, 1966. Government announcement, in Knesset Report 8/11/1966, Vol. 47, p. 228 (Hebrew).

5　Originally named *Usrat al-Ard* (family of the land), the *al-Ard* movement was founded by Sabri Jiryyes, Salah Bransah and Muhammad Mi'ari, members of a group called the Popular Democratic Front. Because of the virulently anti-Zionist propaganda it published, it was banned by Ben-Gurion in 1959. The movement tried to run for Knesset in 1964, but failed to receive permission to register; *al-Ard* was subsequently declared an unlawful association.

6　S. Jiryyes (1996), p. 41 (Hebrew)

7　Knesset Protocol, vol. 9, pp. 1820, 1828 (Hebrew).

8　Knesset Protocol, vol. 33, pp. 1325–1326; 1332–1333 (Hebrew).

9　Rafi – a political party formed in 1965 by David Ben-Gurion and seven MKs from Mapai, as a result of his dispute over a security incident that took place few years before in Egypt.

10　Knesset Protocol, vol. 33, pp. 1325–1326; 1332–1333 (Hebrew).

11　Israel Workers' Party (forerunner of the Labor Party), United Workers' Party and the Israeli Communist Party respectively.

12　To this day, this is the term applied to "experts" on Arab affairs.

13　Golda Meir was Israel's prime minister from March 1969 to April 1974. At the same time she was also general secretary of Mapai.

14　The General Zionists Party was a centrally oriented political party. Later on it became the Liberal Party; in 1965 most of the party joined the Freedom Party to become what is known today as the Likud.

15　These included Hamad Abu Rabia, a Moslem Bedouin from the Negev; Ahmad Dhaher, a Moslem from Nazareth; Fares Hamdan, a Moslem from Baqa al-Gharbiyye in the "Triangle"; Diab Ubeid, a Moslem from Tayibeh; Jaber Mu'adi, a Druze from Yarka; Labib abu Ruqun, a Druze from Isifiya; Elias Nakhla, a Christian from the village Rame; and Mas'ad Qasis, a Christian from Mi'elya.

16　Abu Ghosh (1965), pp. 15–20 (Hebrew).

17　Voting slips bear the code names for the various competing parties. People wishing to vote for the Labor Party posted a voting slip with the letters EMET – the Hebrew word for "truth".

18　They were: Seif al-Din al-Zu'bi's "United Arab List", which won 11,590 votes, Hanna Haddad's "Arab Brotherhood List", which won 8,304 votes, and Nuri al 'Uqbi's "Arab Citizens in Israel Movement", which won 2,596 votes.

19　Zionist parties: Mapai (the Labor Party), Mapam (The United Workers' Party), The Unity of Labor Party, the right-wing Freedom Party (Heruth) – after 1965 it merged with the Liberal Party to form the Likud and the National Religious Party.

20　The Palestine Liberation Organization (PLO) is a multi-party confederation and claims to be the sole legitimate representative of the Palestinian people.

21　See Chapters 3 and 7.

22 Secret meetings had been taking place for several months during 1976–7 between Israeli and Egyptian negotiating teams.

23 Begin took Dayan into his government and appointed him Minister of Defense. The peace treaty was signed 16 months after Egyptian president Anwar Sadat's visit to Israel in 1977, after intense negotiation.

24 The South Lebanon Army (SLA) was a Lebanese militia during the Lebanese Civil War. After 1979, the militia operated under the authority of Sa'ad Haddad's Government of Free Lebanon. It was supported by Israel during the 1982–2000 South Lebanon conflict.

25 A. Yaniv and M. al-Haj (1983), pp. 159–160.

26 Villages which were declared illegal by the national planning and building law of 1965 and usually do not receive municipal services. Many of these villages existed before Israel was established.

27 Before the 1977 elections, the Communist Party joined up with some other minor left-wing and Israeli Arab parties, including some members of the Israeli Black Panthers, to form Hadash (literally "new"), a Hebrew acronym for The Democratic Front for Peace and Equality.

28 The first Arab armed civilian uprising in the occupied territories (*Intifada*) broke out in 1987 and ended in 1991, just before the Madrid Conference.

3   New Political Movements and Trends

1 According to Abd al-Aziz al-Zu'bi's claim, the membership of the three in the Palestine National Council constituted "representation of the Palestinian Arabs living under occupation since 1948" (1971), p. 30 (Hebrew).

2 Y. Harkabi (1975), p. 181 (Hebrew).

3 The strike was announced on March 30, 1976 in protest against the government's decision to expropriate 5,320 dunams of Arab land in the Galilee. Seventy-five percent of all Israeli Arabs participated. Israel's Arabs commemorate the day with demonstrations throughout the Arab sector.

4 This group had broken off from the Sons of the Village (*Abnaa al-Balad*) movement in Umm-al-Fahm during the 1983 local elections. On October 25, 1983, it appeared as an independent list and won 637 votes. The groups called on their supporters to boycott Knesset elections, but supported the "Front" candidate, Umm-al-Fahm mayor Hashem Mahamid, in the elections to the eleventh Knesset.

5 From *al-Arad*'s abortive experience in the 1960s, Arab political leaders learned that if they wanted to avoid being disqualified for being too nationalist, they were better off including Jewish members in their lists, preferably with a sound military career behind them.

6 The PLP campaigned in local elections in the village of Sha'ab (October, 1984) and in the village of Abu Snan (January, 1985) and did not win a single seat.

7 *Al-Ittihad*, May 10, 1985 (Arabic).

8 Uri Avneri, a senior journalist and politician, in a conversation with the author, October 22, 2002.

9 According to this law, all young men and women are conscripted into the military at the age of 18 (unless they are exempt for religious reasons). The

law applied and continues to apply to everyone but Moslems or Christian Arabs are exempted by decision of the Ministry of Defense, although they have the possibility to volunteer for military service.

10 Like *al-Ard*, the Druze Enterprise Committee published a monthly bulletin (under names that were changed frequently to avoid legal issues). The committee had branches in several Druze villages and representatives in local municipal councils.

11 Islamic charitable pious foundation; administers holy sites as well as state lands and other property passed to the Moslem community by its members for public welfare.

12 On the Sons of the Village movement, see J. Landau (1993), pp. 78–82 (Hebrew); I. Reiter and R. Aharoni (1993), pp. 23–25 (Hebrew).

13 The Rejection Front was formed in 1974 by groups within the PLO when a document introducing the concept of a two-state solution was accepted by the Palestine National Council. These groups were backed by Syria, Libya and Iraq and opposed the moderates in the organization.

14 George Habash died in late January 2008 in Jordan. His funeral was attended by members of the Sons of the Village, Arab Knesset members and leaders of the Israeli Arab community. The participation of the Arab MKs was controversial.

15 Translated as "The Objective", also the name of the journal published by the Popular Front.

16 This return to religion was also expressed in municipal elections.

17 Interview in *Yediot Ahronot*, March 9, 1979 (Hebrew).

18 Leket Mihamitrahesh be migzar haArvi be-Israel (A Collection on Events in the Israeli Arab Sector), vol. 2 (March 1981), pp. 22–29 (Hebrew).

19 *Shari'a* is the body of Islamic religious law. It means "way" or "path to the water source" and deals with many aspects of day-to-day life. It is based on the Koran, the saying and doings of the prophet Muhammad, the consensus of the believers and the analogy and centuries of debate, interpretation and precedent.

20 *New Outlook*, September 1979.

21 Sheikh Ra'ed Salah began his political career during the 1970s, as a member of the students' union at the Islamic University of Hebron. It was then that he became acquainted with the ideology of the Moslem Brotherhood, which he has followed ever since.

22 The first *Intifada* began in the West Bank and the Gaza Strip in 1987.

23 The Islamic Movement stood for Knesset in the elections for the fourteenth session, as part of the United Arab List, which included the Arab Democratic Party (led by Darawsha), and won four Knesset seats.

24 *Ma'ariv*, November 1994(Hebrew).

25 For example, the al-Aqsa Foundation, which operates mainly in Germany, the Interpal Foundation that operated in the UK, the Holyland Foundation that operated in the US, and the roof organization known as the Coalition of Charities, which operates mainly in the Gulf States.

26 Sheikh Ra'ed Salah and the leadership of the northern branch of the Islamic Movement were charged on June 24, 2003, but their trial ended in a plea

bargain in January, 2005. They were not charged with aiding terrorist organizations, which was the main reason for their arrest.

27 The idea of establishing an Arab university in Nazareth was raised at the beginning of the 1980s, as one of the Israeli Arabs' tools in their national struggle and in order to express their right to cultural and educational independence.

28 About 6,000 dunams of the 20,000 dunams expropriated were owned by Arabs. The plan was to expand the Jewish settlements in the Galilee and build new ones in order to change the demographic balance in the Galilee in favor of the Jewish sector. The expropriations caused the riots commemorated today as "Land Day".

29 Y. Landau (1981), pp. 205–207 (Hebrew).

30 The status of these NGOs is recognized in international institutions. "The Third Sector" is the name given to voluntary organizations and various kinds of foundations working within the civilian society.

31 For more on approaches to the international community, see Y. Reiter and R. Aharoni (1993), pp. 38–41 (Hebrew).

32 R. Israeli (2002), p. 27 (Hebrew).

33 In 2001, at a memorial service in Damascus for former Syrian President Hafez Assad, Bishara stood next to Hezbollah leader Hassan Nasrallah, in defiance of Israeli law, which forbids meetings with the enemy. He delivered a speech on that occasion, calling on the Palestinians to continue their armed struggle against Israel and expressed his support for Hezbollah. Suspected by Israel's General Security Services of spying for, and providing classified information to, the enemy, Bishara escaped the country in April 2007 and went underground. From his hiding place somewhere in the Arab world, he continues to deliver speeches and lectures, condemning Israel and calling for its downfall.

34 The term "politicization without extremism" was coned in the framework of a lecture given by S. Smooha at a conference on "Primary Solidarities and Elite Groups in the Middle East", University of Haifa, June 12, 2001.

35 The first *Intifada* broke out in the occupied territories in 1987 and the violence dwindled and almost came to a halt in 1991, but the official end came with the signing of the Oslo Accords in 1993.

36 General Security Services, "Shabak".

37 The disqualification was based on Clause 7a, which prevents a candidate list or candidate from participating in an election if "there exists among the objectives or actions of a candidate list a denial of the right to exist of the state of Israel as a sovereign, democratic Jewish state, incitement to racism, support for the armed struggle of an enemy state or terrorist organization against the state of Israel."

38 Oded Shalom, "Even if we are outlawed – we shall continue to act openly." *Yediot Ahronot*, Saturday Supplement, January 3, 2003 (Hebrew).

39 According to the GSS, "the aims and objectives of The Nationalist Democratic Pact is to deny the existence of the state of Israel as a Jewish democratic state, by nullifying its Jewish character and supporting an armed struggle against it. The Nationalist Democratic Pact supports the right of

return of the Palestinian people and the idea of a bi-national state in all parts of "historic Palestine," and thus, in fact, strives to nullify the state and to turn the Jewish majority into a minority, on two levels: first, by recognizing and legitimizing the struggle against and opposition to Israel, in the hope of exhausting Israel and undermining its internal social cohesion and cracking its fortitude, tactics used by the Hezbollah in Lebanon; second, a multi-stage strategy which begins with a model of "Israel as a state for all its people," and ends with a two-nation state from the sea to the river, populated by an Arab majority and a Jewish minority.

40 Yair Ettinger, "Disqualifying the Parties," *Ha'aretz*, January 1, 2003 (Hebrew).
41 Amir Gilat, "It'll Come Back at You Like a Boomerang," *Ma'ariv*, February 1, 2003 (Hebrew).
42 The official commission of inquiry was headed by Judge Theodore Or, in order to study the October, 2000 riots in which a number of Arab demonstrators were killed by Israeli police.
43 Jihad is the Arab word for "struggle."
44 S. Ozacky-Lazar and A. Ghanem, (2003) (Hebrew).

4 Social Rifts in Arab Politics

1 M. Hoexter (1973), pp. 249 – 311.
2 A.M. Lutfiyya & C. W. Churchill (1970), p. 505.
3 M. al-Hajj (1979), p.18 (Hebrew).
4 Extended family – interchangeable with "clan".
5 E. Marx, 1967.
6 On the subject of blood feuds and mutual aid, see E. Gellner (1981), pp. 37–38. According to E. Marx (1973),p. 24, mutual aid is the absolute responsibility of all the members of the mutual aid group.
7 The *Mukhtar* ("chosen" in Arabic) is head of a village or neighborhood. *Mukhtar*s are usually selected by some consensual or participatory method.
8 A. Cohen (1965), pp. 130–173.
9 For instance, As'ad Ghanem failed in an independent attempt to take over the Sha'ab council.
10 The Nassar clan in Tur'an in Galilee, for example, was not the largest clan in the village. Yet Unis Nassar served for 15 years as head of the local council. The clan succeeded in holding on to the post, with the help of agreements forged with most of the small clans in the village and by committing itself to support clan candidates for the local council and refraining from forming an independent list. In return, the small clans promised to support Unis Nassar.
11 A. Ghanem (2001), p. 137.
12 A. Ghanem and S. Ozacky-Lazar (1994) (Hebrew); E. Reches (1985) (Hebrew); D. Elad (1987) (Hebrew) and M. Al Haj and H. Rosenfeld (1990).
13 The Alawites are a prominent Shi'ite Islamic sect in Syria.
14 Mrs al-Zu'bi, the widow of MK Seif al-Din al-Zu'bi, told me in September 1983 that "we Arabs were not born for political parties. Since the beginning of Islam our goal was the religion and the people. These who belonged to a big clan and had land and property were influential. Suddenly we had to

adjust ourselves to a democratic regime, to voting in ballot boxes and this was strange to us."

15 A. Cohen (1965), p. 169 ff.

16 See Official Records, Official Gazette, No. 2996 8/12/195, p. 766 (Hebrew).

17 Data on the Arab population in Israel (Moslems, Druze, Christians, Bedouin and Circassians) was supplied by the Central Bureau of Statistics, 58 (2007), tables 2.2–2.4, pp. 88–90 (Hebrew).

18 Millet is an Ottoman Turkish term for a confessional community in the Ottoman Empire. In the nineteenth century, with the reforms, the term started to refer to legally protected religious minority groups, other than the ruling Sunni.

19 E. Kedourie (1988), pp. 25–31.

20 E. Marx & A. Shmueli (1984), 155 ff.

21 East of Beersheba.

22 In the Circassian language "Adiga" means a whole person, an aristocrat.

23 G. Ben Dor (1979), pp. 161, 235, 240.

24 Voting stations in the Arab sector tend to reflect specific ethnic divisions in the overall voting area.

25 M. Shamir and A. Arian conclude that the ethnic origin of the Jewish voter (specifically among Ashkenazi and Sephardi Jews) plays an important role in determining election results in Israel, especially those of the two main parties, Likud and Labor. See M. Shamir and A. Arian (1982) (Hebrew).

26 Apparently the vote was for the Islamic Movement, which was an important component in this list.

27 During a visit I paid to Umm-al-Fahm, Hashem Mahamid affirmed that there had, indeed, been a pact between the Mahamid and Jabarin clans, notwithstanding that the Jabarin clan held positions on behalf of the Labor Party, whereas the Mahamid enjoyed the support of Hadash and the Sons of the Village.

5 Arab Electoral Power

1 As more Israeli Arabs opt for boycotting the elections, so the Israeli component in their identity becomes more dominant. Abstention is not necessarily testimony to their being more "Palestinian"; rather it indicates the Israeli Arabs' desire and ability to take advantage of being a citizen of the State of Israel. The data in this chapter is supplied by the Central Bureau of Statistics. It is important to mention, however, that in the early years of the state, many difficulties were encountered with regard to registration and updating of voting lists due to the infiltration of refugees, absentee voters, and difficulties in locating names and addresses. Much of the Arab population at that time was under 18 years of age and not eligible to vote.

2 Central Bureau of Statistics No. 58, 2007, pp. 88–91 (Hebrew).

3 Central Bureau of Statistics, No. 58, 2007, Table 2.19, pp. 140–145 (Hebrew).

4 Based on the Central Bureau of Statistics, No. 58, 2007, table 2.26, pp. 159 – 161; A. Sofer, 2003, p. 35 (Hebrew).

5 See Central Bureau of Statistics, work force surveys for late December 2006, No. 1305, table 8.3 (Hebrew). The percentages in the different fields of

employment are calculated out of the number of people who work in the same field in Israel.

6 Parties established to represent the interests of the Arab sector and based on its electoral power.

7 Waves of Jewish immigrants from the former Soviet Union during the 1980s and 1990s constantly reduced Arab electoral power in these years. See Reiter and Aharoni (1993).

8 The Taba Talks took place in January 2001 at Taba in the Sinai Peninsula. Aimed at reaching the "final status" negotiations to end the Israeli–Palestinian conflict, they came closer to reaching a final settlement than any previous or subsequent peace talks yet ultimately failed to achieve its goals.

9 A. Jamal (2002), pp. 64–65 (Hebrew).

10 A drop to an average of 72 percent.

11 A. Arian (1985), pp. 22–23, 221 (Hebrew).

12 G. Ben Dor (1979), p. 182.

13 Anthology of Events in the Arab Sector, vol. 5, June 1981, 18–19 (Hebrew).

14 See the debate in S. Smooha (1999), pp. 39, 42–44 (Hebrew).

15 S. Ben-Ami (1981), pp. 67–84.

16 Interview with Haled Ighbariya from Umm-al-Fahm, August 2003.

17 *Kul al-Arab*, February 2, 2001 (Arabic).

18 It emerged in the author's talks with the Sons of the Village, the Islamic Movement and key figures in the Arab public, that an Elections Boycott Party had actually been established in the sixteenth Knesset elections, since almost 50 percent of the Arab voters boycotted the elections.

19 Author's interview with Arik Barmi, Likud CEO, January 17, 2005.

20 Meretz was formed prior to the 1992 elections by an alliance of three left-wing parties; Ratz, Mapam and Shinui, and was initially led by Ratz's chairwoman and long-time Knesset member Shulamit Aloni.

21 A. Arian (1985), pp. 220–224 (Hebrew).

22 Although no unequivocal studies have been found to verify this, the author bases his opinion on talks with former Arab local council heads, including Ibrahim Nimer Husayn from Shefar'am, MK Saleh Tarif from Julis, Samir Darwish from Baqa al-Gharbiyye, Ahmad Abu Asba from Jatt, As'ad 'Aziza from Daburiyeh, Zaki Jubran from Jish, Muhammad Mana' from Majd al-Krum, and Ahmad Abbas from Nahf.

23 G. Ben Dor (1979), p. 173.

24 The Labor Alignment platform devoted an entire chapter to the minorities issue. See Tenth Knesset: Platform, Tel Aviv, Labor Party Center, June 1981, pp. 91–95 and Eleventh Knesset, Tel Aviv: Labor Party Center, July 1984, pp. 93–96 (Hebrew).

25 D. Rabinowitz and H. Abu Baker coined that generation the "eroded generation" (2002) (Hebrew).

26 See M. Sofer, Y. Schnell, Y. Drori and A. Atrash (1995) (Hebrew). On the lack of industrial development in the Arab sector see R. Jubran (1987) and R. Jubran (June 1987), "A Study of Employment and Unemployment among University Graduates in Arab and Druze Towns," Haifa, Koor Industries Ltd (Hebrew)

27 On problems of employment see A. Fares (1993) (Hebrew) and A. Atrash (1995) (Hebrew). On the lack of industrial development in the Arab sector – "Industrializing the Arab Sector and Binding it to the Israeli Economy," see R. Jubran (1987) and R, Jubran (June 1987) (Hebrew)

28 The subject arose in talks with various figures and clan heads in the Arab sector. These considerations motivated young people, including academics wanting to integrate into public positions. Labor took advantage of these young people in its election campaigns. See R. Cohen, April 1984, Program for Eleventh Knesset Election Campaign, Labor Alignment (Hebrew).

29 Y. Reiter (1989), pp. 345–347 (Hebrew).

30 Author's interview with Jamal Zahalqa, January 23, 2005.

31 Bishara has been accused by the government of Israel of aiding Hezbollah during the Second Lebanon War.

32 Bishara's proposed abolishment of the Jewish National Fund: 5713–1953; World Zionist Federation and the Jewish Agency: P/830, were submitted to the Knesset on November 1, 1999. Ahmad Tibi's amendments to the Citizenship Law: 5760 – 2000 P/1428 was submitted to the Knesset on February 28, 2000.

33 I. Algazi, "Shas also won in Manda," Ha'aretz, May 25, 1999 (Hebrew).

34 On this statistical technique see J. Kmenta (1971), pp. 15–18, J. Johnston (1972), pp. 12–15.

35 The Naser movement caused shock waves in some of the Arab countries and weakened the influence of the Communist parties in the political system of these countries. This weakening did not occur within Israel's Arab population.

36 The 1982 war in Lebanon exposed a hidden ethnic conflict between the Christians and Druze and also the Moslems, especially after the Sabra and Shatila massacre. This conflict was expressed in different interviews given to the author by different personalities from all ethnic groups in the Arab sector. The government of Israel appointed a committee of inquiry to investigate "all the facts connected to the massacre carried out by Christian Lebanese forces against the Moslems in Sabra and Shatila." The conclusions of the committee brought about a government crisis, which forced Minister of Defense Ariel Sharon to resign. Ha'aretz, February 9,1983; also the 13th and 19th (Hebrew).

37 Interview with Jamal Mu'adi, chairman of the Druze Initiative Committee from the village Yarka, March 30, 1989.

38 Muhammad Naffa' of Beit Jann served about two years in the Knesset from February 1990 to July 1992.

39 In an interview October 1988 Dr. Unis Abu Rabia and Sulayman al-Badur, Bedouin from the Negev, claimed that the reason for the low voting participation was inadequate organization of the parties and not necessarily ideological.

40 Talab al-Sani' replaced Abd al-Wahab Darawsha as head of the Arab Democratic Party, which participates together with the Islamic Movement in the United Arab Party.

41 Term used to describe peasant farmers, agricultural laborers in the Middle East.
42 Until 1967 the Christian community was headed by Archbishop George Hakim, who enjoyed close ties with the Israeli establishment and appealed to the members of his community more than once not to vote for the Communist Party and to support the allied Arab lists associated with Mapai because these always assured a place for a Greek Catholic in the Knesset. His appeal also expressed the anti-Communist ideology he advocated.
43 Data received from Knesset elections Committee.

Epilogue: Arabs, Jews and the State of Israel – The Administration, the Establishment and Arab Citizens

1 The reference is to "Area 107," 42,000 dunams (about 10,500 acres) in the region of Ramot Menashe – Iron River.
2 *Ha'aretz*, November 7, 2000 (Hebrew).
3 As told to the author by members of the Arab leadership immediately after the 2001 general elections.
4 Suan (2003), p. 314 (Hebrew).
5 From an opinion poll conducted by the Center for National Security Research, Haifa University, December 2001 (Hebrew)
6 The chairman of the Judicial Commission was former Supreme Court Judge Theodore Or.
7 A commission of inquiry established to investigate the bloody events of January 30,1972 ("Bloody Sunday"), in which 13 Irish demonstrators were killed by British paratroopers.
8 In a rally of the Islamic Movement in Kafar Kanna on October 1,2002, Abd al-Malik Dahamsha said that "the feet and hands of the policemen who want to harm us should be broken."
9 See Y. Boimel, 2000, p. 346 (Hebrew).
10 Conversation with Amram Kal'aji, who was appointed Head of the Abu Basma Regional Council, January 24, 2005.
11 Or Commission Conclusions, Vol. 1, pp. 26–79, September 2003 (Hebrew).
12 U. Benziman, "Through a Bone to the Arab Sector," *Ha'aretz*, August 31, 2003 (Hebrew).
13 As soon as the Or Commission's findings were published, the government decided to adopt its recommendations and establish a Ministerial Committee, chaired by the Minister of Justice (known as the Lapid Commission), in order to study the report and present opinions. See Government Decision 772, dated September 14, 2003.
14 Decision No. Arab/7 of the ministerial commission for non-Jewish sector's affairs dated August 19, 2003. Government decision 735 (Arab/7). (Hebrew)
15 Originally dubbed the "convergence plan", the realignment plan was formulated and introduced to the Israeli public by Prime Minister Ehud Olmert, in a number of media interviews during the election campaign for the Seventeenth Knesset in early 2006. Olmert stated that if he were elected prime minister, within four years he would remove Israeli settlements from most of West Bank (Judea and Samaria) and consolidate them into large

groups of settlements near the 1967 border. The area of removal would correspond to the area east of the route of the West Bank barrier that was begun under his predecessor, Ariel Sharon, or a similar route with national consent and international legitimization.

16 A. Ghanem (1998), pp. 428–448.

17 Interview with Ra'ed Salah, al-Mujtama'a, November 2001 (Arabic).

18 The Knesset Ethics Committee had to discuss many complaints against Arab MKs who blamed other MKs as being racists or Fascists. *Ha'aretz*, January 3, 2005 (Hebrew).

19 Nadim Rouhana, in a lecture at Tel Aviv University, May 4, 2002.

Postscript

1 The new "shelf agreement" concept, advanced by US Secretary of State Condoleeza Rice and Israeli prime minister Ehud Olmert, currently serves as the basis for Israel's negotiations with Palestinian Authority leader Mahmud Abbas. Under this conceptual framework, Israel is to negotiate an "agreement in principle" on an "endgame" solution with moderate Palestinians, but then place this agreement out of their reach – high up on a "shelf" where the Palestinians can see it, but not yet attain it. Only when the Palestinians have matured and fulfilled all their "implementation" obligations will the transcendent trophy come down off the shelf.

2 Also known as Abu Mazen.

3 According to accepted definitions, Indigenous Minority Groups have collective rights that allow them greater equality in the countries in which they are citizens.

4 *The Vision for the Future of the Palestinian Arabs in Israel*, a position paper published by the National Committee for the Arab Local Authorities in Israel, Nazareth, 2006; *An Equal Constitution for All? On Constitution and Collective Rights of the Arabs in Israel*, position paper, by Dr. Yusef Jabarin of the Musawa Center, November 2006; *The Democratic Constitution, March 2007*, Shefar'am, Adala and the Haifa Covenant, the Mada al-Carmel Center, Haifa, May 2007. See S. Ozacky-Lazar and M. Kabha (2008) (Hebrew).

5 "The Future Vision of the Palestinian Arabs in Israel," the National Committee for the Arab Local Authorities in Israel, from the web site: <http://www.arab-lac.org/montada/indexdb.asp>.

6 Published in: Uzi Benziman (ed.), *Whose Land is it? A Quest for Jewish–Arab Compact in Israel*, Jerusalem. Jerusalem: Israel Democracy Institute, 2006 (Hebrew).

Bibliography

Abu-Gosh, S. (1972), "The Election Campaign in the Arab Sector". In: A. Arian (ed.), *The Elections in Israel – 1969* (Jerusalem Academic Press), pp. 242–244.

Al-Haj, M. (1995), *Education, Empowerment and Control: The Case of the Arabs in Israel* (New York).

Al-Haj, M. and Rosenfeld, H. (1990), *Arab Local Government in Israel* (Boulder and London, Westview Press).

As'ad. G. (2002), *The Palestinian Arab Minority in Israel, 1948–2000: A Political Study* (State University of New York Press).

Bailey, C. (1970), "The Communist Party and the Arabs in Israel", *Midstream* (16): 38–56.

Barritt, D. P. and Carter, Ch. F. (1972), *The Northern Ireland Problem – A Study in Group Relations* (Oxford).

Bartolini, S. and Mair, P. (1990), *Identity, Competition and Electoral Availability* (Cambridge University Press).

Ben-Ami, Sh. (1981), "The Catalan and Basque Movements of Autonomy". In: Y. Dinstein (ed.), *Models of Autonomy* (Tel Aviv University), pp. 67–84.

Ben-Dor, G. (1973), "The Military in Politics of Integration and Innovation: The Case of the Druze Minority in Israel", *Asian and African Studies* 9(3): 339–370.

Ben-Dor, G. (1979), *The Druzes in Israel: A Political Study* (Jerusalem: Magnes Press).

Ben-Dor, G. (1979), "Electoral Politics and Ethnic Polarization: Israeli Arabs in the 1977 Elections". In: A. Arian (ed.), *The Elections in Israel, 1977* (Jerusalem: Academic Press), pp. 177–183.

Ben-Dor, G. (1988), "Ethno-politics and the Middle Eastern State". In: M. J. Esman & I. Rabinovich (eds.), (1988), *Ethnicity, Pluralism and the State in the Middle East* (Ithaca and London: Cornell University Press), pp. 71–90.

Bonjour, E., Offter, H. S., Potter, G. R. (1952), *A Short History of Switzerland* (Oxford University Press).

Campbell, A., et al. (1960), *The American Voter* (New York: Wiley).

Cohen, A. (1965), *Arab Border Villages in Israel: A Study of Continuity and Change in Social Organization* (Manchester University Press).

Colbi, S. (1969), *Christianity in the Holy Land* (Tel Aviv: Am-Hassefer).

Connor, W. (1987) "Ethnonationalism". In W. Weiner and S. Huntington (eds.), *Understanding Political Development* (Boston: Little Brown & Co.) pp. 198–220.

Crighton, E. and MacIver, M. A., (1991), "The Evolution of Protracted Ethnic

Conflict: Group Dominance and Political Underdevelopment in Northern Ireland and Lebanon", *Comparative Politics* 23(2): 127–42.

Dalal, M. (2003), *October 2000: Law and Politics before the Or Commission of Inquiry* (Shefar'amr).

Dalton, R. (2002) *Citizens Politics: Public Opinion and Political Parties in Advanced Industrial Democracies,* third edition (New York: Chatham House Publishers)

Dalton, R., Flanagan, S.C. and Beck, P.A. (eds.) (1984), *Electoral Changes in Advanced Industrial Democracies: Realignment or Dealignment?* (Princeton University Press), pp. 454–460.

Drury, M. P. (1972), "Cyprus: Ethnic Dualism". In: J. I. Clarke and W. B. Fisher (eds.), *Populations of the Middle East and North Africa* (London University Press), pp. 81–161.

Eisenstadt, S. (1985), *The Transformation of Israeli Society* (London: Weidenfeld and Nicolson).

Esman, M. J. and Rabinovich, I. (1988), (eds.), *Ethnicity, Pluralism and the State in the Middle East* (Ithaca and London: Cornell University Press).

Esman, M. J. and Rabinovich, I. (1988), "The Study of Ethnic Politics in the Middle East". In: Esman & Rabinovich (eds.), (1988), pp. 3–29.

Esman, Milton, J.(1988), "Ethnic Politics: How Unique is the Middle East?" In: Esman and Rabinovich (eds.), (1988), pp. 287–302.

Franklin, N., Mackie, T, Valen, H. et al. (1992), *Electoral Change: Responses to Evolving Social and Attitudinal Structures in Western Countries* (Cambridge University Press).

Gellner, E. (1981), *Muslim Society* (Cambridge University Press), pp. 37–38.

Ghanem, A. (2001), *The Palestinian-Arab Minority in Israel, 1948–2000: A Political Study* (Albany: State University of New York Press).

Ghanem, A., Rouhana, N., Yiftachel, O. (1998) "Questioning 'Ethnic Democracy'", *Israel Studies* (3): 253–267.

Ghanem, A.S. (1998) "State and Minority in Israel: The Case of the Ethnic State and the Predicament of its Minority", *Ethnic and Racial Studies,* 21(3): 428–448.

Glazer, N. (1957), *American Judaism* (Chicago: University of Chicago Press).

Gordon, M. (1975), "Towards a General Theory of Racial and Ethnic Relations". In N. Glazer and D. Moyniham (eds.), *Ethnicity* (Cambridge, Mass.: Harvard University Press), pp. 84–111.

Greeley, A, and McCreedy W.C. (1974), *Ethnicity in the United States – A Preliminary Reconnaissance* (New York: John Wiley and Sons, Inc.).

Haidar, A. (1987), *The Palestinians in Israel Social Science Writings* (Washington DC: International Center for Public Policy).

Haidar, A. (1990), *Social Welfare for Israel's Arab Population* (Boulder: Westview Press).

Haug, M.R. (1967), "Social and Cultural Pluralism as a Concept in Social System Analysis", *The American Journal of Sociology* (73): 294–304.

Hoexter, M. (1973), "The War of Qays and Yaman Sections in Local Political Decisions", *Asian and African Studies* 19(3): 249–317.

Hofman, J. E. and Beit-Hallahmi, B. (1978) "The Palestinians and Israel's

Arabs". In: G. Ben-Dor (ed.), *The Palestinians and the Middle East Conflict* (Israel: Turtledove Publishing), pp. 217–218.

Horowitz, D. (1982), "Dual Authority Politics", *Comparative Politics* (14): 329–350.

Horowitz, D. and Lissak, M. (1978), *Origins of Israeli Polity – Palestine under Mandate* (University of Chicago Press).

Horowitz, D. and Lissak, M. (1989), *Trouble in Utopia – The Overburdened Polity of Israel* (Albany: State University of New York Press).

Hourani, A. H. (1946), *Syria and Lebanon: A Political Essay* (Oxford University Press).

Johnston, J. (1972), *Econometrics,* second edition (New York. McGraw-Hill).

Kaufman, I. (1999), *Arab National Communism in the Jewish State* (University of California Press).

Kedourie, E. (1988), "Ethnicity, Majority and Minority in the Middle East". In: M. Esman and I. Rabinovich (eds.), (1988), pp. 26–38.

Kleppner, P. (1982), *Who Votes? The Dynamics of Electoral Turnout 1870–1980* (New York: Praeger), pp. 112–141.

Kmenta, J. (1971), *Elements of Econometrics* (New York: Macmillan).

Korbel, J. (1977), *Twentieth Century Czechoslovakia – The Meanings of its History* (New York: Columbia University Press).

Kupferschmidt, U. (1987), *The Supreme Muslim Counsil – Islam Under the British Mandate for Palestine* (Leiden: E.J. Brill Academic Publishers).

Landau, J. (1972), "The Arab Voter". In: A. Arian (ed.), *The Elections in Israel, 1969* (Jerusalem: Jerusalem Academic Press), pp. 157–158.

Lapp, M., "Incorporating Groups in Rational Choice Explanations of Turnout: An Empirical Test", *Public Choice* 98(1–2): 171–185.

Lijphart, A. (1977), *Democracy in Plural Societies: A Comparative Exploration* (New Haven: Yale University Press).

Lijphart, A. (1984), *Democracies* (New Haven: Yale University Press).

Lustick, I. (1980), *Arabs in the Jewish State: Israel's Control of a National Minority* (Austin: University of Texas Press).

Lutfiyya, Abdulla M. and Charles W. Churchill (1970), *Readings in Arab Middle Eastern Societies and Cultures* (The Hague: Mouton).

Maddala, G. S. (1977), *Introduction to Econometrics* (New York: Macmillan).

Marx, E. and Shmueli, A. (1984), *The Changing Bedouin* (New Brunswick and London: Transaction Books).

Marx, E. (1967), *Bedouin in the Negev* (Manchester University Press).

Marx, E. (1973), "The Organization of Nomadic Groups in the Middle East". In: M. Milton (ed.), *Society and Political Structure in the Arab World* (New York: Humanities Press).

Masalha, N. (ed.) (1995), *The Palestinians in Israel – Is Israel a State of All its Citizens and "Absentees"?* (Nazareth: Galilee Center for Social Research).

Nakhleh, K. (1977), "Anthropological and Sociological Studies on the Arabs in Israel: A Critique", *Journal of Palestinian Studies* (6): 41–77.

Peled, Y. (1992), "Ethnic Democracy and the Legal Construction of Citizenship: Arab Citizens of the Jewish State", *American Political Science Review* 86(2): 432–443.

Peres, Y. (1971), "Ethnic Relations in Israel", *American Journal of Sociology* 76(6): 1021–1047.

Rouhana, N. (1984), *The Arabs in Israel: Psychological, Political and Social Dimensions of Collective Identity* (Ph.D. Thesis, Detroit).

Rouhana, N. (1997), *Palestinian Citizens in an Ethnic Jewish State: Identities in Conflict* (New Haven: Yale University Press).

Rouhana, N., Ghanem, A. (1998), "The Crisis of Minorities in Ethnic States: The Case of Palestinina Citizens in Israel", *IJMES* (30): 321–346.

Rumley, D. (1991), "The Political Organization of Space: A Reformist Conception", *Australian Geographical Studies* 26: 329–336.

Sa'di A. H. (1992), "Between State Ideology and Minority National Identity: Palestinians in Israel and Israeli Social Science", *Review of Middle East Studies* 5: 110–130.

Sa'di, A. H. (1996), "Minority Resistance to State Control: Towards a Re-analysis of Palestinian Political Activity in Israel", *Social Identities* 2(3): 395–412.

Shoked, M, (1975), "Strategy and Change in the Arab Vote". In: A. Arian (ed.), *The Elections in Israel, 1973* (Jerusalem: Jerusalem Academic Press), pp. 162–165.

Sivan, E. (1972), "Modern Arab Historiography of the Crusades", *Asian and African Studies*, Vol. 8, No. 2 (Jerusalem Journal of the Israel Oriental Society. Jerusalem Academic Press), pp. 109–149.

Smooha, S. (1978), *Israel: Pluralism and Conflict* (Berkley and Los Angles, CA: University of California Press).

Smooha, S. (1980), "Control of Minorities in Israel and Northern Ireland", *Comparative Studies in Society and History* 22: 256–280.

Smooha, S. (1984), *The Orientation and Politization of the Arab Minority in Israel*, Monograph Series on the Middle East, No. 2, Haifa: University of Haifa, The Jewish–Arab Center.

Smooha, S. (1990), "Minority Status in Ethnic Democracy: The Status of the Arab Minority in Israel", *Ethnic and Racial Studies* 13(3): 389–412.

Tessler, M. A. (1981), "Arabs in Israel", *American Universities Fieldstaff reports*, 1 (Hanover, NH), 21–43.

Trudeau, P. E., (1968), *Federalism and the French Canadians* (Toronto: Macmillan).

Yaniv, A. and Al-Haj, M. (1983), "Uniformity or Diversity: A Reappraisal of the Voting Behaviour of the Arab Minority in Israel". In: A. Arian (ed.), *The Elections in Israel, 1981* (Tel Aviv: Ramot Publishing, Tel Aviv University), pp. 145–149.

Waterman, S. (1987), "Partitioned States", *Political Geography Quarterly* 6: 151–170.

Yiftachel, O. (1994), "Regional Mix and Ethnic Relations: Evidence from Israel", *Geoforum* 25: 41–55.

Zirakzadeh, C. E. (1989), "Economic Changes and Surges in Micro-nationalistic Voting in Scotland and the Basque Region of Spain", *Comparative Studies in Society and History* 31(2): 319–399.

Zureik, E. (1979), *The Palestininas in Israel: A Study in Internal Colonialism* (London: Routledge & Kegan Paul).

Zureik, E. (1993), "The Condition and the Status of the Arabs in Israel", *Journal of Palestinian Studies*, 22(2): 90–109; 22(4): 73–93.

Zuwiyya Y. L. (1969), *The Syrian Social Nationalist Party: An Ideological Analysis* (Cambridge, Mass.: Harvard University Press).

Hebrew Bibliography

Abu Gosh, S. (1965), "Integration of the Arab Clan in a Local Council in an Arab Village," in *Arab Society in Israel – Changes and Trends*, Prime Minister's Office.

Abu Raya, A. (1994), *National Service for Israeli Arabs*, Bet Berl.

Abu Raya, A. (1998), *Rifts in the Islamic Movement in Israel: Its Reasons and Religious and Political Extent* (unpublished Hebrew manuscript).

Al-Asmar, P. (1975), *Being an Arab in Israel*, Shahak Press.

Al-Haj, M. (1979), *Status of Arab Family Clan in Israel* (Hebrew Master's Thesis), Haifa University.

Al-Haj, M. (1996), "Political Organization in Arab Society in Israel: Central/Fringe Development," in Lissak, M. and Knei Paz, B. (eds.), *Israel Facing the Third Millennium*, Magnes Press.

Al-Haj, M. (1996), *Education in the Israeli Arab Sector*, Magnes Press.

Al-Haj, M. (1997), "Identity and Orientation in Arab Society in Israel: a Situation of a Double Periphery," in *State, Government and International Relations*.

Al-Halili, A. (1977), *Palestinian Heritage and Social Strata, Folkloric Study of Arab Palestinian Society through its Catchphrases and Proverbs*, Jerusalem, Salah al-Din.

Amara, M., Kabha, S. (1996), *Divided Identity – Political Divisions and Cultural Reflections in a Divided Village*, Giv'at Haviva Institute for Peace Studies.

Amitai, Y. (1988) *Testing National Solidarity – Mapam 1948–1954: Positions on the Arab–Israel Issue*, Gomeh.

Arian, A. (1973), *The Electing Nation: Voting Trends in Israel*, Massada.

Arian, A. (1985), *Politics and Government in Israel*, Zmora Bitan Publishers.

Arian, A., Nahmias, D., Amir, R. (2002), *Governance and the Governing Authority in Israel*, the Israeli Institute for Democracy, Jerusalem.

Asaf, M. (1967), *History of the Arab Awakening in Israel and their Escape*, Culture and Education and *Davar*.

Atrash, A. (1995), *Day in Day Out – Arab Unemployment in Israel*, Ra'anana: Centre for the Study of Arab Society in Israel.

Atshi, Z. (1981), "Testimony of a Druze Member of Knesset," in Aluf Hareven (ed.), *One Out of Every Six Israelis*, Jerusalem, Van Leer Institute.

Aviv, A. (1993), *Israeli Society, Stresses and Struggles*, MOD Publications.

Baily, Y., Rekhes, A., Sofer, A. (1996), *Israel's Arabs, Where To?* Efal, Yad Tabenkin.

Bar, G. (1973), *Arabs of the Middle East: Population and Society*, second ed., Tel Aviv, United Kibbutz Movement.

Bar, G. (1973), *The Village Mukhtar in the Land of Israel*, Jerusalem, Truman Institute.

Bar-Gal, Y., Sofer, A. (1976), *Horizons in Geography: Changes in Minority Villages in Israel*, Haifa University, Dept. of Geography and the Jewish–Arab Center.

Ben-Arzi, Y. (1980), *Creation of a Living Pattern and Characteristics of Living of Arabs in Haifa*, Haifa, the Jewish–Arab Center and Haifa University.

Ben-David, Y. (1996), *Conflict in the Negev*, Ra'anana: Center for the Study of Arab Society in Israel.

Ben-Dor, G. (1974), *Report of the Commission on the Problems of Druze in Israel*, Haifa, Bureau of the Advisor on Arab Matters.

Bishara, A. (1993), "On the Issue of the Arab Minority in Israel," in Ram, A. (ed.), *Israeli Society: Critical Aspects*, Breirot Publishing.

Bishara, A. (1996), "The Israeli Arab: a Study of Divided Political Discourse," in Ginosar, P., Bareli, A. (eds.), *Zionism: Modern Polemic*, Midreshet Sde Boker: The Ben-Gurion Heritage Center.

Bishara, A., (1996) "A Hundred Years of Zionism," *Theory and Criticism*.

Bishara, A., (1996), "On Nationalism and Universalism," *Zmanim*.

Blank, H. (1984), *The Druze in Israel*, Haifa: the Jewish–Arab Center and Haifa University.

Boimel, Y. (2002), *Attitudes of the Israeli Establishment to the Arabs in Israel, Policy, Principles and Activity: the Second Decade, 1958–1968* (Hebrew doctoral thesis), Haifa University.

Central Bureau of Statistics, No. 58, 2007.

Chamansky, D., Jubran, R., Khamaysi, R. (1984), *Inventory of Enterprises in Arab Towns in Israel*, Haifa, the Center for the Study of the City, Technion.

Chamansky, D., Taylor, T. (1968), "Dynamic Aspects of Entrepreneurship in Arab Towns and Villages in Israel," *Horizons in Geography*.

Cohen, A. (1978), *Economics in the Arab Sector in Palestine During the Mandate*, Giv'at Haviva, the Institute for Arab Studies.

Cohen, A. (1984), *Israel's Arabs, Economic Aspects*, Giv'at Haviva.

Cohen, R. (1982), *Dealing with Arab Towns and Villages Connected to the Labor Councils*, Tel Aviv, Labor Party, Minorities Branch.

Cohen, R. (1984), *Israel's Arabs: Government Policy and Ways of Implementing It*, Tel Aviv, Labor Party, Minorities Branch.

Cohen, R. (1984), *Voting Results to Knesset and Histadrut (General Labor Federation) Elections over Three Election Campaigns: 1973–1981*, Tel Aviv, Labor Party, Minorities Department.

Cohen, R. (1987), *A Thousand Arab Students Studying in the Eastern Bloc*, Tel Aviv, Labor Party, Minorities Department.

Cohen, R. (1989), *Political Development of Israeli Arabs as Reflected in their Voting Patterns for Knesset over Eleven Election Campaigns*, 1948–1984, Ph.D. thesis, Tel Aviv University.

Cohen, R. (2000), *Kiss of the Sabra*, Tel Aviv, Yediot Ahronot Publishers.

Colbi, S. (1969), *The History of Christianity in the Holy Land*, Tel Aviv, Am Hasefer.

Dahr. A. (1977), *Cultural Conflict: Deviation, Conformism and Crime in Arab Society* (M.A. thesis, Tel Aviv University).

Dalal, M. (2003), (ed.), *October 2000: Law and Politics Before the Or Commission*, Shefar'am, Adala, the Legal Center for the Rights of the Arab Minorities in Israel.

Dana, N. (1974), *The Druze, Ethnics and Tradition*, Jerusalem, Ministry of Religion.

Dana, N. (1998), *The Druze*, Ramat Gan, Bar Ilan University.

Diskin, A. (1988), *Elections and Voters in Israel*, Tel Aviv, Am Oved Publishers.

Dotan, S. (1981), *The Struggle for the Land of Israel*, Tel Aviv, Ministry of Defense.

Efrat, A. (1994), "The Rural Minority Population," in Efrat, A. (ed.), *Rural Geography of Israel*, Ahiassaf.

Ehrlich, A. (1993), "Society at War: the National Conflict and Social Structure," in Ram, A. (ed.) *Israeli Society, Critical Aspects*, Breirot (Choices).

Eisenstadt, S. (1967), *Israeli Society: Background, Development and Problems*, Magnes Press.

Elad, D. (1987), "The Local Aspect of Government and Politics in Israel," in Elazar, D., Kalheim, H. (eds.), *Local Government in Israel* (Hebrew), The Jerusalem Center for Public and Political Matters.

Falah, S. (1974), *History of the Druze in Israel*, Jerusalem, Bureau of the Advisor on Arab Affairs.

Fares, A. (1993), Not by Pitah Bread Alone – Poverty and Social Gaps in the Arab Population in Israel, Ra'anana: Centre for the Study of Arab Society in Israel.

Farhi, D. (1979), "The Moslem Council in East Jerusalem and Judea and Samaria since the Six Day War," *The New East*.

Gabizon, R., Hacker, D. (eds.), (2000), *The Arab–Jewish Rift in Israel: a Reader*, Jerusalem, The Israeli Institute for Democracy.

Ghanem, A., (1999), "The Palestinian Minority in Israel: the Challenge of a the Jewish State and its Repercussions," *Studies in Israeli Renaissance*.

Ghanem, A., Ozacky-Lazar, S. (1999), *Local Government Elections in the Arab Sector, November 1993 – Results and Analysis*, Givat Haviva: The Institute for Peace Research.

Ghanem, A., Ozacky-Lazar, S. (2001), "Al-Aqsa Intifada of the Palestinian Citizens of Israel: Reasons and Results," *Reviews of the Arabs in Israel*, No. 27, Givat Haviva, The Institute for Peace Research.

Gilber, G. (1989), *Trends in the Demographic Development of the Palestinians, 1870–1987*, Tel Aviv, Dayan Center, Tel Aviv University.

Ginat, Y. (1980), "Employment as a Social Element in the Arab Village," *a Series of Papers for Discussion, no. 68, the Sapir Center for Development*, Tel Aviv University.

Ginat, Y. (1988), "The Creation of an Israeli Arab," *A Monthly Review*, December.

Ginat, Y., (2000), *Blood Feuds: Ostracism, Mediation and Family Honor*, Tel Aviv, Haifa University and Zmora Bitan Publishers.

Gonen, A., Hamaisi, R. (1993), *The Arabs in Israel in Wake of Peace*, Jerusalem, Florsheimer Institute for Political Research.

Greitzer, D. (1997), "Ben Gurion, Mapai and the Israeli Arabs," in Z. Zameret, Yablonka, H. (eds.), *The First Decade*, Jerusalem, Yad Ben Zvi.

Gutman, A., Klaf, H., Levy, S., (1971), *A Study of Positions, Opinions and Behavior in Arab Villages in Israel – Summary Report*, Jerusalem, The Institute for Applied Research.

Habash, A. (1977), *Processes of Change and Modernization in the Arab Family: a Study of an Arab Village in Israel*, Jerusalem, the Institute for Labor and Welfare Studies, the Hebrew University.

Hadas, A., Gonen, A. (1994), *Jews and Arabs in a Mixed-ethnic Neighborhood in Jaffa*, Jerusalem: Florsheimer Institute for Political Research.

Harari, Y. (1978), *Local Elections in the Arab Sector*, Giv'at Haviva, the Institute for Arab Studies.

Hareven, A. (ed.) (1981*)*, *One Out of every Six Israelis, Interaction Between the Arab Minority and the Jewish Majority*, Jerusalem, Van Leer Institute.

Harkabi, Y. (1975), *Decisions of the Palestinian National Council*, Arabia and Israel, Tel Aviv: Am Oved Publishers.

Hasson, S., Abu Asba, A. (eds.) (2004), *Jews and Arabs in Israel in a Changing Reality*, Jerusalem, Florsheimer Institute for Political Research.

Hochman, R. (ed.) (1979), *Jews and Arabs in Israel*, Jerusalem, Magnes Press.

Idelitz, A. (ed.) (1989), *Plans for Developing the Ajami Quarter in Jaffa*, Tel Aviv Municipality and Ministry of Housing.

Israeli, G.Z. (1953), *Mapas, Pakap, Maki – History of the Communist Party in Israel*, Tel Aviv, Am Oved.

Israeli, R. (1981), "On the Identity Problems of Israeli Arabs," in, Aluf Hareven (ed.), *One Out of Every Six Israelis*, Jerusalem, Van Leer Institute.

Israeli, R. (2002), *The Arabs in Israel: With Us or Against Us?* Jerusalem, Harel Center.

Jamal, A. (2002), "Abstention as Participation: on Confusions in Arab Politics in Israel," in Arian, A., Shamir, M. (eds.), *Elections in Israel 2001*, Jerusalem, Israeli Institute for Democracy.

Jaraisi, S. (1973), *Report of the Committee for Determining the Structure of Expenditure and Sources of Income in Minorities' Local Authorities*, Jerusalem, Ministry of the Interior.

Jaraisi, S. (1976), "Decline of Gerontocracy and Erosion in the Arab Milieu," *Gerentology*.

Jiryyes, S. (1966), *The Arabs in Israel*, Haifa, Al-Athad.

Jubran, R. (1987), *Review: Employment and Unemployment among University Graduates in Arab and Druze Towns*, Haifa, Koor Industries Ltd.

Kamp, A. (1999), "Language of Mirrors of the Border: Territorial Borders and the Establishment of a National Minority in Israel," *Israeli Sociology*, B.

Khamaysi, R. (1984), *Industrialization of the Arab Villages in Israel*, M.A. thesis, Haifa University.

Khamaysi, R. (1990), *Planning and Housing Among the Arabs in Israel*, Tel Aviv: the International Center for Peace in the Middle East.

Khatib, A.S. (1991), *Elements that Influence Geographic Aspects of the Social Networks of Arab Population in the Lower Western Galilee Region*, Ph.D. thesis, Hebrew University.

Kipnis, B., (1989), *Acre – Basic Outlines for Policies of Renewal and Development*, Haifa, the Institute for the Study of Haifa and the Galilee.

Landau, Y. (1971), *The Arabs in Israel, Political Studies*, Tel Aviv, Ministry of Defense Publishing House.

Landau, Y. (1981), "Alienation and Pressures in Political Behavior," in Layish, A. (ed.), *The Arabs in Israel: Continuity and Change*, Jerusalem, Magnus Press.

Landau, Y. (1993), *The Arab Minority in Israel 1967–1991 – Political Aspects*, Tel Aviv, Am Oved.

Layish, A. (1981), "Moslems' Ethnic Organization," in Layish, A. (ed.), *The Arabs in Israel, Continuity and Change*, Jerusalem, Magnus Press.

Layish, A. (1991), "Continuity and Change within the Druze Family," in Shamgar-Handelman, L., Bar-Yosef, R. (eds.), *Families in Israel*, Jerusalem, Akademon.

Layish, A., Falah, S. (1981), "The Druze Ethnic Organization," in Layish, A. (ed.), *The Arabs in Israel, Continuity and Change*, Jerusalem, Magnus Press.

Layish. A. (1965), "The Moslem Waqf in Israel," *The New East*.

Lewis, B. (1988), *Leaves in History – a Collection of Studies*, Jerusalem, Yad Ben Zvi.

Lisskovsky, A. (1989), "The Present Absentees in Israel," in Hochman, R. (ed.), *Jews and Arabs in Israel*, Jerusalem, Magnus.

Lustig, A. (1985), *Arabs in a Jewish State*, Haifa, Mifras.

Man'a, A. (1995), "Identity in Crisis: The Arabs in Israel in Face of the Israel-PLO Accords," in Rekhes, E., Yagens, T. (eds.), *Arab Politics in Israel at the Crossroads*, Tel Aviv, Dayan Center, Tel Aviv University.

Mar'i, S., Tahar, N. (1976), *Facts and Trends in the Development of Arab Education in Israel*, Haifa: The Institute for the Study and Development of Arab Education, Haifa University.

Marx, E. (1974), *Bedouin Society in the Negev*, Tel Aviv: Reshafim.

Medzini, A. (1984), *Mono-Geography – Distribution of Bedouin Settlements in the Galilee as a Result of Spontaneous Settlement and Deliberate Government Policy*, Haifa, University of Haifa.

Meir, T. (1989), "Moslem Youth in Israel," *The New East*.

Mor, Y. (1990), "Strategy of Coexistence in Mixed Jewish–Arab Neighborhoods: Modeled on the Plan for Renewal and Development of the Ajami Quarter and 'Lev Yaffo' in Tel Aviv," *City and Region*.

National Committee for the Defense of Arab Lands in Israel (1976), *The Black Book of Land Day*, Haifa, The National Committee for the Defense of Arab Lands and Al-Ittihad (in Arabic)

Nevo, Y. (1977) *The Political Development of the Palestinian Arab Nationalist Movement 1939–1945*, Ph.D. thesis, Tel Aviv University.

Nevo, Y. (1985), "The Palestinians and the Jewish State in the Years 1947–1948," in Wallach, Y. (ed.), *We Were as Dreamers, Collection of Articles on the War of Independence*, Tel Aviv, Massada.

Ozacky-Lazar, S. (2000), *From Hebrew Federation to Israeli Federation: Integration of Arabs in the Labor Federation, 1948–1966*, Texts in Israeli Renaissance.

Ozacky-Lazar, S., Ghanem, A. (2003), *Or Testimonies: Seven Expert Opinions Presented to the Or Commission*, Giv'at Haviva, Institute for Promotion of Peace and Keter, Jerusalem.

Ozacky-Lazar, S. and Kabha, M, (2008), Between Vision and Reality – The Vision Papers of the Arabs in Israel, 2006–2007, Jerusalem, The Citizens' Accord Forum.

Papeh, A. (1994), "The Birth of the Refugee Problem and its Solution," (Critique of the books by Nur Masalha and Don Peretz), *International Problems*.

Peres, Y. (1977), *Ethnic Relations in Israel*, Tel Aviv, Sifriyat Poalim.

Peres, Y., Yuval-Davis, N. (1968), "On the National Identity of the Israeli Arab," *The New East*.

Porani, P. (1984), *Defending the Roots*, Haifa, the Organization for Islamic Initiative in Haifa (in Arabic).

Porath, Y. (1976), *The Emergence of the Palestinian-Arab National Movement 1918–1929*, Tel Aviv, Am Oved.

Porath, Y. (1998), "What is a State for all its Citizens?" in Rekhes, E. (ed.), *The Arabs in Israeli Politics: Dilemmas of Identity*, Tel Aviv, Dayan Center, Tel Aviv University.

Portugali, Y. (1996), *Inclusive Relations – Society and Space in the Israel Arab Conflict*, Tel Aviv: Hakibutz Hameuhad.

Qahwaji, H. (1978), *The Full Story of the al-Ard Movement*, Jerusalem, Mansourat al Arabi (in Arabic).

Rabinowitz, D. and Abu-Baker, H. (2002), *The Upright Generation*, Jerusalem, Keter.

Rapaport, Y. (1979), "Israeli Arab Youth," *Research Report*, 211, Jerusalem, Henrietta Szold Institute.

Rauhana, N. (1996), "Summary of Research Workshop," in Ossatsky-Lazar, S. (ed.) *Jewish–Arab Relations in the State of Israel*, Giv'at Haviva, the Institute for Peace Research.

Regev, A. (1989), *Israel's Arabs: Political Issues*, Jerusalem, Jerusalem Institute for Israel Studies.

Reiter, Y. (1979), *The Minorities in Israel, Guidelines for Social-Political Development*, Chief Education Officer, IDF.

Reiter, Y. (1989), "Evaluation of Reform in the Moslem Waqf in Israel: the Waqf in Acre," *The New East*.

Reiter, Y. (1995), "Between a Jewish State and a State for its Citizens – Status of the Arabs in a Time of Peace," *The New East*.

Reiter, Y., Aharoni, R., (1993), *The Political World of Israel's Arabs*, second ed., Ra'anana: the Center for the Study of Arab Society in Israel.

Rekhes, E. (1973), *Review of Graduates of Institutes of Higher Education from among the Minorities [...]*, Tel Aviv, Shiloah Institute, Tel Aviv University.

Rekhes, E. (1976), *Israel's Arabs After 1967, a Deepening of the Problem of Orientation*, Tel Aviv, Shiloah Institute, Tel Aviv University.

Rekhes, E. (1977), *Israeli Arabs and Land Appropriation in the Galilee*, Shiloah Institute.

Rekhes, E. (1984), *The Arabs in Israel and the Arabs in the Occupied Territories: Political Yearning and National Solidarity 1967–1983*, Dayan Center, Tel Aviv University,

Rekhes, E. (1985), *The Arab Village in Israel: Centers of Political Nationalist Renewal*, Dayan Center, Tel Aviv University.

Rekhes, E. (1985), *The Arab Village in Israel: Focus of Renewed Political Nationalism*, Tel Aviv, Shiloah Institute, Tel Aviv University.

Rekhes, E. (1986), *Agriculture in the Arab Sector*, Jerusalem, internal study on behalf of the Prime Minister's bureau.

Rekhes, E. (1986), *Between Communism and Arab Nationalism: Rakah and the Arab Minority in Israel, 1965–1973*, Ph.D. thesis, Tel Aviv University.

Rekhes, E. (1989), "Israel's Arabs and Land Appropriation in the Galilee, Background, Events and Repercussions," in Hochman, R. (ed.), *Jews and Arabs in Israel*, Jerusalem, Magnes.

Rekhes, E. (1993), *The Arab Minority in Israel Between Communism and Arab Nationalism 1965–1995*, Tel Aviv University.

Rekhes, E. (1995), "Israel's Arabs as a Bridge to Peace: Evolvement of a Concept," *The New East*.

Rekhes, E. (2000), "The Islamic Movement in Israel and its Relation with Political Islam in the Occupied Territories," in Gabizon, R., Hacker, D. (eds.), *The Jewish–Arab Rift: a Reader*, Jerusalem, the Israeli Institute for Democracy.

Roman, M. (1989), "The Arabs of Israel: Towns and Town Dwellers," in Hochman, R. (ed.), *Jews and Arabs in Israel*, Jerusalem, Magnus.

Rosenfeld, H. (1964), *They were Farm Laborers – Studies in the Social Development of the Arab Village in Israel*, Tel Aviv, Hakibutz Hameuhad.

Rosenfeld, H. (1981), "Change, Obstacles to Change, and Contrasts in the Rural Family," in Layish, A. (ed.), *The Arabs in Israel: Continuity and Change*, Jerusalem, Magnes.

Rosenfeld, H. (1998), "The Economic-Employment Transformation of the Arab Village," in Abuhav, A. et al. (eds.), *Local Anthropology*, Tel Aviv, Cherikover.

Rosenhack, Z. (1995), "New Developments in Sociology of the Palestinian Citizens of Israel: an Analytical Study," *Megamot*.

Sa'adi, A. (1997), "Culture as a Gauge of Political Behavior: the Palestinian Citizens of Israel," *Theory and Criticism*.

Sa'id, A. (1981), *The Question of Palestine*, Jerusalem, Mifras.

Sabri, J. (1968), *The Arabs in Israel*, Haifa, Al-Ittihad.

Schmalz, A. (1980), "Work Force," in Lissak, M. (ed.), *Community, Nationality and Status in Israeli Society*, Tel Aviv, Open University Publishing House.

Schmalz, A. (1981), "The Natural Movement and Population Growth," in Layish, A. (ed.), *The Arabs in Israel: Continuity and Change*, Jerusalem, Magnes.

Schmalz, A. (1981), "Work Force," in Layish, A. (ed.), *The Arabs in Israel: Continuity and Change*, Jerusalem, Magnes.

Schnell, Y. (1980), *Social Regions in Settlements Undergoing Urbanization and Modernization: an Example – Tayibe*, Haifa: the Technion, Israeli Technological Institute.

Schnell, Y. (1994), *Identity Paints Territory*, Ra'anana: Center for the Study of Arab Society in Israel.

Shamir, S. (1976), *The Historic Perspective: Israel's Arabs After 1967*, Shiloah Institute, Tel Aviv University.

Shamir, S. (ed.) (1978), *Decline of Nasserism, 1965–1970, Collapse of a Messianic Movement*, Tel Aviv, Mif'alim Universitaim.

Shapira, G. (1981), "The Right to form an Association and the Organizations Law 1980," *Hapraklit.*

Shebaat, A. (1974), *A Different Israeli Viewpoint,* Tel Aviv, the New Press (in Arabic).

Shiloh, G. (1982), *Israel's Arabs in the Eyes of the Arab States and the PLO,* Jerusalem, Magnes.

Shimony, Y. (1947), *Arabs of the Land of Israel,* Tel Aviv, Am Oved.

Shimony, Y. (1977), *Arab States, Chapters in Political History,* Tel Aviv, Am Oved.

Shimony, Y., Levin, A. (1971), *Political Dictionary of the Middle East in the Twentieth Century,* Jerusalem, Yerushalmy Publishing House.

Shitrit, B. (1949), *Activity between May 1948 and January 1949,* Minorities Office.

Shmueli, A., Schnell, Y., Sofer, A. (1985), The Small Triangle – Course of Events in a Region, Haifa, Jewish–Arab Center, Haifa University.

Shohat, M. (1989), "The Kurds: a Trapped Minority," *Information Paper # 9,* Bet Berl.

Shumaf, A., Hatukai, R. (2000), *The World of the Circassians,* Kafr Kama: the author.

Smooha, S. (1993), "Social, Ethnic and National Rifts and Democracy in Israel," in Ram, A. (ed.), *Israeli Society: Critical Aspects,* Tel Aviv, Brerot.

Smooha, S. (1995), "Jewish–Arab Relations in a Peaceful Era," *The New East.*

Smooha, S. (1998), "The Israelization of the Group Identity and Political Orientation of the Palestinian Citizens of Israel – a New Study," in Rekhes, E. (ed.), 1998, *The Arabs in Israeli Politics: Dilemmas of Identity,* Tel Aviv, Tel Aviv University, Dayan Center.

Smooha, S. (1999), *Autonomy for the Arabs in Israel?* Ra'anana, the Center for the Study of Arab Society in Israel.

Smooha, S. (2000), "Ethnic Democracy: Israel as a Proto-type," in Gabizon, R., Hacker, D. (eds.), *The Jewish–Arab Rift in Israel: a Reader,* Jerusalem.

Smooha, S. (2001), "Arab–Jewish Relations in Israel and a Democratic Jewish State," in Ya'ar, A., Shavit, Z. (eds.), *Trends in Israeli Society,* vol. A, Tel Aviv: the Open University.

Soen, D. (2003), *A Land of Fury and Anger: Rifts and Identity in Israeli Society,* Kiryat Bialik: Ach.

Sofer, A. (1984), "Changing Relations between Majority and Minority and their Regional Expression – the Case of the Israeli Arabs," *Horizons in Geography.*

Sofer, A. (1986), "Territorial Struggle between Jews and Arabs in Israel," *Horizons in Geogra*phy.

Sofer, A. (1988), *On the Demographic and Geographic Situation in Israel, Indeed the End of the Zionist Vision?* Haifa University.

Sofer, A. (1989), "The Israeli Arabs from Village to Metropolis and Then What?" *The New East.*

Sofer, A. (1993), "Full Rights for the Arabs – a Possibility?" *Nativ.*

Sofer, A. (1993), "The Israeli Arabs toward Autonomy: the Case of the Galilee sub-Region," *Studies in the Geography of Israel.*

Sofer, A. (2000), "The Israeli Arabs and the Peace Process – Recommendation for Policy," in Gabizon, R., Hacker, D. *The Jewish–Arab Rift: a Reader,* Jerusalem, the Israeli Institute for Democracy.

Sofer, A. (2003), *Israel Demography 2003–2020, Dangers and Possibilities*, Jerusalem, Zionist Council and Center for the Study of National Security, Haifa University.

Stendel, A. (1968), *The Circassians in Israel*, Jerusalem, Bureau of the Adivisor on Arab Affairs.

Stendel, A. (1973), *The Circassians in Israel*, Tel Aviv, Am Hasefer.

Stendel, A. (1977), *Minorities in Israel*, Jerusalem, Propaganda Center.

Stendel, A. (1989), "Israeli Arabs' Right to Differ – Legal Aspects," *The New East*.

Vashitz, Y. (1947), *The Arabs in the Land of Israel*, Merhavia: Sifriyat Poalim.

Vashitz, Y. (1979), *Studies in the Political Thoughts of the Palestinians*, Giv'at Haviva: Institute for Arab Studies.

Vital, D. (1972), "Small Countries in the Test of Existence," Tel Aviv, Am Oved.

Wallach, Y. (ed) (1985). *We Were as Dreamers, Collection of Articles on the War of Independence*, Tel Aviv, Massada, vol. I.

Winograd, A. (ed.), *Judgments, Collection of Israeli Laws*, Ramat Hasharon, Halachot.

Winter, M. (1981), "Basic Problems in the Education System," in Layish, A. (ed.), *The Arabs in Israel: Continuity and Change*, Jerusalem, Magnus Press.

Yaffe, N., Tal, D. (2002), *Arab Society in Israel*, Jerusalem, Central Bureau of Statistics.

Yiftachel, O. (1988), "State, Space and Ethnic Relations: Lebanon, Cyprus and Israel," *Studies in Geography of the Land of Israel*.

Yiftachel, O. (1993), "A Study of the Arab Minority in Israel and its Relations with the Jewish Majority," *Review and Analysis* no. 12, Giv'at Haviva, the Institute for Peace Research.

Yiftachel, O. (1993), "Model of Ethnic Democracy and Jewish–Arab Relations in Israel: Geographical, Historical and Political Aspects," *Horizons in Geography*.

Yiftachel, O. (1999), "Land Day," in Ofir, A. (ed.), *Fifty to Forty Eight*, Tel Aviv, Hakibutz Hame'uhad.

Yiftachel, O. (2000), "The Ethnic Democracy Model and Jewish–Arab Relations in Israel: Geographical, Historical and Political Aspects," in Gabizon, R. Hacker, D. (eds.) *The Jewish–Arab Rift in Israel*, Jerusalem, the Israeli Institute for Democracy.

Yishai, Y. (1986), *Interest Groups in Israel*, Tel Aviv, Am Oved.

Yom Tov, S. (1984), *Cultural Inhibitions in Promoting Physical Development in the Arab Village in the Galilee*, Giv'at Haviva: The Institute for Arab Studies.

Zbeida, A. (1988), *The Druze in the Golan Heights, a Conflict of Misunderstanding 1978–1982, Statistics and Analysis*, Tel Aviv, Dayan Center, Tel Aviv University.

Zidani, S. (1998), "The Arabs in the Jewish State: their Status in the Present and in the Future," in Rekhes, E. (ed.) *The Arabs in Israeli Politics: Dilemmas of Identity*, Tel Aviv: Tel Aviv University.

Index

Abbas, Ahmad, 237*n*
Abbas, Mahmud, 222, 240*n*
Abbasi, Mahmud, 136
Abd al-Hamid II, Sultan, 133
Abnaa al-Balad (Sons of the Village), 59,
   62, 72–3, 205, 229*n*
  and *al-Ansar* group, 72, 232*n*
  Arab students' committees, 79
  call to boycott elections, 69, 72, 150,
   152, 164, 165
  established in the Triangle, 162, 164
  ideological struggle with Rakah, 63
  influence in Umm-al-Fahm, 72, 138,
   232*n*
  local municipal authorities, 72, 81, 126
  local municipal elections, 72, 127
  Mahamid clan, 236*n*
  and "National Democratic Pact", 104
Abnaa Arrabeh, 166
Abnaa Sha'ab, 116
Abnaa Shafa'amr, 116
Abu al-Asal, Riah, 66, 71
Abu Asba, Ahmad, 237*n*
Abu Baker, H., 237*n*
Abu Basma, 172, 203
Abu Ghosh, 182, 183, *183*
Abu Ghosh, Subhi, 37
abu Husein, Jalal, 116–17
Abu Mokh clan, 116, 120
Abu Rabia, Khalil, 40
Abu Rabia, Sheikh Hamad, 38–41, *93*,
   170–1, 173, 231*n*
Abu Rabia, Unis, 238*n*
Abu Raya clan, 137
Abu Ruqun, Labib, 134, 167, 231*n*
abu Shaiban, Musa, 140–1
Abu Snan, 232*n*
Abu-Ras, Uthman, 55
Abu-Rayh clan, 117
Acre
  Arab Brotherhood List, 49
  Mapam Popular Arab bloc, 43

  as mixed ethnic town, 179, 180, 181,
   182, 188
Adala, 86–7, 109, 198
Adiga, 133, 236*n*
ADP *see* Arab Democratic Party (ADP)
Agudat Israel, 123
al-Ahali, 190
Ahl al-dhimma, 75
Alawites, 121, 235*n*
allied Arab lists *see* Arab allied lists
Allon, Yigal, 29, 44, 48, *93*
Aloni, Shulamit, 237*n*
Alpeleg, Zvi, *91*
Alternative, 56, 66
Am Echad, 140
Anabtawi, Abd, 83
Annapolis Conference (2007), 222, 223
al-Ansar group, 66, 70, 72, 104, 138,
   232*n*
'Aqr, Marr Saleh, 116
al-Aqsa Company for the Rehabilitation
  and Development of Holy Sites,
  77–8
al-Aqsa Foundation, 233*n*
al-Aqsa *Intifada see Intifada* (2000)
al-Aqsa mosque, 77, 108, 198, 199
'Ara, 69
Arab academic associations, 79–80
Arab al-Shibli, 170
Arab allied lists, 36–43
  Bedouin support, 38–41, 170–1, 173,
   174, 175, 184
  Christian Arab community, 49, 135,
   147, 176, 177, 178, 239*n*
  Circassian support, 179, 184
  disappearance of, 119, 130, 145, 153,
   163, 185
  Druze support, 39–42, 167–8, 184
  extended families role, 116
  Galilee Arab support, 163–4, 186
  Knesset elections (1st 1949), 37, 43

Arab allied lists *(continued)*
  Knesset elections (2nd 1951), 43, 167,
    173, 177
  Knesset elections (3rd 1955), 167,
    173, 177
  Knesset elections (4th 1959), 167,
    170, 177
  Knesset elections (5th 1961), 153
  Knesset elections (7th 1969), 37
  Knesset elections (8th 1973), 38, 153,
    170, 173, 177
  Knesset elections (9th 1977), 39–40,
    167, 174, 185
  Knesset elections (10th 1981), 37,
    174, 185
  Knesset elections (11th 1984), 153,
    186
  Knesset elections (12th 1988), 166
  Mapai (later the Labor Party), 36–7,
    38–42, 48, 49, 50, 59, 116, 134,
    135, 145, 153, 166, 185, 186
  military administration (1948-66), 37,
    185, 187
  as the "moderate camp", 157
  the "Triangle" Arab support, 164, 166,
    186
  voting shifts, 185, 186
Arab Brotherhood List, 49, 231*n*
Arab Center for Applied Social
    Research, 105
Arab Citizens in Israel Movement, 231*n*
Arab Civil Rights Organization in
    Nazareth, 86–7
Arab Congress in Israel, 71
Arab Democratic Party (ADP)
  desire to be included in coalitions, 153
  establishment (1988), 38, 48, 126,
    229*n*
  establishment of UAP, 68, 104, 154,
    156, 159, 233*n*, 238*n*
  ethnic voting patterns, 139
  Knesset elections (14th 1996), 104,
    159, 233*n*
  Knesset elections (15th 1999), 139,
    153
  Knesset elections (16th 2003), 140,
    154
  land expropriation, 52
  local municipal authorities, 126
  local municipal elections (1993), 127
  partnership with Islamic Movement,

  68, 104, 105, 154, 156, 159,
    233*n*, 238*n*
  and PLP, 68
  Sani' replaces Darawsha, 238*n*
Arab Front, 60–1
Arab Islamic Bloc, 104
Arab Israelis *see* Israeli Arab community
Arab List for Bedouin and Villagers
    (ALBV), 38, 170
Arab National Party, 154
Arab nationalism
  Bishara's aims, 90
  decisions on Israeli Arabs, 205
  Israeli Arab solidarity, 219
  Israeli Communist Party, 55, 56
  Israeli government policy, 62
  Naser's pan-Arabism, 59–60
  and Rakah, 38, 56–9, 62–3, 65–7
  Umm-al-Fahm at center, 138
  voter participation, 149–50
Arab nationalist movements, 65–8
  see also Abnaa al-Balad (Sons of the
    Village); *al-Ansar* group;
    Progressive Nationalist
    Movement
Arab nationalist parties
  Arab electoral power, 144, 146, 154,
    157–8, 161, 230*n*
  attempts to disqualify, 110
  Christian Arab community, 176, 177,
    178, 184
  Circassian community, 178, 179
  Druze community, 167, 168, 169
  election boycotters, 152
  Galilee Arab community, 163–4, 184
  Galilee Bedouin community, 170, 171
  Knesset elections (9th 1977), 182
  Knesset elections (10th 1981), 175,
    182
  Knesset elections (11th 1984), 65,
    176, 177, *177*, 182, 183, *183*
  Knesset elections (12th 1988), 155,
    174–5
  Knesset elections (14th 1996), 154,
    165, 175
  Knesset elections (15th 1999), 175,
    178
  Knesset elections (16th 2003), 158,
    169, 176, 177, *177*, 178, 179,
    182, 183
  Knesset elections (17th 2006), 158,
    169, 178, 182, *183*

mixed ethnic towns, 181, 182, 187–8
in Nazareth, 177, *177*, 182
Negev Bedouin community, 173, 175,
    176
outlying settlement Arabs, 183–4, *183*
politics of rift, 22
the "Triangle" Arab community, 164,
    165, 166, 184
vote shifts, 185–7
see also Arab Democratic Party (ADP);
    Arab Union for Renewal (AUR);
    al-Ard; Islamic Movement;
    "National Democratic Pact";
    Progressive List for Peace (PLP);
    Progressive National Pact (PNP);
    Progressive Pact; United Arab
    Party (UAP)
Arab political leadership, 87–103
Arab Socialist List, 62
Arab student unions, 73, 79, 125
Arab Union for Renewal (AUR), 104,
    105, 140, 153–4, 159
Arab Workers' Congress, 34
Arab–Israel Bloc, 60
Arab–Israeli War (1948), 1, 29–31, 54,
    132
al-Arad, 232*n*
Arad, 133
Ar'ara, 69, 126, 172, 175
al-Ard, 60, 61–2, 69
    Christian leadership, 71
    disqualification, 68, 109, 148, 231*n*
    ethnic rifts, 148
    founders, 32, 43, 61, 231*n*
    and Israeli Communist Party, 55, 59
    Knesset elections (6th 1965), 62
    Progressive Movement – Nazareth, 66
Arens, Moshe, 206
Arian, Asher, 149–50, 154, 236*n*
Armenian community, 132
Armistice Agreement (1948-9), 4, 30,
    31, 228*n*
Arrabeh, 116, 126
As'ad, Shafiq, 168
Assad, Bashar, 218
Assad, Hafez, 234*n*
Assenara, 99
Association for the Defense of the Rights
    of the Internally Displaced Persons,
    189–90
Atamneh clan, 117
Atawna, Yusuf, 141

Atshi, Zaydan, 134, 168
Australia, consensus model, 10
Avneri, Uri, 56, 66, 67, 68
'Aweisat clan, 117
Awwad, Nimer, 116
'Aziza, As'ad, 237*n*
Azulai, David, 159

Badir, Abdallah, 67
al-Badur, Sulayman, 238*n*
Balad *see* "National Democratic Pact"
Balam *see* Progressive National Pact
    (PNP)
Baltic states, 11
Bangladesh, 11
Baqa al-Gharbiyye, 72, 116–17, 120,
    123, 140
Barak, Ehud, *95, 96*
    Arab voting support, 1, 53, 148–9, 151
    attitude to Israeli Arabs, 1, 149, 190–1,
        201, 202
    election (1999), 149, 151
    loses to Sharon (2001), 148–9
    October 2000 events, 195, 201
    steps down (2000), 159
Baraqa, Muhammad, 105
Bartolini, S., 21
Basmat Tab'un, 170
Basques, 13–14, 22, 152
Bastuni, Rustum, 43
Bat-Yam, 179
Bedouin community, 132–3
    allied Arab lists, 38–41, 170–1, 173,
        174, 175, 184
    Arab nationalist parties, 170, 171, 173,
        174, 175, 176
    blood revenge, 41
    demographics, 133
    government policies, 202–3
    hatred of Druze, 41
    Islamic Movement, 175, 176, 202
    Knesset elections (2nd 1951), 173
    Knesset elections (3rd 1955), 173
    Knesset elections (8th 1973), 135,
        170, 173
    Knesset elections (9th 1977), 174
    Knesset elections (10th 1981), 173–4,
        175
    Knesset elections (11th 1984), 171
    Knesset elections (12th 1988), 174–5
    Knesset elections (14th 1996), 175
    Knesset elections (15th 1999), 175

Bedouin community *(continued)*
  Knesset elections (16th 2003), 140,
    141, 171, 175
  Knesset elections (17th 2006), 150,
    171, 175
  land issues, 135–6, 202–3
  Likud provision of career
    opportunities, 51
  living conditions, 136
  local municipal authorities, 118, 122
  local municipal elections (2000), 126
  "National Democratic Pact", 176
  non-profit organizations, 85
  Orthodox Islam, 135
  support for Zionist parties, 135, 170,
    171, 173, 174, 175–6, 184
  tribal units, 114
  United Arab Party (UAP); (United
    Arab List), 171, 175, 176
  voter participation, 150
  voting patterns, 135–6, 140, 141
  see also Arab List for Bedouin and
    Villagers (ALBV); Galilee
    Bedouin community; Negev
    Bedouin community
Be'er Hail, 203
Be'er Sheba, 179
Begin, Menachem, 48, 50, 232*n*
Beilin, Yossi, 47, 151
Beit Jann, 82, 141, 167, 168
Beit Neqofa, 182
Beit Pelet, 203
Beit Tsafafa, 52, 182
Beitinu party, 107
Belgium, 10, 11, 23
Ben Dor, Gabriel, 155
Ben-Gurion, David
  Arab villages tour (1959), *92*
  banning of *al-Ard*, 231*n*
  first leader of Israeli Workers' Party,
    229*n*
  formation of Rafi, 231*n*
  military administration, 15, 16, 31, 33
  minorities policy, 28
  "voluntary transfer", 28
Ben-Gurion University, 73
Be'neh, 61
Bir al-Maksur, 170
Bir'am, 1, 189
Bishara, Azmi
  abolition of Jewish National Fund,
    159, 238*n*
  Arab nationalism, 90
  Arab pride in, 109
  Arab Union for Renewal (AUR), 159
  autonomy proposals, 90, 152
  Christian Arab support, 178
  Christian identity, 137, 139
  disqualification threats, 107, 108, 109
  extra-parliamentary movements, 104
  Knesset elections (14th 1996), 89
  Knesset elections (16th 2003), 107,
    109, 137, 165
  leaves Israel (2007), 158, 234*n*
  nationalist ideological stream, 158
  Or Commission, 111, 197, 198
  pan-Arabism, 220
  "politicization without extremism",
    103
  "state for all its citizens" theory, 90
  support for Hezbollah, 107, 234*n*,
    238*n*
  Zionism, 90
Biton, Charlie, 56–7
Black Panther movement, 56, 232*n*
blood feuds, 114, 115
blood revenge, 41
blood ties, 114
"Bloody Sunday", 239*n*
Boimel, Yair, 200
Bransah, Salah, 43, 61, 62, 231*n*
British Mandate period, 29, 30, 36, 54,
    55, 113, 118, 152
bureaucratic systems, 34–5
Bush, George W., 221, 222, 223

Camp David negotiations, 3–4, 190, 212
Canada, 10, 23
Carmiel, 65, 179
Central Bureau of Statistics, 107, 236
Christian Arab community
  allied Arab lists, 49, 135, 147, 176,
    177, 178, 239*n*
  Arab nationalist parties, 176, 177, 178,
    184
  cults and denominations, 130, 132
  demographics, 132, 142
  development of separate political
    channels, 130, 131
  electoral power, 147, 148
  establishment of foundations (NGOs),
    127
  ethnic background, 130
  ethnic rifts, 136–7, 139, 147

extra-parliamentary activity, 71
in the Galilee, 162
Knesset elections (1st 1949), 178
Knesset elections (2nd 1951), 177
Knesset elections (3rd 1955), 177
Knesset elections (8th 1973), 177
Knesset elections (11th 1984), 136,
    176, 177, *177*
Knesset elections (15th 1999), 139,
    178
Knesset elections (16th 2003), 136–7,
    176, 177, *177*, 178
Knesset elections (17th 2006), 178
Lebanon War (1982), 238*n*
and Maki, 54, 55, 135, 147
and Mapai, 49, 135, 147, 239*n*
and Mapam, 49
"National Democratic Pact", 176
non-profit organizations, 86
political activity, 135
and Rakah, 49, 135, 176, 178
support for Communists, 49, 54, 55,
    135, 147, 176, 178
support for Zionist parties, 135, 177–8
voting patterns, 135, 176–8
Christian-Moslem list for Arab
    Brotherhood, 49, 231*n*
Circassian community, 133
  Arab allied lists, 179, 184
  Arab nationalist parties, 178, 179
  development of separate political
      channels, 130, 131
  government policies, 202, 204
  Knesset elections (2nd 1951), 178–9
  Knesset elections (3rd 1955), 178–9
  Knesset elections (4th 1959), 179
  Knesset elections (8th 1973), 179
  Zionist political parties, 135, 178–9,
      184
clan system
  Arab allied lists, 37–9
  Druze community, 134
  influence on Knesset elections, 116,
      119–20, 128
  Islamic Movement's attempts to
      undermine, 126, 129, 138
  local municipal authorities, 20, 87,
      115–17, 118–30
  loss of influence, 44
  national political parties, 124–30
  new political leadership, 87
  social and political rifts, 113–18, 186

strength in rural areas, 36
support for Mapai (later the Labor
    Party), 50
ties with Rakah, 57, 129
Clinton, Bill, 4
co-liable groups, 114
Co-operation and Brotherhood list, 38
co-operation model, 10
Coalition of Charities, 233*n*
Cohen, Avner, 115
Cohen, Eliezer, 107
Cohen, Ra'anan, *93*, *94*
Committee for Boycotting the Elections,
    152
Committee for the Management of
    Druze *Waqf* Affairs, 71
Communist parties *see* Democratic Front
    for Peace and Equality (Hadash);
    Israeli Communist Party (Maki);
    Rakah
Complex Loyalties (Cohen), 1
compromise model, 10
consensus model, 10
control model, 11
Coptic community, 132
Cyprus, 23
Czechoslovakia, 11

Daburiya, 153
Dahamsha, Abd al-Malik, 68, 89, 105,
    140, 197, 198, 239*n*
Daliyat al-Carmel, 70, 141, 167
Daqqa, Fathi, 140
dar see nuclear family (*dar*)
Darawsha, Abd al-Wahab
  election to 11th Knesset (1984), 46–8,
      50, 120
  establishment of UAP, 156
  leader of Arab Democratic Party
      (ADP), 48, 68, 104, 105, 153,
      233*n*, 238*n*
  motion of no confidence (1995), 52
Darjat, 203
Darwish, Abdallah Nimer, 77, 105, 148,
    165
Darwish, Ahmad, 68
Darwish, Mahmud, 65
Darwish, Samir, 237*n*
Dash Party, 134, 147, 168
Dayan, Moshe, 48, 232*n*
Dekel, Meir, 45

Democratic Front for the Liberation of
  Palestine, 72
Democratic Front for Nazareth, 57, 65–6
Democratic Front for Peace and Equality
  (Hadash)
  competition from al-Sawt, 71
  desire to be included in coalitions, 153
  dissident camp, 229n
  ethnic rifts, 148
  ethnic voting patterns, 136, 137, 138,
    139
  increasing strength, 57–9
  Israeli Arab elite, 57–8
  Jewish candidates, 145
  Knesset elections (11th 1984), 56–7,
    136, 137
  Knesset elections (12th 1988), 168
  Knesset elections (13th 1992), 159
  Knesset elections (14th 1996), 103–4,
    159
  Knesset elections (15th 1999), 139,
    153, 159
  Knesset elections (16th 2003), 137,
    138, 140, 141, 153–4, 165, 183
  Knesset list in Nazareth, 57
  local municipal elections, 57, 125, 127
  Mahamid clan, 236n
  merger with Black Panther movement,
    56, 232n
  mixed ethnic towns, 181
  political pacts, 105
  support from Rakah, 57
Democratic List for Nazareth and its
  District, 120
Democratic National Pact, 89
Democratic Popular Front (DPF), 60–1
demographic issue, 3, 6–7, 25, 106, 107,
  142–3, 213
Deri, Arye, 51
Dhaher, Ahmad, 231n
al-Dhaher, Kamel, 66
dhimma status, 75
Diab, Saleh, 49
Dichter, Avi, 106
displaced persons, 30
division model, 11
DPF see Democratic Popular Front
  (DPF)
Druckman, Haim, 83, 107
Druze community
  allied Arab lists, 39–42, 167–8, 184
  Arab nationalist parties, 167, 168, 169

autonomy, 131–2
clan rivalries, 134
demographics, 131, 142
development of separate political
  channels, 130, 131
electoral power, 147, 148
ethnic background, 130
ethnic rifts, 134–5, 137, 140, 141, 147
extra-parliamentary activity, 70–1
in the Galilee, 162, 169
government policies, 202, 204
hatred of Bedouin, 41
Israeli Communist Party, 55, 134, 140
Knesset elections (1st 1949), 167
Knesset elections (2nd 1951), 167,
  168
Knesset elections (3rd 1955), 167
Knesset elections (4th 1959), 167
Knesset elections (8th 1973), 167–8
Knesset elections (9th 1977), 167, 168
Knesset elections (10th 1981), 134–5
Knesset elections (11th 1984), 134–5,
  137
Knesset elections (12th 1988), 168
Knesset elections (15th 1999), 168
Knesset elections (16th 2003), 137,
  140, 141, 154, 168, 169
Knesset elections (17th 2006), 168–9
Lebanon War (1982), 238n
Likud Party, 134–5, 152, 153, 168
Likud provision of career
  opportunities, 51
local municipal authorities, 122
Mapai (later the Labor Party), 134,
  168
military service, 70–1
municipality leaders, 82
national identity disputes, 70
Rakah support, 168
support for Zionist parties, 134, 137,
  168, 169, 184
voting patterns, 134–5, 137, 140, 141,
  167–9, 169
Druze Courts law, 131–2
Druze Enterprise/Initiative Committee,
  70–1, 167, 233n
Druze Zionist Circle, 70

East Jerusalem
  Islamic movements, 73
  land appropriation, 51
Eban, Abba, 94

Egypt
  Arab–Israeli War (1948), 29
  nationalization of Suez Canal, 59
  pan-Arabism, 59–60, 162
  revolution (1952), 59
Egypt–Syria pact (1958), 59
Egyptian–Israeli peace talks, 48, 50, 133,
    232n
Ehrlich, Simha, 206
Eilabun, 126
Ein Rafa, 182, 183, *183*
elections *see* Knesset elections; local
    municipal elections; student
    elections
Elections Boycott Party, 237n
electoral behavior theories, 21–7
electoral power, defined, 142
Elissar, Eliyahu Ben, 206
EMET list, 42, 231n
equality issues
  Adala, 86
  Bedouin demands, 136
  Druze demands, 71
  early days of state of Israel, 28–9, 35–6
  Islamic Movement, 77
  Israeli Arab demands, 6, 15, 19, 61, 88
  Israeli Arab leadership, 90–1, 112
  Jewish left, 26
  Likud Party, 51
  Mapam, 44
  October 2000 events, 191–2
  and PLP, 68
"Equality Pact", 90, 104
Eshkol, Levi, 33
Esman, Milton, 12
ethnic rifts, 22–3, 75–6, 113, 139–40,
    147, 148
ethnicity, underlying cause of, 12
Evangelical-Episcopal community, 132
extra-parliamentary movements, 18, 23,
    68–78, 84–7, 104, 157, 185, 188
  see also Abnaa al-Balad (Sons of the
    Village); *al-Ansar* group; Islamic
    Movement; Land Defense
    Committee; National Committee
    for the Arab Local Authorities in
    Israel; Supreme Follow-up
    Committee for the Arabs; Young
    Moslems

al-Fajr, 69
the Family of the Holy War, 75

family reunification, 3
family structures, 113–16, 119, 127, 128
  see also clan system; nuclear family
    (*dar*)
family/tribal system identity, 20
Farah, Bulus, 60
Farah, Ja'far, 86
Farhoud, Sheikh Farhoud Qasem, 70, 71
Fassuta, 135, 176, 177, 178
Fatah, 190, 221
al-Fattah, Awwad Abd, 111
fellahin, 175–6
Fiji, 11
Forward *see* Kadima ("Forward")
Freedom Party, 231n
Furaydis, 182

Galilee
  battles (October 1948), 31
  Druze community, 162, 169
  Islamic Movement, 228n
  Israeli Communist Party, 55
  Knesset elections, 141, 163, 164
  land expropriation, 65, 80, 145, 232n,
    234n
  local authority convention, 82
  local municipal authorities, 118
  non-profit organizations, 86
  terrorist activities, 106
  see also Nazareth; Sakhnin; Shefar'am;
    Tamra
Galilee Arab community, 162–4, *163*,
    184, 186
Galilee Association for Health Research,
    85
Galilee Bedouin community, 133, 170–1,
    172
Gaza
  control by Hamas, 221
  demand for national rights, 190
  Israeli Arab loyalty, 19, 64, 65, 68
  Israeli military activity, 222–3
  military service, 71
  Moslem Brotherhood cells, 74
  open boundaries, 205
  Six Day War (1967), 73, 205
  see also Intifada (1987-93)
Gaza disengagement plan, 1, 6, 153, 210
General Labor Federation (Histadrut),
    34, 37, 44, 47, 120
General Zionists Party, 36, 231n
Ghabsiyy, 189

Ghadir, Muhammad Husayn, 170–1
Ghajar, 121
Ghanaim clan, 117, 137
Ghanem, As'ad, 109, 110, 139–40,
    151–2, 194, 211, 235*n*
Ghosh, Jenny Mancho, *102*
Glazer, Nathan, 22
Golan Heights, 142
Goldstein, Baruch, 229*n*
Greek Catholic community, 132, 135,
    176, 239*n*
Greek Orthodox community, 55, 132,
    135, 176
Greenbaum, Yitzhak, 29
Gulf War (1991), 199, 218, 219
Gur-Arye, Binyamin, 206

Ha'aretz, 109, 151–2
Habash, George, 72, 233*n*
Habbeh, 190
Habibi, Amil, 56, 62
al Hadaf association, 72
Hadash *see* Democratic Front for Peace
    and Equality (Hadash)
Haddad, Hanna, 49, 177–8, 231*n*
Haddad, Sa'ad, 49, 232*n*
Haidar, Aziz, 210
Haifa
    Black Panther movement, 56
    Christian Arab community, 176
    Democratic Popular Front (DPF), 61
    Lebanon War (2006), 219
    Popular Arab bloc, 43
    voting trends, 179, 180, 181, 182
Haifa student union, 79
al-Hajj, Majid, 113, 136
Hajj Yahya clan, 117
Hakim, Archbishop George, 239*n*
Halabi, Sami, 140
Haldani, Bishop, *92*
Halutza Dunes, 3
Hamas, 3, 78, 106, 221
Hamdan, Fares, 32, 120, 231*n*
Hamdan, Munir, 168
Hamis, Walid, 219
hamulas, 32, 114–18
Hamzi, Riad, 42
Hanna, Archimandrit Attala, *102*
Har Homa, 52
al-Haram al-sharif see Temple Mount
Harel, Isser, 33
Harrop, William, 85

Hawatmeh, Nayef, 72
Hazen, Shukri, 71
Hebrew University of Jerusalem, 73
Heshin, Mishael, 108
Hezbollah
    Bishara's support, 107, 234*n*, 238*n*
    Lebanon War (2006), 218–19, 220–1,
        235*n*
    terrorist activities, 106
Hillel, Shlomo, 52, 148
Histadrut *see* General Labor Federation
    (Histadrut)
Holland, 11
Holyland Foundation, 233*n*
homeland groups, 10
homeland minorities, 11, 15, 229*n*
Humanitarian Rescue Committee, 77
Hura, 122, 141, 172, 203
Hurfesh, 167
Husayn, Ibrahim Nimer, 83, 136, 237*n*
al-Huseini, Hajj-Amin, 113
Hussein, Saddam, 218

ideological considerations, 154–61
Ighbaria, Afu, 138
Ighbaria clan, *129*, 138
Ighbariya, Asma, 183
Ikrit (Iqrit), 1, 189
Iksal, 120
I'lam, 86
Independents' Movement, 104
India, 11, 12
Institute for Humanitarian Aid, 77
institutional separatism, 103
intermarriages, 114
Interpal Foundation, 233*n*
Intifada (1987-93), 16, 163, 232*n*, 233*n*,
    234*n*
    activity of Arab MKs, 107
    government decisions, 199, 206
    and Islamic Movement, 77, 78
    Israeli Arab/Palestinian relations, 103
    political reality, 105
    and Rakah, 59
    support for widows and orphans, 78
    suppression by Zionist political
        parties, 48
Intifada (2000), 1, 146, 189–92, 228*n*
    "1948 Arabs" support, 106–7
    Israeli Arab/Palestinian relations, 103
    Israeli/Palestinian relations, 105

voting behavior of Israeli Arabs, 185, 186
Iqrit (Ikrit), 1, 189
Iran, 221
Iranian revolution (1979), 74
Iraq
  Arab–Israeli War (1948), 29
  backing for Rejection Front, 233*n*
  Gulf War (1991), 218
  revolution (1958), 59, 61
irredentism, 13, 229*n*
Isa, Sami, 206–7
Isawi, Freij, 140
Isifya, 167
al-Islah Party, 154
Islam, return to religion of Arab-Israelis, 73–5
the "Islamic Bloc", 126
Islamic Council, 131
Islamic fundamentalism, 75, 108, 135
Islamic ideological stream, 158–9
Islamic Jihad, terrorist activities, 106
Islamic liberation movements, 74
Islamic Movement, 75–8, 89
  ability to cross clan lines, 126, 129, 138
  "al-Aqsa is in danger" slogan, 3, 78, 106, 108
  autonomous society plan, 211
  Bedouin community, 175, 176, 202
  call to boycott elections, 141, 164, 165
  disqualification threats, 108
  establishment of UAP, 156, 238*n*
  ethnic voting patterns, 138, 139
  growing influence, 148, 213–14
  growth of, 16
  ideology, 156
  influence of, 199
  influence in Umm-al-Fahm, 76, 77, 138, 202
  Intifada (1987-93), 77, 78
  Knesset elections (12th 1988), 76
  Knesset elections (13th 1992), 76
  Knesset elections (14th 1996), 76–7, 104, 159, 233*n*
  Knesset elections (15th 1999), 139
  Knesset elections (16th 2003), 138, 140–1, 152, 154, 160–1, 165, 236*n*
  Knesset elections (17th 2006), 165
  local municipal authorities, 69

local municipal elections, 76, 77, 124, 126–7, 140
non-profit organizations, 105
northern branch activities, 3, 69, 77–8, 106, 108, 126–7, 138, 140, 152, 160–1, 165, 228*n*, 233–4*n*
partnership with ADP, 68, 104, 105, 154, 156, 159, 233*n*, 238*n*
political pacts, 104, 105
radicalization, 3
as rival to Rakah, 59
in the "Triangle", 162, 228*n*
two "Sections", 228*n*
unacceptable to Jewish establishment, 148
welfare services, 51
Zaydan's connections, 111
Islamic Revolution, 74
Islamic Support Committee, 78
Islamic University of Hebron, 233*n*
Islamism, 197, 213–14
Israel
  Declaration of Independence, 15, 28–9, 35–6, 43
  demographic issue, 3, 6–7, 25, 106, 107, 142–3, 213
  establishment of state, 29–30
  ethnic policy of "isolation", 130–1
  "gentle" and "strong arm" policies, 28, 33
  Jewish immigration, 3, 6–7, 14, 32, 237*n*
  as Jewish state, 6, 13, 17–18, 30, 107, 194, 213–14
  Lebanon War (2006), 218–21
  military service, 5, 70, 71, 167, 176, 216, 232–3*n*
  monotheistic religions, 9
  recognition of PLO, 214
  split ballot introduced (1996), 53, 103, 151, 163, 165
  as state for all its people, 6, 20, 90–1, 111, 158, 194, 214, 235*n*
  visit of Bush (2008), 221, 223
  voting system, 26, 53, 103, 124, 142, 146, 158, 159, 175
  see also Arab–Israeli War (1948); Oslo Accords; Six Day War (1967); Yom-Kippur War (1973)
Israel Defense Forces (IDF), 131, 133, 167, 176
Israel Workers' Party, 124, 231*n*

Israeli Advisor for Arab Affairs, 1, 16–17,
31, 32, 84–5, 200–1
Israeli Arab community
civil rights issue, 3, 6, 16, 56, 67, 79,
86, 156, 190, 198, 205, 206, 210
demographics, 3, 6–7, 25, 142–3, *143*,
213
disunity, 32
educated classes, 23, 25, 38, 42–3, 58,
79, 87
election boycott, 60, 69–70, 72, 110,
141, 146, 148, 149–52, 160–1,
162, 164, 165, 188, 236*n*, 237*n*
employment issues, 25, 32–3, 143,
143, 192
ethno-religious rift, 130–41, 147–8,
188
female labor, 143
future vision manifestos, 223–6
government policies, 199–209
growing militancy, 69, 79
ideological considerations, 154–61
Islamization, 202, 209
Israeli citizenship issue, 20, 71, 89,
106, 159
Israelization, 15, 19, 180, 210–11
migration to Jewish towns, 215
in mixed towns, 179–82, 187–8
modernization, 37, 38, 73, 87, 128,
180, 187
multiple identities, 18–20
nationalist issues, 58, 79, 82, 156–7
outlying settlements, 182–4, *183*
Palestinian-Arab identity, 19–20, 42,
49, 64, 65, 78–9, 155, 184, 188,
192, 209, 211, 214, 219–20
Palestinization, 19, 210–11
politicization, 19, 82, 103–5
return to religion, 73–5
as rural community, 36
social rifts, 57, 84, 88, 113, 160, 162,
187
as traditional society, 34
"voluntary transfer", 28
voter participation, 145, 149–52
Westernization, 55, 73
see also Christian Arab community;
Circassian community; clan
system; Druze community;
Galilee Arab community; Galilee
Bedouin community; Negev

Bedouin community; the
"Triangle"
Israeli Communist Party (Maki), 54–9,
231*n*, 232*n*
Christian support, 54, 55, 135, 147
co-operation with DPF, 60, 61
desire to be included in coalitions, 153
Druze support, 55, 134, 140
ethnic rifts, 148
Knesset elections (7th 1969), 56
Knesset elections (8th 1973), 55
Knesset elections (10th 1981), 49
local municipal authorities, 124
military administration (1948-66), 34,
35, 185
non-clan lists, 116
struggle against *al-Ard*, 61
struggle against tribalism, 77
unrest amongst members, 67
Israeli Defense Ministry, 29, 31, 48,
233*n*
Israeli Education Ministry, 51
Israeli Finance Ministry, 29, 204, 206
Israeli Foreign Ministry, 29
Israeli General Security Services, 69,
234–5*n*
Israeli Housing Ministry, 203
Israeli Interior Ministry
Bedouin settlements, 203
control by National Religious Party
(NRP), 50–1, 125, 155
control by Shas, 50, 51, 125, 155, 159
local government policies, 24, 82, 204,
206–7
municipal status to Umm-al-Fahm, 52
Taha and Zaydan clans feud, 160
Israeli Ministry of Justice, 84, 86
Israeli Ministry for Minority Populations
(1948-9), 29, 31
Israeli Ministry of Religious Affairs,
50–1, 73, 76, 155
Israeli National Security Council (NSC),
106, 107
Israeli Prime Minister's Office, 29
Israeli, Raphael, 85
Israeli Supreme Court of Justice, 62, 66,
83, 86, 108–9, 146, 192, 215
Israeli–Egyptian peace talks, 48, 50, 133,
232*n*
Israeli–Palestinian conflict, 105, 159,
209, 237*n*

Israeli Arabs, 144, 146, 184, 187–8,
  221–3, 226
Jewish left, 26
"shelf agreement" concept, 221, 240*n*
Israeli–Palestinian peace process, 158,
  222
Italy, 7
al-Ittihad, 55, 63, 89

Jabarin clan, *129*, 138, 236*n*
Jabarin, Hasan, 109, 198
Jabur, Jabur, 60
Jaffa, 179, 180, 181
Jaljulyeh, 75, 77, *97*, 126, 228*n*
Jamal, Amal, 149
Jamal, Mahmud, 138
Jaraisi, Sami, 82
Jarrissi, Rames, 129
Jatt, 72, 120, 123
Jatt-Yanuh, 122
al-Jazeera, 219
Jenin refugee camp, 107
Jerusalem
  Arab population, 142
  Black Panther movement, 56
  Clinton plan, 4
  and Islam, 9
  see also East Jerusalem; Temple Mount
Jerusalem student union, 79
Jesus Christ the Messiah, 9
Jewish Agency, 15, 238*n*
Jewish National Fund, 15, 159, 238*n*
Jewish nationalism, 29, 56, 90
Jezreel Valley, 37
Jihad, 110, 235*n*
Jiryyes, Sabri, 32, 43, 61, 62, 64, 71,
  231*n*
Jish, 135, 182, 183, *183*
Jisr al-Zarqa, 182
Jordan
  Arab–Israeli War (1948), 29
  Palestinians in, 64
  "Triangle" region, 228*n*
Jubran, Salem, 190
Jubran, Zaki, 237*n*
Judea
  "convergence plan", 239–40*n*
  Israeli Arab loyalty, 19, 64, 68
  military service, 71
  Moslem Brotherhood cells, 74
  Six Day War (1967), 73
Judeid, 116

Julis, 141, 167
al-Jurn, Dahud Mahmud, 75

Kabul, 72, 126
Kadima ("Forward"), 164, 165, 168–9
Kafar Barra, 75, 77, 126, 228*n*
Kafar Kamma, 133, 178
Kafar Kanna, 72, 76, 77, 126, 140
Kafar Manda, 160
Kafar Qara, 120, 126, 140
Kafar Qasem
  Bedouin community, 133
  clan rivalries, 123
  Islamic Movement, 76, 77, 126, 207
  Knesset elections (15th 1999), 165
  Knesset elections (16th 2003), 140
  "Little Triangle", 228*n*
  support for UAP, 165
Kafar Yasif, 60, 61, 79, 82, 118, 176
Kan'an, Muhammad, 154, 159
Kana'na, Hatem, 85
Kardush, Mansur, 60, 61, 62, 70, 71
Karman, Haj Taher, 29
Katif bloc, 210
Katz, Israel, 107
Kfar Hittin, *93*
Khalaila clan, 137, 138
Khalaila, Hamad, 49, 137
Khalaila, Muhammad, 46
Khamaisi, Adel, 140
Khamaysi, Rasem, 110
Khamis, Saliba, 62
Khamis, Yusuf, 43
khams, 114
Khatib, Sheikh Atef, 89, 104
Khatib, Sheikh Kamel, 108
Khatib, Tawfiq, 89, 154, 159
Khneifes, Saleh, *92*, 134, 136, 167
Khomeini, Ayatollah, 74
Kisra-Sumei, 122
Kiwan, Muhammad, 72, 150
Kleiner, Michael, 107
Knesset elections
  Arab boycott, 60, 69–70, 72, 110, 141,
    146, 148, 149–52, 160–1, 162,
    164, 165, 188, 236*n*, 237*n*
  clan influences, 116, 119–20, 128
  disqualification issue, 107–10
Knesset elections (1st 1949), 37, 43, 62,
  150, 167, 178
Knesset elections (2nd 1951), 43, 167,
  168, 173, 177, 178–9

Knesset elections (3rd 1955), 60, 167,
        173, 177, 178–9
Knesset elections (4th 1959), 119–20,
        167, 170, 177, 179, 186
Knesset elections (5th 1961), 153
Knesset elections (6th 1965), 32*n*, 56,
        62, 153
Knesset elections (7th 1969), 37, 56, 70,
        179, 186
Knesset elections (8th 1973)
    allied Arab lists, 38, 153, 170, 173, 177
    Bedouin community, 135, 170, 173
    Christian Arab community, 177
    Circassian community, 179
    Druze community, 167–8
    Israeli Communist Party (Maki), 55
    Mapai (later the Labor Party), 38
    Zionist political parties, 135, 170, 173,
        177, 179
Knesset elections (9th 1977)
    Abbasi's list, 136
    allied Arab lists, 39–40, 167, 174, 185
    Arab nationalist parties, 182
    Arab participation, 149
    Bedouin community, 174
    Dash list, 168
    Druze community, 167, 168
    Likud victory, 48, 49, 147, 148, 149,
        163
    Mapai (later the Labor Party), 48, 49,
        147
    mixed ethnic towns vote, 181–2
    Rakah, 185
    United Arab Party (United Arab List),
        120
Knesset elections (10th 1981)
    allied Arab lists, 37, 174, 185
    Arab MKs, 154
    Arab nationalist parties, 175, 182
    clan lists, 120
    Dash Party, 134
    Druze community, 134–5
    election of Khalaila, 137
    independent Arab lists, 42
    Israeli Communist Party (Maki), 49
    Likud Party, 134–5
    Mapai (later the Labor Party), 42, 46,
        49, 54, 120
    mixed ethnic towns vote, 182
    Negev Bedouin community, 173–4,
        175
    Zionist political parties, 50–1, 54, 174

Knesset elections (11th 1984)
    allied Arab lists, 153, 186
    Arab electoral power, 148
    Arab nationalist parties, 65, 176, 177,
        177, 182, 183, *183*
    Bedouin community, 171
    Christian Arab community, 136, 176,
        177, *177*
    Darawsha's election, 46–8, 50, 120
    Dash Party, 134–5
    Druze community, 134–5, 137
    Hadash, 56–7, 136, 137
    Likud Party, 134–5, 148
    Mapai (later the Labor Party), 54, 148
    mixed ethnic towns vote, 182
    Moslem community, 137
    outlying settlement Arabs, 183, *183*
    Progressive List for Peace (PLP),
        66–7, 70, 117, 148
    Rakah, 117, 136, 138, 148
    Sakhnin voting patterns, 117, 137, 138
    Shas Party, 125
    Shefar'am voting patterns, 136, 137
    Zionist political parties, 50, 54, 138,
        155, 171, *183*
Knesset elections (12th 1988)
    Arab allied lists, 166
    Arab nationalist parties, 155, 174–5
    Bedouin community, 174–5
    Druze community, 168
    Hadash, 168
    Hillel as speaker, 52
    Islamic Movement, 76
    Mapai (later the Labor Party), 52,
        120, 166
    Progressive List for Peace (PLP), 67,
        68
    Rakah, 168
    the "Triangle", 166
Knesset elections (13th 1992)
    Arab electoral power, 146
    Arab MKs performance, 161
    Hadash, 159
    Islamic Movement, 76
    Likud Party, 125
    Progressive List for Peace (PLP), 68,
        105
    Socialist Nationalist Front, 70
    unofficial coalition bloc, 18, 53
Knesset elections (14th 1996)
    Arab Democratic Party (ADP), 104,
        159, 233*n*

Arab electoral power, 146
Arab ideological differences, 161
Arab leadership, 88–9, 105
Arab nationalist parties, 154, 165, 175
Arab voter participation, 149, 150,
    163, 165, 230*n*
coalition issues, 199
Galilee Arab votes, 163
Hadash, 103–4, 159
Islamic Movement, 76–7, 104, 159,
    233*n*
Mapai (later the Labor Party), 151
"National Democratic Pact", 103–4,
    159
Negev Bedouin community, 175
parliamentary segregation, 103–4
split ballot introduced, 53, 103, 146,
    151, 153, 163, 165, 199
the "Triangle", 165
United Arab Party (UAP); (United
    Arab List), 159, 175, 233*n*
Knesset elections (15th 1999)
Arab Democratic Party (ADP), 139,
    153
Arab electoral power, 146, 149, 151
Arab nationalist parties, 175, 178
Arab voter participation, 149, 150,
    163, 165
Christian Arab community, 139, 178
coalition issues, 199
disqualification issue, 107
Druze community, 168
ethno-religious rifts, 139
Galilee Arab votes, 163
Hadash, 139, 153, 159
Islamic Movement, 139
Mapai (later the Labor Party), 151
"National Democratic Pact", 153
Negev Bedouin community, 175
Shas, 142, 159
the "Triangle" Arab votes, 165
United Arab Party (UAP); (United
    Arab List), 153, 154, 159, 165,
    175
Zionist political parties, 151, 153, 165,
    178
Knesset elections (16th 2003)
Arab boycott, 146, 151, 152, 160–1,
    237*n*
Arab Democratic Party (ADP), 140,
    154
Arab electoral power, 146, 151, 154

Arab MKs, 154
Arab nationalist parties, 158, 169, 176,
    177, *177*, 178, 179, 182, 183
Arab sector splits, 158
Arab Union for Renewal (AUR), 140,
    153–4
Arab voter participation, 150
Bedouin community, 140, 141, 171,
    175
Christian Arab community, 136–7,
    176, 177, *177*, 178
Circassian community, 179
disqualification issue, 107, 109
Druze community, 137, 140, 141, 154,
    168, 169
ethnic voting patterns, 136–8, 140–1
Galilee Arab votes, 141, 164
Hadash, 137, 138, 140, 141, 153–4,
    165, 183
Islamic Movement, 138, 140–1, 152,
    154, 160–1, 165, 236*n*
Likud Party, 141, 154, 168
Mapai (later the Labor Party), 141,
    151, 154
mixed ethnic towns vote, 182
"National Democratic Pact", 24, 107,
    109, 110, 137, 140, 154, 161,
    165, 176, 183
outlying settlement Arabs, 183
Rakah, 176
the "Triangle" Arab votes, 137, 141,
    165, 166
United Arab Party (UAP); (United
    Arab List), 137–8, 140, 154, 160,
    183
Zionist political parties, 137, 138, 140,
    160, 178, 179, 183
Knesset elections (17th 2006)
Arab boycott, 110, 146, 151
Arab electoral power, 144, 148
Arab nationalist parties, 158, 169, 178,
    182, *183*
Arab sector splits, 158
Arab voter participation, 150
Bedouin community, 150, 171, 175
Christian Arab community, 178
Circassian community, 179
Druze community, 168–9
Galilee Arab votes, 164
Islamic Movement, 165
Kadima list, 168–9
Likud Party, 168

Knesset elections (17th 2006) *(continued)*
  Mapai (later the Labor Party), 168
  mixed ethnic towns vote, 182
  outlying settlement Arabs, *183*
  Rakah, 165
  the "Triangle" Arab votes, 165
  United Arab Party (UAP); (United
    Arab List), 165
  Zionist political parties, 178, 179, *183*
Knesset Ethics Committee, 240*n*
Kollek, Teddy, *95*
Koran, 74, 75, 233*n*
Kseifeh, 126, 140, 172, 175–6
Kusa, Elias, 60

Labor Alignment, 32*n*
labor bureaus, 34
Labor Mapam Alignment (Ma'arakh),
  49
Labor Party *see* Mapai (later the Labor
  Party)
Laborers' Congress, 55
"Land Day" protests, 65, 69, 80–1, *94*,
  137, 145, 163, 184–5, 234*n*
Land Defense Committee, 80–1
land expropriation policies, 25, 30, 80–1
  Arab protests, 69
  Arab student union opposition, 79
  Beit Jann, 168
  Galilee, 65, 80, 145, 232*n*, 234*n*
  military administration (1948-66), 29
  Or Commission, 196
  Shu'fat and Biet Tsafafa, 52
  Supreme Follow-up Committee for
    the Arabs in Israel, 83
Land of Israel Workers' Union, 34
Landau, Ya'akov, 84
Lapid Commission, 207, 239*n*
Laqyyeh, 140, 172, 203
Latin Catholic community, 132, 176
Law of Return, 15, 90, 208
League for National Liberation, 54
Lebanon, Arab–Israeli War (1948), 29
Lebanon War (1982), 163, 238*n*
Lebanon War (2006), 218–21
Levinsky, Goel, *91*
Liberal Party, 231*n*
Libya, backing for Rejection Front, 233*n*
Likud Party, 35, 231*n*
  Arab membership, 49–50, 230*n*
  Arab voting support, 51, 52, 153, 156

Druze community, 134–5, 152, 153,
  168
Israeli Arab policies, 206
Knesset elections (9th 1977), 48, 49,
  147, 148, 149, 163
Knesset elections (10th 1981), 134–5
Knesset elections (11th 1984), 134–5,
  148
Knesset elections (13th 1992), 125
Knesset elections (16th 2003), 141,
  154, 168
Knesset elections (17th 2006), 168
local municipal authorities, 125
national unity government, 48
suppression of *Intifada*, 48
Linn, Amnon, 45
Livni, Tzippi, 222
local authorities, 81–2, 83
  Abnaa al-Balad (Sons of the Village),
    72, 81, 126
  Arab Democratic Party (ADP), 126
  Arab leadership, 88, 185
  Bedouin community, 118, 122
  clan influences, 20, 87, 115–17,
    118–30
  Druze community, 122
  Islamic Movement, 69
  Israeli Communist Party (Maki), 124
  Israeli Interior Ministry, 24, 82, 204,
    206–7
  Likud Party, 125
  Mapai (later the Labor Party), 124–5,
    126
  military administration, 33
  Progressive List for Peace (PLP),
    125–6
  Rakah, 125
Local Authorities law amendment
  (1975), 115
Local Government Center, 82
local municipal elections
  Abnaa al-Balad (Sons of the Village),
    72, 127
  Arab Democratic Party (ADP), 127
  Bedouin community, 126
  Hadash, 57, 125, 127
  Islamic Movement, 76, 77, 124, 126–7,
    140
  national political parties, 124–30
  Progressive List for Peace (PLP), 117,
    232*n*
  split ballot introduced (1975), 115

voter participation, 119, 121
Zionist political parties, 124–5
local municipal elections (1973), 69
local municipal elections (1975), 57, 65
local municipal elections (1978), 57,
    65–6, 72
local municipal elections (1983), 57, 66,
    70, 75, 76, 117, 121
  in Umm-al-Fahm, 129, *129*, 138
local municipal elections (1988), 126
local municipal elections (1989), 72, 77,
    127
local municipal elections (1993),
    115–16, 119, 121, 122, *122*, 126,
    127, 128
local municipal elections (1998), 119,
    121, 122, *122*, 127
local municipal elections (2000), 126
local municipal elections (2003),
    116–17, 121, *122*, 123, 126–7, 129,
    140
local municipal elections (2004), 116
Lod, 61, 133, 179, 180, 181–2

Ma'alot, 179
Ma'arakh (Labor Mapam Alignment),
    49
Ma'ariv, 41
Mada *see* Arab Democratic Party (ADP)
Madrid Conference (1991), 222
Mafdal *see* National Religious Party
    (NRP) (Mafdal)
Mahajna clan, 129, *129*, 138
Mahajna, Wajih, 129, *129*
Mahamid clan, 129, *129*, 138, 236*n*
Mahamid, Hashem, 138, 236*n*
  Knesset elections (11th 1984), 232*n*
  Knesset elections (14th 1996), 159
  Knesset elections (16th 2003), 140,
    152, 154, 165, 166
  Knesset elections (17th 2006), 165
  Progressive National Pact, 154
  Umm-al-Fahm local elections (1983),
    129, *129*
  United National Alliance, 127
Maher, Darash, *97*
Mair, P., 21
Majadlah, Ghaleb, 140
Majd al-Krum, 72, 83
al-Majlisiyyn, 113
Maki *see* Israeli Communist Party
    (Maki)

Malaysia, 11, 23
Malchi, Itzik Ben, *102*
Mali, division model, 11
Mana', Muhammad, 237*n*
Manna', Adel, 109, 210
Mansur clan, 116
Mansur, Iyad, 116
Mapai Committee for Arab Matters, 15
Mapai (later the Labor Party), 35
  allied Arab lists, 36–7, 38–42, 48, 49,
    50, 59, 116, 134, 135, 145, 153,
    166, 185, 186
  Arab Christian community, 49, 135,
    147, 239*n*
  Arab membership, 26, 44–9, 230*n*
  Arab voting support, 36–7, 38–42,
    44–9, 50, 51–4, 149, 152, 153,
    156
  Druze allied lists, 134, 168
  involvement in municipality and
    employment issues, 32–3
  Jabarin clan, 236*n*
  Knesset elections (1st 1949), 37
  Knesset elections (2nd 1951), 173
  Knesset elections (8th 1973), 38
  Knesset elections (9th 1977), 48, 49,
    147
  Knesset elections (10th 1981), 42, 46,
    49, 54, 120
  Knesset elections (11th 1984), 54, 148
  Knesset elections (12th 1988), 52,
    120, 166
  Knesset elections (14th 1996), 151
  Knesset elections (15th 1999), 151
  Knesset elections (16th 2003), 141,
    151, 154
  Knesset elections (17th 2006), 168
  labor bureaus, 34
  local municipal authorities, 124–5, 126
  military administration, 33, 34
  Minorities Department, 2, 17, 202
  national unity government, 48
  Negev Bedouin support, 173
  Or Commission of Inquiry, 195
  security policy, 28
  suppression of *Intifada*, 48
  Supreme Follow-up Committee for
    the Arabs, 83
  ties to Arab sector, 124–5
  the "Triangle" residents, 165
  see also Minorities Department
Mapam (United Workers' Party), 231*n*

allied Arab lists, 36, 43, 49
Arab membership, 26, 43–4, 48
Arab voting support, 36, 43–4, 48
Christian community, 49
formation of Meretz, 237*n*
involvement in municipality and
    employment issues, 32
Knesset elections (1st 1949), 43
Knesset elections (2nd 1951), 43
labor bureaus, 34
military administration, 33, 34
Unity of Labor party, 32*n*
Marx, Emanuel, 114
Masalha, Nawwaf, 47, 120, 165, 200
Masarwa clan, 117
Massarweh, Muhammad, *94*
Mawasi clan, 117
Mawasi, Farouk, 74
May Day demonstrations, 60, 69
Mazra'a, 116
Meir, Golda, 36, 231*n*
Mennem, Carlos, *95*
Meretz Party, 158, 237*n*
  Arab membership, 230*n*
  Israeli Arab municipal scene, 125
  Knesset elections (16th 2003), 140,
      154, 165
  Or Commission of Inquiry, 195
Mghar, 104, 123, 134
Mi'ari, Muhammad, 43, 59, 62, 66, 67,
    68, 104, 105, 231*n*
Mi'elya, 182
  Abnaa al-Balad (Sons of the Village),
      72
  Christian Arab community, 135, 176,
      177, 178
  National Committee for the Arab
      Local Authorities, 82
  Sons of Mi'elya for Tomorrow, 69,
      115–16
Mikunis, Shmuel, 56
military administration (1948-66),
    15–16, 28, 29, 30–4, 35, 231*n*
  Arab allied lists, 37, 185, 187
  Arab clan system, 115
  Arab electoral power, 144–5, 185
  Arab participation, 149
  Arab votes for Zionist parties, 157
  decisions on Israeli Arabs, 205
millet system, 132, 236*n*
Minorities Department, 2, 17, 44, 53–4,
    171, 177, 202, 203

Mormon community, 132
Moslem Brotherhood, 73, 74, 75, 233*n*
Moslem community
  autonomy, 131
  demographics, 131, 142
  electoral power, 147, 148
  ethnic background, 130
  in the Galilee, 162
  Knesset elections (11th 1984), 137
  Knesset elections (15th 1999), 139
  Knesset elections (16th 2003), 137
  Lebanon War (1982), 238*n*
  religious property, 131
  in the "Triangle", 164, 167
  voting patterns, 135
  see also Bedouin community; Islamic
      Movement; Israeli Arab
      community
Mu'adi, Jaber, 39–42, 45, *92*, 120, 134,
    167, 231*n*
Mu'adi, Sheikh Jamal, 71
al-Muaridin, 113
Muhammad the Prophet, 9, 126, 233*n*
al-Mujtama'a, 211
Mukhtars, 127, 235*n*
  Arab vote for Mapai, 50, 124
  military administration, 33, 36, 37
  national Arab leadership, 115
municipal councils *see* local authorities
municipal elections *see* local municipal
    elections
Musawa, 86
mutual aid, 114, 115, 235*n*

Naffa', Muhammad, 168, 238*n*
al-Nahda, 62, 69, 104
Nakhla, Elias, 49, 135, 231*n*
Nakhla, Khalil, 71
Naqba, 5, 29–31, 54, 189, 230*n*
al-Naser, 69
al-Naser, Jamal Abd, 59–60, 61, 69, 162
Naserism, 61, 162, 238*n*
Nashif clan, 119–20
Nashif, Mahmud, 33, 119–20
Nasr al-Din, Amal, 168
Nasrallah, Hassan, 218, 219, 221, 234*n*
Nassar clan, 235*n*
Nassar, George, 43
Nassar, Unis, 235*n*
National Action Front, 72, 73
National Committee for the Arab Local
      Authorities in Israel, 81–2, 83

National Committee of Arab Municipal
Council Chairmen, 57, 185
National Custodian of Deserted
Property, 131
National Municipal Alliance, 126–7
National Religious Party (NRP)
(Mafdal), 27, 50–1, 125, 155
"National Democratic Pact" (Nationalist
Democratic Pact)
Bedouin community, 176
Christian Arab community, 176
disqualification issue, 107, 108, 109,
234–5n
and "Equality Pact", 90
extra-parliamentary movements, 104
Knesset elections (14th 1996), 103–4,
159
Knesset elections (15th 1999), 153
Knesset elections (16th 2003), 24,
107, 109, 110, 137, 140, 154,
161, 165, 176, 183
meeting with Assad, 218
National Municipal Alliance, 127
nationalist ideological stream, 158
pan-Arabism, 220
partnership with Hadash, 103, 104,
105
testimony to Or Commission, 111
Umm-al-Fahm Arab vote, 139
nationalist ideological stream, 158–9
nationalist rifts, 13–14, 21–2
Natur, Humam, 74
Natur, Salman, 86
Nazareth
Arab academic associations, 79
Arab nationalist parties, 177, *177*, 182
Arab university idea, 234n
Christian Arab community, 71, 176–7
ethno-religious solidarity, 134
Independence Day (1954), *91*
Israeli Communist Party, 55
local municipal authority, 118, 125
local municipal elections (1975), 57,
65
local municipal elections (1978), 65–6
local municipal elections (1983), 66
local municipal elections (1989), 77
local municipal elections (2003), 129
Mafdal seat on council, 125
Mapai (later the Labor Party) branch,
46
PLP seat on council, 125

protests (1999), *98*
al-Sawt, 69
see also Arab Civil Rights Organization
in Nazareth; Upper Nazareth
Nazareth Committee for Academics, 57,
65–6
Nazareth congress (2001), 190–1
Nazareth Democratic Front, 57, 65–6
Negev
battles (October 1948), 31
non-profit organizations, 85, 86
territorial exchange, 3
Negev Bedouin community, 133, 172–6,
174
Arab allied lists, 38–9, 40
evacuation, 40
Knesset elections (16th 2003), 141
Knesset elections (17th 2006), 150
land issues, 135–6, 202–3, 217
local municipal authorities, 118, 122
local municipal elections (2000), 126
Orthodox Islam, 135
UN Civil Rights Commission, 212
Zionist political parties, 173, 174,
175–6, 184
Netanyahu, Benjamin, 51, 52–3, *97*, 149
New Outlook, 75
non-governmental organizations
(NGOs), 84, 85–6, 188, 206, 211,
234n
Abnaa al-Balad (Sons of the Village),
72
future vision manifestos, 224
non-governmental organizations
(NGOs), 127
Supreme Follow-up Committee for
the Arabs, 83
Northern Ireland, 11, 12, 15
NRP *see* National Religious Party (NRP)
(Mafdal)
NSC *see* Israeli National Security
Council (NSC)
nuclear family (*dar*), 20, 25, 113, 114

October 2000 events, 1, *99*, 189–94,
199–200, 223
see also Or Commission of Inquiry
Olmert, Ehud, *96*, 164, 200, 210,
239–40n
One Nation list, 165
Or Commission of Inquiry, 7, 86, *100*,
110–12, 189, 194–9, 207, 235n

Oslo Accords, 52, 77, 103, 204, 206,
    209, 214, 222
Ozachy-Lazar, Sarah, 139–40

Pakistan, division model, 11
Palestine *see* British Mandate period
Palestine Liberation Organization
    (PLO), 46, 48, 52, 62
  Barak's history, 190
  control of West Bank, 221
  defined, 231*n*
  international influence, 162–3
  Israeli Arab demands, 222
  as a legal entity, 103
  and Rakah, 59
  recognition by Israel, 214
  and Rejection Front, 233*n*
  reminder calls to "1948 Arabs", 107
  revival (1964), 68
  as sole representative of Palestinians,
    72, 73, 231*n*
  terrorist activities, 106
  see also Oslo Accords
Palestinian Authority, 107, 210, 221, 223
Palestinian Communist Party, 54
Palestinian National Council, 64–5,
    232*n*, 233*n*
Palestinian refugees, 30, 230–1*n*
  Democratic Popular Front (DPF), 60
  refugee camps, 107, 163, 238*n*
  right of return, 3, 44, 222
Palestinian-nationalist issue, 156–7
Palestinians
  collective identity with Israeli Arabs,
    64
  family reunification, 3
  territorial exchange, 3–4
  see also Intifada (1987-93); *Intifada*
    (2000); Israeli Arab community;
    Israeli–Palestinian conflict;
    Israeli–Palestinian peace process;
    Naqba
Palmon, Yehoshua, 16
pan-Arabism, 59–60, 70, 162, 220
parliamentary segregation, 103
Peled, Matti, 56, 66, 68
Peqi'in, *102*
Peres, Shimon, 41, 48, 52, *93, 94, 96*,
    151, 200
Peretz, Amir, 165
PLO *see* Palestine Liberation
    Organization (PLO)

PLP *see* Progressive List for Peace (PLP)
PNP *see* Progressive National Pact
    (PNP)
Poa'lei Zion Left, 43
"politicization without extremism", 103,
    234*n*
Popular Arab bloc, 43
Popular Committee for a Boycott of
    Knesset Elections, 110
Popular Democratic Front, 231*n*
Popular Front for the Liberation of
    Palestine, 72
pragmatic considerations, 155, 157–61
Progressive List for Peace (PLP), 38, 59,
    62, 66–8, 229*n*
  Arab student elections, 73
  disqualification issue, 109
  ethnic voting patterns, 137, 139
  Jewish candidates, 145
  Knesset elections (11th 1984), 66–7,
    70, 117, 148
  Knesset elections (12th 1988), 67, 68
  Knesset elections (13th 1992), 68, 105
  Knesset elections (16th 2003), 137
  lack of "Triangle" representative, 164
  local municipal authorities, 125–6
  local municipal elections, 117, 232*n*
  mixed Arab–Jewish membership, 51
  "National Democratic Pact", 104
Progressive Movement – Nazareth, 66
Progressive National Pact (PNP), 140,
    154, 183
Progressive Nationalist Movement, 73,
    79, 150
Progressive Pact, 104, 105
Protestant sects, 132
"public Jihad", 110

Qahwaji, Habib, 60, 61, 62, 65, 71
Qara, Ayub, 141
al-Qaradawi, Sheikh Yusuf, 108
Qasem, Abd al-Karim, 61
Qasem clan, 116
Qasem, Khalil, 116
Qasis, Mas'ad, 135, 177, 231*n*
Qa'war, Jamal, 71
Qays tribes, 113
Quebec, 23

Ra'am *see* United Arab Party (UAP)
Rabbi Kook Center, 223

Rabin, Yitzhak, 17, 48–9, 51, 52–3, *95*, 190, 204
Rabinowitz, D., 237*n*
Rafi, 33, 231*n*
Rahat, 77, 126, 133, 140–1, 172, 175–6
al-Rahman, Hashem Abd, 127
Rakah
  ability to cross clan lines, 57, 129
  Arab academic associations, 80
  Arab membership, 26, 230*n*
  Arab student activity, 73
  Christian Arab community, 49, 135, 176, 178
  desire to be included in coalitions, 153
  and Druze Enterprise Committee, 70, 167
  ethnic rifts, 148
  Galilee Arab support, 162, 186
  Haifa student union, 79
  ideological struggle with Sons of the Village, 63
  ideology, 104, 156
  and *Intifada* (1987-93), 59
  Knesset elections (1st 1949), 62
  Knesset elections (7th 1969), 56, 70
  Knesset elections (9th 1977), 185
  Knesset elections (11th 1984), 117, 136, 138, 148
  Knesset elections (12th 1988), 168
  Knesset elections (16th 2003), 176
  Knesset elections (17th 2006), 165
  land expropriation, 80
  left ideological stream, 158
  local municipal authorities, 125
  local municipal elections, 117, 129, 139
  mixed ethnic towns, 181
  national leadership of Israeli Arabs, 38, 56–9, 62–3, 65–7
  organizational infrastructure, 104
  Palestinian nationalism, 69
  and PLO, 59
  as rival to Islamic Movement, 59
  support for Hadash, 57
  support to Druze community, 168
  Supreme Follow-up Committee for the Arabs, 83
  al-Tha'ibin's activities, 75
  unacceptable to Jewish establishment, 148
  weakened monopoly, 205

Ramash *see* Progressive List for Peace (PLP)
Rame, 82, 134, 167, 168, 176
Ramla, 61, 133, 179, 181–2
Ramon, Haim, 47
Ratz Party, 237*n*
al-Raya, 72
Rayyan, Kamel, 75
Realignment Plan, 210, 239–40*n*
Reihaniyye, 133, 178, 182
Reiter, Yitzhak, 157
Rejection Front, 72, 233*n*
Rice, Condoleeza, 240*n*
rift
  defined, 21
  see also ethnic rifts; nationalist rifts; social rifts
Roman Catholic community, 132, 176
Rouhana, Nadim, 212
Rubinstein, Elyakim, 108
Rupin, Arthur, 28

Sa'ad, Ahmad, 89
Sabra refugee camp, 163, 238*n*
Sabri, Akhrama, *102*
Sadat, Anwar, 232*n*
Sadeq, Walid, 66
Sa'di, Ahmad, 110–11
Sa'id, Saleh Ahmad, 43
Sakhnin, 72, 82, 117, 119, 129, 137–8, 153
Sakhnin football club, *101*
Sakhnin Progressive Movement, 69
Salah, Sheikh Ra'ed, 77
  arrested (2003), 108, 233–4*n*
  autonomous society plan, 211
  call to boycott elections, 69, 152, 166
  as mayor of Umm-al-Fahm, 130, 138
  Or Commission, 111, 197, 198
  release from jail, *102*
  resignation, 78
Salim, Rashid, 66, 71
Samaria
  "convergence plan", 239–40*n*
  Israeli Arab loyalty, 19, 64
  military service, 71
  Moslem Brotherhood cells, 74
  Six Day War (1967), 73
sanat al marhaba, 37
al-Sani', Talab, 105, 140, 171, 175, 238*n*
Sarruji, Mahmud, 61
Sarsur, Ibrahim, 77, 165

al-Sawt, 69, 71
Sawt al-Haqq wal-huriyya, 108
Scotland, 22, 23
Sderot, 223
sector focusing, 85
security issues, early days of state of
    Israel, 28, 29, 30–1, 32, 33–4
Segev Shalom, 172
Senegal, division model, 11
Sephardi Shas Party *see* Shas Party
Sha'ab, 116, 232*n*, 235*n*
al-shabab a-Muslimin see Young Moslems
Shalhat, Antuan, 86
Shamir, M., 236*n*
Shamir, Yitzhak, 48
Shari'a, 75, 76, 233*n*
Sharon, Ariel, 53, *100*, 148, 153, 164,
    198, 201, 238*n*, 240*n*
Sharon, Moshe, 206
Shas Party, 16
    Arab voting support, 159–60
    Israeli Interior Ministry, 50, 51, 125,
        155, 159
    Knesset elections (11th 1984), 125
    Knesset elections (15th 1999), 142,
        159
    Ministry of Religious Affairs, 50, 51,
        155
    political power, 27, 123, 142
Shatila refugee camp, 163, 238*n*
Shazar, Zalman, *92*
Shefar'am
    Abnaa Shafa'amr, 116
    Arab academic associations, 79
    bus attack, 6, *102*
    Christian Arab community, 176
    Druze community, 167
    ethno-religious solidarity, 134
    local municipal authority, 118
    National Committee for the Arab
        Local Authorities, 82
    voting patterns, 136–7
Shehada, Aziz, 104
Shehada, Shehada, 80
Sheli, 66
Shinui Party, 125, 168, 237*n*
Shu'fat, 52
Singapore, division model, 11
Sirhan, Sami, 116
Six Day War (1967), 64, 73, 155, 184,
    199, 205

Smooha, S., 18, 19, 109, 194, 229–30*n*,
    234*n*
Sneh, Moshe, 56
social rifts, 21–2, 24, 25–6, 57, 69, 88,
    113–41, 157, 160, 187
Socialist Nationalist Front, 62, 70
Socialist Party, 104
Sons of Mi'elya for Tomorrow, 69,
    115–16
Sons of Sakhnin football club, *101*
Sons of Tireh, 69, 104
Sons of the Village *see Abnaa al-Balad*
    (Sons of the Village)
South Lebanon Army (SLA), 49, 232*n*
Soviet Union, 11, 58, 61
Spain, 13–14, 22, 152
Sri Lanka, 11, 12, 15, 23
student elections (1978), 73
student elections (1988), 73
Suan, Dan, 192
Suez Canal, 59
Suhmata, 189
suicide bombers, 3, 78, 106
Sulha, 191
Supreme Arab Committee, 30
Supreme Follow-up Committee for the
    Arabs in Israel (Supreme
    Monitoring Committee . . .), 83–4,
    111, 185, 193, 206
    Arab leadership focus on, 90
    central role for Israeli Arabs, 85, 110,
        130
    future vision manifestos, 224
    recognition of Israel, 222
    replaces Land Defense Committee, 81
Supreme Muslim Council, 29–30
Swed, Hanna, 122
Switzerland, compromise model, 10
Syria
    Arab–Israeli War (1948), 29
    backing for Rejection Front, 233*n*
Syria–Egypt pact (1958), 59

Ta'al *see* Arab Union for Renewal (AUR)
Taba Talks, 146, 237*n*
Taha clan, 160
Tamra, 82, 106, 119
Tamra al Ghadd (Tamra of Tomorrow),
    115
Tarabia clan, 137
Tarif, Saleh, 42, 141, 168, 201, 237*n*
Tarif, Sheikh Amin, 42, *92*, 131, 134

Tarshiha, 177, 179
Tayibeh
  Bedouin community, 133
  Democratic Popular Front (DPF), 61
  Knesset elections (4th 1959), 119–20
  Knesset elections (16th 2003), 140
  municipal elections (1983), 117
  al Nahda group, 69, 104
  Nashif clan, 119–20
  Palestinian heritage fund, 2
  Sons of the Village, 72
  Ubeid Abd al-Qader clan, 38
Tel Aviv, 179, 180, 181
Tel Sheva, 133, 172
Tel-al-Maleh, 133, 203
Temple Mount, 3, 53, 77, 108, 111
Temple Mount incident (2000), 193,
  198
terrorist activities, 3, 75, 78, 105–7, 108,
  220, 222–3
al-Tha'ibin, 74–5
"Third Sector", 84–7, 234*n*
Tibi, Ahmad, 89, 211
  alliances, 104
  Arab Union for Renewal (AUR), 104,
    105, 159
  citizenship amendments, 159, 238*n*
  disqualification threats, 107, 108, 109
  Knesset elections (16th 2003), 107,
    109, 140, 153–4, 166
  "politicization without extremism",
    103
Tireh
  Independence Day (1950), *91*
  Likud Party branch, 153
  local municipal elections (1998), 119
  local municipal elections (2003), 116,
    123, 129
  Mansur clan, 116
  Sons of Tireh, 69, 104
Toledano, Shmuel, 45
the "Triangle"
  defined, 228*n*
  local authority convention, 82
  local municipal authorities, 118
  religious preachers, 73
  territorial exchange, 3–4
  terrorist activities, 106
  al-Tha'ibin's influence, 75
  Usrat al-Jihad activities, 75
the "Triangle" Arab community, 164–7,
  166, 186

Abnaa al-Balad (Sons of the Village),
  162, 164
Arab nationalist parties, 164, 165, 166,
  184
clan system, 115
Islamic Movement, 162, 228*n*
Knesset elections (11th 1984), 137
Knesset elections (12th 1988), 166
Knesset elections (14th 1996), 165
Knesset elections (15th 1999), 165
Knesset elections (16th 2003), 137,
  141, 165, 166
Knesset elections (17th 2006), 165
the "Triangle" Arab community Arab
  allied lists, 164, 166, 186
Tuba, 170
Tuba Zanghariyye, 182, 183, *183*
Tubi, Tawfiq, 56, 62
Tuma, Amil, 62
Tur'an, 235*n*

Ubeid Abd al-Qader clan, 38
Ubeid, Diab, 33, 38, 42, 120, 231*n*
Umm al-Sahali, 83, 86
Umm Batin, 203
Umm-al-Fahm, 138–41
  "al-Aqsa is in danger" rally, 106, 108
  al-Ansar group, 66, 104, 232*n*
  extended families, 114
  Islamic Movement influence, 76, 77,
    138, 202
  Knesset elections (16th 2003), 140
  land expropriation, 81
  local municipal elections (1983), 129,
    129, 138
  local municipal elections (1993), 126
  local municipal elections (2003),
    126–7
  mass rally (2005), *102*
  municipality status, 52, 148
  Sons of the Village influence, 72, 138,
    232*n*
  terrorist activities, 106
  violent clashes (1998), 189
  voting patterns, 138
al-Umur, Ibrahim, 140
Union of Arab Academics, 79
United Arab Party (UAP); (United Arab
  List), 68, 89, 104, 139, 231*n*
  Bedouin support, 171, 175, 176
  establishment of, 156, 165, 238*n*
  ideology, 156

United Arab Party (UAP); (United Arab
List) *(continued)*
Knesset elections (9th 1977), 120
Knesset elections (14th 1996), 159,
175, 233*n*
Knesset elections (15th 1999), 153,
154, 159, 165, 175
Knesset elections (16th 2003), 137–8,
140, 154, 160, 183
Knesset elections (17th 2006), 165
religious-Islamic ideological stream,
158
United Eilabun, 122
United National Alliance, 127
United Nations, 83
Partition Plan for Palestine, 54, 55
United Nations Civil Rights
Commission, 212
United Nations Development Program,
223
United States
consensus model, 10
Israeli–Palestinian conflict, 221
United Workers' Party *see* Mapam
(United Workers' Party)
Unity of Labor Party, 32*n*, 43
involvement in municipality and
employment issues, 32
military administration, 33
University of Haifa, 73
Upper Nazareth, 65, 179, 180
"upright generation", 90, 103
al 'Uqbi, Nuri, 231*n*
urbanization, 21
Usrat al-Ard, 231*n*
Usrat al-Jihad, 75
USSR *see* Soviet Union

Veterans' Committee, 71
Voice of Consent, 104
"Voice of Truth and Freedom", 108

Wadi 'Ara, 114
Wadi Hammam, 170
Wadi Nisnas, 61
Wahba, Majali, 141, 169
Wales, 23
Waqf, 76, 131, 224
War of Independence (1948), 1, 29–31,
54, 132
Warhaftig, Zerah, *93*
Wasel, Taha, 140

Watad, Muhammad, 75, 120
Weizmann, Chaim, 28
West Bank
Camp David negotiations, 212
control by PLO, 221
Israeli Arab loyalty, 64, 65
open boundaries, 205
Realignment Plan, 239–40*n*
religious preachers, 73
territorial exchange, 3
see also Intifada (1987-93)
Wilenska, Esther, 56
Wilner, Meir, 56
World Zionist Federation, 238*n*

Yamma, 140
Yani, Yani, 60
Yarka, 120, 167
Yediot Ahronot, 108
Yemin tribes, 113
Yiftachel, Oren, 10
Yom-Kippur War (1973), 44, 65, 68, 78,
163, 177, 199
Young Moslems, 74–5

Zabarga, Said, 104
Zahalqa, Jamal, 109, 140, 158, 165, 166
Zarzir, 170
Zayad, Taufiq, 55, 57, 65, 105
Zaydan clan, 160
Zaydan, Muhammad, 89, 104, 105, 111,
160
Zbeidat clan, 137
Zionist Council of Israel, 106
Zionist political parties
Arab electoral power, 144
Arab membership, 35, 36
Arab voting support, 140, 152, 153,
155–6, 157, 158, 159, 161,
185–7, 229*n*, 230*n*
Arabs on Knesset lists, 141
Bedouin support, 135, 170, 171, 173,
174, 175–6, 184
Christian Arab support, 135, 177–8
Circassian support, 135, 178–9, 184
Druze support, 134, 137, 168, 169,
184
Galilee Arab support, 163–4
Knesset elections (2nd 1951), 168,
173, 177, 178–9
Knesset elections (3rd 1955), 178–9
Knesset elections (4th 1959), 179

Knesset elections (6th 1965), 153
Knesset elections (7th 1969), 179
Knesset elections (8th 1973), 135,
   170, 173, 177, 179
Knesset elections (10th 1981), 50–1,
   54, 174
Knesset elections (11th 1984), 50, 54,
   138, 155, 171, *183*
Knesset elections (15th 1999), 151,
   153, 165, 178
Knesset elections (16th 2003), 137,
   138, 140, 160, 178, 179, 183
Knesset elections (17th 2006), 178,
   179, *183*
local municipal elections, 124–5
membership drives, 120
military administration (1948-66), 35,
   36, 185
outlying settlement Arabs, 183, *183*,
   184

reasons for electoral support, 139
suppression of *Intifada*, 48
the "Triangle" Arab community, 32–3,
   164–5, 166
see also Freedom Party; General
   Zionists Party; Labor Party;
   Likud Party; Mapai (later the
   Labor Party); Mapam (United
   Workers' Party); National
   Religious Party (NRP); Rafi;
   Shas; Unity of Labor Party
Zirakzadeh, C.E., 22
al-Zu'bi, Abd al-'Aziz, 8, 232*n*
al-Zu'bi clan, 37
al-Zu'bi, Ihsan, 45
al-Zu'bi, Mrs., 235–6*n*
al-Zu'bi, Seif al-Din, 37, 39–40, 45, 120,
   167, 231*n*